Recent Marxian Theory

SUNY Series in Political Theory:
Contemporary Issues

Philip Green, editor

RECENT MARXIAN THEORY
Class Formation and Social Conflict
in Contemporary Capitalism

by
John F. Sitton

State University of New York Press

Cover illustration by Jacqueline Perry
Cover design by Marion Skinner Grelle

Published by
State University of New York Press, Albany

For information, address the State University of New York Press,
State University Plaza, Albany, NY 12246

Production by Christine M. Lynch
Marketing by Nancy Farrell

Library of Congress Cataloging-in-Publication Data
Sitton, John F., 1952-
    Recent Marxian theory : class formation and social conflict in
contemporary capitalism / by John F. Sitton.
            p.   cm. — (SUNY series in political theory. Contemporary
issues)
    Includes bibliographical references and index.
    ISBN 0–7914–2941–5 (cl : alk. paper). — ISBN 0–7914–2942–3 (pb :
alk. paper)
    1.   Social   classes.   2.   Social   conflict.   3.   Proletariat.
4. Capitalism.   I. Title.   II. Series.
HT609.S57   1996
305.5—dc20 95–31700   95–31700
                                                                     CIP

10 9 8 7 6 5 4 3 2 1

Contents

for
Jacqueline Anne Perry

Acknowledgments

This book is largely a work of commentary on various recent Marxian arguments. I very gratefully acknowledge permission to quote from the following copyrighted publications:

• An earlier version of Chapter Three was published in *Critical Sociology* Volume 17, Number 2, pp. 3–33. Reprinted by permission.

• Adam Przeworski, *Politics and Society* 7, 4, pp. 343–401, copyright © 1977 by Sage Publications, Inc.; Adam Przeworski, *Politics and Society* 11, 3, pp. 289–313, copyright © 1982 by Sage Publications, Inc.; John Roemer, *Politics and Society* 11, 3, pp. 253–287, copyright © 1982 by Sage Publications, Inc.; John Roemer, *Politics and Society* 11, 3, pp. 375–394, copyright © 1982 by Sage Publications, Inc.; Adam Przeworski, *Politics and Society* 14, 4, pp. 379–409, copyright © 1985 by Sage Publications, Inc.; Claus Offe, *Political Theory* 15, 4, pp. 501–537, copyright © 1987 by Sage Publications, Inc. Reprinted by permission of Sage Publications, Inc.

• Juergen Habermas, *Philosophy and Social Criticism* 11, pp. 1–17, copyright (1986) by Sage Publications, Ltd. Reprinted by permission of Sage Publications, Ltd.

• Immanuel Wallerstein, *Unthinking Social Science* (1991). Reprinted by permission of Blackwell Publishers, Ltd.

Chapter Six in David Held, ed., *Political Theory Today* (1991). Reprinted by permission of Blackwell Publishers, Ltd., Stanford University Press, and Claus Offe and Ulrich K. Preuss.

• Richard J. Bernstein, ed., *Habermas and Modernity*, copyright © 1985 by Polity Press. Reprinted by permission of Blackwell Publishers, Ltd. and The MIT Press.

• G. A. Cohen, *History, Labour, and Freedom* (1988). Reprinted by permission of the Peters Fraser and Dunlop Group, Ltd.

• Immanuel Wallerstein, *Geopolitics and Geoculture* (1991); Joan Smith and Immanuel Wallerstein, coordinators, *Creating and Transforming Households* (1992). Reprinted with the permission of Cambridge University Press and the author.

• Chapters 2 and 13 in John Roemer, ed., *Analytical Marxism*. © Maison des Sciences de l'Homme and Cambridge University Press 1986. Reprinted with the permission of Cambridge University Press.

• Jon Elster, *Theory and Society* 11, pp. 453–482 (1982); G. A. Cohen, *Theory and Society* 11, pp. 483–495 (1982). Reprinted by permission of Kluwer Academic Publishers.

• Robert Brenner, *New Left Review* 104 (1977), pp. 25–92; Andrew Levine and Erik Olin Wright, *New Left Review* 123 (1980), pp. 47–68; Ellen Meiksins Wood, *New Left Review* 177 (1989), pp. 41–88. Reprinted by permission of New Left Review, Ltd.

• Juergen Habermas, *New Left Review* 151 (1985), pp. 75–105; Juergen Habermas, *New Left Review* 183, pp. 3–21, originally published in *Die Nachholende Revolution: Kleine Politische Schriften vii* 1990. Reprinted by permission of New Left Review, Ltd. and the author.

• Chapter 12 in John B. Thompson and David Held, ed., *Habermas: Critical Debates* (1982). Reprinted by permission of The MIT Press.

• Claus Offe (and John Keane, translator), *Contradictions of the Welfare State*, The MIT Press, © 1984 by Claus Offe and John Keane; Claus Offe, *Disorganized Capitalism*, The MIT Press, © 1985 by Claus Offe. Reprinted by permission of The MIT Press.

• Claus Offe, "New Social Movements," *Social Research* 52, 4 (1985). Reprinted by permission of Social Research and the author.

• Reprinted by permission of Verso/New Left Books: *Classes*, Erik Olin Wright (1985); *The Debate on Classes*, Erik Olin Wright, ed. (1989); *Historical Capitalism*, Immanuel Wallerstein (1983); *Race, Nation, Class*, Etienne Balibar and Immanuel Wallerstein (1991); *Autonomy and Solidarity*, Peter Dews, ed. (1992).

• Claus Offe, *New German Critique* 6 (1975), pp. 139–147. Reprinted by permission of New German Critique, Inc.

Preface

The 'proletariat' is a concept for analyzing the fault lines of capitalist society. As such, it is intended to indicate the most promising political strategy for contesting capitalism and to anticipate the central structure of socialist society, the abolition of social classes based on differential access to productive property. Many have rejected this concept on theoretical grounds, suggesting instead that it is a Hegelian "universal class" in Marxian guise, or a product of Marx's conflation of production and social agency. Others reject it as a politically dangerous abstraction because, as abstraction, the proletariat needs representation—and ultimately substitution—by one vanguard or other. More interesting than *a priori* rejections, however, are the social analyses which conclude that, if the concept proletariat ever had theoretical cogency, this has been irretrievably undermined by the political and social dynamic of contemporary capitalism itself. It is these latter arguments that are the special focus of the present work.

There are several discrete arguments that have led to this conclusion. First, changes in the occupational structure of capitalism, specifically the rise of the "middling classes," have made the application of the traditional Marxian two-class model more and more difficult; a Procrustean bed that does not advance comprehension of the class relations of capitalism. This has stimulated new attempts to further specify the class structure in ways that can theoretically account for these changes. These impressive exertions have nevertheless fallen short in providing a compelling and politically relevant map of contemporary class structure.

The frequent Marxian response to ambiguities in the class structure is to place hope in the possibilities of political mediations for forging a revolutionary agent. This is a response common to both electoral socialists and Bolshevik parties. Political representation can actualize the universality of the interests of the unambiguous proletariat by creating a political coalition with elements from the more ambiguous social categories and other oppressed groups. The "nonantagonistic contradictions" among the "people," to use Mao Zedong's phrase, will be worked out under this umbrella in the process of socialist transformation.

This formula met with many notable, if qualified, revolutionary successes in the twentieth century. However, the bases of these successes have probably been the powerful appeal of national liberation from colonial oppression, the importance of the peasantry in these countries, and the clarity of objectives expressed in the slogan "peace, land, and bread." Therefore the applicability of this model to the political struggles of the working classes in established capitalist democracies has always been doubtful.

When we turn our attention to this different set of circumstances, a number of obstacles emerge for the political representation of a revolutionary proletariat. First of all, the abstract template of citizenship severs the places in production from immediate political communities; a separation reinforced in various other ways. In capitalist democracies, the competition of political parties seeking the real benefits of elected office leads to electoral strategies that undercut class identification. For these and related reasons, political mediations prove inadequate for the creation of a revolutionary socialist agent in advanced capitalist societies.

The failure of traditional Marxian theoretical remedies for actualizing the proletariat has led to a wholesale reconsideration of some of the determinants of the concept, such as the labor theory of value, the meaning of exploitation, and the intentions of the socialist project itself. Many theorists who identify in some manner with Marxian theory conclude that Marxism must be more eclectic in its methods if it is to clarify its perspective on historical change and on contemporary dilemmas. In particular, analytical Marxists employ variants of rational-choice theory to rigorously examine the fundamental theses of Marxism in order to reinvigorate the tradition. One of the major consequences of this, however, has been a further undermining of the status of the proletariat in revolutionary theory.

These cascading weaknesses of the concept, exposed by the development of capitalist democracy in general, are further exacerbated by the historical development of the advanced capitalist welfare state. If the concept of the proletariat ever had some theoretical purchase for comprehending capitalism, it has been eliminated by the political actions characteristic of the interventionist welfare state. The welfare state creates "horizontal cleavages" which shatter forces that previously were thought to have an interest in socialism as well as the potential for political organization to pursue that project. In the process, however, new social and political antagonisms develop due to dislocations engendered by the very activities of the welfare state. There is a shift in both the sites and agencies of struggle against the dynamic of advanced capitalism, clustered around the issues and identities which have emerged as new social movements. The durability of these movements and whether they will eventuate in a real historical challenge to capitalism is in doubt. Nevertheless, they are a matter of important discussion, as is the kind of post-capitalist future implied by these movements. The alleviation of class antagonisms does not mean the elimination of antagonisms of the most profound sort. The advanced capitalist welfare state is not the end of history.

Today any discussion of oppositionist forces in welfare state societies must be immediately qualified in two ways. First, most of the population of the world does not live in capitalist societies that are structured as welfare states. Secondly, the rapid transnationalization of capitalist production places increasing pressure on existing welfare states. The internal fissures of these societies widen as the community of the morally worthy receives an ever more restricted definition. World-system theory attempts to accommodate both of these facts by proposing that the proper unit of analysis for comprehending the prospects of capitalism and the working classes is not the individual nation state. Instead, capitalism is a global social system and it is only from this vantage point that its dynamic and historical trajectory can be revealed. From this perspective, the ubiquitous ethnic, national, and religious struggles of the world are driven by the desperate situation of most of the direct producers of the world and the intense and multidimensional free-for-all of capitalist competition. There is a troubling looseness about many of the theses of world-system theory but it does force us to consider a less restrictive notion of the working classes. However, in the end, even this theory, the one closest to the Marxism of the *Manifesto,* weakens the usefulness of the concept of the proletariat for understanding the sites and agencies for contesting actually existing capitalism.

Although any of these discrete theoretical or substantive arguments taken alone allows considerable rebuttal, taken together it is hard to maintain that the proletariat is still a useful abstraction for organizing our theories about the antagonisms and trajectory of contemporary capitalism. It is for this reason that the present work attempts to bring these arguments together. I do not claim any particular originality in doing so. The work is primarily animated by the belief that it is sometimes useful to bring together the various "obviousnesses" that accumulate in the corners of a tradition.

This work is also animated by the fact that although certain common persuasive themes emerge in recent Marxian theory that provide promising theoretical directions, the depth of these commonalities is often difficult to see because of the specific vocabularies and preoccupations of the variants of Marxian theory. A point of the present undertaking is to reinforce these commonalities by bringing these variants into more contact with each other. Of course the major weakness of a work of this kind is its selectivity. There are many intriguing and relevant perspectives that have had to be excluded. Specifically, the work of many theorists engaged in a critical dialogue with Marxian theory—for example Anthony Giddens, or the self-described post-Marxists Ernesto Laclau and Chantal Mouffe—have only been mentioned in passing. Whether the discussions and arguments that have been selected advance our understanding must be evaluated by those eating this pudding.

It is happily now a cliche to say that traditions, in contrast to dogma, only retain their vitality through internal conflict. But the fact of truisms is that they are true. If Marxism is to have anything to say to the world, it must speak clearly and honestly about the world, even if Marxism must thereby reject as central a notion as the proletariat. Capitalism is not a whit more secure for this loss.

This is not mere whistling past the graveyard. Although the multiple dislocations of contemporary capitalism do not coalesce into class subjects, they do produce searing conflicts. There is no consensus on the exact manner in which these conflicts are systematically grounded in capitalist class relations, however it is still a quite plausible intuition to pursue. Nor would the elimination of class relations mean that all conflicts would disappear. If the intuition is correct, however, they would at least lose their systematic character. That is all that most Marxists have ever expected of socialism. In a world where you must harden yourself in order to walk down the street, watch the evening news, or read the newspaper, that would be plenty.

It is always a great pleasure to publicly acknowledge the many people who, in various ways, sustain an effort such as this one. The everyday kindnesses and generosity of my colleagues in the Department of Political Science, my students, and colleagues in other departments here at Indiana University of Pennsylvania have made the woods of western Pennsylvania a fortunate place to work. This project was also facilitated by two quarter-time releases in different semesters and an IUP Senate Research Grant for one summer. Dr. Hilda Richards, former Provost of IUP (now President of Indiana University at Gary), and Dr. Brenda Carter, Dean of Humanities and Social Sciences, were especially helpful in many ways. In addition, the lively group of theorists and other scholars who frequently attend the Southwestern Political Science Convention aided this work through their comments on papers I presented. I particularly want to mention Sandy Hinchman,

Ted Harpham, Adolf Gundersen, Art Diquattro, and Dan Sabia, Jr. This of course does not mean that any of the above would agree with the arguments presented in this book.

Although the above debts are substantial and clear, there are broader ones that are at least as important. My family and friends have always formed a sustaining community, a community that time, distance, and the difficulties of maintaining contact cannot efface. I think of it as one large home, even though the individual rooms in that home are separated by hundreds of miles. While I was writing this book both my father, William M. Sitton, Sr., and my older brother, Charles Sitton, passed away. Yet this home continues into new generations, in spite of the "thousand natural shocks that flesh is heir to."

It may be an occupational hazard that I am often surprised to learn that there are stonier fields than political and social theory. One of them is painting, the "transfiguration of the commonplace," to employ Harold Rosenberg's phrase. My wife is a painter, but that is not the reason I dedicated this book to her.

One

The Proletariat and Historical Progress

From his earliest work on Hegel, when Marx first puzzled over the working class, the proletariat's role in historical change guided his deliberations. Initially he characterized the proletariat in Aristotelian terms, saying that the propertyless laboring class does "not so much constitute a class of civil society as provide the ground on which the circles of civil society move and have their being."[1] However, slightly later, in the "Introduction" to *A Contribution to the Critique of Hegel's Philosophy of Right,* Marx had already assigned the proletariat a central role in history. The proletariat is a class with "radical chains" whose very existence proclaims the "dissolution of the existing world order."[2]

This famous characterization succinctly expresses the enormous importance of the proletariat in Marx's theory of history. The proletariat is both the living expression of the end of the old order and the indispensable agent of the new. The proletariat reveals the exhaustion of capitalism; its conditions of existence demonstrate the structural inability of capitalism to control and rationally employ the forces it has conjured. The proletariat is therefore both created by and consummates world-historical change, the "gravedigger" of capitalism.

Unlike Max Weber's discussion of social class, which is more taxonomy than theory, Marx's concept of "class" is firmly embedded in his theory of history. In Marxian theory class is the key social relation in society (ownership of productive forces) in that it identifies the conflict potentials of a particular society, predicts the major collective actors who will emerge to struggle over the existing forms and distribution of productive forces, and indicates the new social relations that will free the productive forces for further development. It is not surprising that many have complained of the over-burdening of the concept class in Marxian theory.[3]

In Marx's theory of history the proletariat's struggles are necessary for the abolition of capitalism and the establishment of a society in which pro-

1

duction is directly geared to the satisfaction of needs, i.e., communism. However, Marx was no voluntarist. In his justly famous phrase, "Men make their own history but they do not make it just as they please; they do not make it under circumstances chosen by themselves, but under circumstances directly encountered, given and transmitted from the past."[4] The relative weights of the historical situation (objective conditions) and revolutionary organization (agency) *and* the interaction between conditions and agency have always been obscure in Marx's theory. Consequently the precise role of the proletariat in historical change is equally unclear.

A recent debate, primarily concerned with examining the logical foundations of Marx's "materialist theory of history," has helped to elucidate the role theoretically assigned to the proletariat in furthering historical progress. This continuing debate was originally sparked by G. A. Cohen's *Karl Marx's Theory of History: A Defense.*[5] It is useful at the outset to explore this discussion in order to clarify the importance of the proletariat in Marx's historical theory and to fully appreciate what is lost if the proletariat is judged to be incapable of its revolutionary vocation.

CLASS STRUGGLE AND THE DEVELOPMENT THESIS

Marx's theory of history rests on the distinction and relationship between the "forces of production" and the "relations of production" in an historically specific "mode of production," e.g., capitalism. These are the circumstances over which any generation has no choice, those "directly encountered, given and transmitted from the past." Following Cohen's account, the phrase forces of production refers to instruments of production, raw materials, and the productive capacities of labor-power ("strength, skill, knowledge, inventiveness, etc."). Especially important is labor-power reinforced by "productively useful science." In contrast, the phrase relations of production means the pattern of ownership of the forces of production: "*either* relations of ownership by persons of productive forces or persons *or* relations presupposing such ownership."[6] The pattern of ownership establishes a specific class structure in each historical mode of production.

In his logical reconstruction of historical materialism Cohen emphasizes the objective conditions necessary for revolutionary change. Elaborating Marx's "1859 Preface," Cohen argues that there are two principal theses of Marx's theory of history: the "Primacy Thesis" and the "Development Thesis." The Primacy Thesis states that specific productive relations exist in a certain society because they are "propitious" for the development of the productive forces. As the forces increase they reach a point where they can no longer develop within these relations of production. That is, the existing relations of production (ownership) become "fetters" on the further development of the forces and are replaced by new relations.[7] Therefore in the dynamic of history the forces of production have "primacy" over the relations of production.

This presents an immediate and oft-mentioned problem: how can it be said that the forces have primacy when their development only occurs through the relations of production? Critics of the materialist theory of history argue that since the forces of production only develop within specific relations of production, the latter actually appear to have primacy over the former. At the least, the necessary interaction between the forces of production and relations of production should deny the primacy of the forces of production.

Cohen defends the logical argument of historical materialism by carefully articulating the Development Thesis: there is an autonomous tendency in history for the forces of production to develop, although this development is only realized through specific relations of production. The qualifying phrase distinguishes Marx's position from a claim that the forces of production tend to develop autonomously. The historical *tendency* of development of productive forces is autonomous. This does not imply that the productive forces will develop regardless of the existing relations of production. The forces of production manifest their primacy precisely by selecting the relations of production which are most propitious for their development. Cohen argues in this way that, contrary to the critics, it is not only consistent to argue that forces develop through relations of production but necessary because otherwise the forces of production would not have the effect of selecting optimal relations of production.[8]

According to Cohen, Marx believed that it is this autonomous tendency of the forces of production to develop that makes history "a coherent story."[9] Cohen states that the forces of production manifest this historical tendency because of certain facts of human nature and the human condition: rationality, historical scarcity, and a degree of intelligence that allows people "to improve their situation":

> Given their rationality, and their inclement situation, when knowledge provides the opportunity of expanding productive power they will tend to take it, for not to do so would be irrational. In short, we put it as a reason for affirming the development thesis that its falsehood would offend human rationality.[10]

Cohen admits that what is rational is not always immediately implemented by society. However, history demonstrates the growth of the productive forces and "societies rarely replace a given set of productive forces by an inferior one."[11]

Cohen acknowledges that the materialist theory of history rests on a kind of "functional explanation." The actual mechanism by which productive forces select appropriate relations of production is not specified by Marx but Cohen insists that it need not be specified for historical materialism to be *logically* defensible. He points to the analogous statement that "birds have hollow bones because hollow bones facilitate flight" as a functional explanation that is acceptable although it does not specify the mechanism that caused the development of hollow bones.[12] In this example, Darwin eventually provided the missing causal link through the theory of natural selection. Cohen suggests that Marxists have not yet provided similar mechanisms for elaborating their theses but they are as logically defensible as the statement about birds before we knew exactly how it is that birds came to have hollow bones.

Cohen's elaboration and defense of the key theses of historical materialism are directly relevant to the present topic in the following way. In Cohen's portrayal of historical materialism class struggle does not have the central role in historical change sometimes ascribed to it. Relations of production persist if they further the development of the forces of production. Ruling classes are therefore only in power to the extent that their particular interest coincides with the universal interest.[13] When the relations of production fetter the forces of production, a ruling class will certainly resist the introduction of new relations but the ruling class will fail. This must be true if there is indeed an autonomous tendency in history for the forces of production to develop—if the Development Thesis is true and history is a "coherent story" in the manner argued by Marx.

Cohen strongly insists that he is not a "breakdown" theorist; he does not believe that capitalism will fall without the mediation of class struggle.

> [S]ocialism grows more and more feasible as crises get worse and worse (but not *because* they get worse and worse). There is no economically legislated final breakdown, but what is *de facto* the last depression occurs when there is a downturn in the cycle *and* the forces are ready to accept a socialist structure *and* the proletariat is sufficiently class conscious and organized.[14]

However, the level of the forces of production ultimately decides when a revolution will be successful or not. "Hence to say, as some Marxists do, that 'class struggle is the motor of history,' is to abandon historical materialism."[15] History cannot be explained by class struggle.[16] Rather, history is explained by the fettering of the forces of production by existing relations of production and by the Primacy Thesis, that when fettering occurs the existing relations of production will be replaced by those appropriate to further development. The contrary position is utopian.

Cohen's clarification of historical materialism has been criticized on several grounds: he employs an abstract because unsituated notion of rational action, he neglects the conditions necessary for a revolutionary class to attain the capacity to overthrow the ruling class even when the forces are fettered, and, in trying to support the Primacy Thesis, he consequently misconceives the relationship between forces of production and relations of production. In regard to the first, Andrew Levine and Erik Olin Wright dispute the idea that the impetus behind the historical development of the productive forces is the "rational adaptive practices" of human beings.[17] They argue instead that particular class relations in a specific historical situation always structure individual interests and rationality. The class relations within which persons are situated may actually make it rational *not* to pursue actions which would develop the forces of production. For example, within feudal relations a "rational peasant" would probably have preferred stagnation without exploitation by feudal lords to progress with exploitation. "Class-specific notions of scarcity and rationality" embodied in relations of production always crucially mediate the development of the productive forces.[18]

Robert Brenner elaborates the class-specific rationality argument in his analysis of the transition from feudalism to capitalism in Europe. First of all, he reminds us that only capitalist relations create a situation in which producers are forced to increase the forces of production. Within pre-capitalist relations, lords and peasants had nonmarket access to means of production and to means of subsistence. "[P]roducers will find it in their rational self-interest to specialize only under capitalist property relations, and then *only because they have no choice* but to produce competitively for the market."[19] Since neither lords nor peasants were dependent on the market, there was no competitive pressure to increase the forces of production.

Secondly, Brenner argues that precapitalist relations were actually structured such that the interests of individuals of both classes encouraged them to actively resist changes that would be necessary for economic growth.[20] Obtaining food supplies through the market was uncertain because of low agricultural productivity. Peasants therefore found it rational to diversify rather than specialize in cash crop production, marketing at most specific agricultural surpluses. "The resulting tendency to production for subsistence naturally constituted a powerful barrier to commercial specialization and ultimately the transformation of production."[21] On the other side, the lords also had nonmarket access to means of production from their own land and their extra-economic appropriation from the peasants. They therefore did not have to compete in production. Due to the absence of a class of landless laborers who could serve as tenants or wage laborers, a lord would not find it in his self-interest to expropriate his peasants (nor easy, in any case). Also, lords would find it irrational to devote their resources to bettering productive techniques because of the supervisory costs of a labor force that would have no economic incentive to "work diligently or efficiently" (they could not be "fired").

> Under such conditions, it made little sense for the lords to allocate their income toward investment in the means of production. They found it rational instead to direct their resources toward various forms of unproductive (though reproductively effective) *consumption.*[22]

The lords's situation led them to invest any surplus in military capacity, to maintain their hold on the peasants and to resist the predations of other lords, rather than investing in superior productive forces.

What is rational and what is not is therefore only established within specific class relations. "[P]roperty relations, once established, will determine the economic course of action which is rational for the direct producers and the exploiters."[23] From this Brenner concludes that "pre-capitalist economies have an internal logic and solidity which should not be underestimated" and that "capitalist economic development is perhaps an historically more limited, surprising and peculiar phenomenon than is often appreciated." He suggests that the transition to capitalism may actually have been a result of "unintended consequences."[24]

Assertions of a transhistorical interest in development embodied in human rationality are therefore insufficient to maintain the Development Thesis. Due to the structuring of rational action by specific property relations, action within determinant class structures are central to explaining the course of history. As we will see later, variants of the class-specific rationality argument are the basis for many of the conclusions of analytical Marxists and also for Brenner's rebuttal of world-system theory.

A second criticism of Cohen's interpretation of historical materialism is that a crucial link is missing in his argument. Levine and Wright con-

tend that mere incompatibility of the forces of production and existing relations of production is not enough to produce revolutionary change that
would institute more favorable relations of production. Incompatibility is
not the same as contradiction. The latter requires "endogenously generated imperatives for change" that only exist if a class emerges that is capable of both destroying the old ruling class and of organizing the
productive forces anew.

> Incompatibility leads to contradiction only if there exist class ac-
> tors capable of being bearers of a new society, a new social form
> that would liberate the development of the forces of production.
> Whether or not such a ruling class exists or will be generated de-
> pends not upon a dynamic vested in the forces of production, but in
> the specific historical forms of the social relations of production.[25]

This raises the issue of "class capacities," the "organizational, ideological,
and material resources available to classes in class struggle." If these capacities are not forthcoming, then incompatibility can simply result in
"permanent stagnation."

Levine and Wright argue that the central problem of a materialist theory of history is to show how interests in change promoted by the fettering
of the forces of production "are translated into social and political practices."[26] In contrast, Cohen suggests that class interests will more or less
unproblematically call forth class capacities. For example, Cohen argues
that as the productive forces stagnate, the ruling class will lose its allies
while the rising class will gain support. "The maladies of capitalism and
the development of the forces under it stimulate proletarian militancy."[27]

Levine and Wright criticize this position in two ways. First, they note
that the persuasiveness of Cohen's argument is substantially undercut by
his rejection of the labor theory of value, on which traditional Marxian crisis theory depends.[28] Without it, there is no obvious reason to believe that
capitalist crises grow worse with time. To this we can immediately add
that even if the problems of capitalism do increase in intensity, unless class
capacities are developed, any militancy that may result from economic
stresses will not be *proletarian* militancy but rather violent struggles of an
all too familiar kind.

Secondly, Levine and Wright argue that an existing ruling class and
its relations of production may be maintained just as much by disruption
of oppositional class capacities. The capitalist mode of production itself
contains tendencies which seriously undermine the class capacities of the
proletariat.

> Socialist political strategies must contend directly with the obsta-
> cles in the way of developing appropriately revolutionary class ca-
> pacities: the institutional form of the capitalist state, divisions
> within the working class, and between the working class and its
> (potential) allies, and mechanisms of ideological domination and
> deflection.[29]

Cohen does not elucidate how these divisions will be overcome and therefore does not provide convincing arguments on why these class capacities
will emerge. To this extent, his interpretation of the theses of historical
materialism is at least incomplete.

Levine and Wright's position is again strengthened by Brenner's
analysis of the historical transition from feudalism to capitalism. Brenner
rejects the idea that commercialization (the rise of trade) or population increase ("secular Malthusianism") explains the transition.[30] These "eco-
nomic/determinist" arguments fail when one looks at comparative
historical evidence which shows that commercialization and population increase had different impacts in different parts of Europe.[31] Instead, Brenner presents a kind of class capacities argument. The reason for the
differential impact of these forces is to be found in the existing class relations and the "relatively autonomous processes of class conflict."[32] The
relative strengths of the contending classes decided what the impact of
commercialization or demographic changes would be; i.e., these forces
were refracted through the existing class relations. Moreover, the strength
of the peasants depended especially on the particular structure of the village community (the development of independent political institutions),
and the ability of peasants to obtain political codification of the village
community.[33] Therefore, it is political relations and class struggle that actually determined whether feudal relations would be supplanted by capitalist relations and consequently whether the forces of production would
increase. John Roemer notes that Brenner's analysis "turns classic historical materialism on its head. It is not the level of development of the productive forces that determines the economic structure, but class power that
determines property relations, which in turn determine the speed of development of the productive forces."[34]

These considerations restore the centrality of class struggle to the explanation of why certain relations of production prevail at particular times
and places. The historical interaction of forces of production and relations
of production is mediated by the class-specific rationality engendered by
property relations in specific circumstances and also by the class capacities of the contending forces. If this is true, Levine and Wright argue,

"then it is not the case that the existing relations of production are functionally explained by their tendency to promote the development of the productive forces. They may be just as fundamentally explained by their tendency to undermine the capacity of rival classes to become effective political forces."[35]

In the face of these and similar arguments Cohen has clarified his interpretation of historical materialism. First, he responds to Levine and Wright's criticism of the view that the tendency of the forces of production to develop is a direct consequence of transhistorical "rational adaptive practices" of human beings. Cohen states that he did not intend to imply that rationality in the development of the productive forces (the 'search and select process') is applied directly to the productive forces themselves. Instead, people rationally select *relations of production* which further the development of the productive forces.[36] He agrees that there may be periods of ruling class resistance to the introduction of new productive forces and states that in pre-capitalist societies, productive increase may merely occur within the existing relations of production, not because of them, as in capitalism. He now presents what he calls the "Weaker Development Thesis," that for cultural and other reasons whole societies may lack an endogenous tendency to increase the productive forces but that the Development Thesis may still be true from a global perspective.[37] Finally, Cohen concedes that historical materialism only applies to periods of "epochal development," thereby limiting its "political applicability."[38]

However Cohen's fundamental response to his critics is, first, that although "economic and political structures are not unproblematically congenial to progress," development of the forces of production has taken place. In fact, "the *greater* the propensity of social structures to throw up rationality problems is," the stronger the argument that development of the productive forces ultimately depends on the transhistorical "facts that people are rational, innovative, and afflicted by scarcity." If one rejects this, one must produce another explanation for the "frequency of progress and infrequency of regress."[39]

Secondly, against those who insist on the historical importance of class capacities, Cohen vigorously restates his main point: classes do not create the conditions which occasion their struggles. "[W]hen Marx called on the workers to revolutionize society he was not asking them to bring about what would explain their doing so: the exhaustion of the progressive capacity of the capitalist order, and the availability of enough productive power to install a socialist one."[40] Cohen's position is clearly formulated in his response to Jon Elster's suggestion that game theory would be helpful to Marxian theory in that the Marxian theory of history "centres on exploitation, struggle, alliances, and revolution." Cohen argues that "the items on Elster's list are the actions at the center of the historical process, but for Marxism there are also items more basic than actions at its center."[41] Although "class struggle is always essential for social transformation," this does not imply that class struggle determines the course of history.[42] Classes will emerge to successfully overthrow the existing relations of production only when the forces of production have been fettered by these relations.

> The vicissitudes of class struggle decide just *when* a ruling class is supplanted, once a superior social order is objectively possible. But if one goes beyond that and says that the vicissitudes of class struggle decide whether or not the ruling class is supplanted at all, so that there is no objectively grounded answer to the question of whether it will, in the end, go, then one denies the parameters within which, for Marxism, class struggle operates.[43]

As Cohen argues in various places, if nothing else the class struggle perspective begs the question of why the weaker class is weak.[44] Nevertheless, Cohen admits that if historical materialism is to be a persuasive theory, the functional explanations of historical materialism must be fleshed out by linking them to actions, the "proximate causes of social effects."[45]

In a more recent elaboration of these issues Wright, Levine, and Elliott Sober acknowledge that the historical development of the productive forces is at least "sticky downward" and present several arguments for why this may be the case.[46] Nevertheless, they deny that there is a tendency toward the selection of "optimal" economic relations. They conclude that the tentativeness of the emergence of class capacities makes "suboptimal outcomes" in "unfettering" the forces of production more likely. "It is class struggle that, in the end, determines whether and how we move along the map the theory provides."[47] On these grounds Wright, Levine, and Sober propose a version of historical materialism they call "weak historical materialism," in which "the forces of production only determine a range of possible sets of relations of production; selections within this range are determined by historically contingent causes that bear particularly on the capacities of class actors to transform the relations."[48]

One thing on which Cohen and Wright, Levine, and Sober agree is that the kind of empirical evidence that would test the theory of historical materialism is unclear at present.[49] It is worth noting here that another participant in this discussion, Alan Carling, develops a further version of the

Primacy Thesis that he believes *is* empirically testable. Carling calls his thesis "Competitive Primacy," arguing that when there is competition between two systems of production relations, the one that has promoted a higher level of the productive forces will "prevail" over the system with the lower level. This version of primacy of the forces of production is "deliberately less ambitious" than Cohen's in that it does not require that forces of production select propitious relations in every society. It more modestly states that when there is competition, the society with relations that result in a higher level of productive forces will prevail.[50] One can therefore reasonably propose that history shows a "bias" toward development of the productive forces, grounded in the at least episodic competition between societies with different relations of production and differing levels of productive forces. "Perhaps all that can be said is that history exhibits a *bias* imparted by Competitive Primacy; a bias weaker than a tendency but considerably stronger than nothing at all."[51]

At first glance Carling's perspective is indeed promising for empirically testing the materialist theory of history. However it actually reveals a major limitation of the discussion thus far. When one considers the kinds of productive forces that would allow one set of relations to prevail over another, it appears that Carling's Competitive Primacy is at base a variant of social Darwinism. One major weakness of social Darwinism is that it conflates success with other kinds of superiority. In this way it reduces the theoretical space for evaluating the capacities that are being selected and rewarded.

A similar closing of theoretical space occurs in the preceding discussion. It is assumed that if class capacities emerge when the forces of production are fettered, then revolution will ensue. The meaning of "fettering" and its obverse, "development," has been taken to be tolerably clear. Carling's contribution to the analysis of historical materialism inadvertently reveals that the discussion thus far begs the question of which productive forces are being fettered and the related issue of what "optimal relations of production" means. However, revolutionary motivation depends crucially on the meaning of fettering itself, that is, under what conditions will large numbers of people regard the forces of production as fettered? Asking this question threatens to introduce paralyzing complications for the theses of historical materialism. However, not asking the question would reduce historical materialism to irrelevance for the most important social questions. At the least, discussion of the issue directly opens a much broader perspective on the role of class struggle in the Marxian theory of history.

FETTERING

Fettering of the forces of production can imply several different things. For example, it can mean that the rational use of existing forces is blocked by the relations of production ("use-incompatibility") or that the possible further development of the forces of production is obstructed by existing relations ("development-incompatibility"). Wright, Levine, and Sober argue that Cohen employs both notions in his interpretation of historical materialism but usually stresses development fettering.[52] Three other possibilities are decline of the productive forces, sub-optimal use, and sub-optimal development.

In a more recent essay Cohen explores the multiple meanings of fettering. He notes that the ambiguity stems from the word development itself, in both English and German (*entwicken*). Develop can mean either "improve" or to "bring to fruition." He also agrees with those who argue that Development Fettering is less likely to motivate revolutionary action than Use Fettering, on the grounds that the former is probably less "perceptible" than a "discrepancy between capacity and use."[53]

However, rather than choosing between the two, Cohen proposes a notion of fettering that draws on both use and development.

> [L]ook neither merely at how fast they ["economic systems"] develop the forces of production nor merely at how well they use them but at the trajectories they promise of *used productive power,* which is a multiple of level of development and degree of use. And call a system *fettering* if, given both the rate at which it develops the forces and how well it uses them, the amount of productive power it harnesses at given future times is less than what some alternative feasible system would harness. That is the Net Fettering proposal.[54]

For example, one could argue that although capitalism develops new generations of computing power more quickly than a socialist system, a socialist system could be preferred on the grounds that it uses the productive capacity more fully than capitalism.[55]

However, the idea of Net Fettering raises the clear possibility that the opposite might be true. If capitalism develops forces of production more quickly than socialism, then even if capitalism only uses a percentage of the productive power created it could still be superior in regard to Net Fettering. Due to compounding of development, capitalism would soon have a larger base on which its percentage of use would proceed. It would therefore overtake a socialist society that fully used all of its productive capacity but developed it at a slower rate. In this example, capitalist society would still be superior in net of utilized productive power due to the developmental dimension.[56]

Wright, Levine, and Sober reject the Net Fettering proposal for the reason that it remains less likely to motivate revolution than simple use-fettering. The idea of a use/development trajectory is still more difficult to project than the simpler notion that there are existing capacities that are at present unused due to the existing relations of production.[57] Nevertheless, even if this is true of potential revolutionary motivations, it does not answer Cohen's point regarding the reality of the longterm trajectory of the productive forces if capitalism is indeed superior in development of the productive forces. In this case one must ask how enduring a revolution would be if a socialist society would have to compete with a capitalist one. Elimination of the theoretical importance of development fettering is not so easy to accomplish.

At this point Cohen expands the discussion by stating that there are other criteria for preferring socialism than only this one, specifically "justice" and more "qualitative" aspects of social life. This pointedly introduces new complications to the topic of fettering. We must specify which objective capacities are being fettered, i.e., further development and/or use of which capacities for what ends? In this regard Cohen defines a social "contradiction" as the situation in which "a society's economic organization frustrates the optimal use and development of its accumulated productive power, when prospects opened by its productive forces are closed by its production relations."[58] He argues that capitalism is contradictory in this sense. Capitalism greatly increases the productivity of labor, opening two broad possibilities: increased output and stimulated consumption or increased leisure. However, profits depend on increased consumption, therefore capitalism consistently blocks the prospects of "toil reduction."[59] Historically this bias toward output was progressive, laying the basis for rapid growth and for reducing scarcity.

> But as scarcity recedes the same bias renders the system reactionary. It cannot realize the possibilities of liberation it creates. It excludes liberation by febrile product innovation, huge investments in sales and advertising, contrived obsolescence. It brings society to the threshold of abundance and locks the door. For the promise of abundance is not an endless flow of goods but a sufficiency produced with a minimum of unpleasant exertion.[60]

Cohen argues that the "distinctive contradiction" of advanced capitalism is therefore not "underdeployment of resources" but rather their "grotesque overdeployment in some directions and injurious underdeployment in others."

A more "qualitative" evaluation can admit that capitalism is more productive but prefer socialism on the grounds that it promises "a better way of life."[61] However, Cohen goes beyond mere evaluation to suggest that this is the reason that capitalism will be replaced. "There is much disagreement within Marxism about why capitalism then becomes untenable. In my view, it is ultimately because people no longer have to labour in the traditional sense that they can no longer be made to labour for capitalists."[62] Wright, Levine, and Sober point out that Cohen's view of fettering and contradiction is therefore not blockage of development but "irrational deployment" of existing resources.[63]

From this perspective the notions of fettering, compatibility, and optimality are crucially dependent on an idea of the rational deployment of productive capacity from the standpoint of human preferences. Cohen himself indicates a serious problem with this position. Cohen quite rightly argues that human preferences are conditioned by knowledge of alternatives. People may not choose leisure if the society in which they live has stifled the "theory and practice of leisure." "And this further manifestation of the output bias adds to the explanation of general acquiescence in it. Free time looks empty when the salient available ways of filling it are inane."[64] But if this is true, the movement toward a qualitatively better society becomes considerably more problematic. If the concept of fettering must include human preferences, then whether forces are fettered or not depends on people having the opportunity to rationally assess alternatives. However this is not immediately possible because people live in a system in which the alternatives are not impartially presented.

The collective determination of preferences must be a part of the concept of fettering insofar as people's preferences determine exactly what are the important available objective capacities that are being obstructed. The prospects for socialism therefore depend on a struggle for the constitution of an arena in which such a discourse can unfold. In sum, pushing the topic of fettering in this direction ultimately explodes the objectivistic approach of much of the discussion of compatibility, optimality, and fettering.

The question of preferences is crucially related to one other very important element that must be present for objective capacities to exist: a "feasible alternative set of relations." The above considerations shift the ground of the argument from incompatibility of forces and relations of production in a specific historical system to an evaluation of the relative capacities of alternative systems for advancing the productive forces. The importance of a feasible alternative is often brought out when Development Fettering is being discussed but it is also true that Use Fettering requires conceiving a feasible, even if counterfactual, set of relations.[65] The issue of a workable socialist society must therefore be considered part of the concept of fettering itself in that objective capacities only exist if a feasible alternative exists. Furthermore, the plausibility of the alternative, as we know all too well at this point, clearly influences people's preferences.

From the foregoing it is obvious that the concepts of fettering and development have irreducibly subjective and normative aspects that have not been fully integrated into the theory of historical materialism. It is possible that these aspects cannot be accounted for at the level of abstraction at which such a theory of history must proceed. From their own perspective, Wright, Levine, and Sober conclude that the existence of different historical trajectories based on variable class capacities, along with other considerations, makes the normative defense of socialism inescapable. "It is now clear that the reluctance of traditional Marxism to do so was naive and even pernicious."[66] This is a position shared by a great many recent Marxists, including, as we shall see in a different context, Cohen himself. It is true that this position contains the danger that the normative dimension will be emphasized too much and socialism will be conceived as merely a matter of ethical decision.[67] Since a renewed emphasis on the normative dimension of societal conflict is one of the defining characteristics of recent Marxian theory, further examination of this topic will be reserved until later.

At this point the analysis of the principal theses of historical materialism has clarified one immediate question. Cohen and Wright, Levine, and Sober agree that class struggle has an important role to play if Marx's theory of history is true, although they disagree on the extent of this role. If class struggle is not the motor of history it is at least its necessary transmission. Wright, Levine, and Sober are particularly persuasive that class capacities may be disrupted by existing relations of production and other institutions and processes. If the insurgent class does not develop such capacities, the unfettering of the forces of production (in any interpretation of fettering) is unlikely. If we cannot specify the conditions under which classes will achieve such capacities, then it appears that history is indeed, to borrow Cohen's phrase, not "objectively grounded."

Many recent Marxian theorists have seized on these perplexities in the Marxian theory of history in order to reject the key ideas of historical materialism while still maintaining some kind of anti-capitalist perspective. Marxists like Wright, however, have responded by attempting to establish the conceptual links between class structure and the emergence of class actors in order to theoretically clarify those aspects of contemporary capitalism that obstruct the development of class capacities. This is a necessary first step in formulating a political strategy for collective anti-capitalist action.

Using this approach, the immediate task is to examine what the concept the proletariat itself means in light of various developments in advanced capitalism. The preceding discussion demonstrates the importance of the role of the proletariat in keeping historical materialist theory from disintegrating. However, recent theory has actually been hard-pressed to keep the concept of the proletariat itself from disintegrating. It is to these arguments that we can now turn.

Two

Production, Interests, and Class Capacities

For several reasons the historically central role of the proletariat in furthering progress has become theoretically dubious. First of all, in recent decades other oppositional social movements have apparently displaced the working class in vigorously contesting aspects of advanced capitalist societies. The primary issues and sites of struggle of these movements have not centered on production relations, the *locus classicus* of social movements anticipated by Marxian theory. The intensity of racial and ethnic conflict, battles over gender relations or sexual orientation, the rise of fundamentalist religious movements in all parts of the world, struggles over ecological and quality of life issues, and various community/citizen initiatives (e.g., the anti-war and anti-nuclear movements) cannot be captured by the traditional Marxian focus on production and distribution issues. Attempts to do so seem increasingly to be Ptolemaic exercises; the "groups in motion," as Jean Cohen calls them, are simply not classes.

A second, related, reason is the continuing development of occupational and socioeconomic categories that defy Marxian predictions of the increasing polarization of classes and of clear identification of social groups by ownership or nonownership of means of production. Professionals, technicians, managers, and white-collar workers in general form huge middling classes that at the least require a finer conceptual net than traditional class theory offers. Erik Olin Wright summarizes this theoretical situation as "the embarassment of the middle classes."[1] The theoretical problem is exacerbated by the fact that many participants of prominent social movements are either drawn from or destined to become part of these same ambiguous social categories.

A third reason is the failure of social democracy in advanced capitalist societies to achieve substantial steps toward socialism. This is coupled with the evident limitations of Third World post-liberation governments and the failure of overtly socialist parties (the late Eurocommunism of Spain, Italy,

France, and Portugal) to seriously challenge capitalism. The retrenchment of socialist movements everywhere in the 1980s and 1990s continues to dissipate socialist hopes. The aftermath of the revolutions of 1989 has so far had the same effect. Not only have Marxian theory and practice been vigorously attacked, but the label "socialist" itself is eschewed by many of the dynamic social and political movements of the present.

In light of these developments, there have been several attempts to rethink Marxian class theory in order to invigorate its analytical potential. The most notable and tenacious work in this direction is that of Erik Olin Wright. Wright has made two distinct attempts to reformulate the Marxian theory of the class structure of advanced capitalism, both focused on conceptualizing the structural position of the new middle classes so prevalent in advanced capitalist societies.

As is often noted, Marx created two class 'maps': an abstract class map at the theoretical level of capitalist mode of production, identifying two classes, and descriptions of various actors in his political writings that are alleged to be involved in class struggles. However, Marx never provided a "systematic linkage" between structure and actors.[2] Because social experience is so disjoined from the abstract Marxian concept, many critical theorists have ultimately responded by rejecting the centrality of the concept of class for analyzing the dynamic of capitalist societies. Unfortunately, many of the same theorists confusingly continue to speak of classes and class struggles, employing traditional class language without grounding it in a specific notion of class structure.

Wright argues quite correctly that the specification of class structure is logically prior to discussion of class struggle or class organization.

> To speak of *class* formation or *class* struggle as opposed to simply *group* formation or struggle implies that we have a definition of "class" and know what it means to describe a collective actor as an instance of class formation, or a conflict as a class conflict instead of some other sort of conflict. Elaborating a coherent concept of class structure, therefore, is an important conceptual precondition for developing a satisfactory theory of the relationship between class structure, class formation and class struggle.[3]

Wright distinguishes three ways that one can define class struggle: "by the nature of the *agents* in conflicts, by the *objectives* of the conflict, by the *effects* of conflict."[4] He emphasizes the first, defining class struggles as those in which class actors or organizations clearly representing classes engage in conflict and in which "the lines of opposition in the conflict" are "class lines." Wright wants to exclude the idea that class struggles properly so-called require that the *conscious objective* of the conflict be class relations of distribution or power. This would be too historically restrictive a definition. Nor does he allow that just any conflict which has an effect on class relations is a class struggle. Since innumerable conflicts could have such effects, this would be too loose a definition, tending to reduce the relation between history and class struggle to a "tautology." "The thesis that class struggle is the 'motor' of history, then, means that it is conflict between actors defined by their location within class structures which explains the qualitative transformations that demarcate epochal trajectories of social change."[5]

Wright is quite clear that this is a thesis, not an established fact. He argues that we must test this explanatory thesis in order to clarify the degree to which struggles between actors structured along class lines can actually explain social conflict. To pursue this type of analysis, however, we must be able to clearly define these agents. For this, we have to formulate a strategy for bringing the abstract concept of class structure closer to the observed categories of social life in capitalism. Wright argues that there are two broad strategies one can use to try to link the abstract two-class model with existing collective actors. One can hold fast to the two class model and add additional explanatory mechanisms such as political and ideological variables, or one can try to provide a more complex structural map which could identify the immediate effects of class structure on social struggles. Wright's own work has focused on elaborating the conception of class structure. He wants to produce a more nuanced view in order to see what such a complex structure itself could explain before resorting to political and ideological variables.[6]

Wright has subsequently produced two conceptually distinct maps of the class structure of advanced capitalist society which he calls the "contradictory class locations" approach and the "multidimensional exploitation" approach.[7] Both approaches identify contradictory locations of interests in the class structure, but the particular mapping principle employed in each has important theoretical implications. We will briefly examine each before turning to the broader discussion of the theoretical status of the proletariat that has partly resulted from Wright's work.

CONTRADICTORY LOCATIONS IN THE CLASS STRUCTURE

The contradictory class locations approach provides an alternative to conceiving the "new petty bourgeoisie" (Nicos Poulantzas) or "professional-managerial class" (Barbara and John Ehrenreich) as a new unified class engendered within advanced capitalism.[8] In order to delineate the multiple structural divisions within this group and its relationship to the proletariat Wright adds criteria partly developed through engagement with the class analysis of Poulantzas. Wright especially focuses on "control" or "lack of control" over different aspects of the productive process. He distinguishes "three central processes underlying the basic capital-labour relationship" that can then be used to distinguish different locations: "control over the physical means of production; control over labour power; control over investments and resource allocation."[9]

Wright argues that the separation of these dimensions of production is historically grounded in certain developmental tendencies of capitalism. First, capitalism has progressively eroded the measure of worker control over the labor process—both control over physical means of production and over the pace and direction of their own labor—through the establishment of factories (rather than "cottage" production) and by utilizing technical innovations which resulted in "deskilling" and Taylorist "scientific" management. Secondly, the functions of capital have been differentiated through two kinds of separation of ownership and control: the separation of "economic ownership" ("control over *what* is produced") and "possession" ("control over *how* things are produced"), and the separation of "legal ownership" (ownership of stock) from "real economic ownership" (control of investment and accumulation). The differentiation of these aspects of capitalist accumulation has led to the increase in the numbers of professional managers and coordinators of these various parts of the process of capital accumulation. Finally, the concentration and centralization of capital in large capitalist enterprises has stimulated the "development of complex hierarchies," resulting in layers of middle management, line supervisors ("foremen"), marketing specialists, etc.[10]

Wright anchors this elaboration of class structure in the two conceptually given polar classes of capitalism, the bourgeoisie and the proletariat. The bourgeoisie controls all three aspects of capitalist production whereas the proletariat controls none of them. Although it is not one of the classes of capitalism on the conceptual level of mode of production, he also includes the traditional petty bourgeoisie—owners of means of production who do not control the labor-power of others—as a basic class in his schema because the "simple commodity production" which defines this class persists within the fully developed capitalist mode of production.[11]

Wright uses these three dimensions of the relationship between capital and labor to determine several additional positions within capitalist class relations, defined by control or lack of control of these aspects. Such positions are not actually classes but rather "contradictory locations within class relations." These locations comprise elements of two of the three classes in capitalism and are therefore contradictory between either (1) the bourgeoisie and the proletariat ("managers and supervisors"), (2) the traditional petty bourgeoisie and the proletariat ("semi-autonomous employees"), or (3) the traditional petty bourgeoisie and the bourgeoisie ("small employers").[12]

The first location is constituted of those in capitalist production who generally do not control investment and resources ("money capital") but do have some control over the physical means of production and over labor-power. This location is quite broad depending on the amount of control of these aspects, ranging from top managers to immediate supervisors on the factory floor or in the office. Wright characterizes the second location in this way: "In their immediate work environment, they maintain the work process of the independent artisan while still being employed by capital as wage labourers. They control how they do their work, and have at least some control over what they produce."[13] Such individuals have no control over investment and resource allocation and "minimal control over the physical means of production" but considerable control over their immediate working conditions. Wright suggests that professors, laboratory researchers, some skilled craftspersons, and many technicians should be included in this category. The third location is simply very small employers who control their own investment and physical means of production and have some but minimal control over the labor of others. In all of these categories there is, needless to say, a considerable range and therefore a "certain arbitrariness."[14] However, the utilization of criteria of control allows us to clarify many ambiguous locations in the class structure of advanced capitalism and brings the abstract class map of Marx somewhat closer to the micro-level of specific occupations.

Wright's interest in clarifying positions within the class structure of contemporary capitalism is not an end in itself: "Marxism, however, is not primarily a theory of class structure; it is above all a theory of class struggle."[15] Wright's attempt to further specify the class structure is intended to shed light on potential class struggles. As discussion in the preceding chapter suggests, the central issue here is the relation between class structure and class capacities, or "class formation."[16] Wright defines class capacities as the consequences of social relations within a class that allow it to advance its class interests. In the proletariat traditionally conceived, there are two such aspects: the "structural capacities" of the proletariat that result from the concentration of labor in the workplace, and the "organizational capacities" of a class, the class conscious aspect of class capacities furthered, for example, by trade unions.[17] Wright argues that the structural capacities of a class limit its organizational capacities.

On the basis of this analysis, Wright concludes that class structure does not determine a "unique configuration of class capacities." Instead, class structure sets limits on the possible relations within a class, i.e., on class formation.

> One way of looking at this process is to imagine that every position in the class structure has a certain probability of being organized into a given class formation. The concept of "limits," in these terms, refers to the patterns of these probabilities as they are determined directly by the class structure. . . . In these terms, contradictory locations within class relations can be viewed as those positions which have the least determinate probabilities of being organized into given class formations. They are characterized by multiple potential mappings into class formations, which reflect the objective contradictory character of the class interests of such positions.[18]

Class struggle is consequently expanded in Wright's usage to include struggles over the development of class structure itself, over the structural and organizational capacities of classes, and over the mapping of contradictory locations, i.e., over which of the fundamental classes of capitalism will politically and ideologically absorb those in contradictory locations.

The idea that there is a gap between class structure and class formation is of course implied in the concept of contradictory locations itself. However, Wright's precise point is that there is always such a gap, even between what would usually be considered relatively noncontradictory locations. Wright argues throughout his works that class structure does not immediately issue in collective actors based on class structural position. Instead, the relation between structure and formation has, as he says, a "complex and contingent character."[19] "Class relations may define the terrain upon which interests are formed and collective capacities forged, but the outcome of that process of class formation cannot be 'read off' the class structure itself."[20] Although Wright is not fully clear on why the gap exists for unambiguous locations as well, this is true for several distinct reasons. The structural capacities of a class generated in production could be weakened or strengthened by residence patterns or, as Brenner argues regarding the peasantry, by village structures. This could partially account for national variations in class struggles, an explicit objective of Wright's theory. Secondly, the specific organizational forms of workers such as trade unions—industrial unions or skill-based (craft) unions, company or industry-wide—clearly affect class formation.[21]

Given this analysis, the problem for the socialist movement is how to attract occupants of contradictory locations that are relatively close to the working class into the working class formation. Wright argues that those in contradictory locations have an interest in socialism but also gain "real privileges" from capitalist relations of production. Even if the occupants of contradictory locations are brought into a working class formation, their contradictory interests will not simply disappear. The task of socialists is to develop organizational forms that will finesse the contradictory interests of these locations, in order to bring them into the working class formation, and that will also allow the interpenetration of the immediate interests of the working class with its "fundamental interests" in socialism.[22] The usefulness of elaborating the concept of class structure in this way is that we can then develop a "theoretically specific" role for "political and ideological determinants of class formation."[23]

THE MULTIDIMENSIONAL EXPLOITATION THEORY OF CLASS STRUCTURE

For several reasons Wright later rejected this first approach to clarifying the class structure of advanced capitalist societies. First, there were nagging problems such as the distinction between control of the physical means of production and control of authority relations. He later concluded that these were two species of the same thing: domination of workers.[24] The schema is also complicated by assertions of levels of control: difficulties in defining "autonomous" and "semi-autonomous" in a way that would reveal "contradictory interests" rather than merely "heterogeneous" interests, and the apparent variability of autonomy in specific occupations such that autonomy becomes dubious as a basis for class division.[25]

However, Wright sees the main problem of the contradictory class locations theory in the tendency for the material interests of exploitation to be displaced by relations of domination. Although in this schema the relation to exploitation (in the sense of claim on the surplus) is implied, it is not central to the conceptual map. For example, the two "novel categories"—managers and semi-autonomous employees—are solely defined by their location within domination relations.[26] This is a major failing of the theory, Wright argues, because if one defines classes according to domination or control then the centrality of class structure, i.e., the focus of critical social theory on relations of production, is easily challenged. If domination is the crucial category, then the issue arises of why domination in the work-place should be considered any more important than other relations of domination in society (e.g., gender relations). Workplace relations are thereby displaced as the key relation in society and class theory loses its anchor in production, a theoretical development that is fatal to any Marxi-an account of society. Critical theory then easily slides into a "multiple op-pressions" analysis of society that is very difficult to link with the theory of historical materialism.[27]

Wright wished to retain, if possible, the centrality of class but he ar-gued that the focus on domination, along with its other failings, does not produce a clear conception of "objective," "specific," and "opposed" inter-ests.[28] Therefore Wright returned to an exploitation-centered notion of class in order to anchor the theory in production relations and clarify the concept of interests. However, at the outset this way is blocked by the in-creasing untenability of the traditional basis for theorizing capitalist ex-ploitation, the labor theory of value. The objections to this theory must be briefly noted here because Wright adopted a variant of a new theory of ex-ploitation that does not rely on value theory.

G. A. Cohen states that the classical Marxian theory of capitalist ex-ploitation was actually suggested by the characterization of feudal ex-ploitation. Under feudalism the surplus is clearly extracted by means of surplus labor on the part of serfs.[29] Marx argued that capitalist exploita-tion is also the extraction of surplus labor but it takes the form of the appro-priation of the labor-created surplus value embodied in a commodity. Marx's argument rests on the labor theory of value, i.e., that the rate at which commodities exchange depends on the socially necessary labor time embodied in them. Commodities do exchange at their values (so defined) under competitive capitalism; capitalism is, therefore, as its apologists state, based on the equal exchange of values. Labor-power is a commodity and its value, at which it is purchased by capitalists, is determined like all commodities by the labor embodied in the commodities necessary to repro-duce it. (As John Roemer has noted, this is a supply-side theory in that value is determined by the consumption bundle necessary to produce it, not by demand.[30]) If this is so, it is not immediately clear in what way capital-ism is exploitative.

Marx's answer is that labor-power is a unique commodity that creates more value than is exchanged for it. This rests on the general distinction, originally made by Aristotle, between the exchange-value and the use-value of a commodity.[31] In the case of labor, this distinguishes labor-power (a commodity) from labor (an activity). Due to the competition among workers, capitalists purchase the commodity labor-power at its cost of production (subsistence), but its actual use, concrete labor, creates more value than the cost of labor-power. Profits come from this surplus value that labor creates in its application. This fact is hidden in that the surplus value is embodied in the commodities appropriated by the owners of the means of production. They own the means of production and therefore own the product. In this way the proletariat is exploited: due to the commodification of labor-power and the competitive commodity structure of capitalism, proletarians are not paid the full value of their labor any more than serfs were under feudalism.

Further consequences of the labor theory of value bear on the breakdown thesis discussed earlier, especially the "tendency of the rate of profit to fall." Marx argued that only living labor adds value to a commodity; means of production such as machinery and raw materials merely pass on their embodied value to the commodity. (We can abstract from these in a competitive situation where all will quickly adopt similar machinery and techniques.) Competition causes the increased use of machinery, increasing the "organic composition of capital." Therefore the rate of profit, the surplus over the total investment in constant capital, declines for the economy as a whole. Assuming that the value of constant capital does not fall, this leads to crisis tendencies of capitalism.

Recent arguments reveal several kinds of difficulties with the labor theory of value which reduce its persuasiveness for formulating a theory of exploitation. First, there are technical problems in the application of this theory which make it hard to utilize in economic analysis. The existence of heterogeneous labor (skilled labor), from which Marx abstracted in his economic theory, does not allow us to clearly calculate the value of labor-power by the consumption goods necessary to reproduce it. The value of labor cannot simply be inferred from the wages paid because in Marx's theory value and prices are not identical. This shows the importance of an enduring topic in Marxian economic theory known as the transformation problem, i.e., how to relate value to prices.

Secondly, the labor theory of value appears to be superfluous for critical economic theory. Based on Piero Sraffa's work, Ian Steedman and others show that profit rates can be determined by specifying (in Wright's phrase) "the socio-technical conditions of production and the real wage."[32] If this is true then the labor theory of value is unnecessary for determining profits or appropriation of the surplus, i.e., exploitation. Surplus *extraction* theory therefore does not require a surplus *value* theory of profits.[33]

Thirdly, it is argued that the labor theory of value is logically incoherent. G. A. Cohen has explored the logical inconsistencies in the labor theory of value, especially between the argument that 'labor creates value' and the argument that the "value of a commodity is determined by socially necessary labor-time." If labor creates value, then past labor created the value of present commodities. If this is true, however, then value is not actually determined by currently necessary labor-time. The two statements are simply inconsistent.[34] Exploring these and other logical issues, Cohen concludes that labor does not create value; labor creates what *has* value, and it is the appropriation of the things that have value that is the real basis of the charge of exploitation.

> Yet the workers manifestly do create something. They create the product. They do not create *value,* but they create *what has value.* The small difference of phrasing covers an enormous difference of conception. What raises a charge of exploitation is not that the capitalist appropriates some of the value the worker produces, but that he appropriates some of the value of *what* the worker produces. Whether or not workers produce value, they produce the product, that which has value. And no one else does.[35]

Cohen concludes that the relationship between the labor theory of value and exploitation is one of "mutual irrelevance."[36]

Of course there are defenders of the labor theory of value. For example, M. Morishima has established the "Generalized Fundamental Marxian Theorem" by showing that positive profits only occur where there is a positive rate of exploitation of labor.[37] In response Roemer argues that exploitability is not however a unique characteristic of labor-power: any commodity can be shown to be exploitable in this fashion.

> One can adopt any good as the value numeraire and prove a Generalized Commodity Exploitation Theorem, which states that profits exist if and only if each produced commodity possesses the property of exploitability when it is taken as the numeraire for calculating embodied value. This conclusion is not surprising, because the rate of exploitability can be viewed as a measure of the productive efficiency of a factor.[38]

In a similar vein, Jon Elster remarks that it is actually "man's ability to tap the environment [that] makes possible a surplus over and above any given consumption level."[39] Finally, Marx himself acknowledged that communal labor, i.e., organization of the labor force (scale, technical division of labor), creates a surplus. For all these reasons, then, at the least the surplus need not only result from the difference between the exchange-value and use-value of labor.

Given these serious and varied criticisms of the labor theory of value and the surplus value theory of exploitation, if exploitation is to be used to delineate the class structure of capitalist societies, then exploitation must be reconceptualized. In order to establish a class map based on material interests forged in exploitation relations, Wright adopted a version of John Roemer's general theory of exploitation. We will reserve further discussion of Roemer's revised theory of exploitation to the next chapter because Roemer's thinking on the issue has evolved to the point where he no longer believes exploitation properly so-called is a central issue, a position with which Wright disagrees.

Wright clarifies his own conception of exploitation by first distinguishing it from "economic oppression." Economic oppression exists when a group's material welfare is detrimentally affected by exclusion from control of assets. Although this generates a material interest in change, it is not the same as exploitation.

> In the case of economic oppression, the oppressors' material interests would not be hurt if all of the oppressed simply disappeared or died. In the case of exploitation, on the other hand, the exploiting class needs the exploited class. Exploiters would be hurt if the exploited all disappeared. Exploitation, therefore, binds the exploiter and exploited together in a way that economic oppression need not. It is this peculiar combination of antagonism of material interests and inter-dependency which gives exploitation its distinctive character and which makes class struggle such a potentially explosive social force.[40]

On these grounds, Wright defines exploitation as the "economically oppressive appropriation of the fruits of the labor of one class by another."[41] He adds that "to appropriate the fruits of someone else's labor is equivalent to saying that a person consumes more than they [sic] produce," i.e., that the person appropriates more than her or his share of the surplus.[42] For exploitation to occur, then, both economic oppression and appropriation of labor must occur. Wright acknowledges that, like his contradictory locations formulation, this notion of exploitation depends on an idea of domination. However, he argues, again following Roemer, that this domination is not at the point of production but rather takes place on the level of ownership of assets, i.e., through protection of property rights rather than through the enforcement of authority relations within production.[43]

On the basis of this alternative to surplus value theory, Wright develops his multidimensional exploitation approach to elaborating the class structure of capitalism. Wright argues that contemporary capitalism contains three kinds of productive assets, ownership (exclusion of others) of which allows individuals to appropriate a share of the surplus beyond their productive contribution: "capital assets," "organizational assets," and "skill assets."[44] Ownership of capital assets is still the primary basis of exploitation in capitalism. Ownership of the means of production enables the bourgeoisie to appropriate the surplus through ownership of the product. The originality of this theory lies in the argument that there are two "secondary" forms of exploitation as well.

Again, Wright's theory focuses especially on clarifying the class structural position of the middle classes. Similar to one criticism of the labor theory of value mentioned above, Wright argues that managers control organizational assets that are distinct from ownership of the means of production. Both Adam Smith and Marx acknowledged that "[t]he way the process of production is organized is a productive resource distinct from the expenditure of labour-power, the use of the means of production or the skills of the producer. . . . [O]rganization—the conditions of coordinated cooperation among producers in a complex division of labour—is a productive resource in its own right."[45] Wright admits that saying managers "own" rather than simply "effectively control" these organizational assets is too strong.[46] However, he argues that control of these assets is indeed a basis for exploitation of the labor of others.

Another part of the middle class is distinguished by ownership of the third kind of exploitation-generating productive asset. Experts and especially "credentialled" employees own "skill assets" that allow them to exclude others, bid up the price of the asset, and thereby appropriate part of the surplus beyond their contributions to production. "For this reason, possessors of credentials have interests in maintaining skill differentials as such, in maintaining the restrictions on the acquisition of credentials."[47] Wright acknowledges that in the case of all three of these productive assets, "the thesis that exploitation is rooted in the monopolization of crucial productive assets" is quite close to Frank Parkin's notion of group strategies of "social closure," derived from the work of Max Weber.[48] The importance of this admission will be demonstrated shortly.

Utilizing this conceptualization of multiple production assets, Wright elaborates a complex class map based on asset exploitation which, unlike the contradictory locations approach, is rooted in a fairly clear notion of opposing material interests. Because there are differing kinds of assets, individuals can be exploited through exclusion from one type of asset but simultaneously be an exploiter by ownership of another type. The middle class of managers and experts are exploited by capitalists (owners of capital assets) but are in turn themselves exploiters of those who lack organizational assets (in the case of managers) or lack skills (in the case of experts). Advanced capitalism is therefore characterized by multidimensional exploitation or contradictory locations within exploitation relations.[49] Wright expects that the material interests generated by this class structure are revealed in individual attitudes and will in this way condition class capacities.

> I am assuming, therefore, that one's location within the structure of class relations is an important mechanism determining forms of consciousness. This assumption is based, at least in part, on the view that class locations objectively structure the interests of actors and that people are sufficiently rational to come to know those interests. There should, therefore, be at least a tendency for those aspects of consciousness which revolve around class interests to be structured by class location.[50]

In a survey of Sweden and the United States Wright finds statistical support for this relation, although he admits that the empirical differences with the prior contradictory locations approach are minor.[51]

Besides the above, Wright draws certain political conclusions from this analysis. Wright conjectures that more than one post-capitalist future is possible, that differing anti-capitalist political projects might be promoted because of the existence of different kinds of exploitation, not all of which would be eliminated by the elimination of private ownership of capital assets. Since two types of exploitation exist beyond capital assets exploitation, Wright argues that exploitative post-capitalist societies are theoretically and politically explainable. For example, Wright argues that under certain conditions managers could become anti-capitalist—because they are exploited by owners of capital—and promote a statist mode of production that would leave their particular exploitation-generating asset secure.[52] Similarly, skill exploitation would exist even under a socialism in which organizational assets had been democratized ("democratic socialism"). However, Wright does not consider this as difficult a problem because if capital assets are not privately owned and organizational assets are democratically diffused, the residual exploitation based on skills would be more tractable.[53]

A related political implication of this new conceptualization concerns the likelihood of different class alliances, given the multiple interests based on asset exploitation. Wright argues that the capitalist class is usually able to exert hegemony over those in contradictory locations within exploitation relations because the capitalist class has the means to bind their respective material interests together. Elimination of net exploitation through high salaries for some of those in contradictory locations and the creation of opportunities for advancement into the "dominant exploiting class" reduce conflicts of interests between the capitalist class and individuals in contradictory locations. "When such 'hegemonic strategies' are effective, they help to create a stable basis for all exploiting classes to contain struggles by exploited classes."[54] The problem with this strategy is that cooptation is very expensive. Wright argues that the stagnation of capitalist economies will reduce the surplus available for distribution in this manner. In this case it is possible that the statist anti-capitalist interests of managers, perhaps in alliance with managers and experts in the state sector, would become more pronounced.[55]

An alternative is that the working class will forge an alliance with those in contradictory locations within exploitation relations. Wright argues that this is more difficult but possible, especially when contradictory locations are being degraded through "deskilling, proletarianization, routinization of authority, etc.," and when their situation is such that they are "net-exploited."[56] Forging such an alliance is in Wright's opinion crucial for the prospects of democratic socialism.

It is difficult to imagine a scenario in which socialism would become a real possibility in these societies without the co-operation of a significant segment of the people in such contradictory locations. Yet, at least in terms of their material interests, the incumbents of these contradictory locations are either directly threatened by socialism, or at least have relatively ambiguous material interests in a socialist transformation. This poses a deep dilemma for socialists: socialism is achievable only with the co-operation of segments of the population for whom socialism does not pose clear material advantages.[57]

Wright suggests that such an alliance could be formed around other interests than simply interests in consumption, e.g., "the quality of life, the expansion of real freedom, the reduction of violence."[58] On this point Wright's argument converges with the discussion of fettering in the previous chapter.

However Wright argues that such an alliance also poses dangers to the interests of the working class. As in his previous schema, the material interests of those in contradictory locations will not simply disappear if they form an alliance. These interests will persist and will lead to struggles over what kind of post-capitalist society will be established. The multidimensionality of exploitation indicates that the range of alternatives is such that the working class could still be exploited after capitalism.[59] We could add that if the alliance is formed around non-class issues, the indeterminacy of the result increases regarding the specific class interests of the proletariat. As we will see later, Adam Przeworski has explored the logic of this dilemma at length.

After Wright has further specified the class structure, he then acknowledges the inescapable role of politics. Wright argues that the prospects for all class alliances or class formation is "heavily mediated by politics and ideology."[60] He invokes Lenin to the effect that the political terrain greatly influences the conditions of struggle and possibilities of class formation. For example, Wright argues that some of the survey differences between Sweden and the United States can be attributed to differences in labor law, electoral arrangements, and the design of welfare provision—all of which can facilitate or obstruct class formation.[61] Struggles over these organizational forms are crucial to advance the possibilities of a broadened working class formation and therefore class capacities.

CRITICISMS OF WRIGHT'S THEORY

Two kinds of criticisms have greeted Wright's multidimensional exploitation theory of class structure in advanced capitalism. First, there are objections to specifics of the theory. Secondly, critics have argued from various theoretical perspectives that interests within capitalism have multiple determinations and therefore cannot serve as a coherent basis for identifying classes. Regarding the first, many theorists have argued that Wright does not clearly establish that skilled workers or experts actually exploit others. Instead, it could be that their marketable skill assets simply allow them to reduce their own exploitation, i.e., to escape superexploitation. Exploitation rests on excluding others so that a person can consume more than he or she produces. However in the absence of the labor theory of value, Wright does not provide clear criteria nor a "unit of measure" for analyzing an individual's contribution to production. Therefore, exploitation in the sense of appropriation of a surplus one did not produce cannot be persuasively argued.[62]

In response Wright acknowledges that it is difficult to say when one is appropriating the surplus produced by one's own skills (the surplus beyond the costs of reproducing one's labor-power) or is appropriating part of the surplus produced by others. His original position was that if one appropriates beyond the costs of reproducing one's own skilled labor, then one is an exploiter.[63] Wright now acknowledges that one can appropriate beyond one's own cost of reproduction but still be only appropriating the surplus one's skills have contributed in the labor process, not the contributions of others. On this basis, he agrees that it may be more accurate to say that the skilled are simply "less exploited" than the unskilled. He also concedes, perhaps too readily, that the material advantages of especially the "credentialled" do not necessarily imply "antagonistic material interests" regarding other workers.[64]

Beyond problems of operationalizing skill exploitation, Wright now apparently believes that the skilled benefit from exclusion of others but not from the actual effort of the unskilled. This would then be a case of economic oppression rather than exploitation. These can be easily confused: "In both instances, the inequalities in question are rooted in ownership and control over productive resources."[65] Since it cannot be determined if the skilled do appropriate the surplus produced by others (rather than that produced by their own skilled labor), the most that could be claimed is that monopolies on credentials are a species of economic oppression. However, Wright seems to be conceding too much in that "legal monopoly" and "closure strategies" do indeed imply antagonistic interests, even if one cannot construct a clear class division on these interests. Wright probably accepts the criticism because criteria which establish class divisions, not merely antagonistic interests, are his real concern.

As with skill exploitation, some have doubted that a distinct kind of exploitation based on organizational assets exists under capitalism.[66] It is quite difficult to actually separate organizational assets from capital assets in capitalism. Wright attempted to do so for two related reasons: to contribute to an analysis of the particular kind of exploitation in state socialist societies, and to argue the case that managers in capitalism may under certain conditions be drawn toward a statist post-capitalist society which would maintain their privileges. Peter Meiksins argues that it is more likely that under conditions of capitalist crisis managers would push for a kind of "managed capitalism" rather than become anti-capitalist.[67] Wright now agrees that managers are unlikely to be drawn toward an anti-capitalist politics. Regarding both "skill exploitation and organization exploitation (or, equivalently, skill-generated scarcity rents and organization-generated loyalty rents)," Wright now argues that these should be regarded as "the basis for *strata* within classes rather than for class divisions as such."[68]

Both of these emendations of Wright's theory result from a more pervasive difficulty of the multidimensional exploitation approach: as he partly admits, Wright does not actually clearly establish exploitation itself. "While it was still the case that I never attempted to directly operationalize exploitation as such—the class map is built around relations to exploitation-generating *assets* rather than exploitation *per se*—nevertheless, exploitation was the organizing principle for the overall class structural analysis."[69] However, since Wright has not clearly shown in what ways these assets generate exploitation, it is more accurate to say that he has at best mapped assets. Wright suggests that the problem lies in operationalizing exploitation by being able to distinguish between appropriation of one's own surplus and appropriation of the surplus produced by others.[70] Rather the problem appears to stem from retaining a labor surplus appropriation conception of exploitation after discarding the labor theory of value. Wright's difficulties actually result from the hole left in Marxian theory by the unpersuasiveness of the labor theory of value.

Several critics suggest that Wright's difficulties in establishing exploitation have an additional source in his individualistic premises. Wright is intent on showing how an individual owner (or controller) of assets exploits by consuming more than she or he contributes to the surplus. However, it can be argued that in contemporary capitalism it is impossible to measure individual contribution in this manner. Since all contribute to production in manifold ways, not individuals but the collective laborer is exploited.[71] This criticism is tantamount to repudiation of Wright's entire theoretical strategy of further specifying the class structure of advanced capitalism by linking the abstract concept of classes with economically ambiguous individual locations.

Beyond the specifics of Wright's theory, a second set of criticisms focuses on the general position that interests are sufficiently determinant to ground a conception of class structure. Wright's own reasoning on the matter is quite clear.

> Marxist treatments of class structure can be seen as emphasizing one or more of three types of effects: material interests, lived experience, and capacities for collective action. While theorists generally do not use precisely this language, implicit in most elaborations of the concept of class structure is one or more of these kinds of class-generated effects. In each case, these effects

are seen as directly generated by class structural mechanisms as such and, therefore, as providing the basis for the theoretical relevance of the concept of class.[72]

Class position need not be ultimately determining in order to be of explanatory importance. Class theory simply argues that class structure has causal effects in at least one of these three areas, even if these effects are blocked by intervening variables.[73] Therefore understanding class structure is always of at least methodological importance for analyzing social conflict. Substantively, a detailed class structural map would help us evaluate the probabilities and political strategies for forming radical coalitions to contest capitalism.

Wright argues that in the abstract concept of class bequeathed by Marx the three dimensions of class—material interest, lived experience, and collective capacity—"coincide." Marx's thesis of the increasing polarization of classes is partly based on a belief that these dimensions would converge. However, in the particular social relations and experiences of advanced capitalist societies, these three dimensions actually become separated. For this reason, the abstract concept is increasingly difficult to relate to the micro-level of experience and locations in capitalism.

Many socialist theorists have suggested that the lived experience of individuals be used as an alternative approach for analyzing working class identity and class action, and especially for conceptualizing the middle class. They argue that it is the different workplace experiences of workers that established the original intuition of the class location of the middle class, as demonstrated in the phrase "white collar."[74] Even the Ehrenreichs, in their attempt to theorize the "professional-managerial class" on the basis of interests, mention workplace experiences, although this does not play a primary role in their theory.[75] Discussions of the "service class" also focus especially on the situation and nature of this kind of work. This is shown in Anthony Giddens's summary of theories of the "new working class," although he criticizes the proposed homogeneity of the service class.[76]

Wright himself proposes three aspects of lived experience that could be considered commonalities forming the working class: compulsion to sell labor-power, experience of domination in the workplace required to transform labor-power into concrete labor, and powerlessness regarding control of the surplus.[77] However, Wright concludes that lived experience, unlike material interests, does not allow a level of abstraction capable of defining class structure on the micro-level. "[W]hile there are a range of strategies for deriving concrete material interests from the abstract concept of class relations, I know of no parallel way of deriving concrete lived experiences and collective capacities."[78] We should also point out that the focus on domination, compulsion, and powerlessness transcends production relations and would again strengthen the multiple oppressions approach, an approach that ultimately undercuts the importance of production relations altogether. It was on these grounds that Wright rejected his first theory of contradictory locations.

For these reasons Wright takes it as "axiomatic" that the most important commonality of class is material interests and therefore that this is the "most coherent basis" for analysis.[79] Production creates a set of commonalities of positions which entail certain material interests. This does not mean that individuals necessarily react the same way to their interests structured by production. They are not a class because they respond in the same ways to their situation but because, "by virtue of their relationship to the underlying mechanisms embedded in the social relations of production," they face the same objective "structure of choices and strategic tasks when attempting to improve their economic welfare—that is, the package of toil-leisure-income available to them."[80] Wright himself points out that workers's interests are affected by their choices regarding collective action, e.g., organize, take a second job, or move someplace else. He insists that the commonality of their interests does not therefore reside in identical "distributional outcomes" but in "the common material conditions which shape the available choices and strategies with respect to those outcomes." It is not that all workers are compelled to do the same thing or to face an unalterable fate that grounds their common interest; it is that they face the same structuring of alternatives, the same "trade-offs" and "dilemmas."[81] Again, Wright is quite clear that the explanatory primacy of specifically material interests is not to be inferred from his focus.[82] He uses the concept of material interests to map classes for methodological reasons: only in this way can we determine if interests or something else is explanatory and establish a theoretically precise place for other motivations.

The thesis that common location in production generates a class interest, advanced by Wright but also taken for granted by other Marxian theorists, is often criticized for failure to appreciate the differing individual and fractional interests among workers. In response Wright acknowledges that class interests on the immediate level are fractured "by particular markets, particular working conditions, particular forms of competition, etc." However, he insists that "members of a given class share common *fundamental* interests, interests over how the basic property relations of the society should be organized."[83] Utilizing the language of rational choice, Wright explains that immediate interests are interests structured within a certain game (or set of social relations) whereas fundamental interests concern which game should be played.

Wright argues that the Weberian definition of class situations as life chances, unlike the concept exploitation, does not lead to a conception of antagonistic interests. He notes that Weberians utilize a concept of material interests in discussing classes but, since these material interests are derived from market position rather than position in production, the typical Weberian argument (1) leads to a multiplicity of interests and class positions, and (2) material interests so conceived are not inherently antagonistic because they are not based on a notion of exploitation. Consequently: "In the Weberian approach, there are as many classes in a society as there are types of market capacities that generate common life chances."[84] As Anthony Giddens says, the Weberian market definition of classes leads to a *reductio ad absurdum* in that individual market situations always differ somewhat, thereby ultimately reducing market (class) situations to individuals.[85]

However, some theorists suggest that Wright himself opens Marxian theory to what Wright calls "the Weberian temptation"[86] by utilizing concepts such as assets that focus too much on distribution rather than production. In both theoretical approaches Wright employs Weberian criteria of authority in the workplace or credentials for affecting market chances. Wright himself admits that generally his empirical differences with Weberian theorists regarding the class structure are not large.[87] Carchedi blames this intrusion on Wright's adoption of Roemer's approach and game theory. To expose the limitations of Wright's conception of exploitation, Carchedi considers a hypothetical situation in which capitalists returned the surplus to the laborers. This would eliminate exploitation in distribution without altering production relations. Nevertheless, Carchedi argues, "the exploitative relations at the level of production, the fact that the workers would still have no say as to what to produce, for whom to produce it, and how to produce it" would remain.

Both the distribution and the production aspects of exploitation are necessary. But Wright's "game theory approach" simply erases the latter, specific, one. As a result, there is implicit in this approach to exploitation the notion that if the rich would disappear there could be an equitable redistribution of wealth produced *in the same way,* that is, in a capitalist way, under a system of capitalist production relations. The congeniality between game theory and reformist policies becomes then clear.[88]

Carchedi argues that Wright's theory is consequently a version of Weberian stratification theory. Although Carchedi does not pursue it here, this issue is extremely important in that it determines one's conception of the socialist project itself. If one defines class structure according to distribution, then one's conception of socialism could leave production relations untouched.

Although, as we will see, this focus on distribution not only applies to Roemer but is embraced by him, it is not completely accurate regarding Wright's theory. Wright argues that his concept of exploitation links both economic welfare and economic power, i.e., "interests in securing the conditions for material welfare and interests in enhancing economic power. . . . For the exploited, economic welfare is depressed by virtue of having surplus appropriated from them, and economic power drastically curtailed by being excluded from control over the allocation of the surplus."[89] In capitalism the extraction of the surplus places control of investment in the hands of the owners. Workers must be concerned not only about exploitation in the narrow sense but also about the uses to which the surplus is put. Material interests are structured around "both deprivations and powerlessness."[90] Overcoming powerlessness is therefore also a part of Wright's conception. It is true that by discussing *distribution* of power, the actual structuring of power in production receives less attention. However, regardless of its weakness for establishing an independent extractive notion of exploitation under capitalism, Wright's discussion of organizational assets and definition of democratic socialism as the dissolution of this kind of asset demonstrates at least his sensitivity to the issue.

This specific exchange nevertheless raises a crucial issue for determining the ultimate direction of socialist theory itself. Much socialist discussion focuses on exploitation as some sort of violation of equal reward. Distributional questions rely on a principle of equality and Marxian theory is then interpreted as reducible to a critique of inequality. We will see Roemer's explicit reasoning on this matter. However, we cannot simply ignore Marx's criticism of the egalitarian emphasis of certain conceptions of socialism, as opposed to defining socialism as the rational ordering of production. The two conceptions may be reconcilable but they are not identical. We must reserve further discussion but it needs pointing out here that this criticism of Wright actually poses deep unresolved questions in Marxian theory.[91]

From the other side, Frank Parkin, a Weberian theorist, argues that Wright's particular strategy for producing a more persuasive Marxian account of the class structure is not surprising. According to Parkin, it was

Weber who originally proposed the relation between class position and authority.

> The fact that these normally alien concepts of authority relations, life-chances, and market rewards have now been comfortably absorbed by contemporary Marxist theory is a handsome, if unacknowledged, tribute to the virtues of bourgeois sociology. Inside every neo-Marxist there seems to be a Weberian struggling to get out.[92]

Similarly David Rose and Gordon Marshall complain of the "irritating way" Marxists have of introducing Weberian criteria of class analysis as if they were new discoveries.[92]

Be that as it may, Wright's argument that Weberian theory does not yield a concept of antagonistic interests is not accurate. Parkin's elaboration of the Weberian conception in terms of "closure strategies" is clearly an account of antagonistic interests generated by market capacities. It is true that these material interests are not antagonistic along the lines of production classes, i.e., as classes defined according to position in production, but rather are based on credentials and other ascriptive (or, in Parkin's preferred usage, "collectivist") attributes.[94] But this only establishes that the antagonistic interests typically generated in capitalist society cannot be captured by the Marxian concept of class, thereby eroding the theoretical importance of class structure for analyzing social conflict in capitalism.

Moreover, Wright's theory appears to underestimate the degree to which interests are crucially determined by the political and organizational structures of workers. For example, many have pointed out that uneven trade unionization intensifies the material interest conflicts within the proletariat. Trade unions are quite often defensive, protecting the jobs of their members against the reserve army of the unemployed.[95] Along these lines, Philippe Van Parijs has recently proposed a different fundamental interest faultline in advanced capitalist societies, one which casts doubt on the very definition of the proletariat. Van Parijs argues that since having a job is still the key to having a good standard of living, the "central class divide" in "welfare-state capitalism" is actually formed by the conflicting material interests of the employed and the unemployed.[96] He shows that the unemployed would benefit more from the equal distribution of jobs than the equal distribution of wealth.[97] Since full employment is less and less likely in contemporary capitalism, the crucial material struggle is over jobs, with the employed and unemployed holding opposed material interests.[98] Using similar reasoning, Arthur Stinchcombe suggests that the real "class conflict" today is over income distribution through the welfare state.[99]

Other socialist theorists have evinced additional arguments that lead to the abandonment of the concept of objective class interest altogether. For example, Uwe Becker rejects Wright's idea of "fundamental interests" partly because of the absence of a clearly defined socialism on which these interests are allegedly based.[100] We can add that if an alternative to capitalism cannot be specified, struggles over multiply fractured immediate interests will be intensified. Similarly, Paul Hirst insists that the concept of class interest is faulty because political mediation is inescapable for interests to be formed. "Classes do not have given 'interests,' apparent independently of definite parties, ideologies, etc., and against which these parties, ideologies, etc., can be measured. What the means of representation 'represent' does not exist outside the process of representation."[101] Finally, giving voice to the doubts of many contemporary socialist theorists, Ernesto Laclau and Chantal Mouffe dismiss the concept of objective interest as simply arbitrary. It is "a concept which lacks any theoretical basis whatsoever, and involves little more than an arbitrary attribution of interests, by the analyst, to a certain category of social agents."[102] According to Laclau and Mouffe, this concept is generated by a "Diogenes-like search for the 'true' working class."

It is possible that the very focus on interests is fundamentally flawed. Several theorists contend that the concept interest is itself a capitalist structure and therefore cannot be used for charting a path beyond capitalism. For example, Agnes Heller argues that the concept interest actually reflects the alienation of bourgeois society. For this reason Marx himself rarely referred to class interest. For Marx, the proper category for imagining a qualitatively different society is "human need," not interest. The prospects for transcending capitalism depend on the generation of "radical needs."[103] Elaborating this perspective, Jean Cohen insists that struggles over interests cannot challenge the logic of capitalism. Only *"radical needs* that point beyond the competitive egoistic and economistic structure of interest and production specific to capitalist society" can do so.[104] Heller pointedly adds that these needs are not necessarily generated within the working class: "It does not detract from Marx's greatness that the bearers of these radical needs today are not, or rather not exclusively, the working class."[105]

Taking all of these criticisms together, the theoretical situation appears to be as follows. Marxian theory has been forced to introduce criteria such as market capacities and organizational control in order to produce a more useful and detailed analysis of the class structure. Marxian concepts of exploitation and the focus on relations of production simply are not closely enough related to the real experiences of individuals in advanced capitalism to produce a persuasive account of the class structure. Therefore, at the least, market capacities (even in the rather restricted notion of credentials) have to be taken into account.

Nevertheless, the Marxian criticism of market capacities and life-chances is correct: market capacities do indeed lead into multiple fragmentations. Therefore the admission of Weberian criteria for theorizing class structure actually seems to show the bankruptcy of the sphere of production as a whole for producing classes, except in the most abstract sense. Capitalist production does not clearly structure individual interests in class ways and therefore production does not provide stable class identities nor perhaps even the basis on which the elements of class identity could be forged through other mediations. Wright's interchanges with Weberian and other critics reveal that neither neo-Marxian nor Weberian theory is capable of adequately identifying classes. We may simply have to acknowledge, as Becker encourages, that individuals have a variety of interests that they weigh differently.[106]

Given the problems of the contradictory class locations approach, the weaknesses of the multidimensional exploitation analysis, and the multifarious objections to the idea of class interest, Wright admits that he is unclear how to proceed from here.

> In each case I tried to build a differentiated map of the class structure on the basis of a single principle. I cannot at this point offer a third general strategy of this sort which will dissolve the anomalies and difficulties of the previous two. Indeed, it is not obvious that the proper way to proceed is to search for a new, unitary principle for solving the puzzle of the middle class(es).[107]

However, he does advance certain observations at a lower level of abstraction, staying closer to the lived experiences of individuals but still focusing on material interests. In his most recent work, Wright develops further criteria for distinguishing the class positions of individuals, e.g., "multiple locations" as a consequence of holding several jobs, "mediated class locations" from being a part of "kinship networks," and an unavoidable class indeterminacy that stems from "temporal dimensions" of certain career tracks. He also mentions that many should be considered to belong to a "shadow class," resulting from the fact that a change of personal situation (such as divorce) could drastically affect one's material situation and interests. Finally, there is a general indeterminacy especially among experts and professionals in that ownership of capital assets sometimes depends irreducibly on the choices one makes in life, e.g., to invest or consume extra income, or the choices of managers and professionals to become self-employed. For this reason many professionals and experts, who face such choices in a typical career, must be considered to be in "objectively ambiguous locations."[108]

Wright's attempts to further specify the class structure have always been guided by the hope of theoretically advancing our comprehension of the class capacities of the proletariat. He now admits to doubts about the explanatory potential of the class structure in this regard. "While I continue to believe that solving the conceptual issues in class structure analysis is important, I no longer believe that this provides the key to understanding the more general problem of variations in class formation and possibilities for the creation of radical coalitions."[109] At this point in his work Wright is nevertheless still holding onto two key elements of all of his theories: first, he continues to attempt to map the interest structure of advanced capitalism, showing the subtleties of the material interests of individuals in different locations; secondly, he still employs a notion of contradictory locations. However, it must be acknowledged that the manner in which these locations can be considered locations within a class structure is becoming less clear as more and more criteria are utilized.

REJECTIONS OF PRODUCTION AS THE PRIVILEGED SITE FOR CONTESTING CAPITALISM

Wright's analyses of the class structure of advanced capitalism are driven by the intuition common to Marxian theorists that the concept capitalism itself somehow requires that revolutionary agents must be generated in the sphere of production. Many of Wright's critics conclude that this is untrue because the experience of capitalism transcends class categories. Becker succinctly states this position.

> Class struggle is not the motor of the history of capitalist society. If there is any such motor, and only in the sense of the central initiator of societal change, it is the dynamics of the capitalist economy, of which the structural antagonism between labor and capital is only one aspect.[110]

Wright himself appears to have at least partly conceded this position with the recent remark that, "Today, relatively few Marxists still believe that class analysis alone provides a sufficient set of causes for understanding the historical trajectory of capitalism."[111]

Although their reasoning differs, two prominent and self-described post-Marxian theorists, Andre Gorz and Jean Cohen, have forcefully rejected production as the crucible in which revolutionary agents are forged. Their arguments and similar perspectives open new doors for socialist theory and are now quite pervasive. Before considering the possibilities of political mediations for overcoming the multiple fragmentations engendered by the sphere of production, it is appropriate to examine these wholesale rejections of the very expectation that production will produce agents to challenge capitalism. Besides chastening further the hopes for the development of class capacities of the proletariat, the arguments of Gorz and Cohen imply additional dimensions of the meaning of fettering. In this way their theories amplify aspects of the discussion of the previous chapter and anticipate some of the themes of later chapters.

As suggested earlier, the idea of class capacities must include a realistic probability that the revolutionary class can organize production in a more fruitful fashion. In his book *Farewell to the Working Class,* Gorz argues that the primary reason Marxism identified the proletariat as the subject of revolution is its collective ability to take over and manage the means of production. Marx believed that the technological development of capitalism simplifies the majority of tasks in production, tendentially destroying the basis of skilled labor. Moreover, the vicissitudes of the labor market necessarily teach workers flexibility in employment. Marx's vision is that of the "polytechnic" worker, equipped for a variety of tasks and conscious of the capability, with her or his fellow polytechnic workers, to manage the process of production.[112]

Gorz states that even if we accept the "deskilling" of labor, it has not led to the consequences Marx expected.[113] Changes in the workplace and especially in the *social* division of labor have reduced the possibility of initiative by individual workers, groups of workers, or even whole units of production. Factories today do not even produce a whole product; they make a part of a product for other factories hundreds or thousands of miles away. This is made possible especially by technological developments in the communications and transportation infrastructure. The result for the individual workplace is even less flexibility over schedules, supply, and outlets than previously.[114] The ability to collectively appropriate the means of production has therefore remained a property of an abstract collective, "abstract" partly because it is inaccessible from the experience of the individual worker.

The important point for Gorz is that because the power of the collective only exists above and beyond individual abilities, the individual worker does not identify with the category "potential masters of production."

"Capitalist development has endowed the collective worker with a structure that makes it impossible for real, flesh-and-blood workers either to recognize themselves in it, to identify with it or to internalize it as their own reality and potential power."[115] The very developments which have increased the power of the collective to transform and control nature have reduced the capacities of individuals to recognize themselves in this power. The ubiquitous proposals for self-management can provide no remedy for this situation. The traditional problem of self-management, how to integrate the various units of production without statism, has intensified because of the extension of the social division of labor. Gorz argues that the institution of workers's councils today only leads to their reintegration as local arms of the trade union apparatus.[116]

In sum, according to Gorz new "imperatives" inscribed in developments of technology and in the elaboration of the social division of labor have made the phrase "realm of necessity" even more appropriate from the standpoint of the individual worker. Even those "in power" in the workplace have at most a kind of functional power, i.e., they are formally in the position to command but actually have little flexibility, initiative, or capacity to pursue alternatives. From this standpoint, the only hope for a freer society is not in attempting to change the organization of production, but in restricting its scope and importance for social life as a whole.[117] This means struggling for the expansion of free time by breaking the logic of capitalism as "productivism," especially by weakening the present support of productivism in modes of consumption. To be sure, the realm of necessity will continue. For Gorz, the first step toward liberating areas of social life is to always recognize the realm of necessity as necessity.

The conscious response of workers today to the above developments is to decisively reject production as a meaningful sphere of life activities. "For workers, it is no longer a question of freeing themselves *within* work, putting themselves in control of work, or seizing power within the framework of their work. The point now is to free oneself *from* work by rejecting its nature, content, necessity, and modalities."[118] Not only do workers not identify with their class, they do not even identify with the traditional site of class formation, i.e., production. This is true of the increasing numbers of those who only find occasional or marginal employment, but also of those whose capacities are under-employed due to the deskilling of the labor process. Gorz contends that for a majority of the population,

[a]ny employment seems to be accidental and provisional, every type of work purely contingent. It [the 'neo-proletariat'] cannot feel any involvement with 'its' work or identification with 'its' job.

Work no longer signifies an activity or even a major occupation; it is merely a blank interval on the margins of life, to be endured in order to earn a little money.[119]

Compared to this group of workers, the traditional working class of better paid steady employment is a privileged minority. Furthermore, "[n]othing indicates that this total alienation of socialized work can be reversed."

In Gorz's discussion the considerable literature on alienated labor takes an interesting turn. Work is *so* alienated that it loses all importance for self-definition. Modern production excludes any conception of a class subject whose identity is formed by its role in production. The accidental and contingent possibility of finding work and the meaninglessness of work for those who do find employment results in only one certainty: "that they do not feel they belong to the working class, *or to any other class*."[120] Therefore the site of struggle for identity through meaningful activity shifts to areas of social life outside of production.

Gorz refers to this new group of contingent workers as "a non-class of non-workers," "prefiguring a non-society within existing society in which classes will be abolished along with work itself and all forms of domination."[121] This group is a non-class in that their rejection of capitalist society is a rejection by individuals, not as a class. Their activities focus on attempts to carve out areas of individual autonomy (a non-society), separate from production and from the state. The goal is the development of individuality *"alongside* and *over* that machine-like structure."[122]

This attempt to create spaces of individual autonomy challenges capitalism in that the non-class no longer sees the development of the forces of production as progress. Not only does capitalism merely offer more of the same (productivism and consumerism), its future development presages worse: "more destruction, more waste, more repairs to destruction, more programming of the most intimate facets of individual life." The logic of capitalism, development of productive forces for its own sake, has reached its limits. "We are not going anywhere. History has no meaning."[123]

The creation of this "non-class of post-industrial proletarians" prefigures a new society only as the possibility of rupture with productivist consciousness. A new society is possible because this group rejects capitalism *as* individuals and *for* individuality. The rupture can be decisive because, although recognizing the permanence of at least a limited realm of necessity, this group rejects the sphere of production and its compulsions as the locus of emergence of a new society. However, this is only present as possibility because the new society must be a conscious creation of individuals, essentially without guidance.

[T]he crisis of the industrial system heralds no new world. Nothing in it is indicative of a redeeming transformation. The present does not receive any meaning from the future. The silence of history therefore returns individuals to themselves. Forced back upon their own subjectivity, they have to take the floor on their own behalf.[124]

Unlike Marxist accounts, class action is not necessary nor possible for individual goals. Only individuals can create spheres of individual autonomy; end and means are identical in this transformation. In Gorz's conception, there is no room for "representatives of class interests."

It is clear that Gorz has adopted aspects of Marx's description of the dialectic of alienated labor and utilized it for his own presentation of the phenomenology of workers's consciousness. He imitates the phraseology of Marx in describing the non-class: "a class of civil society which is not a class of civil society, a class which is the dissolution of all classes." But for Gorz, the non-class dissolves classes by stepping outside of the class framework itself, i.e., by denying production to be the site of social transformation. Gorz even parodies Marx's famous "fisherman, shepherd, critical critic" passage in order to underline the extreme alienation and sheer contingency of all work, i.e., its unimportance for individual identity.[125] Alienation theorists have done their work too well: only by abandoning the sphere of production altogether can individuals build meaningful and free lives.

Since the realm of production in even the most democratic socialism would still not be an arena of fulfillment and formation of identity, the goal of struggle must be to limit the range of operation of production. A new, emancipated society can only be achieved if socialist theorists recognize the profound "cultural mutation" that has taken place. " 'Real life' begins outside of work, and work itself has become a means towards the extension of the sphere of non-work, a temporary occupation by which individuals acquire the possibility of pursuing their main activities."[126] Capitalism can be challenged only if socialist theorists take this fact of cultural consciousness as their starting point and seek its "political extension."

In contrast to Gorz, Jean Cohen's critique of the importance of the sphere of production relies on more strictly theoretical considerations. Cohen is fully aware that our assumptions regarding oppression—or, in the terms of our previous discussion, fettering—determine our conceptualization of emancipated society. In criticizing the focus on oppression in production, she reveals the theoretical bases of certain debilitating silences in Marxian theory, especially on the traditional concerns of political theory.

Cohen's argument takes the form of a critique of the various reductions involved in Marx's class analysis. Cohen disputes the "assumption that *relations of domination* in modern society can be reduced to *social relations of production* and thus comprehended as *class relations*. . . ."[127] According to Cohen, this conflation of domination with "relations of production," expressed in Marx's class theory, yields a general identification of civil society with capitalism, entailing the primacy of the relations of production with regard to all other social institutions and processes. First, the "logic of the economy" is taken for the "logic of society as a whole"; and, secondly, domination is reduced to class relations such that political processes can only be seen as "epiphenomena of socio-economic relations."[128] Cohen exposes both of these reductions so that the institutions of civil society, the positive accomplishment of "modernity," can be appreciated for their role in advanced capitalism and as potential sites of struggle.

There are several reasons why Marx conflated "civil society" and "the economy." Marx accepted the classical liberal notion of the economy as a "self-regulating, self-reproducing" system when he formulated his critical social theory as an *immanent critique* of political economy.[129]

> [T]he theoretical reproduction of the logic of capitalism through the critique of the categories of political economy . . . has inherited its most basic proposition—that the capitalist economy can be analyzed as a self-sufficient, albeit contradictory, system, with its own internal dynamics and reproductive mechanisms.[130]

This focus on production was reinforced by Marx's intellectual background in Hegelian philosophy, especially the concerns with labor, alienation, and a "universal class in particularity." Like Gorz, Cohen argues that: "In effect, the universality and emancipatory role of the proletariat are logically and not sociologically derived."[131]

Cohen acknowledges that it was legitimate of Marx to consider capitalism as an abstract system, divorced from state action and actual historical development, in order to reveal its system logic. However, "to move from here to sociological predictions regarding class formation is a category mistake."[132] The fruit of Marx's abstract analysis of this system logic of capitalism and his residual Hegelianism was a confusion of the logic of the system with a theory of the formation of collective socioeconomic actors: "He assumed that the capitalist mode of production reproduces itself, its social actors, and their necessary motivations out of its own economic logic."[133]

All of the above resulted in Marx's "overburdened" and "too ambitious" class theory.[134] Furthermore, Marx's class theory and his conflation of capitalism and civil society kept him from seeing the *"positive achievements* of modern civil society" and in this way contributed to dangerous political tendencies in the socialist political tradition.[135] The first danger is easily identified. According to Cohen, because of the disjunction of what the proletariat is supposed to be and do, following the analysis of the abstract system logic (common interests, homogeneous, the "negation of the negation"), and what the proletariat actually is (internally stratified by position in the division of labor, by ethnic group and gender, by region), a representative of the common class interest becomes necessary. That is, Marx's conflation of the abstract system logic and the formation of social actors is the conceptual basis of Leninism.[136]

Secondly, Marx's identification of domination with class relations projects a vision in which the state will no longer be necessary.[137] The identification of civil society and capitalism results in communism being conceived as the "de-differentiation" of state and civil society.[138] This de-differentiation is inherently authoritarian in that it eliminates the space for civil society. Cohen's main theoretical concern in her work as a whole is to explicate the relationship between the development of democracy and freedoms in modern society and the emergence of an autonomous civil society.[139] Marx's confusion of civil society with capitalism means that the institutional bases of freedom are jeopardized in the development of socialism.

In order to elaborate the institutional bases of an emancipated society, what we need, as the title of one of Cohen's articles has it, is "more political theory." Cohen believes that Marx's various reductions obstruct the inquiry of political theory in a number of ways. Marx's economic determinism, which reduces politics and ideology to superstructures, clearly rules out independent reflection on political structures and their possibly autonomous role in the future. Furthermore, the critique of political economy focuses on the restraining effect of the relations of production on development of the forces of production. Cohen argues that exclusive attention to this conflict in the sphere of production leads to the postulation of communism as the free development of the forces of production: "productivism." Instead of political reflection, one gets a "mythology of abundance in an Eden of harmony" in which needs and their interpretation are unproblematic.[140] This takes the place of

(a) a practical philosophical reflection on "the good life" or the value choices involved in interpreting and acting upon needs and
(b) a social and political theory of democratic association and in-

stitutional forms necessary to make the concept of social individuality meaningful.[141]

In Cohen's opinion, reflection on the role of political institutions and institutions of civil society for the articulation and interpretation of needs simply becomes superfluous in Marx's project. Political theory was thereby falsely and dangerously deprived of its *raison d'être*.

If we expand the concept of fettering as discussed in the previous chapter, we can immediately dismiss Cohen's simplistic interpretation of abundance. Her perspective can actually be more easily accommodated to recent debates on historical materialism than she presumes. However, Cohen's central point is quite sound. Marx's class theory and focus on production lead to the attribution of the emergence of "radical needs" to only one site in society, i.e., production, and one group, i.e., the proletariat. Like Heller, Cohen insists to the contrary that modern capitalism is a system in which radical needs can arise in many different places, production being only one of them.[142] Marx's denigration of the "superstructural" moments of politics and civil society forecloses the possibility of comprehending radical contestation of the logic of capitalism outside of the realm of production. For this reason Marxian theory cannot develop an adequate appreciation of particularity and of new social movements as forces, albeit limited, for emancipation.[143]

In light of these arguments, Cohen rejects Marxian class analysis, although accepting production as one site of stratification and therefore a possible site for the development of radical needs which would challenge capitalism. She firmly rejects any notion of a "universal subject" and concentrates instead on the possibilities and institutional mediations necessary for uniting various particular social emancipatory struggles. Her interest in social movements stems especially from their potential to construct counter-institutions of civil society which can lead to the transformation of capitalism and to the democratization of all spheres of society, without de-differentiation of state and civil society.

Additional arguments which reject production as the primary site for contesting contemporary capitalism will be explored in later chapters. There, some of the themes of Gorz and Cohen—the declining importance of work, the emergence of radical needs, and the renewed importance of normative and political discussion—will be given more detailed and critical attention. To round out our discussion of the specific topic of class structure, what is important is the unavoidable conclusion that the sphere of production does not create interests nor identities in class ways. If one thinks of classes in terms of a "cluster of forms of structuration," and not as an "all-or-nothing phenomenon,"[144] at the very least one has to acknowledge that, although there are social experiences and structural positions that can be conceived in class ways, these are not usually exclusive enough to establish class collective action. Classes exist only in the abstract. Whether they will congeal into collective actors is conjunctural or dependent upon other conditions.

In the Marxian tradition, the other conditions that promise to establish the class capacity of the proletariat are various political mediations. These are mediations in that political organization and strategy are not presumed to be creating a class subject *ex nihilo*. Rather, political action intends to draw on and clarify existing social relations and experiences so as to form the revolutionary proletariat. However the arguments of the next chapter strongly suggest that these hopes, at least in the context of capitalist democracies, are misplaced.

Three

Citizens and Classes

Following Marx and Engels it is a widely held socialist belief that the development of democracy under capitalism creates greater possibilities for the organization of workers to pursue their class objectives. There are now a considerable number of discrete arguments that suggest that this belief is at least partly false. Although in some ways capitalist democracy establishes a space for furthering political class organization, in other crucial respects capitalist democracy actually disorganizes the working class as a class, thereby obstructing the development of working class capacities. This chapter attempts to bring together the various strands of this thesis by examining the arguments of several classical and current theorists who have contributed to it.

The Marxian analysis of the effects of democracy on class formation originated in a concern to identify and remove obstacles to the formation of the working class as a political actor, i.e., to facilitate the development of a class 'for itself.' Although mediations have always been considered necessary for political class formation (e.g., the development of unions, the creation of an independent workers party, the establishment of the International), Marx largely considered this task to be unproblematic.[1] The primary reason for the latter is that Marx believed the proletariat to be substantially forged as a class by its existence in the sphere of production. As the preceding discussion demonstrates, we do not have the luxury of this assumption. Class formation therefore depends crucially on the possibilities for developing effective political mediations.

Some of those who have pursued the topic of political mediations take their inspiration from a comment by Antonio Gramsci that the structures of capitalist democracy protect the hegemony of the capitalist class. "The massive structures of the modern democracies, both as State organizations, and as complexes of associations in civil society, constitute for the art of politics as it were the 'trenches' and the permanent fortifications of the front in the war of position . . ."[2] In his commentary on Gramsci Perry

50

Anderson asserts that the "representative State" is the "principal ideological lynchpin of Western capitalism," "the formal framework of all other ideological mechanisms of the ruling class," "the general code in which every specific message elsewhere is transmitted."[3] It should be added that this is not merely ideology, or, more precisely, that ideology is not as separate from material practice as is sometimes implied.

We can summarize the main points of the argument of this chapter in the following way. The characteristic political forms and processes of advanced capitalism endow individuals with a status and powers—citizenship—that further fragment class identity. Contrary to liberal political theory and its theoretical cousin, the base/superstructure dichotomy, polity and economy interpenetrate even under capitalism. This interpenetration paradoxically takes the form of the juridical creation of legally equal, rights-bearing individuals, resulting in the relative autonomy of both economy and polity. Capitalist democracy is established through an abstraction from class relations, necessitating political action for individual workers to be forged into a class. However, the primary capacity for political action open to individuals under capitalist democracy is electoral politics, making class formation subject to the constraints of electoral politics. In turn, the logic of electoral participation under the circumstances of capitalist democracy encourages strategies which reduce the political salience of class.

In order to evaluate the prospects of working class capacities we need to explore these arguments in some detail. After an early statement by Lukacs, and similar comments by Luxemburg and Sartre, we will examine Pashukanis's analysis of the juridical establishment of individuals, some criticisms of that analysis by Hirst, and Poulantzas's alternative conception of classes and political individualization. Secondly, we turn to Przeworski's utilization of aspects of Poulantzas's work, especially the objectivity of political and ideological relations in structuring and destructuring classes. Przeworski's argument is strengthened by his specific analyses of how the electoral dynamic of capitalist democracy disrupts the development of class parties. Finally, we will see how the recent historical work of Katznelson and his colleagues support the theoretical conclusions of Przeworski and consider Katznelson's own argument of how the concept class should be construed given these historical conditions. Needless to say these various arguments do not fit seamlessly together. Nevertheless, the whole should help clarify the specific mode of existence of classes under the conditions of capitalist democracy, a situation that has very serious implications for the project of class formation itself.[4]

CAPITALIST DEMOCRACY AND THE BOLSHEVIK RESPONSE

Georg Lukacs's early Marxian critique of capitalist democracy is important because it initiates many of the themes of later analyses. Lukacs argues that "bourgeois democracy" disorganizes the proletariat in several
ways. First, this democracy is built on an abstraction: individuals are directly linked to the state, unmediated by their existence in real life.[5] This
is of course a position shared by both Marx and Hegel in their respective
critiques of liberal political theory. Lukacs adds that this "pulverizing" is
furthered by the separation of economics and politics, one of the most important structural characteristics of capitalism. It is also reinforced by the
action of the bureaucracy, bourgeois political parties, the press, schools,
religion—that is, those agencies that Louis Althusser later characterized
as "ideological state apparatuses."[6]

The importance of this for working class politics is that the working
class is not a pre-existing collectivity. The working class must be forged
into a class through political organization. For this, bourgeois democracy
is not only un-usable but actually fragments the working class by fixing its
members as citizens. The various political and social institutions of existing democracy further the aim "of binding the individual members of these
classes as single individuals, as mere citizens, to an abstract state reigning
over and above all classes; *of disorganizing these classes as classes* and
pulverizing them into atoms easily manipulated by the bourgeoisie."[7]

Lukacs's primary target here is not the existence of "formal democracy" but those socialists who believe that these existing democratic forms
can be utilized by the working class to achieve class power. Because it appears that a majority of the population can be won to the "ideals of social
democracy," many believe that peaceful agitation can result in an "evolution into socialism." However, as Lukacs says, "The moment of deception
lies in *the undialectical concept of 'the majority.'*" In order to struggle successfully for socialism the working class must be organized as a class and
this cannot take place through the structures of existing democracy. For
this we need the political form of "soviets," which unify the proletariat by
immediately bridging the division between economy and polity and in-
stalling the class power of the proletariat in the organs of government.

This analysis is repeated in Lukacs's criticism of the organizational
form of existing parliamentary parties, another important theme of this
general discussion. In these organizations the party is divided into leaders
and followers; it therefore does not engage the "total personality" of the
members. The freedom of its members is the freedom of "more or less pe-

ripheral and never fully engaged *observers* to pass judgement on the fatalistically accepted course of events or the errors of individuals."[8] This of
course leads into an argument for the Bolshevik form of political party.

Jean-Paul Sartre agreed with this analysis of both the isolating character of capitalist democracy and the importance of the mediation of the political party. Existing democratic forms are a part of the "processes of
massification"; "democratic rights" contribute to the mechanization of social relations. "The right to vote is the last straw: the worker finds in these
mechanical summations called elections no trace of the solidarity he is
seeking. It is a matter of voting *in isolation,* for a program which he did not
draw up and which he found out about in isolation: and the greatest number of isolations wins, in the name of the majority."[9] Again, to overcome
this isolation the working class must have its own political party. It is only
through this party that it can act as a class. "It is true that the C. P. is nothing outside of the class; but let it disappear and the working class falls
back into dust particles."[10]

The political implications of this kind of criticism of electoral democracy is well known. It leads to a "class instrumentalist" view of universal
suffrage. Given the class struggle, it is necessary to destroy the class
power of the capitalist class, and in a war you do not allow the enemy
weapons if it can be avoided. It is perhaps best to recall the words of someone who is usually cited against Bolshevism, Rosa Luxemburg.

> It makes no sense to regard the right of suffrage as a utopian prod
> uct of fantasy, cut loose from social reality. And it is for this rea
> son that it is not a serious instrument of the proletarian
> dictatorship. It is an anachronism, an anticipation of the juridical
> situation which is proper on the basis of an already completed so
> cialist economy, but not in the transition period of the proletarian
> dictatorship.[11]

Luxemburg's analysis is more nuanced than suggested in this brief quote
but for her also, the measure of bourgeois democracy is taken only in the
context of a class society and what is necessary to overthrow it.

Lukacs's analysis is important for broaching many of the general
themes of how capitalist democratic forms can be conceived as obstructions to the organization of individual workers into the 'proletariat.'
Democracy based on the representation of individuals separated from their
social context actively disorganizes the working class. These difficulties
cannot be overcome by representation through parliamentary parties
which are shaped by the structure of capitalist democracy.[12]

However, Lukacs does not exactly explain how these abstract individuals who are institutionalized in capitalist democracy are formed. They are not conjured out of thin air as the very word abstraction suggests. In fact, to insist on their abstract character runs the risk of underestimating the real practical effects of individualization in a capitalist democracy. This topic is explored more fully in a classic account by Lukacs's contemporary, Evgeny B. Pashukanis.

THE ORIGIN OF THE RIGHTS-BEARING SUBJECT

Pashukanis argues that abstract individualization originates in commodity relations. This is also the structural basis for the characteristic separation of polity and economy in capitalist societies which contributes to the disorganization of the working class. The specific topic of Pashukanis's work is the development of a Marxian theory of law. As an important part of his theory he examines the social structural origins of the "rights-bearing subject." His analysis allows us to raise the general question of "rights" and the ways in which "rights" can contribute to a mode of political action that to some degree may hinder working class organization. Pashukanis's discussion also creates a framework for pursuing other accounts with the same object, especially the work of Nicos Poulantzas.

Pashukanis argues that the individual institutionalized in capitalist democracy is the product of the development of commodity relations for mediating social production. Specifically, the category of the legal subject is a necessary concomitant of the development of alienable property, i.e., freedom to dispose of property on the market. From the standpoint of a capitalist economy, the "chief failing" of feudal property is its inertia, the fact that it cannot circulate.[13] The development of alienable property is simultaneously the creation of the legal rights-bearing subject.

> [T]he necessary condition for the realization of the social link between people in the production process—reified in the products of labor and disguised as an elementary category—is a particular relationship between people with products at their disposal, or subjects whose 'will resides in those objects'. . . . At the same time, therefore, that the product of labor becomes a commodity and a bearer of value, man acquires the capacity to be a legal subject and a bearer of rights.[14]

As Pashukanis puts it, the legal subject is "an abstract owner of commodities raised to the heavens."

In the development of a capitalist polity in accord with a capitalist economy, the legal right to own is extended to all. Essentially, the necessary juridical conditions of the bourgeois class are generalized. It does not matter from the standpoint of law that all are not owners and in fact cannot be owners if there are to be those who, separated from the means of production, are forced to sell their labor. The important point is that a legal status common to all citizens is established, differing from feudalism in which specific privileges are mediated by group membership.

The development of this legal status creates a notion of a capacity to act separated from one's real capacities, the latter of which are determined by one's position in the social division of labor. "At this point the capacity to be a legal subject is definitively separated from the living concrete personality, ceasing to be a function of its effective conscious will and becoming a purely social function. The capacity to act is itself abstracted from the capacity to possess rights."[15] This juridical individual is akin to "a mathematical point, a center in which a certain number of rights is concentrated." To a great extent Pashukanis's argument thus far is simply an elaboration of Marx's well known sardonic comment in *Capital* that commodity relations are "a very Eden of the innate rights of man."[16]

However, Pashukanis suggests that this is not mere ideology in that this ideological creation is institutionalized and therefore practically efficacious. He of course recognizes that these formal freedoms of equality and "autonomy of the personality" are "an instrument of deceit and a product of the hypocrisy of the bourgeoisie," wielded to defend class relations. But the "principle of legal subjectivity" is much more than this. It is a "concretely effective principle" that structures bourgeois society "from the moment it emerges from and destroys feudal-patriarchical society." Therefore, "the victory of this principle is not only and not so much an ideological process (that is to say a process belonging entirely to the history of ideas, persuasions, and so on), but rather is an actual process, making human relations into legal relations, which accompanies the development of the economy based on the commodity and on money." As such, it "is associated with profound, universal changes of an objective kind."[17] Legal subjectivity achieves an institutional embodiment in legal regulations, rights, law courts, trials, lawyers, and prisons. One of the major weaknesses of Pashukanis's theory is that this point is not fully developed.

Pashukanis relies on the labor theory of value for explaining the separation of polity and economy. This separation is made possible under capitalism because exploitation, the extraction of surplus labor, takes place through exchange, as surplus value. The commodification of labor becomes the avenue of exploitation. Since exploitation is hidden in the employment of labor itself, in Marx's phrase "other than economic pressure"—the direct intervention of political authority—is unnecessary.[18]

However, Pashukanis notes that this only establishes the possibility of the separation. The separation of polity and economy is made necessary for two other reasons. First, the competition of capitalists among each other requires an autonomous state in order to create the capacity of the bourgeoisie to act as a class. Secondly, value cannot function as a regulator of the economy if political authority intervenes, therefore the economy must be autonomous.[19]

Pashukanis's conception of the origin of the legal personality and of the individual as a rights-bearing subject has been criticized especially well by Paul Hirst. There are two aspects of Hirst's critique that are elaborated by others in analyzing the ways in which the fundamental structures of capitalist democracy disorganize the proletariat. First, Hirst argues that Pashukanis's derivation of the concept of legal personality is "economistic." By this Hirst means that Pashukanis presupposes a realm of production that is constituted prior to its legal determination, "an economy which generates and determines its own conditions of existence."[20] As we will see, the conception of a self-constituting economy is a particularly important object of criticism by Nicos Poulantzas.

Secondly, Pashukanis seeks to ground the legal form in commodity relations because he wants to establish the historical specificity of the legal form of social regulation in contrast to feudal regulation through privileges granted to social corporations. In doing so he presupposes the unity of the concept legal form, i.e., he tries to discover its essence, its "differentia specifica" in Pashukanis's own phrase. Hirst objects to this essentialism on the grounds that any attempt to reveal the essence of law by determining its origins implies that the content of law is substantially pre-given. This leads to an underestimation of the real objective efficacy of law in capitalist societies.[21] "Socialists confronting the particular legal-economic forms of modern capitalism, attempting reforms through legislative procedures or defending political practices against the courts can only be blinded and lose by subscribing to an essentialist doctrine of law."[22] An essentialist notion of law causes socialists to misunderstand history in that they then tend to conceive legal struggles—for example those concerning the incorporation of businesses—as inherently limited, pre-ordained, and therefore relatively unimportant struggles. In this way socialists fail to realize the actual stakes involved in such legal struggles.

Contrary to Pashukanis, Hirst argues that insofar as law has unity it does not derive from its origin in commodity relations but rather from its location in the legislative process and legal apparatuses. The legal form is socially objective in that it channels activity through legislative processes governed by legal procedures that are objective to the content of law.[23] Pashukanis's analysis is limited in that, for all of his remarks to the contrary, he still conceives the politico-legal processes of capitalism to be primarily ideological. This is revealed in his suggestion that the legal capacity to act is abstracted from the status as a rights-bearing subject, that it has no basis in a person's real capacities for action determined by her or his position in the social division of labor. In contrast, Hirst insists that the legal capacity to act is a real capacity; it is not an illusion but is rather action through a different form. Hirst's analysis establishes the general objectivity of the institutions of capitalist democracy relative to class formation. This institutional objectivity is crucial to the arguments of both Poulantzas and Adam Przeworski.

It has been difficult for Marxian theory to acknowledge and integrate the political implications of the institutionalization of this "rights-bearing individual." Many Marxists have denigrated the importance of rights on the grounds that appeals to rights propagate illusions about the neutrality of public authority and also because such appeals fail to recognize that rights are limited to a specific historical form of society. Although this is now subject to considerable debate, Marx himself generally rejected moral appeals and from "On the Jewish Question" to the "Critique of the Gotha Programme" tried to demonstrate the historically limited nature of rights.

It is now clear that this position begs important questions. First, the significance of rights is obscured by categorizing rights as merely an expression of the social structure. The implication of the latter phrase is that the political form of rights has no objective, autonomous relation to other social structures. However, even if rights are fundamentally grounded in capitalist social relations this does not necessarily mean that they cannot have an independent reciprocal effect on the social structure. Marx himself suggests this in one well known passage: "The specific economic form, in which unpaid surplus-labour is pumped out of direct producers, determines the relationship of rulers and ruled, as it grows directly out of production itself and, in turn, reacts upon it as a determining element."[24] If the latter possibility is admitted, then socialist theorists must fully integrate into their theory the political importance of assertions of rights and the manner of the institutionalization of rights. Only this can capture the specific, rather than abstract, existence of classes in capitalist societies.

Secondly, the general failure of Marx and earlier generations of Marxists to 'take rights seriously,' aside from the barriers this position presents for analyzing the structures of actually existing socialism, makes it very difficult to comprehend the fact that rights are the fundamental language of revolutionary movements in the world. Samuel Bowles and Herbert Gintis have recently reminded us of the importance of the assertions of rights not only for various liberation movements but also for the history of the labor movement itself through much of its history.[25] The central point of their analysis has been supported by more specific historical investigations. Both the French and American workers movements drew heavily on their respective national revolutionary traditions to formulate the demands of the movement.[26] For example, in regard to nineteenth century France William H. Sewell, Jr. remarks that: "Class consciousness, in other words, was a transformed version of liberal revolutionary discourse."[27]

Some of the difficulties of the topic are a consequence of the amorphous character of rights, as noted by both Eric Hobsbawm and T. H. Marshall.[28] However a full analysis of rights is necessary if Marxian theory is to be able to politically evaluate the importance of the language of rights in the history of the labor movement, in Soweto, in China, or in the United States. The reconsideration of Marx's position on moral argument, explored in a number of recent works, is for this reason alone quite welcome.[29]

One of the reasons that the appeal to rights is so common to oppositional movements is that assertions of rights clearly have a mobilizing and organizing potential. In a stray comment in *The German Ideology* even Marx acknowledged this, doubly surprising because it is one of the very few instances in which he ascribes a positive role to moral appeals.

> Saint Sancho [Stirner] again presents the proletarians here as a "closed society," which has only to take the decision of "seizing" in order the next day to put a summary end to the entire hitherto existing world order. But in reality the proletarians arrive at this unity only through a long process of development in which the appeal to their right also plays a part. Incidentally, this appeal to their right is only a means of making them take shape as "they," as a revolutionary, united mass.[30]

Even against other, better known positions of Marx, this is undoubtedly correct. The primary issue in the present context is whether mobilization through appeals to rights also has deleterious effects on workers pursuing their class interests.

It is clear that at least in one way the question of rights poses a practi-

cal difficulty for class formation. If the appeal is made to a specific authority such as a court, this reinforces the idea that political authority in capitalism is neutral. Hugh Collins has explicated this through the dilemma of
a radical lawyer who tries to defend a client by appeal to the law. Victory
tends to reinforce the idea that the law is neutral because it protects even
the rights of radicals.[31] Although appeals to rights have mobilizing potential, in this way they also may contribute to the illusion of classless society.

However, rights can lead into more complications for class formation
than this. Although rights are an abstraction based on the legal capacity to
alienate property, they generalize the conception of the rights-bearing subject. The autonomy of the individual implied in this conception historically eventuated in—after enormous struggles—the full political inclusion of
the working class as individuals. Although the typical political structure
of capitalism is based on an abstraction, the right to participate in political
institutions is a real capacity, not an illusion.[32] It is from this actual political situation that the actions of members of the working class proceed. For
example, the right to vote is a real power and rational individual workers
take advantage of this power, with consequences that are elaborated in the
work of Przeworski.

Before we turn to the arguments of Przeworski, however, we must consider an alternative way of conceiving the origin and institutionalization of
the individual. Whatever the limitations of his theory, Pashukanis was correct in his choice of questions. The individual is the atom of capitalist
democracy and as such the institutionalization of the individual must be of
prime concern in attempting to unravel the disorganizing effects of capitalist political forms on the working class. While rejecting certain aspects of
Pashukanis's conception, Nicos Poulantzas deepens our understanding of
the central role of the state itself as an objective determinant of class formation.

THE STATE AS UNIFIER OF NATION/CITIZENS

Poulantzas argues that one of the primary functions of the state is precisely
the disorganization of the working class through the representation of individuals. Unlike Lukacs, Poulantzas discusses in detail the relation between the political institutionalization of individuals and the topic of class
formation. It would be an understatement to say that there are perplexities
in Poulantzas's account but there are also certain relatively clear arguments on which we can focus our attention.

In order to reveal the relationship between politics and classes

Poulantzas rejects the base/superstructure model as being a misleading metaphor, a survival from liberal ideology. Poulantzas specifically rejects Pashukanis's commodity exchange theory of the state, i.e., the derivation of the state from the relations of circulation.[33] However, he is also opposed to deriving the state from the relations of production. Classes are not constituted by the relations of production and then disorganized by the state and ideology. Rather, the state is always immediately present in the very constitution of the relations of production and therefore always directly involved in class organization and disorganization.[34] In Poulantzas's conception, the state's relation to the relations of production is its primary relationship to social classes and class struggle.

Poulantzas argues that individualization is developed from certain fundamental characteristics of the capitalist labor process. Specifically, he argues that two characteristics of the capitalist labor process provide a "primal material framework" for elaboration: the separation of the direct producer from means of production, and the fact that workers perform their labors in private. This is the emergence of the "naked individual" of which Marx wrote.[35]

However, Poulantzas insists that these dependent/independent workers are not by the above two facts constituted as individuals. That position would theoretically restore the separation of the state from the relations of production by presuming a pre-existing substantive autonomy of the economy. In Poulantzas's conception these agents are not yet constituted at this point as "individuals/subjects" but are merely "supports of a structure of the labor-process." "The term 'bare individual' as a historical condition does not therefore in any way mean that agents, who were previously 'organically' in unities, arise *in reality* as atomised individuals, to be *later* inserted into combinations of capitalist relations of production, and then gradually to constitute social classes."[36] Instead, individuals are constituted directly by the state from this "mold of social atomisation and splintering."

According to Poulantzas, the social division of labor in capitalism is structured in distinct and multiple ways: economically, politically, and ideologically.[37] Economic structure is primary but this is not to say that relations of production (social relations) are constituted solely by the economic structure. The relations of production are structured simultaneously by economic, political, and ideological relations/structures, which Poulantzas refers to as the "constitutive role" of "political and ideological relations." "These relations are not simply added on to relations of production that are 'already there,' but are themselves present, in the form specific to each mode of production, in the constitution of the relations of production."[38] The idea that the relations of production form and maintain themselves naturally is simply a holdover from liberal ideology.

It is the state, not the sphere of circulation nor the sphere of production, that constitutes "the socio-economic monads as juridical and political individuals-persons-subjects."[39] Poulantzas refers to the state's individualization of agents of production as the "effect of isolation." As Poulantzas says in several places, although isolation is an effect of "the State's material ideological practices," it is nonetheless "terrifying real."[40] It manifests itself as competition. Competition is not given by the capitalist labor process; it is an "effect of the juridical and the ideological on *socio-economic* relations." Because of this effect, socio-economic relations are not experienced as class struggle but rather as competition among wage-earning workers and among capitalist owners, i.e., as intra-class competition.[41] "This ideology of individualization not only serves to mask and obscure class relations (the capitalist State never presents itself as a class State), but also plays an active part in the divisions and isolation (individualization) of the popular masses."[42]

Although the state has the primary role in producing the effect of isolation it simultaneously appears as the unifier of these isolated, competing individuals, as the "representative of the 'general interest.'" "This state presents itself as the incarnation of the popular will of the people/nation. The people/nation is institutionally fixed as the ensemble of 'citizens' or 'individuals' whose unity is represented by the capitalist state: its *real substratum* is precisely this isolating effect manifested by the CMP's [capitalist mode of production] socio-economic relations."[43] The state therefore creates a unity out of an isolation that is "largely" its own effect. Marx referred to this as the "dual movement" of the state and so does Poulantzas.[44]

It is this isolation caused by the immediate presence of political relations in determining the relations of production that constitutes the specific conditions of existence of classes in capitalism.

> There can be no question of first 'deducing' the state organizational framework from individualization of the social body over which power is exercised, and afterwards bringing it into relation with the class struggle and political domination. For in its relation to the capitalist process and division of labor, this process of individualization is nothing other than the outlining of the terrain on which classes and the class struggle are constituted in their capitalist specificity.[45]

There is no "outside the state" in which classes could organize themselves to then join in struggle with the economic and political relations of capitalism. To clarify this point it is necessary to face directly what Poulantzas meant by social classes. Although his argument is often frustratingly obscure, in the process it will become clear in what ways Wright, Przeworski, and others have found Poulantzas's perspective instructive.

There are three major aspects of social classes in Poulantzas's use of the term. First, classes are the effects of the structures of a social formation. "At every level the relation of conflict of the practices of different classes, the 'struggle' between classes, the very existence of classes themselves, are the effect of the relations of the structures, the form assumed by the contradictions of the structures in social relations."[46]

Secondly, classes are "practices." The contradictions of the structures give rise to specific opposing practices, such as the practices attempting to realize profit versus practices attempting to raise wages, or practices aimed at maintaining existing social relations versus those aimed at their transformation. "Social classes do not cover structural instances but social relations: these social relations consist of class practices, which means that social classes are conceivable only in terms of class practices."[47]

The word "practice" has a specific meaning in the Althusserian terminology employed by Poulantzas. A practice is a kind of production, that is, it is a work of transformation of some raw material. So the term social classes designates practices aiming at the transformation of structures. However, to avoid voluntarist implications, Poulantzas insists that these practices are determined. Although practices aim at transforming structures, they are in some unclear fashion also structured.

Finally, and following from the above, classes are not "subjects"; they are structured practices. The practices that aim at transforming the structures of capitalism "coincide with [the] supports" or agents in the capitalist labor process but these practices are not originated by these "supports." As Poulantzas says, these "supports . . . cannot theoretically be conceived as subjects."[48]

Although these statements are extremely compressed and correspondingly vague, Poulantzas's approach to the topic of social class persistently opens new doors, only a few of which we can enter here. We can flesh out these arguments somewhat by examining how Poulantzas utilized this perspective in defining the proletariat. According to Poulantzas, classes are only principally, not exclusively, determined by ownership of productive resources, therefore the usual way of defining the proletariat will not do. Classes receive their specificity from all of the structures of capitalism.

"The working class is not defined by a simple and intrinsic negative criterion, its exclusion from the relations of ownership."[49] Classes are defined by their places in the capitalist social division of labor as a whole and, like the social division of labor, are determined economically, politically, and ideologically.[50]

In this way Poulantzas adds further criteria to pare down membership of the proletariat. For example, productive labor is a criterion that can help delimit the concept of the proletariat: "that labor is productive which corresponds to the relations of production of the mode in question, i.e., that which gives rise to the specific and dominant form of exploitation."[51] The specific form of exploitation in capitalism is the appropriation of the surplus-value contained in commodities. Therefore, on Poulantzas's conceptualization, all wage-earners are not workers. Workers produce surplus-value; people who do not produce commodities may be exploited, i.e., may perform surplus-labor (above costs of reproduction), but they are not part of the proletariat.[52] Those who perform supervisory labor are also not part of the proletariat because they enforce the capitalist labor process. This is an example of political relations participating in the determination of the social division of labor. "The reason why these agents do not belong to the working class is that their structural class determination and the place they occupy in the social division of labour are marked by the dominance of the political relations that they maintain over the aspect of productive labour in the division of labour."[53] (Poulantzas specifically rejects the idea, elaborated by Wright, that this is a "contradictory location.") Finally, the division between mental labor and manual labor, an example of "ideological relations" in the social division of labour, excludes others from the proletariat.[54] The division of mental and manual labor is reproduced in production but also "functionally" in ideological apparatuses such as schools.[55] Engineers and technicians are excluded by the first, and teachers by the second.

These criteria for defining the proletariat are not as arbitrary as they first appear. They are firmly grounded in the multiple relations which constitute capitalism as a class society. Capitalism is a system of particular social relations—separation of some from means of production, extraction of surplus-value, a specific labor process, and the division between mental and manual labor. All of these characteristics of capitalism together generate places which define the class structure, not simply the bare economic structure of ownership or non-ownership.

Thus the fundamental reproduction of social classes does not just involve places in the relations of production. There is no economic self-reproduction of classes over and against an ideological and political reproduction by means of the apparatuses. There is, rather, precisely a process of primary reproduction in and by the class struggle at all stages of the social division of labor.[56]

It follows that class struggle takes place across all of the social structures of capitalism, involving struggle over surplus-value, supervision, and the mental/manual division, as these are incorporated in specific institutions. Poulantzas's vision of socialist practice is the struggle against these multiple determinants of capitalist class society.

It also follows from the above that class formation is not an issue for Poulantzas. Class struggle always exists even if it is not manifested in class consciousness or an independent political party. It exists as class practices: "there is no need for there to be 'class consciousness' or autonomous political organizations for the class struggle to take place, and to take place in every domain of social reality."[57] Institutions are riven by class conflict and receive their animating principles from this struggle.

In sum, Poulantzas sees capitalism as an ensemble of political, economic, and ideological structures. The contradictions of these structures reveal themselves in opposing practices, that is, in social relations conceived entirely in a dynamic, not static, sense. These opposing practices are class practices in the sense that these practices (social relations) aim at the transformation of the fundamental structures of capitalism. Class is therefore a *concept* for analyzing the dynamics of capitalist social formations. History is not the struggle of *classes* in the sense of formed subjects, but the history of class *struggles,* that is, of a particular set of practices which aim at transforming fundamental structures. History has no subject; it is the outcome of structured practices.

This formulation fosters the complaint that in Poulantzas's work structures yield practices without the mediation of subjects. For example, Przeworski argues that "these classes remain suspended in the air. They never acquire bodily representation; they are never more than 'effects' that in turn affect something else."[58] Nevertheless, in his own work Przeworski appropriates certain conceptions of Poulantzas, specifically the key notion that politics and ideology are objective in their relation to the formation of classes. We will soon examine his (much more accessible) theory in some detail.

Leaving aside the hyper-structural complications and irremedial obscurities of Poulantzas's analysis as much as possible, we can extrude some very useful arguments from his work. Classes in capitalism have a specific mode of existence, as individuals forged through the operation of the state in shaping the raw material of the capitalist labor process into specific relations of production. The apparatuses of the state are modelled on the capitalist labor process, reproducing and intensifying the divisions of the capitalist labor process. Poulantzas clearly presents this argument as an avenue for further research in attempting to comprehend in exactly what ways the capitalist state *is* a capitalist state. The only example he pursues in demonstrating these research possibilities is that of the division of mental and material labor, a division present in the capitalist labor process that is reproduced and institutionalized in the structure of state apparatuses.[59]

The state materializes or "realizes" the capitalist labor process in its own apparatuses, therefore socialist struggle partly entails challenging the structure of the state itself. More generally, following Lenin, Poulantzas describes the state as "the condensation of a particular class relationship of forces." The struggle of the workers for their interests must therefore be a democratic struggle to shift the balance of forces on the terrain of the state. However, because a statist transformation of the state is contradictory and any attempts in that direction are dangerous, Poulantzas insists that struggle for workers's class interests within the state apparatuses must be constantly supported by popular movements.[60]

Compared to Pashukanis's account of individualization, Poulantzas's view is more persuasive. Pashukanis assumes a self-generating economy, i.e., one whose essential structure is fixed before and outside of political intervention. This perspective is rooted in the capitalist ideological distinction between polity and economy. To the contrary, the state appears to play a more direct role in establishing political individuals, not only through the juridical creation of rights-bearing subjects but also through the particular configuration of its apparatuses. As Poulantzas says, "the state also acts in a positive fashion, *creating, transforming and making* reality."[61]

There are obvious difficulties with Poulantzas's analysis, which are perhaps partly indicated by the density of his prose. The most glaring is the apparent ineffability of 'structures.' Poulantzas insists that structures are not the same as institutions; they are in some manner the organizing principles of institutions.[62] Poulantzas needs the notion of structures in order to keep the relatively autonomous determinations of politics and ideology from becoming absolutely autonomous. He also requires this argument in order to maintain a view of history as determined, not subject to the merely contingent actions of social participants. This is his theoretical strategy for keeping history grounded. However, the notion of structures is never actually explained. Therefore the key concept of Poulantzas's class theory always seems to be more a rhetorical gesture rather than part of an argument. Nonetheless, the concentration on class relations and class practices, instead of a focus on class formation and class subjects, is an enduring contribution to which we will return.

Whether one believes that political individualization results directly from capitalist relations of production or from a more direct role of the state in some manner working up aspects of capitalist production into individuals, the consequence is that of a state as representative/unifier of the body of citizens. This state is not an illusion; it creates a concretely effective terrain of action for contending social forces. As Pashukanis puts it: "The state is not merely an ideological form, but is at the same time a form of social being. The ideological nature of the concept does not obliterate the reality and the material nature of the relations which it expresses."[63] Since the working class exists in individualized fragmentation, it requires political mediation to achieve class expression. On the terrain created by political individualization, the working class can easily fail to achieve the status of political actor. If this is so, then the sense in which classes actually exist under the conditions of the capitalist polity becomes unclear. This perplexity, which results from acknowledging the objective effects of ideological and political structures in class formation, has been directly confronted by Przeworski.

POLITICAL PROCESS AND CLASS FORMATION

Although he utilizes elements of Poulantzas's argument, Przeworski is critical of Poulantzas's conception of classes on the grounds that human agency is eliminated in Poulantzas's conception of history.

> Poulantzas rejects the view, which he terms "historicist," according to which classes as historical actors spontaneously appear in one way or another out of the relations of production. He emphasizes the independent role of ideology and political organization in the process of class formation. Yet in the heat of the polemic against historicism, history seems to be scorched with the same flame. It becomes a history that proceeds from relations to effects without any human agency.[64]

Przeworski wants to restore human agency in the processes of class organization and disorganization but also retain Poulantzas's insights into the objective effects of autonomous political and ideological relations. In

Przeworski's analysis, classes are the "effects of struggles." These struggles are structured by "objective conditions that are simultaneously economic, political, and ideological."[65] Classes are not uniquely determined by any one sphere of social life (e.g., production) but rather, insofar as they are determined, are codetermined by all three spheres of the economic, the political, and the ideological.

The starting point of Przeworski's analysis is that the classes in capitalism cannot be determined once and for all. The conception of classes as occupants of certain positions in production ignores the dynamic of capitalist development. This development has generated new positions, in both the productive process and in the sphere of the realization of capital, which are theoretically uncertain. Capitalism, through the increasing productivity of labor, does not produce enough places of productive employment, i.e., positions that could be intuitively considered proletarian in the noncontroversial sense of manual, industrial laborers. Przeworski especially has in mind white collar workers and also those who are separated from employment altogether—students, retirees, housespouses, the unemployed, those on welfare, etc. Consequently, proletarianization has two meanings which have become disjoined. Separation from independent means of production does not necessarily mean becoming a productive worker. "The source of the ambiguity of the concept of the proletariat lies in the dynamic of capitalist development itself."[66]

Przeworski is firmly opposed to any attempt to theoretically resolve what has become known as the boundary question, for example by asserting that certain middle strata have an objective interest in socialism and therefore can be included with the proletariat. "On paper one can put people in any boxes one wishes, but in political practice one encounters real people, with their interests and a consciousness of those interests. And these interests, whether or not they are 'real,' are not arbitrary; their consciousness is not arbitrary; and the very political practice that forges these interests is not arbitrary."[67] Attempts to theoretically resolve the boundary question easily fall prey to a new form of economistic understanding of class formation that fails to appreciate the autonomous effects of political and ideological structures.

Przeworski argues instead that the economic relations, ideological relations, and political relations established by the capitalist production process all objectively structure the field within which class struggles unfold. However, the relationship between class struggle and these relations is "reciprocal" in that class struggles can challenge these relations. "In other words, while objective conditions determine the limits of class struggles, these struggles can transform such determinants by altering economic, ideological, or political relations."[68]

Since classes are not uniquely determined at the level of the relations of production (as in economistic notions) nor even by the objective effects of political, ideological, and economic relations taken together, Przeworski's answer to the boundary question is that the "classification" of positions in the productive process is "immanent to the practices that (may) result in class formation."[69] Przeworski insists that: "Classes are not a datum prior to political and ideological practice." Whether people are defined as "workers" or as "individuals, Catholics, French speakers, Southerners, and the like" is an intrinsic aspect of "struggles to maintain or in various ways alter the existing social relations." For this reason classes must be conceived as being "organized and disorganized as outcomes of continuous struggles."[70]

Many different agencies and organizations participate in "ideological struggle" in regard to how society is itself to be portrayed, e.g., as a class society, a collection of individuals, or a nation of ethnic groups. To this extent all of these organizations participate in class formation. Social differentiation only coalesces into social "cleavage" as a consequence of political and ideological struggle. "The ideological struggle is a struggle *about* class before it is a struggle *among* classes." Przeworski argues that even economic struggles are not necessarily class struggles; they may simply take the form of protectionism for certain industries or struggle between industries. In this way economic struggles are also structured by ideology and politics. For example, Przeworski notes that the very right to strike or form unions is conditioned by political struggles.

In arguing that classes are a consequence of struggles *about* 'classes' we must not fall into the opposite of economism, that is voluntarism. Przeworski asserts that only a limited number of practices are "historically realizable" at any particular moment. Existing "positions" or "places" within the relations of a specific capitalist society delimit the range of possible projects of class formation.[71] Within this range, however, classes are an outcome of struggles. What is present is a structure of choices, limited but real, embodied in strategies. It should be mentioned that although this is a necessary point for Przeworski's theory, it is not fully defended in this place.

If class struggles are struggles about class before they are struggles between classes then the question arises of who is struggling before classes are formed. Przeworski suggests that at any particular moment some "carriers of the relations of production are organized as such," some are unorganized, and others are organized under different interpretations of social cleavages. "Indeed, the bourgeoisie is successful in the struggles about class formation when social cleavages appear at the phenomenal level in forms that do not correspond to positions within the relations of production. Thus, in each concrete historical conjuncture struggles to organize, disorganize, or reorganize classes are not limited to struggles between or among classes."[72]

This formulation raises a central problem in the very posing of the question of class formation. If classes as historical actors are not given by places in production, that is, if Przeworski and Poulantzas are correct that political and ideological structures, although in some way fashioned from capitalist production, are objectively determining (to some extent) of collective actors, then why should we focus on class formation at all in attempting to understand the various struggles within capitalist society? As Przeworski himself notes, if all struggles in society are class struggles only in the sense that these struggles have an impact on class formation, then Marx's classic statement that history is the history of class struggles is a tautology. (We have already mentioned a similar argument by Wright.) Once political and ideological relations are considered to objectively structure the struggles of collectivities in capitalist society, understanding the theme of history as class struggle becomes labored, or at least radically unclear.

Przeworski argues that we should still seek connections between positions in production and collectivities in struggle because only then can these struggles be understood in historical terms.

> What is lawful about historical development is the development of the forces of production, specifically, the process of capitalist accumulation. The places-to-be-occupied by concrete individuals become transformed in the process of development of the forces of production, and they become transformed in a manner characteristic of the organization of a capitalist system of production. . . . The assumption of class analysis is thus that the historical development of capitalist societies is to be understood in terms of the development of a capitalist system of production . . .[73]

The attempt to analyze collectivities in struggle by their relations to the capitalist system of production broadly conceived rests on the "hypothesis" that the "continuity of history" is to be found in the particular process of accumulation engendered by the social relations of capitalist production.

Some of the vagaries of Przeworski's theory of class formation are dispelled by his historical analyses of the socialist movement. In these analyses Przeworski shows specifically how the structures of capitalist democracy have had an autonomous effect on working class formation. He attempts to demonstrate how the choices of socialists within the constraints of democratic ideology and politics are not arbitrary and how these choices affect class organization and disorganization.

The major choice made by the socialist movement was whether or not to participate in the electoral process. This decision was fundamental in that it structured later choices. The importance of this decision was clearly recognized by many in the socialist movement and Przeworski reviews the various debates on whether or not to participate.[74] In his opinion, however, for several reasons, abstention was never a viable alternative for socialists seeking to represent workers. Through electoral participation workers-as-citizens can make claims for goods and services denied them by their position in the relations of production.[75] Through participation workers could also secure the right to organize and the right to strike. Another consideration was that if socialists did not field a political party then the masses may become politically organized under a different party and under different issues, making it more difficult to organize them as workers challenging capitalism. Particularly pressing was the fact that through participation workers could achieve immediate benefits. Przeworski quotes Schumpeter's argument that, "No party can live without a program that holds out the promise of immediate benefits."[76] Nonetheless, this was—and is—a fateful decision in that, "Participation imprints a particular structure upon the organization of workers as a class."

Capitalist democracy has two fundamental features that structure workers participation and therefore their organization as a class. One primary feature of capitalist democracy is that economy and polity are separated. We have already explored the classic argument of Pashukanis of how this is both possible and necessary. This division results in the development of two organizational forms of the working class, trade unions and political parties. Trade unions and political parties have different constituencies and therefore can and do clash. Because there are two distinct realms of activity, the working class never appears as a unified actor under conditions of capitalist democracy. Although it is not inconceivable for them to be unified, we will see later how this division in capitalist democracy was organizationally solidified in the history of the United States's working class movement.

The second feature is electoral participation through political parties.

Participation through parties has certain immediate effects. As Lukacs (and Roberto Michels) argues, electoral parties lead to a division between leaders and masses which tends to demobilize the masses. Furthermore, political parties, even workers parties, require the development of a party apparatus filled with people performing *petit bourgeois* functions. Electoral participation also means a commitment to legality.[77] Parties nevertheless appear necessary because of the competition of individuals within the class.

More broadly, there is a logic of electoral participation that immediately weakens the prospects for class formation. Przeworski argues that historically socialist parties became "workers parties" because of an ideological constraint, the clear distrust of workers of socialism as an alien ideology. The decision to become workers parties was accepted easily because of two considerations. First, it was widely believed that pursuit of immediate goals or reforms posed no danger to ultimate goals because reforms were believed to be "irreversible" and "cumulative."[78] Secondly, it was firmly believed that workers would soon become a majority.

The problem is that workers, in the uncontroversial sense of manual laborers, never became a majority. As argued above in regard to the two meanings of proletarianization, the middle classes did not become workers even when the traditional middle class occupations declined. Przeworski argues that the persisting minority status of workers altered the "very logic" of transformation with profound effects on class organization. A workers party is forced to seek allies, which means it must appeal to nonworkers. It does so by appealing to issues and criteria that are not specific to the working class, that is, it must become a "people's party" (Volkspartei). This appeal has the effect of reducing the salience of class for voters in that the party is now no longer identified as a class party. Furthermore, social democratic parties can no longer solely pursue workers's interests but only those interests that "workers as individuals" have in common with potential allies. "What they cease to be is the organization of workers as a class which disciplines individuals in their competition with each other by posing them against other classes. It is the very principle of class conflict—the conflict between internally cohesive collectivities—that becomes compromised as parties of workers become parties of the masses."[79] The appeal to allies is an appeal to individuals and this "reinstates a classless vision of politics."

In this way under conditions of capitalist democracy and worker minority there is a trade-off between seeking support of workers and support of allies. Przeworski and John Sprague have pursued these kinds of considerations utilizing elaborate statistical and historical data on socialist electoral participation.[80] They show under what conditions the electoral trade-off between maintaining worker support for the party by class-based appeals and seeking allies by appeals to non-class issues is more or less severe. Przeworski and Sprague argue that the loss of working class voters is less where (1) strong trade unions exist to take some of the burden for organizing workers as workers (under the limitations of this form of organizing mentioned above), and is even less where corporatist political structures are in place; and (2) where there are few competing parties for organizing workers along other lines, specifically ethnic-based parties.[81]

Although these specific analyses show that there is some variability in organizing workers as workers, the logic of electoral participation in general makes political class formation extremely fragile and ephemeral. Given the specific structure and constraints of capitalist democracy and the fact that those who can unambiguously be classified as workers are a minority, Przeworski concludes that, "Social democrats will not lead European societies into socialism."[82] As he states even more pointedly in another place, "Elections are just not an instrument for radical transformation."[83]

At this point we can summarize the major points of Przeworski's argument. Classes are the effect of struggles that are constrained but not determined by economic, ideological, and political structures. This makes class organization crucially dependent upon the strategies utilized to attempt class formation. Classes are not given by the relations of production nor even by economic, political, and ideological structures taken together. Neither classes nor any other social identification is given by "the immediate experience of social relations." "[T]he experience based on income, the character of the work, the place in the market, the prestige of occupations, and so on, does not of itself become transformed into collective identification since this experience is mediated by the ideological and political practices of the movements engaged in the process of class formation."[84] In Marx's phrase, which Przeworski (and Gramsci) is fond of quoting, it is in the realm of ideology that people become conscious of social relations. There is nothing that preordains that this consciousness will be of class. That depends on political strategy and ideological struggle.

There is, however, an important ambiguity in Przeworski's analysis of the conditions of class formation. As Wright pointed out, a central question of class formation is exactly how the word class is to be construed. Although there are many passages in which Przeworski suggests that classes are subjects or at least theoretically can become historical collectivities, in one place he specifically rejects this use of the term class.

"Class" then is a name of a relation, not of a collection of individuals. Individuals occupy places within the system of production; collective actors appear in struggles at concrete moments of history. Neither of these—occupants of places or participants in collective actions—are classes. Class is the relation between them, and in this sense class struggles concern the social organization of such relations.[85]

This appears to be quite close to Poulantzas's idea that classes are not subjects but rather the name of a kind of relation, a way of characterizing certain actions or practices.

From this perspective one can conceive an alternative way of speaking of class that would focus specifically on social relations. The social relations of capitalism could be characterized as class relations because of differential control over investment, command of the immediate workplace, private appropriation of the collective product in the form of profits, and the respective political and ideological practices that maintain this differential control, for example the separation of manual and mental labor (or, better expressed, between execution and control). In this usage the term class would clearly be an adjective for describing relations between individuals; it would not be a noun referring to collective actors. Class struggle could then be used to describe any action by any collectivity to transform these relations. Class struggle would be defined solely by the object of certain practices—transformation of the differential social relations which sustain capitalism—not by reference to a specific group of individuals. In fact, under this definition people could be engaged in class struggle without even being aware of it. It is unclear if this is what Przeworski has in mind, but it is a promising alternative to chasing after the proletariat.

THE HISTORICAL CONTINGENCY OF WORKING CLASS FORMATION

Without specifically referring to his work, Ira Katznelson and many historians of the labor movement in the United States have provided evidence for some of the theoretical theses advanced by Przeworski. In a study of urban politics Katznelson, with a nod to Gramsci, refers to the ideological and political structures of capitalist democracy as "city trenches." He singles out three key elements as having independently shaped class organization and disorganization in the United States: "trade unions at the workplace," a decentralized political party system, and the existence of "new governmental

services" delivered at "residential communities."[86] The separation of residence and work in capitalism creates the possibility of organizing each sep-
arately and in the United States led to a radical distinction between a
politics of work and a politics of residence community. In the history of the
United States the separation of these two realms of politics was "crystal-
lized" by the organization of trade unions and urban machines.[87]

The development of urban machines illustrates well how political organizations directly and multiply affect working class formation. Along
with ethnic neighborhoods, machines were a consequence of two features
of the American political system: the early development of the franchise
for workers and the decentralized political party system. To obtain votes,
machines organized workers as residents, members of an ethnic group,
even though their constituency was largely working class. Machines con-
spicuously avoided fracturing their power base by organizing according to
class.[88]

The national situation of workers further encouraged the development
of multi-class parties and therefore reduced the possibilities of a specifically working class political representation. For example, workers were isolated in cities, a political situation made worse by malapportionment and
single-member districts. To achieve any legislation helpful to workers they
had to seek allies.[89] Specific political events solidified these cross-class
political identifications, especially the Civil War and Reconstruction.[90]
Finally, several comparative labor historians have emphasized the importance in United States history of the fact that the franchise arose before
class divisions. Aristide Zolberg even states that "the single most important determinant of variation in the patterns of working-class politics" in
capitalist countries is whether at the time the class emerged "it faced an absolutist or a liberal state."[91]

For their part, trade unions in US history developed their own independent, organizationally non-political strategy for two main reasons. First,
some trade union leaders expected that state intervention into production
relations would most likely be against the unions, not in their favor. Secondly, given the politically partisan identifications of workers for the reasons noted above (as Democrats and Republicans), trade unions sought to
protect their organizational integrity, to defend themselves against political fracturing, by being non-partisan.[92]

Moreover, the mode of delivery of public policies also undoubtedly influences social divisions and therefore class formation. Urban machines
were successful because they could provide services. The provision of services at the local level helped separate a politics of residence from a poli-

tics of work. This is only one example of the important truth that public policy can crucially shape the divisions of society. For example, it is entirely to be expected that gender-specific policies, racially-specific policies, industry-specific policies, policies aimed exclusively at students, policies aimed exclusively at retirees, etc., would help shape the development of non-class political collectivities. For an obverse example in German labor history that supports this thesis, Mary Nolan argues that Bismarck's welfare policies aided working class formation because these measures were aimed specifically at workers as 'workers.'[93] As we will see later, the effect of public policy on collective identity is a central part of Claus Offe's analysis of the welfare state.

These historical examples bolster Przeworski's theoretical arguments regarding class formation. As Przeworski says: "The organization of politics in terms of class is not inevitable. There is nothing inherent in capitalism and nothing in the logic of history that would make inexorable the emergence of classes as collective subjects."[94] Drawing the same conclusion, Katznelson suggests that we understand class in terms of four "layers" or "levels": "structure, ways of life, dispositions, and collective action."[95] He thereby distinguishes several levels of, or ways of thinking about, the existence of classes. The first level, structure, is the abstract configuration of capitalism, in Przeworski's terms, places in the production process. "Ways of life" refers to the concrete social relations of individuals in a particular situation, dispositions to the frequency with which individuals respond to their changing conditions in ways consistent with class position, and collective action refers to the organizations through which individuals pursue class interests. To understand class history, Katznelson insists that these levels be kept analytically distinct. He further argues that the relation of any one level with another must be considered "contingent"; there is no necessary development from one level to another.[96]

Katznelson's differentiation of ways of using the term class provides a way out of some of the ambiguities of Przeworski's analysis. In particular it allows us to avoid conflating class *relations* with class *subjects*. In capitalist society classes always exist on the level of structures: "Class society exists even where it is not signified."[97] Classes may or may not exist on the other levels. Capitalism is a kind of society that can be characterized as a class society regardless of whether its development in specific historical circumstances eventuates in class disposition to action or concrete class-based organizations.

THE PROSPECTS FOR POLITICAL MEDIATIONS

Based on the arguments of the various theorists in this chapter, we must acknowledge that class formation through political mediations is at least radically contingent. This contingency is exacerbated by the typical forms and processes of capitalist democracy. Capitalist democracy is characterized by the juridical establishment of workers as equal individuals in the market, the relative autonomy of polity and economy, the disjuncture of work and residence, and the creation of a polity uniting these individuals as citizens. This polity provides individuals with arenas in which they can be aggregated under non-production based identities and short-term interests, reinforced by public policies which isolate these identities. Capitalism creates the working class in its own image, under specific conditions and within particular relations.

Given this we have to reconsider in what sense classes exist in capitalist democracies. This is clarified by distinguishing class relations from the formation of class subjects. Capitalism is indeed a class society; class relations exist even if class subjects do not. There are two primary relations of this kind: the control of property (and therefore investment and workplace relations) and the commodification of labor. However, individualization through capitalist legal relations and the logic of electoral participation—both comprised under citizenship—create a situation in which social and political identities are not given but are constructed in the course of various social struggles, including struggles over class relations.

Przeworski and Poulantzas both mention that political forms structure the field of struggles only to the point where these struggles transform these forms. Capitalist democracy is not the only conceivable kind of democracy. Functional representation of a variety of sorts, not just "soviets," promises to overcome the fragmentation of the naked individual. However, given the real accomplishments of even limited capitalist democracy (civil liberties, the autonomy of the personality), such proposals must be given the most careful evaluation. After examining certain additional perspectives we will briefly raise this topic again. Suffice it here to say that in the contemporary world functional representation is more likely to strengthen other kinds of identity than class identity.

In fact, the arguments of this and the preceding chapter strongly suggest that the project of class formation is a dead end. The social and political dynamic of advanced capitalist societies resists being captured by more traditional Marxian approaches, especially in regard to the capacities of workers for collective action. Key aspects of conceptualizing the proletariat—such as exploitation, interest, and class structure—remain quite problematic. For this reason many theorists who identify with the Marxian tradition have concluded that clarification of the central theses and concepts of Marxism requires the utilization of methodological tools developed outside the Marxian tradition. The arguments generated within analytical Marxism do indeed help clarify some of these issues, although the approach itself is subject to continuing and heated debate. However, if Marxian theory is to continue to be useful for comprehending contemporary capitalism, it is time for new departures.

Four

Reason, Revolution, and 'Rithmetic: Analytical Marxism

Analytical Marxism, or "rational choice Marxism," has a relationship to traditional Marxism that is quite perplexing, not least of all to its practitioners. It is in the Marxian tradition insofar as its central concerns are the classical topics of Marxian theory: the dynamic of forces of production and relations of production, the relation between property forms and social change, the importance of exploitation for defining social classes, analysis of the capacity of the working class for collective action, and the prospects for socialism. However, "analytically sophisticated Marxism" distinguishes itself from traditional Marxism by adopting the research strategies of analytical philosophy, methodological individualism, game theory, and the mathematical techniques of neo-classical economics for elucidating and evaluating the claims of Marxian theory, especially in order to provide the "microfoundations of Marxist social theory."[1]

Although the theorists usually included under the rubric of analytical Marxism are quite varied in their conclusions, they are united in rejecting the idea—especially associated with Georg Lukacs—that Marxism should be committed to a particular method. Erik Olin Wright, Andrew Levine, and Elliott Sober, who embrace a version of analytical Marxism, affirm this "wholesale embrace of conventional scientific and philosophical norms." "The view that Marxism should, without embarassment, subject itself to the conventional standards of social science and analytical philosophy implies a rejection of the thesis that Marxism as a social theory deploys a distinctive methodology that differentiates it radically from 'bourgeois social science.'"[2] Wright, Levine, and Sober argue that opening up Marxian theory to the methodological concerns of other traditions does create the danger that a specifically Marxian approach to social change will be effaced. However, they insist that the danger must be courted if we are to critically examine and further elaborate the substantive claims of Marxism, the "valuable" aspect of Marxian theory. Similarly, John Roemer argues that "Marxism should be distinguished from other social thought, not by its tools, but by the questions it raises."[3]

Conceptual rigor needs no defense, especially in a theory with the responsibility of practical intent. However, at first glance methodological individualism appears uncongenial to a theory primarily concerned with supra-individual entities such as classes, social structures, and the broad sweep of history. As mentioned earlier, Jon Elster argues to the contrary, stating that game theory based on methodological individualism "is invaluable to any analysis of the historical process that centers on exploitation, struggle, alliances, and revolution." He defines methodological individualism as "the doctrine that all social phenomena (their structure and their change) are in principle explicable only in terms of individuals— their properties, goals, and beliefs."[4] It is, therefore, as Elster acknowledges, "a form of reductionism."[5] Although there are variations, in the main rational choice tries to explain social interaction by assuming that individuals have choices and that they will be guided in these choices by the optimization of individual utility.

Although it is easy to see why Marxian theorists would be dubious especially regarding methodological individualism, in appraising this approach it must be kept firmly in mind that this is a method, that the characterization of people as "rational self-interested optimizers" is a methodological postulate, not a description of reality. For example, in constructing an explanation of collective action Elster says we should "first assume that behavior is both rational and self-interested; if this does not work, assume at least rationality; only if this is unsuccessful too should one assume that individual participation in collective action is irrational."[6] In places, Adam Przeworski criticizes the abstract conception of the individual employed by game theory. Nevertheless, he also persuasively argues that: "The strength of methodological individualism is methodological . . . To introduce descriptive realism is to cut Samson's hair."[7] Indeed, rational choice theorists compellingly argue that if we reject the imputation of self-interested rationality to agents, it is unclear with what theoretically productive alternative hypothesis we should replace it.[8]

Although much of the literature on analytical Marxism is concerned with methodological disputes, that is not the primary concern of this chapter. Following the dictum of Henri Theil that "models are to be used, not believed"—frequently quoted by Przeworski[9]—we will focus on the arguments of analytical Marxists which they intend to help elucidate the problems of proletarian identity and historical agency. Specifically, this chapter examines the arguments of this school regarding three topics: (1) the relation between exploitation and classes, (2) problems of the constitution of classes as collective actors, and (3) the prospects of socialism. Although there are good reasons for grouping these theorists under the same broad description, this should not lead us to assume that they come to the same conclusions. In fact it is precisely in their disagreements that this approach is often the most enlightening.

EXPLOITATION AND THE WORKING CLASS

In a previous chapter we briefly summarized the many problems of the labor theory of value that have led to a re-examination of the Marxian theory of exploitation. In light of these difficulties, Roemer has attempted to formulate a "general theory of exploitation" which would allow us to then specify different kinds of exploitation, including types of exploitation that occur in state socialist societies. By developing several simplified mathematical models of subsistence economies he demonstrates that, given differing initial endowments of means of production, exploitation can take place purely through the exchange of commodities. In his first model, for example, Roemer shows that even without a labor market, production for exchange by two individuals with different capital endowments allows the wealthier one to work less than the socially necessary labor-time. "A wealthy producer will, therefore, have more production options than a poor one and hence will be able to produce goods worth the market value of his subsistence needs by working less time than the poorer producer. (He can, essentially, choose capital intensive activities to operate.)"[10] Since they are producing for exchange, the wealthier individual exchanges goods which embody less labor than the poorer individual's goods, which is what Marx meant by exploitation. Therefore Roemer's model reveals that "we can produce a theory of exploitation, defined as the expropriation of labor, even in the absence of an institution for labor exchange. Exploitation can be mediated entirely through the markets for produced commodities."[11] This rebuts the traditional Marxian thesis that "extraction of surplus labor" requires a labor market. However, the first model is not sufficient to establish classes, defined as hirers and sellers of labor-power, therefore Roemer proceeds to generate models that include a labor market and then an alternative simplified society without a labor market but with credit markets where means of production can be rented at interest.

Using a model with differing levels of wealth and with a labor market, Roemer shows that optimizing individuals will sell or hire labor as a mere consequence of competitive markets and differential endowments of capital. The reason that some will sell labor is that by working for another they can receive more in wages than they could produce using their own capital stock.[12] Depending on their endowment, five optimal strategies based on the alternatives of "work in their own shop, hire labor, sell labor, or do some combination of these" will be generated. The important point here is that, given differing levels of wealth and competitive markets, the poor will choose to be exploited in order to optimize.

> Their problem is to optimize, in this case a labor-minimizing program of production choices, subject to a capital constraint. All that is specified a priori is the optimizing behavior of agents and their differential initial endowments of capital stock. Given this, some producers must hire labor power to optimize (the two top classes) and some must sell labor power to optimize (the two bottom classes).[13]

Therefore this model results in an "endogenous" emergence of classes that corresponds to exploitation.

Following these results Roemer then produces a third model that assumes individuals with differing levels of wealth and no labor market, but with a credit market where individuals can rent capital at interest. In this model he shows that the same classes will emerge with the same correspondence between class position and exploitation. "The heresy is complete. Not only does exploitation emerge logically prior to accumulation and institutions for labor exchange, but so does the articulation of exploitation into class."[14] The implications of Roemer's models are intuitively plausible because we speak of wealthy countries exploiting poorer countries purely through exchange of commodities or through credit arrangements. Jon Elster, Immanuel Wallerstein, and even Marx discuss exploitation in this way.[15] This appears to be the relationship Marx has in mind when he describes the French peasantry as exploited.[16]

These models establish two important points that Roemer uses in his later deliberations on the topic of exploitation. First, a labor market is unnecessary for society to be divided into classes and for class and exploitation to coincide. These will result simply from differential ownership in the context of competitive markets. "Exploitation can be mediated entirely through the exchange of produced commodities, and classes can exist with respect to a credit market instead of a labor market—at least at this level of abstraction." Secondly, the real origin of exploitation appears to lie in the differential ownership of means of production. "It is a mistake to elevate the struggle between worker and capitalist in the process of production to a more privileged position in the theory than the differential ownership of productive assets."[17]

Although these preliminary models are useful for bringing out these points, they are wanting in that, since the poor individual chooses to sell labor or borrow capital at interest, it is not yet clear on what grounds this unequal exchange of labor should be morally condemned. "The bourgeois thinker argues that the proletarian is gaining from trade, and his trade of labor power is voluntary, and so the transfer of 'surplus' labor time should not be considered exploitative. The quid pro quo is surplus labor in exchange for access to the means of production."[18] To clarify what Marxists intend when they claim exploitation in other than a purely "technical" sense, and to further develop a "general" theory of exploitation, Roemer resorts to game theory.

> I propose that a group be conceived of as exploited if it has some *conditionally feasible alternative* under which its members would be better off. . . . Formally, this amounts to specifying a game played by coalitions of agents in the economy. A coalition can either participate in or withdraw from the economy. To define the game, I specify what any particular coalition can achieve on its own if it withdraws from the economy. Given these specifications, if a coalition can do better for its members by "withdrawing," then it is exploited.[19]

This is a very innovative strategy for clarifying what it is we actually mean when we say that people are exploited. Roemer argues that a group is exploited if it would be better off withdrawing from its present situation and pursuing a feasible alternative. If the imagined—counterfactual—situation is not feasible for one reason or another, then we must say that the exploitation is "socially necessary" at this stage of social development.

This game theoretic definition advances a general theory of exploitation in that it allows us to distinguish different types of exploitation by specifying different withdrawal rules. "Feudal exploitation" is established if a coalition could do better by withdrawing with its assets (as serfs would have), whereas "capitalist exploitation" exists if a coalition would do better by withdrawing with a "*per capita* share of society's alienable productive assets." Along these lines Roemer also develops a notion of "socialist exploitation."[20]

This approach is also useful in that it allows Roemer to answer the justification of capitalism that everyone gains from trade. It is true that the proletarian is better off selling her or his labor than starving due to lack of means of production. However, the proletarian would be better off still by withdrawing with a per capita share of productive assets. The game theoretic definition allows us to clearly see that the difference of opinion regarding exploitation here rests on which withdrawal rule one thinks is relevant. In turn, this reveals that what underlies the Marxian charge of exploitation is unequal access to the means of production. The game theoretic approach thereby not only provides an alternative to the surplus value theory of exploitation but also, like the previous labor exchange models, focuses our attention on the real source of capitalist exploitation: inequality in the distribution of property.

On this basis Roemer argues that the crucial form of domination under capitalism is that which maintains property relations, not domination in the workplace as is commonly assumed. "Domination at the point of production is neither sufficient nor necessary for capitalism. It is not sufficient, because many would claim that such domination exists in socialist countries as well. It is not necessary, because it is possible for trade unions to be strong enough that workers effectively control conditions on the factory floor, but capitalists' ownership of the means of production is uncontested."[21] Roemer acknowledges that there is domination in the workplace but argues that it is derived from the domination upholding property relations. To directly challenge class relations, the capitalist distribution of property must be the object of struggle.

Roemer sees conceptual confusion and faulty conclusions when socialist theorists focus on domination in the workplace. The primary confusion is a conflation of "socialism and industrial democracy."[22] Against those who would argue that his conception of exploitation without regard to domination in the workplace ignores important aspects of working class existence, he insists that they are confusing exploitation and alienation. Identifying alienating work with exploitation forces us to conclude that capitalist and socialist exploitation are "essentially the same" because of the similarity of workplace conditions.[23] Socialists who reject the socialist character of existing socialism for this reason implicitly break with the materialist theory of history in that they are then defining modes of production by their labor relations rather than property relations. In contrast, concentrating on property relations allows us to connect the theory of exploitation with differing property forms and therefore historical materialism.

Przeworski criticizes Roemer's argument by raising the importance of workplace domination from another angle. He states that Roemer's models assume that the extraction of labor will be effortless. That is, the models assume that people working for another will work as hard as for themselves.[24] It is possible that extraction of surplus labor will be more problematic when one works for another and therefore the proposed relation between wealth and income is not as conceptually tight as the models suggest. In response, Roemer defends his procedure on methodological grounds. Domination at the workplace only exists because of the "impossibility of writing a perfect contract."[25] We can avoid this difficulty by imagining a situation in which there are no "market frictions," where contracts are "costlessly enforceable."[26] Roemer argues that this is a defensible assumption because it is the customary level of abstraction of Marxian value theory; Marx himself abstracted away issues of contract enforcement and cheating.

In this first attempt to reformulate the concept of exploitation, Roemer develops two different reasonable alternatives: the "unequal embodied labor" conception and the game theoretic notion. Both show the importance of inequality of property but he prefers the latter because of its more general applicability in analyzing kinds of exploitation under differing property relations, such as feudalism and socialism. This is the theory of exploitation Erik Olin Wright adapted for analyzing classes. In further investigations of the idea of exploitation, however, Roemer elaborates a number of additional considerations. As a consequence, having already disputed the surplus value theory of exploitation, Roemer also rejects the unequal labor theory as providing an important definition of exploitation.

First, Roemer argues that receiving through exchange goods embodying more labor than the goods one exchanges, due to the inequality of wealth, is only unjust if one establishes that the original distribution of resources is also unjust. If one does not establish this, then exploitation is merely "technical exploitation."[27] Secondly, Roemer adduces a model that shows that, given differing preferences for leisure and income, a poorer individual can actually exploit a wealthier individual by loaning the latter his smaller endowment and living modestly off the proceeds.[28] Therefore there are conditions under which the relationship between exploitation and wealth do not hold.

At first this would seem to strengthen reasons for employing the game theoretic definition of exploitation. However, this procedure is weakened by the fact that which rule one chooses appears rather arbitrary.[29] Roemer also shows that using this definition yields certain hard cases, e.g., whether employed proletarians could be considered exploiters in situations where per capita distribution would worsen their situation.[30] As seen earlier, from a related perspective Philippe Van Parijs argues that the real class divide in advanced capitalist societies is the division between the employed and unemployed. Both Claus Offe and Juergen Habermas also incorporate this consideration into their analyses of advanced capitalist societies.

For his part, in light of these further investigations Roemer concludes that the concept of exploitation is not actually of central concern to critical social theory. Roemer acknowledges that discussions of exploitation have highlighted several interesting and important topics: unequal access to the means of production, domination, alienation, and the various irrationalities of capitalist accumulation. However he believes that we can and should explore these bases of critique directly, foregoing the "circuitous route" through technical exploitation.[31] "[E]xploitation theory is a domicile that we need no longer maintain: it has provided a home for raising a vigorous family, who now must move on."[32]

G. A. Cohen reaches conclusions similar to Roemer's through different reasoning. As previously mentioned, he argues that it is not that workers produce surplus value that makes them exploited, but rather that they make things of value that they do not appropriate. Like Roemer, Cohen points out that whether the appropriation of things of value constitutes exploitation depends on whether the original control of the means of production, i.e., distribution, is justified or not. "The question of exploitation therefore resolves itself into the question of the moral status of capitalist private property."[33]

In contrast, some have argued that exploitation consists in the fact that workers are excluded from control of investment decisions. This is the definition of Leszek Kolakowski, flirted with by Jon Elster.[32] G. A. Cohen criticizes this notion on the grounds that this is subordination, not exploitation, and that control over investment is a consequence of prior appropriation in the labor process.[35] If this is so, then once again the justice of control of investment depends on whether the original appropriation is just or not. After considering some additional alternative definitions, Elster himself ultimately concludes that exploitation is not "a fundamental notion in moral theory."[36]

Besides the perplexities of exploitation that Roemer's analyses reveal, another reason for rejecting the classical Marxian conception of exploitation is that it is not likely to be a motivation for collective action. According to Marxian theory itself, exploitation as unequal labor exchange is hidden in capitalism by the commodification of labor. "[O]ne cannot use *exploitation* as an explanation of class struggle unless it is perceived by the workers as an injustice they wish to erase. It is hard to make this case, when one simultaneously wishes to claim that capitalist relations obscure relations of exploitation."[37] Roemer does believe, like many analytical Marxists, that the issue of justice is a prime motive in class struggle.[38] He argues that it is possible that the links between justice and class struggle could be developed by elaborating a "sociology of injustice."[39] Furthermore, Roemer contends that issues that have been historically confused with exploitation—issues such as inequality, alienation, or domination in the workplace—may be of greater importance in generating class collective action than technical exploitation.[40]

The work of Roemer and other analytical Marxists in conceptually disentangling exploitation from associated notions of alienation, domination, and other forms of inequality certainly deflates the importance of the concept. In general, analytical Marxists present strong arguments that the discussion of exploitation is a detour from the fundamental issue of unequal access to means of production. In this way the normative dimension of Marxian theory is given center stage, albeit in a new guise. However, whether normative motivations can actually be accommodated by the rational choice framework is an issue to which we will return.

THE DILEMMAS OF CLASS-BASED COLLECTIVE ACTION

As strongly suggested in previous chapters, the weakest link in Marxian theory is the relationship between class structure and the formation of collective actors. Przeworski states bluntly that "[t]he relation between social relations and individual behavior is the Achilles heel of Marxism."[41] It is precisely on this issue that rational choice theory claims to make a contribution in that it focuses on the conditions, dilemmas, and dynamic of collective action. Rational choice theory rejects the view that people simply "act out" structural positions or internalized norms.[42] Rather, people are presumed to be rational self-interested "optimizers," acting within constraints. The explanation of the success or failure of collective action therefore lies in specifying the effects of the constraints on the actions and strategic interactions of rational optimizers.

According to rational choice theory, the chief obstruction to collective action is the "free rider" problem. Simply stated, it is irrational for self-interested individuals to participate in collective action if they will receive the benefits whether they participate or not. The rational thing to do in this situation is to not participate and gain the benefits of the collective action of others, i.e., to "ride for free." However, since each individual will reason the same on this question, all will abstain and collective action will not occur. A corollary to this argument is that a rational individual will recognize that her or his individual contribution will not make a difference on whether a collective action succeeds or fails. It is therefore irrational to contribute in that there is a cost without any real effect or benefit. Again, since each will reason the same, no one will contribute.

Elster interprets Marxian theory to say that the "reality" of classes depends on their propensity to congeal into collective actors under certain conditions and defines "class consciousness" as the ability of the working class to overcome the free rider problem and act on its class interests.[43] The conditions he lists for overcoming this problem are the usual ones in rational choice theory: workers must find themselves repeatedly in the same situation (iterated game), they must not know how long they will be in this situation (unknown duration), and individual workers must not pursue an immediate payoff (low rate of time discount). To participate in collective action the individual must be assured (the assurance game) that others will do so as well, through reliable information of workers about each other or through threats of coercion. Another requirement of collective action specifically to oppose capitalism is that workers must have an understanding of the "causal context," that is, they must know the situation they are in and who actually are the opposing classes, a condition which Elster suggests is unlikely.[44]

Elster remarks that there are so many conditions necessary for the collective action of workers to emerge that "it is a wonder that it can occur at all."[45] Since it does occur, Elster relaxes the methodological restrictions and briefly considers the possibility of unselfish behavior, the impact of leadership on forging collective action, and even the possibility of irrationality.[46] He concludes that the Marxian theory of class is very weak as a guide to the likely collective actors, that Marx's "two maps"—one of classes, the other of collective actors in history—never converge. The major collective actors in history simply are not classes nor does history show non-class actors to be ephemeral. For this reason he argues that we must reject "the centrality of class in social conflict."[47]

Allen Buchanan raises additional rational choice objections to the idea that individual workers will engage in class-based collective action. According to Buchanan, Marx believed that the struggle for socialism would be engaged because it is in the interests of individuals of the working class. Buchanan argues that both the capitalist class and the working class have a free rider problem and, in brief, Marx's theory of the eventual defeat of capitalism comes down to the assumption that the capitalist class will find its free rider problem insoluable whereas the proletariat will not.[48]

In regard to the free rider problem faced by workers, Buchanan contends that various proposed solutions are either false or not open to Marxian theorists because these proposed solutions would contradict other Marxian theses. For example, those who argue that "in-process benefits" (the camaraderie of organization), will overcome organizing obstacles, beg the question of getting started: people cannot know of these benefits until there already exists such organization.[49] To the argument that moral principles may inspire collective action, Buchanan replies that this is a non-Marxian argument and therefore not available given the theory.[50] Furthermore, those who suggest that workers will not utilize "bourgeois rationality" in seeking answers to their predicament presume that socialist rationality (whatever that might be) has somehow already developed before socialism itself.[51]

One seeming weakness of the free rider argument is that it makes a key assumption that group utility is the sum of individual utilities. There is no place in this conception that the whole may be greater than the sum of the parts in that one more contribution might actually determine whether the whole is successful or not, 'the straw that breaks the camel's back.' Rational choice theorists call this a "threshold effect." In a footnote, Buchanan anticipates this objection and argues that in large-scale revolutionary action, every individual will realize that the likelihood is that his contribution will not determine whether the threshold is reached or not, and therefore will conclude that his contribution will not be necessary.[52] The result will be the same as before. Therefore under various conditional assumptions, Buchanan argues that collective action of workers will not occur.

The arguments of Elster and Buchanan cast serious doubt on the probability of collective action by workers. Elster concludes that Marx simply neglected the microfoundations of the development of the working class as a collective actor, relying instead on a type of functional argument, i.e., that workers would organize because of the benefits they would receive in so doing.[53] From the above it is clear that this position has a rather large hole in it.

Much of Elster's work on these topics is clearly animated more by a desire to dismiss Marx than improve Marxian theory through critical engagement.[54] Although basically supportive of applying rational choice methods to traditional issues of Marxian theory, Adam Przeworski provides a more balanced appreciation of the strengths and weaknesses of both Marxism and rational choice theory. In the previous chapter we presented Przeworski's arguments that class formation is contingent on the political strategies and dilemmas of electoral democracies. Here we need to examine his more general but forceful arguments for the further development of analytical Marxism.

Przeworski's support for what he would prefer to call the "strategic action perspective"[55] flows from his conception of Marxism itself. "Marxism for me is an analysis of the consequences of forms of property for historical processes. Any Marxism, as far as I am concerned, is a theory of history, . . . of the lawful reproduction and transformation of social relations."[56] Przeworski agrees with Elster that Marxism has failed to develop a persuasive theory of history because it has not rigorously engaged the microfoundations of such a theory, "the explanation of individual acts under particular conditions."

In practice Marxists usually rely on a functionalist explanation of individual action. "Functionalists explained that people behave in accordance with shared values because individuals are taught norms and values, which they first 'internalize' and eventually act out. Functionalists viewed all individual behavior as an act of execution of the internalized society, with the implication that all persons exposed to the same norms and values should behave in the same manner."[57] Sharing this conception of the springs of individual behavior, Marxists previously have at most thought of individuals as "acting out" their class positions. More commonly Marxists did not even pursue the question because of the theoretical focus on "forces, structures, collectivities, and constraints, not individuals." The consequence of neglecting the necessary microfoundations of social action is that "Marxism was a theory of history without any theory about the actions of people who made this history."[58]

By adopting game theory and methodological individualism we can develop a different, more dynamic analysis of social action and interaction that takes account of the fact that individuals have choices, rather than merely acting out some sort of prior imprinting. "Social relations are the structures within which actors, individual and collective, deliberate upon goals, perceive and evaluate alternatives, and select courses of action." Furthermore, these social relations are not simply given.

> [S]ocial relations must themselves be viewed as a historically contingent outcome of, to use Marx's phrase again, "men's reciprocal actions." That is, while social relations constitute a structure of choices within which actors choose, their choice may be to alter social relations. Social relations are not independent of human actions. It is not in this sense that they are "objective." They are objective, indispensable, and independent of individual will only in

the sense that they constitute the conditions under which people struggle over whether to transform their conditions.[59]

Przeworski's conception of social relations is therefore more dynamic in that these relations constitute a structuring of choices that is in turn altered by these choices, thereby creating a new set of conditions within which further choice takes place. The structure is objective in that it is indeed given at any particular moment; it is the set of constraints for any particular strategy. However, structure is itself alterable by the choices that may then ensue. Contrary to Marxian "essentialist" conceptions of social structure, "structure is an attribute of recurrent interactions."[60]

Although he is sympathetic to rational choice theory and forthrightly states that "the critique of Marxism offered by methodological individualism is irrefutable and salutary," Przeworski nevertheless criticizes these approaches on a number of grounds.[61] First of all, Przeworski argues that rational choice theory employs a conception of "undifferentiated, unchanging, and unrelated 'individuals'" that, to be persuasive, at the least requires "more contextual information."[62] In another more recent place, he comes close to traditional Marxian critiques of game theory by stating that this specific "ontology" of individuals is "ideologically derived and patently unreasonable."[63]

Przeworski's second criticism of game theory is that it methodologically regards as fixed (exogenous) the preferences by which individuals make their choices. Traditional Marxism at least raises to central importance the question of the historical and social formation of preferences, even if it does not have a persuasive theory for explaining them. In fact, Przeworski states that, "Marx was the last thinker who simultaneously viewed behavior as a rational, strategic conduct and sought to explain how people acquire their historically specific rationality, including preferences."[64]

In both its conception of individuals and in its treatment of preferences as given, game theory does not yet fully incorporate the specific historical situations in which individuals choose.[65] The limitation of the "equilibrium" models of Roemer or the "isolated, singular events" of game theory is that we cannot explain "how the actions of individuals under given conditions produce new conditions."[66] Therefore game theory "has nothing to say about history." Methodological individualism is stronger in its critique of Marxism than in establishing convincing alternative explanations.

Przeworski's final criticism of game theory is that at this stage in its development it must employ models in which there are either a great number of actors or only two, whereas most politically and socially relevant strategic interactions involve some number of actors between these two extremes.[67] Przeworski argues that the tools of game theory are "almost unusable" for situations involving an intermediate number of actors. He is therefore "not particularly optimistic" about future "applications of game theory to the study of intergroup conflicts and, in particular, to the study of class alliances."[68] This is actually a further criticism of methodological individualism in that Przeworski's objection is explicitly based on the consideration of organizations as strategic actors. In a recent analysis of transitions to and the stabilization of democracy he basically excludes individuals as important actors: "Democratic societies are populated not by freely acting individuals but by collective organizations that are capable of coercing those whose interests they represent."[69]

All this said, Przeworski believes that rational choice theory is powerful for dismantling certain Marxian conceptions. If rational choice has been salutary in general for Marxian theory, it is "exceedingly salutary" for revealing the weaknesses of certain Marxian assumptions regarding "class action."[70] However, Przeworski immediately raises an important objection to the way in which the collective action difficulties of workers is typically described. The choices are usually presented as 'to join' or 'not to join,' establishing the free rider problem. If this is intended to imply that workers have the luxury to act or not act, it is simply untrue. Przeworski insists on the importance of the fact to the strategic calculations of workers that they are already in the difficult situation of competing against each other. For this reason there often is no comfortable "pre-strategic status quo" on which individual workers could depend: "there are situations in which the choice is only between acting for or acting against."[71] This is therefore an additional spur for workers to attempt collective action that is not considered in Elster's critique of Marx.[72]

Rational choice theory is attractive to Przeworski primarily for two reasons: it helps explain (1) why class formation is contingent and, (2) why the working class has more options than suffering or socialist revolution, i.e., it helps explain the historical existence of "social democracy." In the previous chapter we discussed Przeworski's argument concerning the contingency of class formation. It is useful to again raise the topic of classes here in order to further specify Przeworski's conception of capitalism itself and the choices it presents.

Many Marxists, analytical or not, have come to the conclusion that the relationship between class position and class action is radically contingent. However Przeworski has made this contingency the center of his conception of capitalism and criticizes Roemer's early models on this account.

Roemer does not demonstrate "any logical correspondence between exploitation and class struggle" because there is no such correspondence.

> [T]he organization of classes as historical subjects, collectivities-in-struggle, is not determined by the places occupied by individuals within the realm of property relations. There is no relation to be deduced here. The history of capitalism need not be a history of class struggle between the exploited and the exploiters, although it may happen to be that if workers and capitalists organize as such and if everyone struggles only in their capacity of workers or capitalists. The history of capitalism may be a history of struggle *among* exploiters; it may be a history of struggle among women, nations, races, or religious groups.[73]

Przeworski argues that because the presumed correspondence is mistaken, Marxists have no theory of the conditions necessary for the emergence of class actors or other kinds of actors. Under capitalism individuals relate to each other in a "multidimensionally described social structure." Which actors emerge at particular times depends on the political strategies of organizations and political parties.

In Przeworski's view, classes only have a rather attenuated existence under capitalism. They only exist in that "the structure of property characteristic of capitalism makes everyone's material conditions contingent upon the privately made decisions of owners of wealth."[74] This "structural dependence on capital" results from the fact that capitalism is a system of production in which people must exchange in order to satisfy their needs and in which means of production are privately owned. Investment is required for the improvement of material conditions and these decisions are based on the prospects of profit. "[A]ny demands that threaten the profitability of investment cause the rate of investment to fall; therefore, whether any particular interests can be satisfied depends upon their compatibility with the privately appropriated profit of the owners of wealth."[75] This argument is familiar in contemporary politics as the insistence on maintaining a good business climate or, more critically, as the threat of a "capital strike." Przeworski notes that it is this structural dependence on capital that allows capitalists to appear as the "bearers of universal interests."[76]

It should be noted that Przeworski's position is actually more cautious than that of many who discuss the danger and inherently undemocratic nature of the threat of a capital strike, e.g., John Roemer and Claus Offe.[77] First, Przeworski refers to it as an "empirical hypothesis, the validity of which is not certain." Secondly, many proponents of this thesis speak as if capitalists are free to invest or not invest. However, this assumes that capitalists, unlike workers, inhabit a pre-strategic situation wherein they could simply consume their investment capital. In contrast, Przeworski suggests that, due to competition among capitalists, they are not completely free in this regard.[78]

For Przeworski, the importance of this structural dependence on capital is that it fundamentally conditions the choices workers make regarding capitalism as an economic system. Przeworski says that Marx "never developed a theory that would relate the social processes of accumulation and class struggle."[79] He even argues that any discussion of class struggle in *Capital* is only "lip service" because Marx suggests that these struggles cannot fundamentally alter the process of accumulation.[80] On the same grounds Przeworski criticizes Roemer's argument about exploitation, especially his game theoretic definition specifying withdrawal rules to define specific kinds of exploitation, because it presents the choices of workers as either/or: either they agree to their present material benefits under capitalism or they choose the overthrow of capitalism.[81] However, if we include a temporal dimension to this game, and the possibility of democratically affecting patterns of investment through mass political participation, the calculus is substantially different. There arises a third option: capitalist democracy gives workers the opportunity to increase their utility by weighing the effects of present restraint on future benefits. Przeworski develops arguments that show when workers would rationally choose a "class compromise."

Democratic capitalism creates conditions for a class compromise in that, although capitalists maintain control over the means of production and investment, workers have power to influence investment and distribution through the vote. Przeworski's argument is rather obvious, once stated, but nonetheless true and important. In a capitalist system economic expansion is financed out of profits. Because of this fact workers must calculate that wage losses to profits in the present may lead to greater opportunities for employment and consumption in the future and, obversely, that wage gains at the expense of profits in the present may lead to losses in the future. This much is given by capitalist control of investment.

However, although profit is a necessary condition of future prosperity it is not a sufficient condition. Profit may not be reinvested productively: it may be spent on luxury goods for capitalists, it may be invested in a way that is less productive (mergers), it may be invested in other countries, or it may be invested in ways that will not increase future employment, e.g., jobless growth through mechanization, without social provisions for handling the consequences. Przeworski argues that through political participation workers can have an effect on whether profit is reinvested productively or not.[82] It is therefore rational for workers to participate in politics under democratic conditions because, contrary to the presumptions of many Marxists, political outcomes are truly uncertain.

The coexistence of democracy with capitalism gives workers the possibility of altering the distribution of goods and making choices in regard to present consumption and investment for the future. This is demonstrated by the fact that capitalist economies in the world are "extremely heterogeneous."[83] There are great distributional differences even among the advanced capitalist countries. Although it is true that capitalism is irrational, "[t]he degree of irrationality in capitalism is not a given."[84] It can be affected by working class action through democratic forms.

Stated another way, Przeworski's point is that there are conditions under which workers will consent to exploitation, contrary to the usual Marxian idea that they will not if they become conscious. Even if workers were collectively organized as a class actor they would not necessarily pursue socialism, at least if solely motivated by potential material benefits. This is the case for at least two reasons. Due to their capacity to democratically influence investment and other aspects of social welfare, the following paradox appears.

> [T]hose working-class movements that may have the political muscle to bring about some form of socialism by legislation have no incentive to do so, while those movements that have much to gain by transferring productive wealth to the public realm have no power to do it. Hence, socialism as a program for public ownership of productive wealth is the political project of only those movements that cannot bring it about.[85]

Secondly, Przeworski argues that even if there was a workable example of socialism that is productively superior to capitalism there would necessarily be a transitional period when economic control would still be in the hands of the capitalists. Any moves in the direction of public ownership would provoke divestment and an economic crisis because rational capitalists would not invest if their investment were likely to be nationalized in the near future. These "transition costs" to socialism would deter rational materially-interested workers as long as there is likelihood that material conditions will improve under capitalism. As a whole the above explains the rational basis for the historical development of social democracy.

Given this analysis, Przeworski concludes that if workers are inspired solely by the prospects of material advancement, "the question of the superiority of socialism may simply be moot."[86]

THE LIMITATIONS OF 'ANALYTICALLY SOPHISTICATED MARXISM'

The theorists reviewed above criticize traditional Marxian theory on three important points: (1) exploitation is neither a necessary nor sufficient basis for the critique of capitalism and in its classical version is unlikely to serve as a motive for collective action by workers, when that occurs; (2) collective action by workers faces a host of obstacles, illuminated by rational choice theory, which traditional Marxian theory is ill-equipped to analyze or appreciate; and (3) even if workers were organized there are rational grounds for them not to pursue socialism. Although these points are powerfully argued from a fresh perspective, each has important limitations as well.

The concept exploitation plays a key role in classical Marxian theory by binding together 'interest' and 'right.' It implies both a material interest among workers in the development of socialism and suggests that capitalism is morally wrong. Although it is not explicitly argued this way by Marx, G. A. Cohen and others are persuasive that this moral evaluation provides the real reason why many have supported the Marxian project, which they themselves would recognize except for "ill-conceived philosophical commitments."[87] However, Roemer's critique of the concept of exploitation reveals that Marxists have misconceived the basis on which capitalism is unjust. This has prevented them from confronting the key ethical issue of capitalism, the distribution of property, and from directly engaging the ethical arguments of those who defend capitalism.[88] Cohen bolsters Roemer's case by arguing that "one thing which helps to consolidate the ruling order is confused belief about its nature and value, in the minds of members of *all* social classes, and also in the minds of those who have dedicated themselves against the ruling order."[89]

The most contentious conclusion that emerges from Roemer's discussion is the deflation of the importance of the capitalist labor process. Roemer rejects the importance of workplace relations partly on the grounds that we can methodologically dispose of the problem of extracting labor from labor-power. However, even if the assumption of a "costlessly enforceable contract" is acceptable for the specific argument regarding the technical conception of exploitation, it is neither acceptable nor possible when we turn to motives for collective action and for the establishment of socialism. In their haste to reject the labor theory of value some theorists have also mistakenly rejected the distinction between labor and labor-power. Although the "General Commodity Exploitation Theorem" may well show that labor-power is not unique in exploitability, labor is nevertheless unique in that the cooperation of the worker is necessary to make labor-power useful. The importance of the distinction between labor and labor-power is therefore not exhausted in the labor theory of value and should not be cast off with the latter.[90]

Claus Offe develops an argument that helps explain why we cannot even in principle imagine a fully specified labor contract. Flexibility of the worker is precisely what makes living labor valuable; if the task could be perfectly specified it would probably be mechanized. Some measure of autonomy is intrinsic to the usefulness of labor, a fact which Offe refers to as the "inextirpable subjectivity of labor-power."[91] One could perhaps respond that corn, steel, energy, or any other commodity also needs flexibility in order to be useful. But to state the obvious, corn, steel, energy, or any other potential *value numeraire* does not care how it is utilized: people do. Roemer himself acknowledges that, "It is much more likely that workers struggle against capitalists in part because of the methods of control that are used against them in the workplace, to extract their labor."[92] Nevertheless, this point does not seem to be integrated into his amended theory, which is now oriented almost exclusively to analyzing the effects of the distribution of property on welfare.[93]

The point here is that one of the specific reasons that people may prefer socialism is that people are treated as commodities, due to the specific structure of capitalist labor relations. Capitalism is a social form in which things that are not commodities must be regarded as if they were; in Karl Polanyi's phrase, they are "fictitious commodities."[94] Labor is the crucial example. Once Roemer has sundered exploitation and the labor process he appears incapable of restoring the labor process even after exploitation has been dispatched as an important concept. This is not to suggest that democratic control of the workplace and democratic control of the economy as a whole can be easily integrated. Indeed there are unintended effects of the rational choices of workers in a specific workplace on the economy as a whole that would plague any self-managing socialism. Neither does it mean that syndicalism or industrial democracy is sufficient to establish socialism. However, industrial democracy is necessary to any version of socialism that is constructed on the basis of identifying the specifically repellent features of capitalism and also wishes to focus on probable motivations for collective action. The discussion of industrial democracy has persisted because the underlying claims are simultaneously material and ethical: people should not be treated as commodities.

It is untrue that the ethical critique of capitalism resolves itself into an inquiry into the justice of the original distribution of resources. This turns anti-capitalist struggle into just another variety of the struggle between rich and poor. It is not simply the unequal distribution of resources but the specific distribution of resources that has led to the majority being forced to sell their labor-power and therefore enter conditions of capitalist production and authority relations. These authority relations can be criticized on their own grounds, as proven by the workers opposition literature that has dogged the steps of existing socialism from its earliest days.[95] It is illegitimate to argue that these production conditions depend upon prior distribution and therefore the 'real' ethical question is prior distribution. The *real* question remains the historically specific form of distribution that produced and reproduces these *specific* productive relations and the multiple ethical problems they pose.

The issue to be confronted is therefore the specificity that ties together the distribution of resources, the capitalist labor process, and other aspects of welfare outcomes. Marx's way of theoretically unifying these phenomena may no longer be persuasive but the alternatives are rather pallid. As Ellen Meiksins Wood argues,

> [Roemer's] theory of exploitation entails breaking the connections among the various 'moments' of capital—production, distribution, exchange, consumption—and destroying any conception of capitalism as a *process,* in which these analytically distinct moments are dynamically united. In other words, there has been a complete reversal of the theoretical advances which Marx so painstakingly laboured to establish in his critique of political economy. That this represents progress in our understanding of capitalism, and not a regression to the worst simplifications of pre-Marxist political economy, remains to be demonstrated.[96]

Whether capitalism is a just system or not does not depend solely on whether inequality of resources can be defended. Its justice depends partly on the life it provides for human beings. It can be faulted on the grounds that workers are "brutalized" in the labor process, generally treated as commodities and without respect. For this reason the question of efficiency—and the concept of fettering—cannot be neatly separated from issues of justice. The efficiency of capitalism is partly defined by our moral evaluation of the kind of life it entails.

This criticism would not find its target if Roemer defined classes in

terms of wealth. However, he explicitly (and rightly) rejects this definition. Although the distribution of individuals among class positions in a
society is a consequence of the distribution of resources, Roemer defines
classes by a common position in respect to production, specifically as sellers and hirers of labor.[97] However, if this class division is a necessary or
at least likely consequence of inequality of resources, and if domination
in the workplace is still important even after it has been conceptually separated from exploitation, then a specific characterization of capitalism
and the probable motivations for challenging it depends upon analyzing
workplace relations even if exploitation is not sufficiently defined by what
happens there.

In regard to anti-capitalist struggles, it is quite difficult to reject some
of the arguments of Elster and Buchanan on the obstructions to collective
class action and of Przeworski on the prospects for socialism. Elster,
Buchanan, and Przeworski are helpful in clarifying the logical dilemmas
of collective action and showing how these pose grave difficulties for the
socialist movement. However, a troubling aspect of the rational choice approach is raised by Daniel R. Sabia, Jr. and is alluded to by Elster himself.
This approach would perhaps be better named the "logic of inaction."[98]
The situation reminds us of Galileo's legendary remark after being forced
to confirm an earth-centered view of the universe: "And yet, it moves." Elster's arguments on the persistence of non-class social actors are a case in
point. Granted the insights of the free rider problem and other rational
choice constructs, why do we see so many collective actors, although not
class-based ones? Rational choice arguments do indeed help clarify the
reasons why collective action will not occur but less attention is given to
explaining why collective action does occur, and so frequently. It is not
enough to explain why the emergence of class-based collective actors is unlikely or episodic. We need to articulate the conditions under which the
collective actors that do hold the stage emerge. Przeworski's argument of
the radical contingency of class-based collectivities does not prejudge this
question as do Elster's usual arguments.

This issue can be further explored by considering a recent discussion by
G. A. Cohen. As seen from some of the preceding, Cohen is something of a
distant cousin in the family resemblance that holds the rubric "analytical
Marxism" together. Although on occasion he denigrates the importance of
game theory for elucidating the central theses of historical materialism, his
arguments are also often based on the presumption of rational optimizers.[99]
However, one recent argument by Cohen appears to be incompatible with
this methodological assumption of rational choice theory.

In order to account for the enduring non-economic phenomena of nationalism, ethnic identity, religious communities, etc., Cohen proposes that
there is a human need for identity. "I claim, then, that there is a human need
to which Marxist observation is commonly blind, one different from and as
deep as the need to cultivate one's talents. It is the need to be able to say
not what I can do but who I am, satisfaction of which has historically been
found in identification with others in a shared culture based on nationality,
or race, or religion, or some slice or amalgam thereof."[100] Cohen says that
we do not actively seek an identity, because a capriciously seized identity
would not satisfy the need. It is not necessary to seek an identity anyway
since we are born with an identity, at the very least on the basis of gender.
He is simply arguing that a person's identity affects motivations for action,
which he calls generally "the potent force of familiarity."

Although Cohen does not pursue it, it is very difficult to fit this conception into the rational choice framework. This may help explain why
people do what they do even if such action has great costs in other ways.
If people are motivated by their identity, they act in ways that are not
amenable to the cost/benefits calculations on which rational choice analysis is based. In particular, it is hard to measure the strength of this need
and therefore it is hard to predict what choices a rational person would
make. The problem lies in the fact that the costs in this situation are not
commensurable, utilities cannot be compared. As Elster himself admits,
if utilities are not comparable then a rational choice calculation cannot be
made.[101]

Characteristically, Elster actually speaks in these cases of the "non-
existence of rational behavior" but this is because he believes that rational
choice exhausts the concept of rationality. If identity is indeed a human
need then its satisfaction is not irrational nor even arational behavior. It is
true that a rational *choice* cannot be made because there is no commensurability and if commensurability is denied then so is the "transitivity of
preferences." But this does not entail that the pursuit of either of the options is arational. It is simply the rational pursuit of something that cannot
be fitted into the categories of rational choice theory.

Sometimes people apparently engage in action for its own sake.
Again, Elster himself notes this, pointing to the persistence of voting even
though rational choice calculations suggest that it is individually irrational
behavior since the single vote has costs with no impact in most cases. "Indeed, voting behavior provides one of the strongest cases against the om-
nipotence of rational-choice explanation. Voting does seem to be a case in
which the action itself, rather than the outcome it can be expected to pro-

duce, is what matters."[102] Elster interprets these cases as a following of community norms, "internalized" in one's "self-image." We may restate it as affirming one's identity.

This broaches the general question of acting so as to advance certain values. Rational choice theorists claim to be able to incorporate this topic but when they relax the methodological stricture of *self*-interested behavior, they typically resort to the idea of altruism, i.e., that my preferences are to optimize the preferences of others.[103] This is, however, a much too restrictive way to consider the issue. Indeed, Elster and other analytical Marxists must broaden the discussion in so far as they consider justice or any other ethical value to be a possible or even probable basis for revolutionary motivation.[104]

Ethical motivation is difficult to analyze through rational choice theory. First, it is hard to see how values could be regarded as commensurable, therefore again a rational choice may not be possible. Secondly, ethical values may not even be compatible. Elster occasionally defines a rational desire as one that is achievable, invoking the postulate that "ought implies can." Contrary to Elster, it is quite common for individuals to be in situations where they believe themselves to have conflicting moral responsibilities, all of which cannot be fulfilled. The fact that they cannot fulfil them does not, however, release them from the obligation; this is therefore a 'tragic' situation.[105] On the face of it this would be hard to accommodate to the rational choice framework because it is uncertain that the conception of individuals employed by this theory even allows the very notion of obligation. If analytical Marxists appeal to ethical principles at all—as they do—they need a much more sophisticated moral philosophy than the one employed here.

Przeworski criticizes the poverty of the view of society that conceptualizes agents as merely executing norms but that is not precisely the case here. People are not acting out norms but acting on them, choosing a course of action on the basis of norms. For his part, in one place Elster criticizes explanations of actions based on norms as "ad hoc and ex post facto" but, given the ubiquity of collective action, the same can be said of rational choice responses to these questions.[106] Utilitarians have always been very adept at redescribing motivations as variations of self-interest, but establishing the truth of the matter is something else again. In any case, the reformulation of the nature and importance of the normative concerns of Marxian theory, to which analytical Marxists have made such a powerful contribution (presumably motivated by something other than self-interest), does not appear to be compatible with the narrow notion of interest utilized by rational choice theory itself.

Elster is correct that we do not know how to explain or predict when normative motivations will supercede calculations of interest, nor what happens when traditional ways of doing things are no longer possible, i.e., when "the feasible set contracts so that the formerly chosen behavior becomes impossible."[107] However, the conditions under which motivations for action can be transformed has long been a topic of socialist discussion. In response to the free rider problem of collective action by workers, some have argued that the preferences of workers can be altered by the creation of organizational forms which would expand the feasible set. In rational choice theory this possibility is again understood in an unnecessarily restrictive fashion, as in-process benefits or selective incentives. Contrary to this perspective, which merely proposes variations of what is still individual self-interest, participation can foster feelings of solidarity or in other ways transform the motivations of individuals by creating a common identity.

For example, Claus Offe and Helmut Wiesenthal argue that the different structural situations of workers and capitalists create different logics of collective action. For workers, the forging of a collective identity is crucial for collective action in that it alters "the standards according to which these costs are subjectively estimated within their own collectivity."

> No union can function for a day in the absence of some rudimentary notions held by the members that being a member is of value in itself, that the individual organization costs must not be calculated in a utilitarian manner but have to be accepted as necessary sacrifices, and that each member is legitimately required to practise solidarity and discipline, and other norms of a non-utilitarian kind.[108]

This argument provides an alternative to the belief that all in-process benefits can be calculated according to individual utility. Offe and Wiesenthal contend that one can develop a new identity that is inextricably bound with a collectivity, such that the measurement of individual costs and benefits is altered. The "I" which is the referent of utilities is now part of a "we"; the self which is to be advanced through self-interest is transformed. If G. A. Cohen is right about a human need for identity, then the emergence of collective identities should be neither arduous nor rare.

However, Buchanan is still correct that even if there are transformations once an organization is begun, the beginning itself still presents rational choice problems. In response, Sabia suggests that working class conditions can generate solidarity as a motive in small scale situations (e.g., neighborhoods) and that these smaller scale efforts can be built upon in establishing larger scale actions.[109] Elster himself agrees that "[s]olidarity can substitute for material incentives," although he argues that such motivation is conditional.[110] Nevertheless, if we acknowledge that lesser communities always exist on which larger collective efforts can be constructed, i.e., if we dismiss the Hobbesian conception of society, the collective action problems of workers and others are at least reduced.

On occasion Elster too registers some surprising doubts about rational choice theory. In regard to contextual information, Elster suggests that the sheer complexity of bargaining situations and potential alliances of the working class, bourgeoisie, or fractions of either overwhelms understanding.[111] He also recognizes that game theory takes preferences as an exogenous given, which begs the question of the social origins of preferences, perhaps rooted in class position.[112] In one place Elster even calls for "explanatory pluralism," although still in the framework of methodological individualism: "*A priori* there is no reason to believe that any single model for individual-level behavior will be the best in all cases of collective action. Explanatory pluralism should not be eschewed. On the other hand, one should beware of the dangers of *ad hoc*-ness."[113] Finally, in one place Elster argues that we should avoid a "premature reductionism." "Collective action may simply be too complex for individual-level explanations to be feasible at the current stage."[114] All we need add is that the complexities are multiplied when one considers a possible need for identity, the origins of ethical motivation, and the sources of solidarity.

Even if the collective action problems of workers were overcome, we would still have to face the dilemmas posed by Przeworski. Przeworski's elaboration of the rational, strategic grounds of the class compromise which originated and maintains the interventionist welfare state is logically compelling. It is also a powerful explanation for the historical turn of the socialist movement to social democracy rather than socialism. There are, however, several additional considerations that at least modify the analysis, all of which are in places raised tangentially by Przeworski but should be amplified here.

First, there are many reasons why the class compromise explained by Przeworski may not be stable. The most important is the international fluidity of capital. Workers are constrained not only by capitalist control of investment and the threat of divestment if there are any moves toward public ownership, but also by the threat of capital to move to more congenial venues if the workers ask 'too much.' The internationalization of capital means an improved bargaining position for capital and increased pressure on the living standards of workers. This may eventually lead to a recalculation of the costs of a transition to socialism. There is no doubt that capitalism does not deliver the goods on a world scale. Przeworski himself quotes a Brazilian business leader to this effect: "Our businessmen think that communism has failed. They forget that our capitalism is also a monstrous failure."[115] The internationalization of capital seems to require an internationalization of the workers movement simply to preserve the status quo, and that presents extraordinary collective action problems, rational choice or otherwise.

A second qualification must be added to Przeworski's analysis. The crucial condition of the class compromise of social democracy is the efficacy of democratic control. Democracy must be real and it must be enduring for the compromise to persist. Przeworski himself has noted the pressure on democracy in the United States and the consequent endangering of the compromise under the onslaught of the New Right beginning in the late 1970s.[116] Processes that hollow-out democratic influence on the economy therefore would work against an enduring class compromise and the rational calculus that maintains it.

There are two things to be noted in this regard. First, Przeworski has recently brilliantly analyzed the problems of transitions to democracy in the South and East. To be stable, democracies must be "fair" in that all the "relevant political forces" must have a real possibility of winning on occasion. Furthermore, democracy must be "effective" in that losing is "more attractive than a future under nondemocratic alternatives." However, "[f]airness requires that all major interests must be protected at the margin; effectiveness may necessitate that they be seriously harmed."[117] Przeworski admits that it is difficult to strike a balance between fairness and effectiveness. "This is why democracy has been historically a fragile form for organizing political conflicts."

The strong democracy necessary to affect investment in the ways required for the class compromise is inherently fragile. However, the power of democratic government is also increasingly limited in a second way. With the intensification of global production, a hollowing-out of democracy occurs not simply because of any domestic changes but because of the reduced sovereignty of national governments over their own economies, increasingly determined by global economic rhythms. Globalization may mean the end to the historic bases and rational calculus underlying social democracy.

Globalization of production may therefore undermine the class compromise in advanced capitalist countries in two ways: by increasing the

bargaining position of capital and by reducing national governmental control over the determinants of the domestic economy. Needless to say, there
is considerable evidence that these are occurring in the world today. In
sum, using Przeworski's own criticism of game theory, he fails to fully
specify the context and conditions that result in the class compromise insofar as the globalization (or even regionalization) of production is not fully
considered.

PREFERENCE FORMATION AND SOCIALISM

Analytical Marxism should be judged by whether it illuminates central
questions of Marxism. The abstractions employed by analytical Marxists
are necessary and fruitful for generating hypotheses about the logical basis
of social action in contemporary capitalism. Marxian theory today is not
in any position to reject out of hand new methodological approaches to its
leading questions, as many are still wont to do. Contrary to Margaret Levi
(in her review of one of Roemer's earlier books), Marxism entered "the
second half of the twentieth century" before Roemer's work. However,
contrary to Ellen Meiksins Wood, rational choice theory does not land us
back in the nineteenth century (or earlier) by its employment of a "banal
and shrivelled *homo economicus*."[118] The strengths of analytical Marxism
are methodological. Analytical Marxism shows us that some things can be
explained if we assume that individuals are rational and self-interested.
The application of their method also frequently shows us the opposite as
well. As Wright noted, a theory is good if it also clearly reveals what it
cannot explain, thereby providing us with precise grounds for seeking additional explanations. From this perspective, rational choice is an extremely productive theory.

Analytical Marxists have contributed to restoring the ethical question
to Marxian theory, partly by destroying the importance of the chief (although largely unacknowledged) Marxian ethical category: exploitation.
However, as argued above, this bold reinstatement of the question of justice calls into question the application of rational choice theory itself. Ethical questions often do not allow the commensurability on which rational
choice depends. This is not to say that pursuing a normative path is irrational but that the choice of one ethical path over another cannot be defended according to criteria that would be acceptable to a rational choice
theorist. The word commensurability is used on purpose because much recent discussion on the commensurability of theoretical paradigms would
have something to contribute to this line of analysis.[119] So also would

Juergen Habermas's two volume critique of functional reason and Alasdair MacIntyre's analyses of the concepts of justice and rationality in the history of moral philosophy.

This raises from within analytical Marxism itself a problem endemic to rational choice theory: where do preferences, i.e., conceptions of welfare, come from? As noted by Przeworski and Elster, in game theory preferences are treated as given (exogenous, rather than generated from within the theory itself, i.e., endogenous). Roemer acknowledges that at present economics offers no "useful theory of endogenous preference formation." Although in his investigations he considers possible origins of endowments and how these origins might affect the legitimacy of property, "hardly any space has been devoted to discussing where people's preferences come from. My topic has been the inequality of welfare produced by private ownership of the means of production, but I have taken as given and unanalyzed the utility functions—the conceptions of welfare—that people have."[120] As noted, Roemer has indicated in a few places the necessity of a "sociology of injustice" for helping to uncover the determinants of preferences.[121]

Roemer has theoretically deprived himself of perhaps the richest source of preference formation under capitalism by deflating the theoretical importance of the commodification of labor. Resistance to capitalism is not only based on calculations of material benefit. When people resist capitalism they undoubtedly do so partly because of its effects on social life and because of conceptions of how people ought to live. The treatment of laboring people as a commodity—labor-power—is one of the key motivations for socialism. At least it was seen as such by Karl Polanyi in his account of emergent capitalist society.

> In spite of exploitation, [the worker] might have been financially better off than before. But a principle quite unfavorable to individual and general happiness was working havoc with his social environment, his neighborhood, his standing in the community, his craft; in a word, with those relationships to nature and man in which his economic existence was formerly embedded. The Industrial Revolution was causing a social dislocation of stupendous proportions, and the problem of poverty was merely the economic aspect of this event.[122]

It is for normative reasons such as these that the project of industrial democracy has always been central to socialist theory, even if in its earlier expression the proponents believed this could be satisfied through mere central government ownership. The problem, from a rational choice perspective, is how these individual experiences of the social dislocation essential (not accidental, nor a consequence of immaturity) to a market economy can become a motivation for collective action. Elster is undoubtedly correct, following what appears to have been the implicit position of Marx (or explicit opinion of Aristotle, for that matter), that revolutionary motivation would most likely have to be a combination of interest and right.[123] The concept of radical needs, vague as it is, contains in one phrase both of these dimensions. This would alter the weights in the evaluation of social democracy versus some form of socialism. It would not, of course, solve the problem of working out a feasible kind of socialism.

On the relations between preference formation and socialism, some other reflections of Przeworski are relevant. Przeworski restores a historical dimension to the discussion by reminding us of the hopes of previous generations of socialists that have been more or less effaced from contemporary socialist theory. "Socialism was not a movement for full employment but for the abolition of wage slavery; it was not a movement for efficiency but for collective rationality; it was not a movement for equality but for freedom."[124] Like Allan Wood and others, Przeworski rejects the argument that equality is at the center of the socialist project. Under socialism, "Equality ceases to be a meaningful term: it is an issue only in an unfree society."

Similarly to Heller, in several places Przeworski states that socialism could be oriented to "the satisfaction of different needs," e.g., free time. He describes at some length the original vision of socialism as a society in which free time has been extended to the point where society is only minimally "institutionalized."[125] In any case, the experience of needs under socialism is likely to differ from capitalism. "As long as the satisfaction of needs is externally constrained, we cannot tell what human needs are." Rational choice theorists might still respond that even if this is true under socialism, getting there is a difficult collective action problem. However, although Przeworski does not pursue this point, there are reasons to believe that the development of radical needs could begin within capitalism, perhaps as a reaction to its dessication of individuals. If this is true, then G. A. Cohen's argument concerning fettering would have considerably more currency.

In this way Przeworski ably criticizes the renewed socialist focus on distribution. He argues—as do Gorz, Offe, Habermas, and others—that, "Since the efforts to secure full employment are becoming increasingly quixotic," we must reconsider the possibility of reducing labor-time.[126] We may not be able to see at the moment how we can get there but, as Cohen counsels regarding market socialism, this should not cause us to surreptitiously engage in "Adaptive Preference Formation," i.e., regard the second-best as best because it is attainable.[127]

All of these considerations taken into account, there are three extraordinarily interesting topics illuminated by analytical Marxism: the normative grounding of capitalism, the conditions of collective action by workers, and the class compromise that led to and stabilizes the interventionist welfare state. Claus Offe shows how all of these issues are bound together in the dynamic of the welfare state. Offe argues that the welfare state in its very mode of operation displaces social conflict into the political realm, but, contrary to some arguments within analytical Marxism, this presents new problems of administrative rationality and creates an entirely new set of legitimation difficulties for advanced capitalism. Social democracy can therefore be destabilized from more grounds than have been suggested thus far. It is to this intriguing analysis we must now turn.

Five

The Political Displacements of the Welfare State:
The Theory of Claus Offe

Many theorists working in the Marxist tradition have long suspected that, whatever may have been the case in the past, the modern welfare state fundamentally alters the dynamic of social conflict in advanced capitalist societies. Claus Offe's work represents the most probing and comprehensive exploration of this thesis. Offe argues that the specific character of contemporary capitalism displaces production as the primary site of conflict potentials as a consequence of the politicization of production by the interventionist welfare state. The crisis tendencies of capitalist society are not thereby eliminated but rather are in diverse ways transmuted into "second order crises" of the "political administrative subsystem" and the "normative subsystem" of capitalist society. The specific dynamic of this displacement and the manner in which the state attempts to handle its new tasks further undermine the conditions of working class formation. However in the process other oppositional forces are produced, organized on different grounds. This chapter examines Offe's arguments on the effects of this political displacement on social conflict in contemporary capitalism and on the theoretical status of the proletariat.

Some socialist theorists have welcomed the repoliticization of production in advanced capitalism, arguing that it opens new possibilities for class struggle.[1] In contrast, because of his analysis of the specific ways in which the interventionist state intervenes, Offe is more or less agnostic regarding the potential for socialist transformation. He concentrates on the political dynamic initiated by the responsibilities of the welfare state, its struggle to develop new policies and strategies and the need to establish new administrative forms to handle these tasks. Only a detailed analysis of this specific dynamic will allow us to judge the opportunities and obstructions it creates for the socialist project. Until then these prospects must remain an open question.

108

Offe's work is extraordinarily rich and traverses many of the concerns of the social sciences. For this reason many interesting arguments and discussions can only be indicated rather than explored. We will reconstruct his basic argument from the many essays in which it is developed and consider some of the ambiguities that emerge. There are five broad aspects of Offe's theory that are of interest here: (1) Offe's analysis of the situation of 'actually existing capitalism' and the functional reasons for the development of the interventionist welfare state, including an account of its specific activities; (2) the political administrative problems these new tasks create for the state and the strategies the state utilizes to handle these difficulties; (3) how these problems, public policy strategies, and political dynamic affect working class formation; and, (4) Offe's argument of how conflict is displaced to new sites and new collectivities in advanced capitalism. Finally, (5) we must examine Offe's more recent reflections on the decline of political support for the welfare state and how this political turn can be accommodated to his previous arguments on the functional necessity of the welfare state for contemporary capitalism.

ACTUALLY EXISTING CAPITALISM

Offe defines capitalism as a system of production based on exchange in the context of an unequal distribution of property. "This principle of exchange, which also includes the commodification of labor power, becomes *dominant* because it is freed from normative and political-coercive restraints."[2] Especially important for our purposes and for Offe's conception of capitalism is the existence of a labor market, which in another place he refers to as "the most significant feature of capitalist social structures."[3]

Although later the approach is de-emphasized, Offe generally utilizes a broad systems theory in analyzing capitalism. Capitalism is a system the identity of which is determined by its dominant subsystem, production mediated by exchange. To analyze the existing situation we must forego the immediate discussion of collective actors and examine the functional requirements of contemporary capitalism and the ways in which these requirements are handled.[4] Offe recognizes the dangers of this approach, that the "functional imperatives" of the capitalist system are thereby analytically divorced from the social actors which place these *as* "imperatives" for the system.[5] However, immediately focusing on social actors would beg the question of their formation. It should be noted at the outset that Offe's focus on system imperatives introduces a fundamental ambiguity as to the actual supports of system imperatives.

Capitalism is a system identified by the dominance of the subsystem of production mediated by exchange. Nevertheless, as Offe argues, no society could be totally regulated by exchange relations. Therefore even liberal capitalism entailed "flanking subsystems" for its existence, at least social-ization through the family and a legal order for establishing contracts, re-spectively the "normative" and "political-coercive" subsystems.[6] The latter subsystems operate according to different principles than exchange and, although they are necessary for the persistence of the system as a whole, it is important that they not be allowed to interfere with the ex-change principle of the economic subsystem.[7] Offe's thesis is that this be-comes increasingly difficult with the development of advanced capitalism. How the state in particular tries to support capitalism without endangering the dominance of the exchange principle, and the specifically political ad-ministrative dynamic this engenders, is the center of Offe's work.

Like others discussed previously, Offe rejects many aspects of Marxi-an economic analysis such as the labor theory of value and the thesis that the rate of profit tends to fall. He does accept what is in a broad way the overall Marxian economic critique of capitalism: the essential "anarchy" of production mediated by exchange.[8] The development of the exchange relations of capitalism necessarily means division, differentiation, and specialization of the economy and a corresponding interdependence of the various parts, in sum, the "socialization" of the means of production.[9] The economy becomes increasingly sensitive to disruption and requires coor-dination. However this coordination cannot issue from the sphere of ex-change because of private appropriation and investment. The argument is, of course, quite familiar.

These various difficulties necessitate an increased role for a "flanking subsystem," namely the political administrative subsystem, i.e., the state. To pursue this role the state requires increased autonomy in order to steer the system as a whole. "The more that steering problems result from the failure of the exchange mechanism to integrate the process of socializa-tion, the greater is the degree of independence or relative autonomy re-quired by the political-administrative center if it is to repair, or compensate for, these problems."[10] Although his discussion is compressed at this point, Offe has in mind not only the usual regulatory policies but also Key-nesian demand management for steering the system.

Over time these policies prove to be insufficient, however, and in fact the economic problems intensify. Increasingly capitalism ("late capital-ism") appears to suffer from "self-paralyzing laws or tendencies." "The key problem of capitalist societies is the fact that the dynamics of capitalist development seem to exhibit a constant tendency to *paralyze* the commodity form of value."[11] Although he discusses this "paralysis" in various places, the specifics remain, as John Keane says, "obscure."[12] Offe indicates the origins of the problem in monopolization of the economy, economic differentiation, saturation of the demand for durable goods, and even the blocking of the effects of economic crisis by Keynesian policies themselves. The latter is important to our specific topic and must be examined in greater detail.

According to Offe, Keynesian policies are themselves obstructive in a number of ways. Most importantly, Keynesian policies create disincentives to work and invest. The disincentives to work are a consequence of the improvement of the relative bargaining position of labor caused by welfare policies.[13] This bargaining position causes wages to be "sticky" and "downwardly inflexible." State protection of labor consequently makes employment more costly to capital thereby encouraging jobless growth and increasing unemployment.[14]

Offe also agrees with supply-side theorists that Keynesian policies result in disincentives to invest, caused especially by deficit-spending which drives up interest rates, discouraging investment by increasing costs. In addition, Offe argues—similarly to Friedrich A. Hayek—that countervailing Keynesian policies of incentives for investment are only effective so long as they do not become a "matter of routine."

> As soon as that happens, however, investors will postpone investment because they can be reasonably sure that the state will intervene by special tax exemptions, depreciation allowances or demand measures, if only they wait long enough. The spread of such 'rational' expectations is fatal to Keynesianism, for to the extent it enters the calculations of economic actors, their strategic behavior will *increase* the problem load to which the state has to respond . . .[15]

The intensifying demands on the state "exhaust" further possibilities along those lines.

Offe broadly agrees with conservative theorists who argue that the interventionist welfare state is quite burdensome for capitalism.[16] In general, state intervention ameliorates the "[p]ressures to adjust to changing market forces," reducing the "adaptation potential of capitalism."[17] The crucial difference is of course that Offe also sees the welfare state as responding to functional needs of advanced capitalism. Therefore this amounts to an objective political economic contradiction of advanced capitalism. Whether this is properly described as the self-paralysis of the commodity form is disputable, although in one place Offe directly places it under that rubric.[18]

Many might find this analysis objectionable, again for reasons of Offe's objectivist systems level approach. For example, the obstruction of the "purgative effects" of "unfettered economic crises" by Keynesian economic policies is no doubt to some extent the consequence of a large part of the population, workers and capitalists, refusing to put up with widespread economic dislocation and cannot be explained without referring to these actors. This leads to reservations in describing these difficulties as *self*-paralyzing. Regardless of these objections, however, Offe is correct in his main point that, "there is plenty of everyday evidence to the effect that both labor power and capital are expelled from the commodity form, and . . . there is little basis for the liberal belief that they will be reintegrated automatically into exchange relationships."[19] It is also true that, "[a]lthough this argument is hard to *develop,* it is even harder to *reject*" in the face of various sorts of social disorder evident today.

It is very important to Offe's characterization of the specific activities of the interventionist welfare state that the economic contradictions of capitalism be described as a crisis of the commodity form of value. The commodity form of value is what distinguishes the capitalist mode of production from other modes. If the system is to maintain its identity as capitalist, accumulation must continue through exchange relations, as opposed to forced labor or state command of production. The state must therefore find a way to "recommodify" capital and labor so that the paralysis is overcome without breaching the principle of exchange.

To keep this discussion from turning into an entirely functionalist argument, Offe does indeed allow that there are specific social forces which channel state action in the direction of recommodification. Most important of these forces is the structurally privileged position of capital. One of Offe's central arguments is that state action is constrained by the perpetual threat of divestment by business, that is, by "capital's power to obstruct." "The foundation of capitalist power and domination is this institutionalized right of capital withdrawal, of which economic crisis is nothing but the aggregate manifestation."[20] This "blackmail capacity" of capital is strengthened by the fact that it is businesses that determine whether profits are sufficient or not:

> That is to say, whatever they *consider* an intolerable burden in fact is an intolerable burden which will *in fact* lead to a declining propensity to invest, at least as long as they can expect to effec-

tively reduce welfare-state-related costs by applying such economic sanctions. The debate about whether or not the welfare state is 'really' squeezing profits is thus purely academic because investors are in a position to *create the reality—and the effects—of 'profit squeeze.'*[21]

As briefly mentioned in the previous chapter, there are certain limitations on the feasibility of the use of the "capital strike" in the long run, limitations suggested by Offe's qualification "at least as long as they can expect . . ." The conditions for effective use of this weapon depend upon competitive pressures on capital (willingness of some firms to accept a lower rate of return), demand, and the ability of capital to outwait its opponents by foregoing investment.

As we have seen, variants of this argument on the potential of a capital strike are important to a number of recent theorists.[22] However, this thesis is difficult to reconcile with Marx's conception of capitalist dynamics. For Marx, capital *had* to invest because of the nature of capital as many competing capitals. The capitalist who did not invest would lose in the competitive struggle. The fluidity of capital certainly allows a flexibility of investment decisions so that capitalists can play one community against another or even one country against another. But the idea that capital as a whole can simply refuse to invest for any length of time is something that Marx would have had difficulty conceiving. Needless to say, it also begs a number of immediate collective action questions.

The possibility of a capital strike is certainly increased by the development of monopoly capitalism. Nevertheless, the importance of this notion for Offe's analysis (and that of others) demands a more thorough explication of the conditions under which this threat must be taken seriously. However in the present context, the *threat* of a capital strike, i.e., its generalized manifestation as a state concern with "business confidence," is sufficient to carry Offe's argument.

Policies for the recommodification of capital and labor are encouraged by the fact that the state depends on taxes for its institutional resources. Taxes are skimmed from accumulation, which in turn depends on investment. The "institutional self-interest" of the state therefore requires no interruptions of accumulation.[23] This in turn sensitizes the state to the conditions of business confidence. The state fashions its policy in accord with accumulation based on exchange because it is too expensive fiscally and politically to simply distribute use-values directly to those who cannot find employment.[24]

Similarly to Adam Przeworski, Offe argues that a "Keynesian class compromise" has also made the recommodification strategy acceptable to labor. As long as this policy is successful and economic growth is maintained, labor and capital are involved in a "positive sum game." Each class acknowledges the interests of the other class. On the one side, workers see that profitability is the condition of job security and increased income. On the other, capitalists recognize that they "must accept the need for wages and welfare state expenditures, because these will secure effective demand and a healthy, well-trained, well-housed and happy working class."[25] This compromise has served as a peace formula since World War II. Needless to say, this accord is now under considerable strain, a fact we will explore later.

Due to the above considerations, state intervention is oriented toward the revitalization and maintenance of the dominance of exchange relations. The focus on exchange relations and the importance of channeling state action through them allows Offe to specify exactly what forms state intervention takes. Offe distinguishes two types of state interventionist policy: "allocative" policies and "productive" policies.[26] The importance of this distinction for Offe's general theory is that these two "modes of state intervention" have very different internal effects on the state, posing new problems for public administration and presenting new opportunities for conflict in advanced capitalism.

Offe characterizes the allocative mode or method of state intervention as state distribution of resources already under its control. Specifically, he argues that allocative policies utilize taxes and governmental spending (Keynesian parametric policies), sovereign authority over land, and repressive force to shape the conditions under which accumulation takes place. As discussed above, these policies prove insufficient to maintain accumulation and a new political strategy must be devised.

Interestingly, the major reason for the emergence of a new kind of policy is the internal competition of capital. Offe says that at some point in development the required inputs to continue exchange simply are not forthcoming, indicating problems of costliness of new inputs, risk and uncertainty of capitalist firms in providing these inputs, and the inability of individual capitalist firms to ensure exclusive exploitation of inputs provided. For these reasons "the quantitatively and qualitatively sufficient supply of variable and constant capital fails to appear on the market."[27] The ability of capitalist firms to innovate inputs as a defensive measure against competition drastically declines. Productivity gains therefore come to depend on sources outside of the accumulation process itself, i.e., the task falls to the state. "At this point, productive state activities, in addition to

the allocative ones, emerge, since the state is the only organization in capitalist society that could provide such inputs that are required in order to
sustain accumulation and production."[28] The development of productive
policies is not only broader in scope but is also state intervention in a "new
way," qualitatively different from allocative policies. As such they place
qualitatively new demands on state administration.

The types of policies that Offe has in mind are "education, skills, technological change, control over raw materials, health, transportation,
housing, a structure of cities, physical environment, energy, and communication services."[29] The state also engages in direct stimulation of new
possibilities of investment by "forced consumption" through armaments
production. Finally, the state allows those regions that appear incapable
of revitalization to simply decline (known in urban policy as triage). In
general, the state takes on the function of shaping all the factors of production.[30] State policy takes this form "when the state is required to produce (rather than merely decide upon) the conditions of continued
accumulation."[31]

In later discussions Offe describes productive policies more specifically as the "administrative recommodification" of capital and labor.[32] The
goal is to "create and universalize the commodity form of value, in whose
absence values become non-existent in a capitalist society." Offe argues
that, given existing conditions, this administrative recommodification is in
the general interest. The state is not directly promoting the interest of a
particular class through these policies. "[R]ather it sanctions the general
interest of all classes on the basis of capitalist exchange relationships."

> For instance, it would be a mistake to argue that state policies of
> education and training are designed to provide the necessary labor
> power for certain industries, since no one, least of all the state bu-
> reaucracy, has any reliable information concerning the type, tim-
> ing and volume of skills required by capitalists. Such policies are
> instead designed to provide a *maximum of exchange opportunities*
> for both labor and capital, so that individuals of both classes can
> enter into capitalist relations of production. Similarly, research
> and development policies designed and funded by the state are by
> no means directed towards concrete beneficiaries, such as indus-
> tries which can use the resulting technologies.[33]

Offe's point is to underline what he considers to be the crucial difference
between allocative and productive policies in their demands on public administration. Allocative policies, utilizing resources already under the

control of the state, are determined by the usual give and take of politics. This is because interest groups demand of the state (or its specific agencies) something that it already has. However, productive policies are qualitatively different in that they are "avoidance" actions, a response to *"negative events*, namely, the absence or disturbance of an accumulation process." In this case there is no "clear-cut course of action." Since the problem is one of restoring the accumulation process as a whole, the state cannot rely on the recommendations of dominant social groups. "The rules and laws that govern *politics* are not sufficient to solve this problem. An additional set of decision rules is required that determines *policies*."[34]

Because of an inherent lack of consensus ("class consciousness") of the "ruling class,"[35] the state has no cues as to how it is to proceed in developing productive policies. Therefore it must invent its own "decision rules" or "production rules." The state's relative autonomy is stretched remarkably by the fact that it must devise its own rationale and plan for productive policies. This is what Offe indicates when he says that state policies of administrative recommodification are guided by the general interest, albeit under conditions of an exchange society. However, these new demands pose a danger to the dominance of the exchange principle in society as a whole. Offe suggests that relative autonomy threatens to become absolute autonomy as the state must call on its own administrative creativity for productive policies. We will explore the specific difficulties this poses for state administration in the next section.

Since our present concern is the theoretical status of the proletariat, we need to examine a few more details of Offe's argument, specifically on the administrative recommodification of labor power. In one place Offe increases the historical depth of his discussion by arguing that even in the earlier history of capitalism, depriving individuals of independent means of subsistence was not enough to turn them into workers, that is, the "mute compulsion" of economic forces (Marx's phrase) was not and is not sufficient to force individuals into the labor market. He argues this by distinguishing between "passive proletarianization" (depriving individuals of independent subsistence) and "active proletarianization" (their entry into the labor market). As is well-known, historically many individuals deprived of subsistence actively resisted their transformation into wage workers by resorting to migration, crime, begging, and Luddism. Contrary to common conceptions, "the rise of a labor *market*" is not "natural." "Even if the destruction of traditional forms of subsistence is presupposed as a fact, the process of industrialization is inconceivable without also presupposing massive 'active' proletarianization."[36] Changing dispossessed labor power into *wage*-labor is "a constitutive socio-*political* process whose accomplishment cannot be explained *solely* by the 'silent compulsion of economic relations.'"

There are three specific things that the state must do to accomplish this purpose. First, it must encourage values that make the risks of wage-labor relatively attractive compared to the alternatives. It does this through ideology and repression, but it is a continuing battle. Secondly, the contemporary state must provide support systems for labor power such as schools, family, and health facilities.[37] Under modern conditions these functions must become state functions because of the inefficacy and decay of traditional forms of support caused by the "disaggregation and mobilization of whole populations" for economic activity. Offe specifically mentions the decline of guilds, churches, communities, and, especially, the extended family.

Thirdly, and very importantly for Offe's argument, the state must take on the function of actively regulating which individuals are to be included in the labor market. That is, in providing support services the state must directly decide who will have access to alternatives to participation in the labor market. This function stems particularly from the fact that labor is only a fictitious commodity. Offe borrows Karl Polanyi's phrase to indicate that labor power does not obey the usual dynamic of commodities. "[L]abor power is indeed treated *as a commodity* but, unlike other commodities, its coming into being is not *based on* strategic expectations of saleability."[38] Unlike other commodities it does not appear only when there is a possibility for sale, i.e., it does not obey the laws of supply and demand like ordinary commodities (unemployment establishes this fact). Neither does the supply of labor diminish when the price of labor declines; in many cases it rises. The state must thus provide for the "storage" of labor power until it is needed. It regulates the supply of labor by directing it especially toward education and training so that it can be properly fitted while awaiting employment. Also, some potential labor is simply excluded by child labor laws and mandatory retirement. (There are other aspects of this fictitious commodity that will be utilized in criticism of Offe's theory later.)

In sum, Offe insists that labor is not naturally a commodity but must actively be commodified. In many ways the state has always been actively involved in the constitution of the labor market, especially through criminal penalties for the indigent and ideological promotion of the moral worthiness of work. Due to the various economic and political changes that contribute to the self-paralysis of the commodity form, these commodifying activities are enormously extended and intensified today, requiring qualitatively new state policies.

This discussion opens a number of interesting theoretical possibilities. It can be easily extended to the other two fictitious commodities mentioned by Polanyi: land and capital.[39] If we did so it would sharpen our understanding of the role of politics and policy in creating even liberal capitalism, increasing the specificity of the phrase relative autonomy. However this is clearly beyond the present discussion. The point here is merely to underline Offe's insistence that "[t]he most decisive function of social policy is its regulation of the process of proletarianization," such that we can explore its ramifications for class formation.

From these various arguments about the state's new role we can understand Offe's thesis that the "first order crises" of production give way, under advanced capitalism, to "second order crises" of political administration in handling these tasks. According to Offe, "second order crises are more relevant than those of the first order, although they are, of course, produced by the latter."[40] Unable to rely on the usual cues of politics, it is necessary for the state to provide its own "production rules," thereby displacing the "objectivity of capitalist development" to the politico-administrative sphere. The ambiguity involved in insisting, on one hand, that the dynamic of advanced capitalism has shifted to political administration but, on the other, that this has "in no sense neutralized the politicized economy as the ultimate regulator in the functioning of political institutions"[41] will have an important bearing on our evaluation of Offe's argument that the potential for conflict in contemporary capitalism has been displaced to the state and normative spheres. However, before that we must examine in more detail the problems that these new tasks cause for the political administration of the state.

EFFECTS OF STATE INTERVENTION ON PUBLIC ADMINISTRATION

There are three primary political consequences of the assumption of these new tasks by the state. The first is the intensification of demands made on the state, threatening to overburden it, known in conservative theory as "ungovernability."[42] According to Offe, ungovernability is primarily a consequence of the increasingly generalized and accurate perception that "[e]conomic growth . . . has become a matter of political design rather than a matter of spontaneous market forces."[43] In order to reduce these demands the state is continually pushed toward policies of "reprivatization"[44] and "scientization." The latter is the increasing reliance on experts in determining which opinions are relevant for policy formation, "rejecting potential claims of 'non-experts' to be heard."[45]

However, Offe suggests that these strategies for reducing demands on the state will be a failure. The interdependency of the economy as a whole means the proliferation of veto-groups who can insist on a voice. He even argues that in advanced capitalism these groups are so ubiquitous that the effectiveness of public policy is not actually under the control of the state. Rather, the impact of state policy is crucially dependent on the cooperation of the affected groups themselves. "[T]he administration can fulfil its concrete goal-oriented functions, by which it responds to the need for authoritative solutions to specific societal problems, only to the extent that it can rely on the readiness of its societal target groups to cooperate voluntarily in the attainment of administrative goals."[46] For this and other reasons, the state finds itself pursuing "empirical consensus formation." This casts doubt on the likelihood of success of strategies to improve governability by restricting the scope of the state or by reducing the number of opinions that will be heard.

Instead, the favored strategy has actually been the opposite of relative autonomy: corporatist interest intermediation. Offe discusses corporatist arrangements in a variety of places and refers to them by a variety of names—" 'liberal corporatism,'" "neo-corporatism," "modern corporatism," etc.[47] Offe insists that this "creeping corporatism" is extended to many groups beyond business associations and organized labor. "Such state-sanctioned schemes of mutual accommodation among associations and collective actors (recently described as neo-corporatism) are to be found not only in the area of wage-bargaining, but equally in areas like housing, education, and environmental protection."[48] Groups are included on the grounds of their "functional indispensability" or "considerable 'obstruction potential.'"

Although some critics of corporatism have denied it, Offe argues that the delegation of decisionmaking to private organizations suggests the expansion of corporatist structures beyond labor and capital.[49] Nevertheless, as is customary in corporatist theory, Offe focuses most of his attention on business associations and organized labor. He argues that the state strategy of corporatism differs in this case from the self-administration or delegation of powers to interest groups. In regard to wage-labor and capital, the real object of corporatist arrangements is "restraint," not delegation.

Offe insists that corporatist institutions are not just a response to the need for increased economic steering but are also elicited by the ineffectiveness of modern "catch-all" political parties for "will-formation."[50] For this reason parties are "increasingly by-passed and displaced by other practices and procedures of political participation and representation." However Offe is not entirely consistent on this issue, arguing in at least one place that the "characteristic feature of modern corporatism, in contrast to authoritarian models, is the *coexistence* of the two circuits with only a limited substitution of functional for territorial representation."[51] Offe's actual position would be important in assessing the recent arguments that corporatism is an entirely new form of polity, but this is not essential for the present discussion.[52] What is important here is Offe's argument that the state attempts to respond to increased political demands through corporatist forms and the consequences of this strategy.

Offe believes that this utilization of corporatist forms is inadequate for at least three reasons, causing corporatist structures to be "unstable" or "limited."[53] Speaking specifically of the inclusion of capital and wage-labor in corporatist institutions, Offe argues that the situation is unstable because the arrangement is inherently biased against labor. Organized labor has much more disciplinary control over its membership than business associations do. Business associations cannot direct the economic activities—primarily, pricing and investment—of their constituents because the control of investment is in individual hands, whereas organized labor can make its restraint agreements effective by its organizational control over wage and benefit demands. Organized labor is called upon to effectively give up more simply because it can command obedience of its membership and capital cannot.[54]

Secondly, corporatism raises several kinds of legitimacy problems. Corporatism is a kind of functional representation and functional representation always faces the immediate difficulty of justifying which groups are to be included, or why certain issues are considered relevant and not others. "The viability of this solution depends on how the political system manages to deal with the basic theoretical (as well as highly practical) deficiency of corporatist arrangements, namely, that no legitimizing principle can be provided for this particular fusion of private power and public authority."[55] Offe remarks that the "fragile reconciliation" established by these "parademocratic political structures" will no doubt be weakened when serious material interests of the excluded are affected.

To the extent that political parties and parliament are bypassed by corporatist arrangements, the struggle over material interests becomes a struggle over the ground rules of institutions designed to ameliorate these conflicts. "The pervasive shift is from conflict over group interest to conflict over ground rules, from the definition of claims to the definition of legitimate claimants, from politics to metapolitics."[56] The resort to corporatist institutions thereby intensifies fundamental arguments over the efficacy and legitimacy of political institutions.

Finally, the parcelling out of state functions and the inclusion of groups in decisionmaking because of their obstruction potential may well not increase the steering capacity of the state. Nevertheless, the functional need of increased autonomy for the politico-administrative subsystem as a response to increased political demands is a real need. Therefore the state is caught in the following dilemma:

> ... in an advanced industrial economy, interest organizations have the power to interfere with public-policy making in highly dysfunctional ways; hence the desire to 'keep them out.' At the same time, however, such representative organizations are absolutely indispensable for public policy, because they have a monopoly of information relevant for public policy and, most important, a substantial measure of control over their respective constituencies.[57]

The state's attempt to pursue both global direction of the economy and empirical consensus is at least inconsistent, if not contradictory.

Along with the dilemmas of corporatist inclusion, the second political consequence of the new tasks of the state is the emergence of "rationality" problems in public administration. The bureaucratic state is not structurally equipped to handle the development of productive policies. As mentioned earlier, the distinctive characteristic of productive policies is that they require the administration to invent its own decision rules or production rules. However, bureaucracy is a mode of organization designed to follow fixed, legal structures in processing certain inputs. The premises of its decisions must be clear for its actions to be rational. "Its outputs are, in the ideal case, and for all those involved, calculable reflexes of legal norms, organizational programmes, codified procedural rules, and routines."[58] Bureaucracies are not constructed so as to be creative, i.e., taking an instrumental view of their procedures in attempting to contrive inputs themselves. However, this is precisely what the modern state is required to do in developing productive policies which will maintain accumulation as a whole.

Offe argues that public administration in advanced capitalism is measured not by its ability to follow procedures in processing given inputs but by its "concrete results." "Efficiency is no longer defined as 'following the rules,' but as the 'causing of effects.'" "[A]dministration often turns from implementing given rules in compliance with established routines towards an active search for the *acquisition* of inputs which are adequate to the fulfilment of these concrete tasks and quasi-autonomously interpreted goals."[59]   Again, in pursuing the acquisition of inputs the administration must appeal to various groups and interests, building an 'empirical consensus' on which the success of its policies will crucially depend. This means that it must take a more flexible, utilitarian approach to the rules on which its organizational structure and legitimacy are based.

Offe argues that this ultimately leads to the decay of the rule of law itself in at least two related ways: laws must be written more broadly, giving the administration greater flexibility of interpretation in its search for an input package; and, consequently, legal authority cannot be the ultimate appeal of an administration in legitimating its choice of policies.[60] Again, to compensate for the decline of the traditional basis of its legitimacy, public administration must build an empirical consensus which grants it legitimacy on the basis of its success at maintaining accumulation.   Adherence to the formal rationality of bureaucracies—being sharply circumscribed by clear, fixed rules—under the changed tasks of the state in advanced capitalism would be functionally irrational. Simply put, the new tasks of the state entail a repudiation of Weber: "Bureaucratic domination is not, as Weber supposed, the irrevocable structural feature of all future societies."[61]

These rationality problems of public administration under the conditions of advanced capitalism reveal themselves in an even more pointed fashion, directly bearing on the issue of class formation. This results from the fact that, as Offe puts it, the new tasks of the state contain no inherent "stop rule" in regard to productive policies. The state activities designed to "recommodify" labor and capital are themselves "decommodified," i.e., not constrained by saleability or other structural criteria, and "decommodified state institutions tend to develop an independent life of their own."[62] Although productive policies are intended to revitalize capital and labor as commodities, these support systems are difficult to "switch off" and can grow beyond what is functionally necessary.

Since there is no inherent stop rule of state productive activities, the fact that these activities operate according to a different principle than exchange poses a threat to the dominance of the exchange principle itself. The boundary question of subsystems is intensified. By their principle of operation, and because they are charged with regulating the economic life of the nation as a whole, these "administrative organizations represent the most advanced forms of erosion of the commodity form within capitalist exchange relationships themselves."[63]

The most active state policies that try to maintain and to restore exchange opportunities for every citizen through a huge variety of economic and social strategies of intervention are—by their form and according to the image they project of themselves—a model of social relations that is liberated from the commodity form. In actual fact, however, these policies are forced to operate as supportive mechanisms of the commodity form, and within the fiscal and institutional limits of the universe of commodity relationships.[64]

This situation creates a "dual and inconsistent standard of 'goodness' in policy making." State activities productive of health, education, and other social services are supposed to pursue these policies in service of the commodity form but also to satisfy the basic needs of the people. This creates an inherent tension in the setting of goals for public policy. Although Offe later denies that these decommodified activities should be considered "harbingers of socialism,"[65] the fact that state productive policies have no stop rule and also imply a dual standard of goodness establishes them as potential sites of conflict in challenging the capitalist principle of exchange itself.

The third problem that the new tasks of the state produce is a generalized crisis of legitimacy, a consequence of having to discard or bypass traditional political institutions such as political parties, parliament (the necessary broadness of law), and bureaucratized public administration. We have already mentioned legitimacy problems that accompany the resort to corporatist forms, but Offe also argues a broader legitimation crisis. The politicization of production in advanced capitalism weakens the customary bases of legitimacy on two levels. First, Offe frequently argues that the more the state intervenes, the less there is that stands outside the state to which it could appeal for justification of its activities. Offe contends that the extension of public policy into more areas of social life is, "rather paradoxically, both a gain and a loss of state authority." It is a gain in that more aspects of society "can and must be manipulated." It is a loss in that there are fewer "uncontested and noncontroversial" foundations for its actions. "As the *functions* and responsibilities of the state expand, its *authority* (i.e., its capacity to make binding decisions) is debased."[66]

Offe is arguing two closely related points. The more the state intervenes, the more the various aspects of social life are designed rather than 'naturally given,' increasing the areas of contestation in politics. Also, the more social structures themselves are seen as politically designed, then the more the goals of politics are detached from any possible reference to outside structures. In fact, there is no outside of politics. Politics tends to become self-referential, and therefore increasingly difficult to justify. As Offe puts it, the more the various elements of society are "manipulated," political authority "subverts its nonpolitical underpinnings, which appear increasingly as mere artifacts of the political process itself."[67]

The second level of legitimacy problems which emerge from the general politicization of production concerns how individuals see themselves in the system. According to Offe, capitalism requires that individuals orient themselves to social life through the subjective prism of "possessive individualism." However, welfare state interventionism tends to subvert this principle as well. The more exchange relations are maintained by state action, the clearer it becomes that the "exchange value of any unit of labor or capital on the market" is at least as dependent on public policy as individuals's choices regarding their "resources." Opportunities for employment and the level of wages and salaries "increasingly become—at the level of normative orientation and actors's self-understanding—a matter of adequate or inadequate state policies in such areas as education, vocational training and regional economic development." From the standpoint of capital, "market success depends less upon such factors as the willingness to take risks, inventiveness and the ability to anticipate changes in demand, and more upon state policies in areas such as taxation, tariffs, research and development, and infrastructure investment."[68] The more the state attempts to stabilize the commodity form through intervention, the more the commodification of labor and capital is seen as an artifact of politics. In Offe's view, this is nothing less than the "structural weakening of the normative and moral fibres of a capitalist commodity society." Taken together with the other difficulties of the state, entailed by the assumption of the new tasks of maintaining the capitalist productive system as a whole, it is also an invitation to profound social and political conflict.

ADVANCED CAPITALISM AND WORKING CLASS FORMATION

It is obvious, however, that in Offe's opinion, this conflict will not revolve around classes rooted in production. As the above discussions demonstrate, for many reasons Offe believes that the conflicts of advanced capitalism have decisively been displaced to political administration and normative concerns. Offe argues that the interventionist welfare state has challenged the classical Marxian notion of class formation in at least four major ways. First, as indicated in the last point, public policy, not position in production, largely determines how individuals fare in advanced capitalism.[69] Various welfare transfers such as health insurance, pensions, and unemployment insurance have to a great extent disjoined individual living conditions from one's position in production. Besides these, collective goods have taken on an increased importance for an individual's life chances, undermining the importance of income derived from work. "For many inhabitants of over-crowded urban centers, it is already the case that they could not 'purchase' satisfying living conditions, to say nothing of other, less 'purchasable' aspects of the quality of life, even if their income was suddenly doubled."[70] Citing Juergen Habermas, Offe argues that individual identification with one's position in production is vitiated by the fact that the "work role is neither the exclusive nor the basic focus of the experience of deprivation."[71]

In addition, the proportion of an individual's life-time engaged in the work world is declining.[72] Extended time in school, increased leisure time, longer life-span after retirement, and unemployment are all life experiences not governed by one's role in production. In regard to the latter, Offe argues that unemployment is an increasing phenomenon and full employment is now impossible.[73] Semi-permanent unemployment especially for certain social categories defined by ascriptive criteria (women, youths, race or ethnic background, and immigrants) is increasingly likely.[74]

Offe concludes from the above that the individual's life chances in advanced capitalism are less determined by her or his position in exchange relations than by the individual's status as a citizen. "[T]he provisions of the welfare state have partly 'decommodified' the interests of workers, replacing 'contract' with 'status,' and 'property rights' with 'citizen rights.'"[75] Simply, the "potential to organize social life" carried by the exchange principle is drastically reduced with the development of advanced capitalism and the welfare state. Especially important for considering the relevance of class position for life chances, Offe argues that the labor market will continue to decline in its potential for determining the individual's mode of life, speaking of the eventual "replacement or, more likely, a supplementing of the labor market as the dominant principle of allocation."[76]

A second way in which class formation is disrupted in advanced capitalism is a consequence of the specific mode of political intervention. Offe frequently discusses the well-known fractures of the working class under advanced capitalism: the existence of dual labor markets which increase fragmentation according to ascriptive criteria, the employed versus the unemployed, etc. However he also argues that intervention in general is fragmenting and that specific political modes such as electoral parties and corporatism intensify it.

State intervention in general is fragmenting because labor policies have become more particularized. "[T]he growing 'disaggregation,' together with the increased 'depth of intervention' of these policies leads to legislative decisions that affect and/or favor ever-smaller groups of social categories (defined by profession, income level, age, residence, family status, line of business, etc.)."[77] Essentially, classes are fragmented into interest groups by the specificity of intervention. In this way state action creates "horizontal cleavages" of industries, regions, and workers frequently defined by ascriptive categories (gender, race, age).[78]

Furthermore, the politicization of production is partly a consequence of a labor movement that develops electoral political parties. However, like Przeworski, Offe argues that these political parties themselves disrupt class formation by reducing class identity. In order to obtain an electoral majority, political parties must become catch-all parties, de-emphasizing their class identification by appealing to broader, non-class specific, issues.[79] The structure of political parties also generally deactivates the rank and file, making it quite difficult to reorient the labor movement as a movement, rather than simply as a particularly large interest group in an erstwhile socialist party.

Finally, corporatist forms themselves can lead to the deactivization of the rank and file, partly by creating a logic of opportunism on the part of union leaders. Corporate inclusion substitutes legal status for the threat of social struggle for workers's interests. The more a union depends on legal status to guarantee its interests, the less it relies on a mobilized membership. Without an active rank and file, however, unions have reduced power to maintain these legal guarantees. The survival of the organization therefore becomes conditional on the union leaders ensuring as best they can the "cooperative, responsible, etc. behavior of the organization." As Offe puts it, "survival" is gained at the expense of "success."[80] Although Offe does not say so, it is not surprising if workers then become disenchanted with unions.

As briefly mentioned in the previous chapter, Offe argues that unions require reflexivity and identity to be effective. Union strength depends on solidarity and solidarity depends on an organization that encourages the creation of identity through the articulation of common interests of which workers are not naturally aware.[81] On the other hand, corporatist inclusion takes the form of representation through union leadership. It thereby obstructs union organizational forms which help formulate—not just convey—workers's interests.

The third principal source of disruption of class formation is easily the most contentious. Offe argues that the very concept of a "unified working class" has been dealt a fatal blow by the development of service employment, a development which is necessary to satisfy the general needs of modern capitalism and the specific administration of recommodification. Offe has in mind both the providers of state services and those performing "integrative" functions in private industry. This attempted conflation can be challenged in its details, but Offe's arguments as a whole are quite intriguing.

Offe believes that for several reasons the "logic" or "rationality" of service work is qualitatively different from other kinds of work. Ordinary work in the "secondary" sector (manufacturing) is structured by the needs of "technical-organizational productivity and economic profitablity."[82] In contrast, service work cannot be evaluated by the usual concepts of efficiency for two related reasons. First, often this work can only be "defined negatively, namely, as the 'prevention' of disorders and irregularities." Secondly, to a great extent the goals of such work are under the direct control of the worker. "[N]ot only the instrumental actions oriented to a pregiven goal, but also the goal itself are largely subject to the independent definition and control of service workers according to the circumstances of the particular case under consideration."[83] Service work is essentially synthetic and interpretive: "It is always necessary to simultaneously normalize 'the case' and individualize the norm." Since their work is preventative, service workers require much more autonomy for flexibility of response, i.e., they require room for "ad hoc" judgments.

The similarity of this argument to the previous discussion regarding the rationality problems of state bureaucracy is reinforced by Offe's insistence that service workers, in both public and private, are concerned with and oriented to "concrete uses," not "monetary profit." "[S]ervice work differs from productive work in the lack of a clear and uncontroversial 'criterion of economic efficiency,' from which could be strategically derived the type and amount, the place and timing of 'worthwhile' work."[84] The relation between the essential quality of service work and the tasks of public administration is clear in that both are concerned with prevention, a task that requires autonomy and also whose efficiency at providing success is hard to evaluate. This argument by Offe presents a problem in that in his book *Industry and Inequality* he insisted throughout that this characteristic of prevention is a quality of many kinds of work today, not just service work. This is only one indication of Offe's ambiguity on a central point.

On the basis of this attempt to give a unified and distinct definition to service work, Offe argues that under advanced capitalism the "category of work" has "imploded": "one can no longer talk of a basically unified type of rationality organizing and governing the whole of the work sphere."[85] Offe even suggests that the increasing importance of service labor is a kind of "return of the repressed," that a new substantive rationality must emerge in the work world in order to compensate for the extension of technical rationality in the use of labor in general.

> The normatively based 'substantive' rationality which had been successfully repressed in productive work and in the transformation of labor power into a marketable 'commodity' resurfaces, so to speak. Indicting the repression of 'substantive' rationality in the sphere of wage labor, it takes the form of growing numbers of service workers and professionals, whose special task is that of institutionally securing social existence through a special type of work.[86]

Here Offe connects the rationality problems of public administration and the development of service labor with a specific group of people who embody, in their work, an awareness of the limitations of technical rationality. As we shall see, this is crucial for Offe's conception of the new issues and actors which challenge advanced capitalism.

Finally, these three developments of advanced capitalism—the disjunction between living conditions and position in production, the fragmenting and non-class politics of catch-all political parties and corporatist arrangements, and the apparent dissolution of a unified rationality at work—contribute to a decline in identification with one's role in production and a corresponding decline in work-centered motivations. In *Industry and Inequality* Offe argues that the "achievement principle" by which capitalism was historically legitimated no longer operates as traditionally conceived. One reason among many is simply that in complex productive systems the individual's contribution to the functioning of the whole is becoming invisible, and therefore the individual cannot be rewarded on the basis of his or her contribution.[87]

However in later works Offe has gone far beyond this position. In *Industry and Inequality* Offe suggests that the achievement principle could still be reinterpreted; it is not dead. With the above arguments he is stating, on the contrary, that the achievement principle is indeed dead for an increasing proportion of society. There is a value change emerging in significant parts of the population that erodes the motivations necessary to work. At the least this intensifies demands on the welfare state. It also portends the destruction of what he earlier described as the "central institution of capitalism." "What can be expected, however, is an erosion of the cultural foundations, and hence the acceptability, of the labor market as the dominant pattern of allocating labor power as well as of distributing income."[88] It bears repeating that in Offe's view this normative change results from the objective change of the position of production in the system of advanced capitalism as a whole. Wage workers "no longer subjectively see the work sphere as the central fact of life, as the dominant reality from which the social interests, conflicts and communicative relations of the individual are derived. As much as society may 'objectively' remain a 'work society,' it nonetheless nourishes and provokes subjective orientations that do not correspond to it."[89] This indicates clearly the culmination of the above described processes in a battle over normative orientations which Offe sees as one of the primary arenas of conflict in advanced capitalism.

SOCIAL CONFLICT AND NEW SOCIAL MOVEMENTS

A basic thesis behind all of Offe's work is that "under state-regulated capitalism, all-out class conflict is no longer the driving force of social change."[90] Given the political and economic dynamic of advanced capitalist welfare states there are a multiplicity of cleavages along which social collectivities in conflict can and do form. This does not mean that the conflicts are any less severe. "But, in spite of the highly fragmented nature of modern political conflict, its outcomes may well involve fundamental changes in either the economic or the political order of society: changes that have, for just a limited period of time, been inconceivable under the unchallenged reign of competitive party democracy and the Keynesian welfare state."[91] Offe argues that in analyzing the potential for conflict in advanced capitalism we must allow for "contingency concerning the areas and methods in which such change might be accomplished."[92] According to Offe, classical Marxism allowed for no such contingency.

The principal reason why conflict is now decentered is that the experience of deprivation is generalized, not directly traceable to one's position in production. Offe refers to the "increasingly 'social' character of deprivation," "a fact that would render plainly inadequate any traditional Marxist view of 'core conflicts' and core contradictions inherent in specific institutional settings."[93] However another reason for the development of non-class conflict is that as identity with work declines, people seek other forms of identity. "Highly mobile populations" have a reduced feeling of "belonging" to traditional collectivities (families, communities, professions, etc.). This is a consequence of other social changes, e.g., variety of occupational experience (multiple careers in a single life), the decline of traditional living arrangements (experience with "more than the 'normal' two families"), and in general different styles of life.[94] The consequence is that people tend to form their identity on the basis of the " 'permanent' parameters of social identity," i.e., age and gender.

This latter argument is part of a recurring discussion by Offe of the contemporary forces which are resuscitating ascriptive identities at the height of modern society, contrary to classical sociology. He states this in *Industry and Inequality* as one of the bases that employers use to recruit employees, given the difficulties of actually measuring achievement in modern industry. In general he believes that the persistence of ascriptive categories is an "embarassment" to mainstream sociology.[95]

Besides multiple identifications forming the basis of multipolar conflict, Offe contends that the existing political forms and dynamic also provide multiple sites of conflict in advanced capitalism. First, for reasons described above, Offe believes that the possibilities for economic growth increasingly depend on state-imposed "forced consumption" in the form of various projects carried out by the state intended to stimulate private investment, for example nuclear energy and armaments production. State investment projects of this type open up new areas of resistance to capitalist growth, which no one would doubt given the experiences of the anti-nuclear energy and peace movements in Europe and the United States. It is important to his entire argument that Offe characterizes this as a "new politics of production during the 1980s, that is, the rise of forms of struggle that effectively block the opening up of new outlets for private capitalist investment."[96] Although Offe's remarks here are focused on the major movements of the 1980s, it is easy to see that this structuring of protest has been prominent from the 1960s to the present in struggles against new highways, power dams, airports, shopping malls, convention centers, etc.

A second site of conflict is a consequence of the state's strategy of recommodification of capital and labor. As indicated, the fact that there is no stop rule for the productive policies of the state makes possible a conflict over whether state activities should be guided by the commodity form or not. Offe argues that conservative critics of the welfare state have rightly feared "that the administrative form of control over material resources could become politicized to such an extent that it is no longer subservient to, but subversive of the commodity form." Battles over expansion of services and infrastructure development continually provoke the contrast between the goal of commodification and the decommodified form in which this goal is pursued. "There is no accepted formula by which it could be decided what is to be learned at school, how many miles of highways should be built in what region, and so on."[97]

Offe points out that many of the conflicts since the 1960s have taken place at decommodified institutions: the patriarchal family, universities and schools, prisons, armies, "and the more custodial and oppressive parts of the welfare state apparatus."[98] These decommodified institutions are filled with decommodified individuals, individuals who do not depend for their subsistence on the labor market. They hold their positions and their mode of life on the basis of their status (not contract) and quite often on the basis of ascriptive criteria (age or gender, not achievement). Furthermore, these institutions are frequently operated in an authoritarian manner, stimulating revolt. Their "conditions of life and life chances are shaped by direct, highly visible and often highly authoritarian and restrictive mechanisms of supervision, exclusion, and social control, as well as by the unavailability of even nominal 'exit' options."[99] As Offe correctly notes, the decommodified also have more time to engage in politics, something they have in common with "the often flexible time schedules of middle class professionals."

Offe believes that decommodified institutions present an "opportunity for the Left." They provide a site for a struggle to redirect state productive activities in ways that are freed from subservience to the commodity form. Offe acknowledges, as some critics have charged, that these institutions and programs are often run in a fashion that attempts to de-politicize the "inmates," through "bureaucratic disabling of the clientele" by the administrative determination of needs.[100] However these institutions are also an occasion for struggle, an "opportunity," and that is all Offe claims.

The central political forms of advanced capitalist states also provoke conflict and the possibilities of serious change. For example, Offe argues that citizen action groups are a response to the unresponsiveness of catch-all political parties and to being closed out of participation in corporatist institutions.[101] In one place Offe even suggests that modern political parties are in a certain sense "irrational." "If one regards the principled maintenance of established goals and priorities over a long time-period and the consistency and continuity of action over time as a sign of political rationality, then it turns out that the struggle for a majority conditions the action of voters, parties and candidates in such a way that *this* rationality is not *required*."[102]

Offe also often suggests in passing that corporatist institutions, based on functional representation, could possibly be related to the various functional representation schemes developed in the history of the left.[103] The connection between existing corporatist forms and left-wing functional representation institutions has been denied by Leo Panitch and conflicts with Offe's own argument that corporatist forms deactivate the rank and file. However, any socialist political theory has to seriously analyze how territorial representation individualizes and even privatizes people under capitalist democracy, and consider how forms of functional representation might overcome this fragmentation.

The resort to corporatist arrangements indicates quite clearly the depth of the political legitimation problems of the modern capitalist state. Such arrangements are an aspect of the breakdown of the institutional separation of society and politics that is at the center of traditional legitimation of the capitalist state. By dispersing political power through delegation and by including social actors in decisionmaking, new areas of political action are established. "[T]he shift from representative to 'functional' forms of representation breaks down the bourgeois definition of politics as the struggle for institutionalized state power. As the realm of *politics* transcends *state* institutions, new arenas of resistance are opened up."[104] This breaching of the wall between state and civil society is clearly a consequence of the need for empirical consensus building, described earlier, which challenges the bureaucratic mode of public administration and the legitimation on which it rests. It is also related to fundamental characteristics of the new social movements that will be discussed shortly. Offe is quite persuasive when he predicts an intensified conflict over political ground rules, that is, the rise of new issues of meta-politics.

Finally, the persistence of economic problems, particularly unemployment, may result in a direct challenge to the "dual allocative" function of the labor market: its allocation of social labor and its allocation of income. Further growth, where it occurs, will not be able to absorb all of the unemployed. Offe repeatedly mentions the possibility of institutionalizing the "informal sector" such that people will be allowed to perform socially important work without their remuneration being tied to the labor market. Offe argues that it is likely that there will be increasing demands for the "partial uncoupling of useful activities from the nexus of monetary remuneration." Not only would work no longer be the only source of money, but the product of "self-organized, independent labor" could be allocated without the medium of money.[105] In several places Offe relates this idea of granting a base income to people so that they can participate in cooperatives, community housing projects, etc. to "old socialist ideals" and forms. To keep the labor market from being depopulated by the possibility of alternative means of subsistence, Offe argues that some regulation would be needed, however he is quite vague and inconsistent on this point. (In one place he even expresses doubts that the informal sector could absorb very many people.[106]) Nonetheless Offe's main point is that there may emerge increasing demands to break down the wall between remunerated (labor market) labor and presently unremunerated (community forms, household) labor.

These various conflict potentials are the basis upon which the new social movements have emerged. Although these movements are as diverse as the issues and sites of conflict described above, they do share certain important characteristics, an identifiable constituency, and, according to Offe, a general thrust that places in question the continued existence of advanced capitalism. In some ways Offe believes that the new social movements are the "heirs" to the broad concerns of the traditional labor movement and challenge the logic of capitalist development. They therefore establish the possibility that capitalism could be seriously contested without class organizations.

Offe's argument about the development of multiple sites of contestation of the structures and dynamic of advanced capitalism, of multi-polar conflict, is clearly intertwined with an attempt to understand contemporary social movements. The usual groups referred to are the anti-nuclear energy groups, peace movement, environmentalists, feminists, youth, citizen action groups, and various smaller issue groups (squatters, cooperatives), which have partially coalesced into the Green Party in Germany. (Juergen Habermas includes conservative groups in his analysis; Offe does so only marginally.[107])

These movements are largely concerned with quality of life issues, with the defense of a "life-world" against encroachments by large technological and economic forces. Specifically the groups Offe discusses are resisting the effects of economic growth. They emerge as "new types of social and political conflicts, whose emergence Raschke [and Habermas] has characterized in terms of a transition from a political paradigm of 'distribution' to one of 'form of life.'" The issues of these groups are at least thematically related by the fact that "they cannot be interpreted plausibly as derivative conflicts, whose 'real' point of origin is to be found in the sphere of production."[108] Indeed, they often face the unified opposition of capital and labor.

Although Offe has argued that these groups express "post-material" values, he appears to qualify this characterization later. Offe suggests that these movements should be seen as "a 'modern' critique of modernization, rather than an 'antimodernizing' or 'postmaterialist' one."[109] He insists that they do not reject the normative tradition but rather respond to inconsistencies in the modern value system, posing a kind of immanent critique or "selective radicalization of 'modern' values."[110] Offe makes this distinction in order to defend the new social movements against the frequent charge of pre-modern romanticism. The new social movements Offe considers are opposed to future economic growth that threatens the quality of life, weak and uninstructive as that phrase may be.

Offe argues that although these groups are not class-specific, i.e., defined by their position in production, they nevertheless challenge the productive system of advanced capitalism. Their political project is to expose "the *structural incapacity* of existing economic and political institutions to perceive and to deal effectively with the global threats, risks, and deprivations they cause."[111] As suggested above, a primary political focus is on "forms of investment and consumption that are administratively imposed on the population."[112] These forms are resisted on the grounds of their disruptive and wasteful aspects regarding the environment and their effects on communities. Again, as argued above, Offe believes that state-designed investment is the primary source of new economic growth, therefore this amounts to a serious challenge to the existing capitalist dynamic.

The political methods of this "anti-productivist" protest movement are of particular interest. Existing political institutions are not applicable to their set of concerns for several reasons. First, these are frequently single-issue groups that do not address the full range of issues and policies that must be the concern of a political party. Secondly, for this reason—as is so familiar with single-issue groups—their demands are often considered "non-negotiable."[113]

> All major concerns of new social movements converge on the idea that life itself—and the minimal standards of "good life" as defined and sanctioned by modern values—is threatened by the blind dynamics of military, economic, technological, and political rationalization; and that there are no sufficient and sufficiently reliable barriers within dominant political and economic institutions that could prevent them from passing the threshold to disaster. This view also provides the basis for the adoption and legitimation of unconventional *modes* of action.[114]

If survival is the issue, the "rules of the game" easily lose their hold on many participants. Existing political institutions are perceived to be too rigid to address these problems. Consequently the demands of new social movements cast doubt on the legitimacy of the majority principle itself, an example of the rise of meta-political issues.[115]

Their values of "autonomy and identity" could not be implemented through state power in any case. Instead these values must be articulated through mass protest and direct participatory forms, a "noninstitutional politics"[116] or, in Habermas's phrase, a "politics of the first person." Furthermore, this form of politics follows the developmental tendencies of the interventionist welfare state itself. "At a time when capitalist societies themselves, under the pressure of social and economic crises, are forced to give up their own fundamental distinction of state and civil society, the insistence upon statist strategies of socialist transformation is rendered both unrealistic and anachronistic."[117] Offe says that it would not be too much to suggest that "politics and the state have become divorced from each other."[118]

Of particular importance to our topic is who these participants are. Offe argues that there are three principal social groups in the new social movements: (1) the decommodified (students, youths, house-spouses, retired persons, the unemployed and marginally employed); (2) the "new middle class"; and (3) parts of the old middle class who feel threatened. The shrinking capacity of the labor market to absorb the population leads to a growth in the decommodified sector, described as a transformation of "workers" into "clients."[119] The growth of this category is directly related to the growth of the second, the new middle class of the "human service professions and/or the public sector," performing major social functions such as "teaching and the distribution of information; the provision of health services; social control and administration."[120] The new middle class is relatively well-educated and economically secure. Although in various places Offe acknowledges that the continued growth of the new middle classes is constrained by fiscal problems, the general dynamic suggests they will grow apace with the decommodified.

In one place Offe suggests a parallel between the rise of the new middle class and the early working class movement and that the former is picking up issues—"the forgotten agenda"—that have been dropped by traditional working class organizations in the course of establishing institutional recognition and of struggling for material benefits for their constituents. At the same time these middle class radicals "revitalize some of the non-institutional forms of politics that were characteristic of earlier periods of the working class movement itself."[121] As it presently stands, the working class has been excluded from social change by being included in the institutional arrangements that satisfy certain of its interests at the expense of neglecting others. This is one of the things providing the impetus for the new social movements.

Offe argues that this parallel between the rise of the new middle class and the early working class movement would be strengthened if it were the case that their issues are "the intrinsic and continuously reproduced outcome of the established modes of rationality of production and domination."[122] The above account of Offe's analysis leaves no doubt that he believes this to be the case. However the parallel holds not only on the issues but also regarding the manner in which the new middle class is centrally located in these modes of rationality and their administration. Establishing the link between the earlier described rationality crisis of state production and the distinct rationality of service work, Offe argues that the new middle class is the group in the belly of the beast. "[T]hose parts of the new middle class working in social services and administrative functions are confronted most closely and immediately with those irrationalities through their occupational practice and experience."[123] However, to keep this from becoming another substitutionist argument with which the history of socialist theory is littered, Offe also argues that although this class has roots in a specific position in the reproduction of advanced capitalism, its demands are either baldly universalistic (e.g., peace) or narrowly particularistic in non-class ways (e.g., an issue regarding a specific locality). It is "class aware" but not "class conscious"; it is "typically a politics *of* a class but not *on behalf of* a class."[124]

It must be quickly added that the new social movements are not made up solely of the new middle class. The new social movements are composed of the new middle class in coalition with the decommodified—who are structurally related to them by being on the other side of the desk—and also elements of the old middle class. It is also becoming clear that the attempt to establish the structural position of the new middle class involves Offe in a contradiction, a point to which we will return shortly.

Judging the potential for success of the new social movements partly depends on what these movements would consider success. Their oppositional character and non-negotiable demands result in their goals being largely defensive. As Offe notes, most frequently the issues of new social movements are expressed in negative terms: "key words such as 'never,' 'nowhere,' 'end,' 'stop,' 'freeze,' 'ban,' etc." Given this, it is perhaps unsurprising that: "They also typically lack a coherent set of ideological principles and interpretations of the world from which an image of a desirable arrangement of society could be derived and the steps toward transformation could be deduced."[125] Jean Cohen has argued that the "self-limiting" aspect of these movements is in fact one of the key features contributing to their novelty.[126]

Although the new social movements challenge the existing dynamic of production, Offe argues that they "do not claim to know what the future will look like."[127] Apparently the only terms in which their resistance can be positively expressed is to "help to increase the learning capacity of political systems by diminishing their degree of 'blindness' or unawareness of fore-seeable and often catastrophic consequences," or, more strongly, to "resist the blind logic of development of the capitalist system by forcing it to develop greater learning capacities." Offe even remarks that the basic difference between capitalism and socialism is socialism's "superior and expanded capacity for learning."[128] This formulation raises questions about Offe's conception of social change that will be addressed in the last section.

Offe suggests that any real possibility of success by the new social movements will depend on their ability to forge a political coalition with the labor movement and its traditional representatives; in Germany the SPD. The major obstacle to this is the orientation of the labor movement to productivism, the "growth-and-security game," with security referring to both welfare state measures and the promotion of investments for national defense.[129] A second obstruction is that the new social movements, regardless of the Green Party, are, from a normal political perspective, fundamentally anti-organizational. This is of course connected to their emphasis on direct participation, defensive demonstrative style, and non-negotiable demands. Several commentators have noted that whether the latter difficulty can be overcome or not will depend at least on the outcome of the conflict within the Green Party between the "fundamentalists" and the "political realists."[130] However, on the other hand, Offe states that perhaps this fragmentation and eclecticism are the most promising approach for increasing learning capacities.

At the very least the possibilities of political coalition would require a fundamental change of orientation by the labor movement: it must become "more than a labor movement." "[T]he historical aspirations of the workers' movement can only be continued if they abandon the idea that all immiseration and domination derive from wage-labor."[131] Regardless of how the possibilities of political coalition play out, this succinctly states Offe's fundamental reason for believing that the working class has been displaced as the privileged oppositional collectivity under the conditions of advanced capitalism.

THE EROSION OF SUPPORT FOR THE WELFARE STATE

Offe has frequently argued that for several reasons the welfare state is an "irreversible" development. First, the welfare state is a response to the multiple problems of the "collective reproduction" of advanced capitalist society discussed above, including the declining ability of "oligopoly capital" to provide employment. Secondly, the political force of unions is such that abolition of the welfare state would require a veritable political revolution, including the "abolition of political democracy." Thirdly, attempts at the " 'dismantling' of the welfare state would result in widespread conflict and forms of anomic and 'criminal' behavior that together would be more destructive than the enormous burdens of the welfare state itself." For these reasons, the welfare state is actually a "highly efficient and effective means of resolving problems of collective reproduction." This does not mean that there will not be repeated attempts to reduce its scope nor that it will ever have an uncontested existence.[132] Nonetheless, Offe typically argues that the efforts of the New Right will be successful only at chipping away at the welfare state at its edges. For all of the fiscal problems generated by the welfare state, the functional needs of advanced capitalism to which the welfare state is a response ensure that these efforts will fall short of a project for abolition.

However, there are more recent places in which Offe actually suggests that the existence of the welfare state is rather precarious. In an analysis that is partly a deliberation on rational choice theory and partly an attempt to understand the animus toward the welfare state that intensified in the 1980s, Offe undercuts each of the arguments above that he himself advances. It is actually unclear why individuals would consent to welfare state policies if they could provide for some of these needs themselves, e.g., through private pensions or insurance. Offe states that generally in a democracy there is "zero-cost" for individuals if they should on these grounds defect from supporting the welfare state. Given this, Offe concludes that the ultimate reason individuals support welfare policies in a democracy is normative. "The only alternative seems to be to hypothesize that actors produce collective goods not because of the rational capacity to maximize utility and to avoid punishment, but because of their normative disposition to do so, or because of the relationship of trust, reciprocity, sympathy, and fairness that they have experienced between themselves and their fellow contributors."[133] The basis for support for welfare state policies rests fundamentally on a "shared notion of sameness or nonrival commonality of interest," i.e., on a conception of "collective identity."[134]

This notion of a shared collective identity is subject to erosion in times of social change in a way that Offe did not fully take account of in his earlier work. In these conditions, strategic action by individuals becomes more pronounced and thereby erodes support for welfare state policies. In particular, policies that previously had been widely judged as necessary to equity, maintaining effective demand, developing human capital, or collectively maximizing opportunities—for example, support for unemployment insurance or for public education—are reinterpreted as redistribution to the undeserving or as policies primarily designed to advance the interests of limited status groups (e.g., teachers). The "parameters of sameness" constrict "from the universalist notion of human rights of all human beings to the interest of the nation to the interest of certain categories of taxpayers, professional groups, and cultural communities, and finally to the interests of the individual." This "narrowing" is not primarily caused by change "on the level of objective events and facts" but by change in "interpretive frameworks" that encourage other changes in "beliefs and expectations." "The calculative attitude toward individual and short-term costs and benefits is therefore nothing that is inherent in human nature or an eternal standard of rational action; to the contrary, it is the product of disintegration and decomposition of cultural and structural conditions that constrain and inhibit such utilitarian orientations."[135]

Offe's argument about the decline of support for the welfare state includes references to fiscal problems and ideological problems in legitimizing welfare state policies. However, this is not the center of his analysis nor what is original about it. Offe also rejects the frequent complaint that the intensification of individual cost-benefit calculations is caused by the political assault of the New Right on the welfare state. Instead he argues that specific recent social and political developments have led to this "*Gestalt*-switch," thereby allowing the political-ideological arguments of neoconservatives to find "fertile ground." Although neoconservative divisions of society according to "moral worthiness and unworthiness" contribute to the decline, they are not primary for understanding the deterioration of support. Conversely, neither will moral appeals reverse it.[136]

Offe argues that collective identity is especially conditioned by the existing forms of the division of labor, "cultural differentiation," and (like Adam Przeworski) "political organization and representation." It is these that are the "underlying determinants of what kind and scope of collectivity people refer to when using the word 'we.'"[137] It is changes in these structural aspects of social life that have led to the restriction of the referent of the word "we" and therefore the waning support for the welfare state as traditionally conceived.

Generally, the "destructuration of collectivities" is caused by the decline of "commonalities of economic interest, associational affiliation, or cultural values and lifestyles." However, Offe also mentions several specific causes stemming from some of the developments he analyzed earlier. For example, there are "increasing disparities of life-chances among the totality of wage workers," resulting from uneven sectoral development, region, skill, ethnicity, and gender. Secondly, the emergence of jobless growth not only further divides workers among themselves but increases the vulnerability of the unemployed. This division is costless for the employed in that a stratified job market reduces the tendency of the unemployed to exert downward pressure of wages due to the existence of this reserve industrial army. Thirdly, the fiscal problems of the welfare state, the long-term decline in real wages, and the weakness of the political response of traditional defenders of the welfare state all make the future of the welfare state uncertain. These reasons encourage more individualistic calculations of gains and losses, further undercutting defenses of the welfare state. Fourthly, the bureaucratic means of the welfare state are increasingly considered ineffective or even counterproductive (creating dependency). The welfare state's policies are clearly incapable of getting at the roots of social problems, stimulating "ex post and compensatory" policies which simply throw "ever-rising amounts of money" at problems.[138] Fifthly, Offe argues that large segments of the middle class defect because of the availability of private alternatives, questions of the worthiness of recipients of welfare, and other reasons.

A very interesting point Offe makes in this regard is that one of the reasons for the decline in support for the welfare state is that many members of the middle class have shifted their participation to conflicts regarding "nonclass, nonredistributive" issues of the sort associated with new social movements. These issue areas are in accord with the general decline of the "egalitarian-collectivist" aspect of the traditional Left and a resurgence of the "libertarian, antietatist, and communitarian ideals and projects."[139] This shift in the Left's ideological orientation is coupled with a failure of the Left to articulate a plausible mobilizing alternative that would appeal to the traditional constituency of socialist, social democratic, and labor parties. It at best leaves the Left in the defensive position of trying to 'maintain what we have.' In sum, doubts about the effectiveness and legitimacy of the welfare state reinforce a dynamic which encourages many to abandon it.[140]

The perceived realities and experiences of the welfare state and the many aspects of social restructuring elaborated above have caused a de-structuration of the collectivities that formerly politically supported the welfare state. "Structures do not *directly* translate into outcomes and developments; they do so by virtue of the responses, interpretations, memories and expectations, beliefs and preferences of actors who *mediate* the link between structure and outcome."[141] The major reason for the waning of support for the welfare state is the increased *persuasiveness* of individual rational choice calculi, in turn caused by the decay of the structures that maintained a more universalistic normative orientation. However, Offe argues that this corrosive individualist calculus is not necessarily openly expressed as such.

> It seems that dissolving "traditional political identities" are not openly replaced by pure individualism, but that such a shift to individualism is provided with a justification by the formation of identities of a moralizing and/or particularistic kind. What is least popular with the "middle mass" are programs that benefit those supposedly *morally* inferior categories (such as unemployed youth and single parents) and ascriptively defined minorities (such as ethnic or national ones).[142]

Besides its political importance, this is an intriguing analysis of the reasons behind the resurgence of rational choice approaches in sociology and contributes to a consideration of the preference formation problem discussed in the previous chapter.[143]

One of the primary consequences of these structural and cultural changes is the "virtual evaporation of classes."[144] This does not mean that conflict has disappeared, of course. In fact, Offe again argues that the new conflicts can be as severe as those in a class model but the actors in contemporary conflicts are a "plurality of relatively small groups and categories rapidly shifting in size, influence, and internal coherence with no dominant axis of conflict."[145]

Given these arguments, one wonders about the status of Offe's previous analysis of the functional need for collective reproduction and the dangers of social disruption from any attempt to dismantle the welfare state, i.e., the thesis of the irreversibility of the welfare state. In the place in which these later arguments are made, Offe specifically brackets the issue of functional utility of welfare state policies. However, the two arguments must be brought together in a persuasive fashion if his overall theory is to make sense.

Offe's discrete discussions can perhaps be reconciled in the following way. First of all, essentially the collective that needs to be reproduced has become more restricted in the minds of many social actors today. The individual rational choice orientation encouraged by structural developments allows many to be excluded, always bolstered by—but not created by— neoconservative arguments of moral worthiness. Secondly, all parts of the welfare state are not equally under attack, only those that are perceived as redistributive in effect and not those for which no cost-effective private alternatives are readily available. Offe mentions old age pensions and health care as being relatively more popular for these reasons.[146] Thirdly, regarding the probability of social unrest on the part of the excluded, Offe simply appears to have changed his mind. Speaking specifically of the unemployed, he states that "there is little reason for the middle class and employers to fear that the existence of a growing 'surplus class' could lead to disruptive forms of social unrest and conflict, the prevention of which could be 'worth' a major investment in welfare policies—or even the full maintenance of those that exist."[147] For this reason Offe says that the assumption of irreversibility of the welfare state appears "rather heroic today."[148]

AMBIGUITIES AND ADDITIONAL CONSIDERATIONS

It goes without saying that Offe makes a penetrating and multidimensional contribution to our understanding of the dynamic of the contemporary welfare state. However, it is necessary to briefly explore a few ambiguities in important aspects of his argument. Offe is very insightful in analyzing the particular modes of operation of the interventionist welfare state and the internal dilemmas these tasks pose for political administration. However it is not quite accurate to say that second order crises of public administration "are more relevant" than first order crises of production, especially since, as he quickly adds, the former "are produced by the latter." Like many theorists already discussed, although Offe forcefully argues that the working class is displaced in challenging contemporary capitalism, he nonetheless frequently resorts to the customary terminology of class analysis: "ruling class control," ungovernability caused by "class conflict," "class interests," "class compromise," and "class struggle."[149] Given our previous discussion, we can argue that this is not an inconsistency. Class relations continue to define capitalist society even if class subjects "evaporate."

Nevertheless, this specific ambiguity is exacerbated by the fact that, although as presented above Offe generally argues that the labor market is rapidly declining in significance for the social experiences of a large proportion of the population, in at least two places he suggests the contrary. For example: "To be sure, not every individual is always exposed *directly* to the dynamics of the labor market. Nevertheless, the labor market is a power relationship that touches, permeates and envelops *all* forms and spheres of social life."[150] However the contrary assertion, the one Offe usually makes, is essential to the idea that the economy has been displaced as a primary site of conflict.

Rather than assigning priority to the differing crisis tendencies, it is more appropriate to say that the multiple problems of the state detailed by Offe are the problems of managing advanced capitalist production. What is evident from Offe's analysis is that a new category has emerged from the collapse of the barriers between economics and the state, a collapse he describes well in his discussion of corporatist arrangements. The crisis is not primarily of political administration but of *state capitalist production*. State capitalist production confronts problems that differ substantially from a more liberal capitalism but they cannot be described as problems largely of political administration, especially considering that these intense difficulties are set in train precisely by production structured by capitalist class relations.

In this regard, Offe's superb resurrection of Polanyi's analysis of the fictitious commodity labor is very much to the point. This analysis throws doubt on the belief, expressed in many Marxian works, that, whatever the case now, at one time the economy was autonomous. This was never more than relatively true. The *laissez faire* economy, in so far as it existed, was historically created and maintained by political institutions (especially law) and political decisions. The alternative view necessarily accepts the fundamentally ideological self-interpretation of capitalism: that the self-regulating market economy is more natural than state-controlled production. To the contrary, regardless of the merits of either one, both are established by political institutions, and are neither more nor less natural than any other social arrangement.

The relationship between polity and economy in capitalism was earlier described by the metaphor 'interpenetration.' Our discussion of the differing arguments of Pashukanis and Poulantzas demonstrates that the metaphor does not take us very far. In contrast, Offe employs a systems analysis of society in order to think through this relation. The distinction between first order and second order crises stems from conceiving society as a system constituted of subsystems. However, the uncertainty of the relations between these subsystems simply reproduces the ambiguity of the relationship between polity and economy in advanced capitalism. Systems theory plays a much more central role in the analysis of Juergen Habermas and the relation among subsystems is directly confronted in his theory. Therefore we can reserve further comments on this topic until we have examined his arguments.

On the other hand, Offe's specific analysis of the fictitious character of the commodity labor must be further explored here because it exposes a certain exaggeration—promoted in places by Offe himself—of the extent to which the site of normative challenges to advanced capitalism has shifted away from production. Elaborating on Polanyi, Offe argues that the commodity labor is fictitious for at least two basic reasons. The first was utilized above in Offe's discussion: in capitalism labor is regarded as a commodity, that is, something produced for sale. However, it is not produced for sale; it is produced for many reasons. The second reason is more probing. It is a unique characteristic of the commodity labor that it cannot be separated from its owner and therefore can be "set in motion only by its owner."[151] This characteristic of labor clarifies the classic distinction between labor and labor power.

> What the procurer of labor purchases in the labor market is not 'labor' but, rather, labor *power.* The question is always the extent to which labor power is transformed successfully into labor actually performed. . . . Every buyer of labor power must rely on the 'participation' of the worker since, on the one hand, that buyer cannot exclusively control the purchased commodity, and, on the other, the utilization of labor power is linked inextricably to the cooperation of the owners. The worker must also *want* to work; the fundamental problem of every company or organization consists accordingly in inducing the worker, as the subject of labor power, to this cooperation.[152]

Neither could the buyer control the worker through greater specification of task because, as noted earlier, it is the flexibility of the worker that makes her or him valuable.

Offe argues in *Industry and Inequality* that the importance of this subjectivity has increased under modern conditions of production. In the modern industrial process functional differentiation has been extended to the point that supervisors quite often do not have extensive knowledge of the tasks of their subordinates and correspondingly have a lessened ability to direct their work. Supervisors are frequently not recruited from the ranks but rather are recruited from outside on the basis of different qualifications. Therefore, in the modern "task discontinuous" organization, "the possibility of external control has been reduced," requiring a new emphasis on inculcating a "normative commitment" of the worker to work. "[I]nstructions now refer much more to the desired *results* of courses of action. As far as the separate phases of their execution are concerned, orders necessarily include 'discretion' and room for interpretation, so that the subordinates *must* develop their own complementary goal interpretations and their own independent commitment if the planned result is to be achieved."[153] Offe also argues here that, because of the complexity of modern productive processes, increased emphasis is placed on "preventive influence," i.e., prevention of problems. Especially in capital intensive processes, failure to prevent problems cannot be easily punished because it cannot be easily ascertained. (Offe suggests that even sabotage could be blamed on "technical trouble."[154]) For this reason the success of the enterprise depends crucially on supportive normative orientations.

There are two important points that follow from this discussion. First, as mentioned above, in *Industry and Inequality* Offe ascribed to modern labor in general what he later described as evidence of the different rationality of service work: discretion, preventive action, and normative commitment as important to the job role. If one believes that he is accurate to some degree in ascribing these characteristics to modern work in general, then serious doubts are raised about his argument that the category of work has "imploded" under the development of two different rationalities of work.

Secondly, and much more importantly for the fundamental orientation of Marxian theory, here we see that production in the interventionist welfare state cannot simply be reduced to struggle over distribution. In so far as labor is a fictitious commodity which requires participation and willingness of its owner in order to be useful, and in so far as the modern task discontinuous work organization stresses even greater discretion and normative support of her or his work by the worker, there is an ineradicable basis for normative conflict at the very heart of modern production. If Offe (and Andre Gorz) were right about the modern worker not identifying with her or his job, modern industry, as Offe argues so persuasively in *Industry and Inequality,* would immediately collapse.

In other places Offe offers a much more subtle and potentially fruitful analysis of the issues involved directly in production. In his argument about the two logics of collective action of workers and capitalists (mentioned in the previous chapter), Offe insists that because of the fictitious character of the commodity labor, unions must take an expansive, multidimensional view of workers's interests. "Since the worker is at the same time the subject and the object of the exchange of labor power, a vastly broader range of interests is involved in this case than in that of capitalists, who can satisfy a large part of their interests somewhat apart from their functioning as capitalists. . . . Unions are, therefore, confronted with the task of organizing the entire spectrum of needs that people have when they are employed as wage workers."[155] Offe then proceeds to argue that workers's needs are interpreted in a narrow fashion, as a struggle over distribution, primarily because of the constraints on union organization and the articulation of interests by corporatist agreements. Simply, if workers's interests in production are limited to a struggle over distribution, that is a consequence of union organization and existing political demands on unions for responsibility, not anything inherent in the productive process itself. Again, precisely this is indicated in the above citations of Offe on the reasons for considering the new social movements in some sense the heir of the labor movement. However, Offe's emphasis is clearly on the opposite view, that production is basically a battle over distribution and therefore lacks the depth for challenging capitalism as a kind of civilization.

The limits of Offe's position are seen in a contradiction in his argument regarding the principal social group of new social movements. After arguing at length in various places that one's position in production no longer serves as a basis for identity (even referring to Gorz's "marvelous book"), as shown above he explains the central role of the new middle class in the new social movements by stating that its identity is formed by its position in advanced capitalism, by its members's first-hand experience in their work of the irrationality of advanced capitalism. If this is so, we have to reconsider the widespread belief among socialist theorists that production is no longer important for forming identity.

If Offe and Polanyi are right about the fictitious commodity, capitalist production is not, never was, and never can be simply a struggle over distribution of the product. Labor is a commodity that cannot be separated from its owner. For this reason the conditions and structure of production will always be directly related to the individual's quality of life. As Offe suggests in places, it will always be a site of conflict, and in fact conflict is institutionalized in that the worker must be induced to work. Also for this reason we can assume that it will always play an important role in forming the worker's identity (the unemployed are a different situation). Emancipation of the working class is not a sufficient condition for the emancipation of society, but it is still a necessary condition. In so far as this is the case, the specific structure of production retains its relevance in analyzing the possibilities of social change.

Offe's recognition of these issues makes it quite curious why he seems to believe that the important challenges to capitalism will come at its margins, i.e., in resistance to further growth and investment. It is true that in many places he argues that there are opportunities for challenging capitalism directly over the state policy of recommodification and the fact that such policies have no stop rule. State policies for maintaining capitalist production relations are also exposed to contestation by the multiple legitimacy questions they provoke, questions that cannot be easily avoided because of the need for empirical consensus formation. However, Offe's political commitment seems to clearly be to the extra-institutional forms of the new social movements. This needs to be clarified because, as Jean Cohen states, resistance at the margins is not enough. "The sovereign power of the state and the coercive power of the capitalist economy they hope to bypass have the nasty habit of returning to frustrate their projects."[156] There seems to be a considerable amount of historical evidence to support this position. Statist strategies may not be sufficient, but non-statist strategies are also questionable. Perhaps the need for empirical consensus building and the interpenetration of economy and polity have made the very metaphor of margins inappropriate. Immanuel Wallerstein also supports a non-statist strategy for antisystemic movements, therefore we will discuss this further after we have explored his provocative position.

Two additional points need to be made in regard to the conjunction of Offe's analysis of the functional imperatives to which the welfare state has been an historic response with his more recent argument that the political forces and normative orientations that maintain the welfare state are quickly eroding. Both do indeed appear to be true. If this is the case, we are faced with a social contradiction at the heart of welfare state capitalism, as sometimes suggested by Offe.

> The embarassing secret of the welfare state is that, while its impact upon capitalist accumulation may well become destructive (as the conservative analysis so emphatically demonstrates), its abolition would be plainly disruptive (a fact that is systematically ignored by the conservative critics). The contradiction is that while capitalism cannot coexist *with,* neither can it exist *without,* the welfare state. This is exactly the condition to which we refer when using the concept 'contradiction.'[157]

Although Offe now appears to believe that disruption by the excluded is less threatening, if the welfare state does indeed respond to pressing problems of advanced capitalism then there are other potential disruptions of perhaps an even more paralyzing sort on the horizon.

It also needs to be noted that Offe does not address how the erosion of the welfare state affects what is widely considered to be the single most important reason that capitalists acceded to it: welfare policies help maintain effective demand through mass consumption. It may be, as Mike Davis argues, that a restructuring of consumption focusing on luxury goods reduces the need for mass consumption.[158] Wallerstein, on the other hand, contends that the single most enduring—and irresolvable—problem of capitalism is declining demand. We will examine the response to this underconsumptionist crisis theory in the context of Wallerstein's theory. However, any thorough analysis of the prospects of the welfare state would have to include this topic.

Finally, whatever merit there is in a political project aimed at increasing the learning capacities of society, it is a dubious project unless it is clearly connected with specific social and political institutional change. Offe's more recent work addresses this topic by reiterating the need for a learning process in regard to the formation of preferences. For some of the reasons given above and for additional reasons we will not engage here, Offe concludes that, contrary to much socialist discussion, extending participation will not in itself necessarily improve collective decisionmaking. Therefore he focuses his attention on improving democratic will-formation. "What are needed for effective implementation of policies, in addition to legal regulation, are enlightened, principled and refined preferences on the part of citizens."[159] This will require a new set of political institutions that will encourage "reflective preferences, rather than 'spontaneous' and context-contingent ones."[160] Offe is not implying that the judgements of actors can be or should be completely desituated. However, if a "civilized democratic polity" is to be maintained, more emphasis must be placed on developing institutions that can facilitate "dialogical forms of making one's voice heard."

Once again, the new social movements and civil society appear to be at the forefront of this project. Offe contends that in recent decades "most of the new issues and problems concerning the 'common good'" have been raised "by new social movements working outside the formally constituted political system, while the representative institutions have often been *more* myopic, *less* other-regarding and fact-regarding, than parts of their constituencies."[161] Although interesting, Offe's arguments are admittedly sketchy on this topic. His reference to the common good also seems to contradict Offe's argument that the new social movements have contributed to the erosion of support for the welfare state by downplaying the egalitarian-collectivist projects of the Left in favor of the libertarian and particularist ideals that practically define the identity politics of the new social movements. This apparent inconsistency may partly be a result of the essential contestability of the phrase "the common good." In any case, this analysis of the promise of new social movements and civil society is open to many additional criticisms. Habermas also explores the topic of learning processes, social movements, civil society, and a similar Arendtian conception of "representative thinking" necessary for judgement, therefore we will leave this topic for our examination of Habermas's theory.[162]

None of these considerations casts doubt on Offe's central achievement. He brilliantly illuminates the rationality problems of political administration that emerge with the displacement of problems of production in advanced capitalism through the development of the interventionist welfare state. The typical mode of operation of the welfare state further provokes multiple legitimacy issues that are irresolvable within the welfare state. These legitimacy issues in turn generate political fragmentation in organization and around issues that undercut the support for the welfare state. All of these difficulties are then intertwined with a shift of normative orientation regarding collective identity that lead to the overall decline, even exhaustion, of the welfare state as an answer to the functional requirements of advanced capitalism. However, whether this will engender effective oppositional movements against capitalism is unclear from Offe's analyses. We must also allow for the possibility that Marx referred to as "the common ruin of the contending classes." We have abundant and increasing evidence today that societies do sometimes commit suicide.

Beyond his analyses of the interventionist welfare state Offe's arguments deepen our understanding of issues raised by other Marxian theorists discussed above. Offe is concerned to lay bare the societal conditions under which an individual rational choice calculus actually becomes pervasive. He is also fully convinced of the importance of normative issues, examining the social dynamic that generates new normative orientations in the general public and those that animate the new social movements. For this reason his discussion of normative issues is not that of a moralist judging society from the outside, as sometimes appears to be the normative framework of analytical Marxists. Therefore he concretely contributes to the "sociology of injustice" called for by Roemer. He does so by discussing normative issues in the context of the generation of collective identity, an approach that avoids the theoretical impotence of the "thou ought."

For all his discussion of service labor and new social movements, however, it is ultimately unclear how Offe relates the dynamic of advanced capitalism to social actors. Specifically, it is unclear whether a society of individualistic rational actors is possible, that is, whether some underlying normative consensus is necessary for society to cohere. Unless society is held together by autonomic processes that can operate behind the backs of the participants, the coherence of society is jeopardized by the widespread development of self-interested rational actors. The relation between the cultural/normative framework of society and the functional connections of its subsystems is at the heart of the theory of Juergen Habermas. In the next chapter we will discuss Habermas's own version of the displacement of problems of capitalist societies and his attempt to articulate the relationship between the functional requirements of advanced capitalism, the normative and identity problems that ensue, and his political proposals for responding to these conflicts.

Six

Reification Without the Proletariat:
The Argument of Juergen Habermas

For over thirty years Juergen Habermas has been developing a theory of advanced capitalist welfare states that attempts to "overcome the paradigm of production, without abandoning the intentions of Western Marxism in the process."[1] Utilizing both systems theory and phenomenological analyses of the "lifeworld," Habermas sketches a logic of the dynamic of advanced capitalism that indicates new sites for contesting capitalism while demonstrating the diminished importance of the concept of class. To a certain extent Habermas follows Claus Offe's analysis of the difficulties of the interventionist welfare state of advanced capitalist societies. Habermas agrees with Offe that class conflict has become latent because of political intervention and that intervention to a large degree displaces production as the primary determinant of the life chances of individuals. He also agrees that the latter leads to a rationality deficit within public administration, renews the issue of political legitimation, and creates new, nonproduction based, oppositionist forces.

Although Habermas acknowledges that there is indeed a displacement of conflict into the political sphere, he does not believe that the rationality deficit necessarily leads to a crisis. Instead, Habermas argues that the crisis tendencies of advanced capitalism are further displaced into the cultural sphere, broadly speaking, i.e., into the lifeworld. As indicated by Offe, political legitimation problems are a part of this displacement. Habermas goes beyond this analysis by exploring the ways in which legitimation problems ultimately rest on a "motivational crisis" and how the motivational crisis is one of several manifestations of a general disruption of culture in advanced capitalism. These arguments are explored in *Legitimation Crisis* and *The Theory of Communicative Action,* respectively.

Habermas's primary social theoretical statement is the two volume *The Theory of Communicative Action: Reason and the Rationalization of*

Society (Volume One) and *Lifeworld and System: A Critique of Functionalist Reason* (Volume Two).[2] In this work he draws together arguments and the theoretical perspectives of Weber, Marx, Parsons, Mead, and Durkheim in order to analyze the "reification" of social relations—their alienated, objective, "thing-like" character—in advanced capitalist welfare states. Specifically, he elaborates and links together four topics: a theory of rationality, the theory of communicative action, the dynamic of societal rationalization under capitalism, and a conceptualization of society that combines systems theory and action theory. The result is a social theory that proceeds at a very high level of abstraction.[3]

Although Habermas says that the *Theory of Communicative Action* is not a "directly political" book, his political perspective directly proceeds from the theoretical edifice constructed in this work.[4] The abstraction of this work is more manageable if we first examine his earlier argument in *Legitimation Crisis*. The discussion in *Legitimation Crisis* is explicitly related to the theses advanced by Offe and others concerning class and crisis in the welfare state. By reviewing that discussion we can see Habermas's reservations about certain crisis theories, his own preliminary statement of the likely source of societal crisis, and how these themes are extended and deepened in *The Theory of Communicative Action.*

In all of his works, but especially in the two of primary concern here, Habermas's analysis is extraordinarily multifaceted, intervening in several debates at once and replete with methodological arguments. In this chapter we will focus on Habermas's more substantive argument on (a) the political displacement of class conflict in advanced capitalism, as argued in *Legitimation Crisis,* and (b) how political conflicts are actually quickly transformed into normative (legitimation and motivational) crises. We will then turn to the discussion in *The Theory of Communicative Action* regarding (c) Habermas's distinction between system and lifeworld, and how the former is precipitated from the latter with the modernization of society; (d) the ways in which conflict develops between these two aspects of social life; (e) the sites of conflict and new social actors that emerge in advanced capitalism; and (f) Habermas's political proposals for reorienting socialist theory in light of his analysis.

THE BASES OF THE LEGITIMATION CRISIS

In *Legitimation Crisis* Habermas begins his argument by accepting the common notion of "organized capitalism."[5] Advanced capitalism is dominated by a large oligopolistic sector and a large public sector, in both of which workers are unionized. The public sector intervenes in the economy through "global planning," alterations of the "boundary conditions" within which private enterprise operates. Like Offe, Habermas reminds us, however, that even in liberal capitalism the state was charged with the function of maintaining the "social foundations" and other supporting conditions of the competitive production of surplus value.[6]

The interventionist state is distinguished by the fact that it not only secures the general conditions of production but is also involved in the capitalist "reproduction process itself." Such intervention partly displaces the labor market such that the theory of value can no longer be used to "comprehend" economic movement.[7] Economic movement is a consequence of economic driving forces and political counter-controls. State support for the qualification of labor (education) and for science and technology improves productivity, thereby increasing the use-value of capital. This alters "the form of production of surplus value."[8] In this way there is a "displacement of the relations of production" and a repoliticization of the class structure, i.e., a partial return to the politically constituted classes of precapitalist societies as contrasted with the economically constituted classes of capitalism.

The repoliticization of production does not result in heightened political consciousness of classes. To avoid a crisis of the entire system, all resources are focused on keeping class conflict "latent."[9] A "quasi-political wage structure" is developed in both the oligopolistic sector and the public sector which pass on increased wage costs, so that they "externalize class conflict." This "immunization of the original conflict zone" has indeed a number of deleterious consequences: differential wage developments, the intensification of wage conflicts within the public sector, permanent inflation, a permanent fiscal crisis of the state, and sectoral and regional economic disparities. However, class conflict is kept latent because capital devaluation occurs through inflation rather than economic crises and the dysfunctional effects of these arrangements are dispersed over "quasi-groups" such as consumers, schoolchildren, and users of public transportation. "In this way the social identity of classes breaks down and class consciousness is fragmented." However, this should not be taken to mean that class structure has ceased to exist. Habermas specifically refers to the "temporarily suppressed, but unresolved class antagonism" as having set in motion the dynamic of advanced capitalism.[10]

Habermas argues that it is an empirical question whether the tendencies toward economic crisis have been solved. It is dependent on whether the growth of science and technology, supported by the state, increases productivity enough to insure loyalty of the population as a whole and also keep accumulation going. At the very least, inflation and a permanent fiscal crisis result, although these cannot properly be called a "system crisis." These are a consequence of the fact that government bears the costs of "more and more socialized production," besides expenditures on armaments, space exploration, "imperialistic market strategies," and maintaining the infrastructure.

Due to its new tasks, however, there are two other crisis tendencies of the interventionist state: a rationality crisis of the administration and a legitimation crisis due to the transformed relation of the state to production. In advanced capitalism, the state is directly involved in the process of the realization of capital. This position, along with the class compromise in the monopoly sector of the economy, gives the state a "limited planning capacity." However, the state still has to negotiate its way between two kinds of enduring conflict. First, there is continuing competition between "collective-capitalist" interests and individual capitalist groups; secondly, there is conflict between collective-capitalist interests and "the generalizable interests, oriented to use-values, of various population groups."[11]

This state has two primary tasks: on the one hand, it has to raise and utilize taxes "so rationally that crisis-ridden disturbances of growth can be avoided." On the other hand, it must raise and utilize taxes in such a way that "the need for legitimation can be satisfied as it arises."[12] Failure in the former results in a "deficit in administrative rationality"; failure in the latter results in a "deficit in legitimation." Habermas argues that state intervention, even if it develops a rationality deficit because of the demands for state planning of the economy, does not necessarily result in a system crisis. Disorganization of certain areas of life may be tolerable and compromises of some sort that allow rational planning cannot be *logically* precluded. He insists that "government activity can find a *necessary* limit only in available legitimations."

According to Habermas, state intervention does directly court a legitimation deficit in that such intervention makes the state responsible for managing the economy. The argument is quite similar to that of Offe.

> Because the economic crisis has been intercepted and transformed into a systematic overloading of the public budget, it has put off the mantle of a natural fate of society. If governmental crisis management fails, it lags behind programmatic demands *that it has placed on itself*. The penalty for this failure is withdrawal of legitimation.[13]

Furthermore, the dynamic is such that precisely when the state is most in need of legitimation, when it is failing, legitimation demands increase.

The state cannot avoid these demands because it seeks to maintain capitalist production. The class structure of capitalism again shows here its continued importance for the crisis tendencies of advanced capitalism. The state continues to attempt to manage the economy within the still existing but "transformed fundamental contradiction of social production for non-generalizable interests."[14] It is true that state intervention weakens class formation, that social conflict does not assume class-conscious forms because of administratively "scattered secondary conflicts." However, these secondary conflicts themselves "directly provoke questions of legitimation" of public policy.

There is a solution to these immediate legitimacy problems that maintains the appearance of universalism. This is the establishment of "formal democracy," a kind of democracy structured such that elections do not interfere with public administration. "Substantive democracy" must be avoided in that it "would bring to consciousness the contradiction between administratively socialized production and . . . private appropriation."[15] Instead, it is necessary to create a situation in which "civic privatism" and a "passive citizenry" are encouraged, a situation that can produce "diffuse mass loyalty" without participation. In such a "structurally depoliticized public realm" the need for legitimation is answered through the provision of social welfare policies which Habermas and others call the "welfare-state substitute program." People are steered toward consumption of goods, achievement through education, and the rewards of careers. The depoliticization itself is legitimated through theories of democratic elitism and variants of technocratic theory.

Nevertheless, even if the formalization of democracy insulates public administration from the need for immediate legitimation, administrative planning of various areas of social life itself resurrects the need for the state to justify its actions. As part of its intervention into production, the state must invade areas that used to be "self-legitimating," for example curriculum planning required by its intervention in the qualifying of labor, city planning, health planning, and family planning. "At every level, administrative planning produces unintended unsettling and publicizing effects. These effects weaken the justification potential of traditions that have been flushed out of their nature-like course of development."[16]

Besides the general legitimation problems provoked by administrative intervention, there are also specific pressures. As Offe noted, administrative planning requires the participation of at least some of those affected.

Planning thereby engenders an increased need for "consensus formation" that produces demands which the administration cannot solve "under conditions of an asymmetrical class compromise."[17] Furthermore, political conservatives vigorously object to planning. In sum, administrative management of economic problems requires consensus which in turn provokes demands for justification.

The key question for Habermas is whether these various legitimation difficulties actually lead to a legitimation crisis, i.e., whether they become "insoluable." Authentic legitimation of this system is ruled out by Habermas because of the continued existence of class structure. Even if growth without crisis is achieved, the real problem is that the priorities of this system are based not on "generalizable interests" but on the "private goals of profit maximization."[18] The priorities that drive public policy result from "a class structure that is, as usual, kept latent." As Habermas says succinctly, "In the final analysis, *this class structure* is the source of the legitimation deficit."[19]

Since the system cannot be legitimated, the political administrative subsystem could attempt to alleviate its input difficulties by trying to dominate and manipulate sociocultural production. However, in an argument that is too brief to be persuasive in *Legitimation Crisis* but is greatly expanded in *The Theory of Communicative Action,* Habermas states that there is a "structural dissimilarity" between administration and culture such that there can be "no administrative production of meaning."[20] The sociocultural system is "rigid" enough that it cannot be "randomly functionalized for the needs of the administrative system."[21] Therefore the administration seeks to substitute social welfare policies and production for the meaning-giving traditions it has weakened. As Habermas puts it: "The fiscally siphoned-off resource 'value' must take the place of the scanty resource 'meaning.'"[22]

The system must channel demands in ways that are in conformity with its operation. Given this, Habermas concludes that a legitimation crisis would develop if one of two conditions emerge. "A legitimation crisis arises as soon as the demands for such rewards rise faster than the available quantity of value, or when expectations arise that cannot be satisfied with such rewards."[23] Habermas argues that it is an open question as to whether the political-economic system could keep up with rising demands for use-values. However he is convinced that the second condition does appear, that there are "systematically produced" needs or expectations that cannot be filled with "rewards conforming to the system." "A legitimation crisis, then, must be based on a motivation crisis—that is, a discrepancy between the need for motives declared by the state, the educational system and the occupational system on the one hand, and the motivation supplied by the socio-cultural system on the other."[24] Therefore the probability of a legitimation crisis actually resolves into the question of the probability of a motivation crisis. On this issue Habermas's argument is quite compatible with G. A. Cohen's elucidation of fettering and with the many theorists who discuss the possible emergence of radical needs.

Drawing on systems-theoretic categories, Habermas defines a motivation crisis as a situation in which the sociocultural system changes such that its "output" is "dysfunctional for the state and for the system of social labor." The motivations most important for advanced capitalism are "civil and familial-vocational privatism." The former refers to the depoliticized public realm, i.e., mass, diffuse loyalty in the context of formal democracy. The latter refers to family and "career orientation suitable to status competition" organized through "educational and occupational systems that are regulated by competition through achievement." He states that a motivation crisis results when the traditions that provided the context for these attitudes have been eroded, and when no "functional equivalents" are forthcoming because of the "logic of development of normative structures."[25]

Habermas advances three primary theses regarding the failure of the socio-cultural system to provide the needed motivational inputs for the advanced capitalist polity and economy. First, Habermas contends that capitalistic societies have always to some extent depended on pre-capitalist culture for its traditions, feeding "parasitically on the remains of tradition."[26] He argues that the dynamic of capitalism erodes this "traditionalist padding" of bourgeois society because of the expansion of the "rationalization of areas of life once regulated by tradition." Examples of this expansion are the scientization of professional practice, the commodification of services, the "administrative regulation and legalization of areas of political and social intercourse previously regulated informally," the general commercialization of culture and politics, and "scientizing and psychologizing processes of childrearing."[27] This argument is expanded in a more discriminating manner in *The Theory of Communicative Action*.

More generally, the rationalization of worldviews, analyzed by Weber, has led to a "ruling scientism" that creates dissonances with traditional ways of understanding the world without being able to replace many of the functions of the latter, especially to give meaning or make sense of life. For example, religious beliefs have been relativized; religion has "retreated into the regions of subjective belief." As a consequence, bourgeois egoism has become "common sense," effacing the comprehensive views of religion and philosophy. "Bourgeois ideology" is no functional replacement for traditional worldviews in that it cannot connect us with an objectified nature, creates no basis for solidarity, and is simply inconsolate in regard to the "basic risks of existence."[28]

Secondly, the key elements of bourgeois ideology itself—achievement, possessive individualism, and orientation to exchange value—are being undermined by social changes. Like Offe, Habermas argues that these aspects of bourgeois belief are increasingly disabled as the market becomes less important as the regulator of social life.[29] Formal law and bourgeois ethical theory contribute to the disorientation by retaining universalism but more or less severing it from motive formation. The separation of formal law from morality excludes motive formation in that only permissions are created: "Actions may not be commanded, but only left to choice or forbidden."[30] This leaves the individual uncertain as to what path should be followed. The universalistic ethics of utilitarianism, which attempts to formulate a basis for motives, cannot fill this gap. "Utilitarianism clearly falls below the stage of internalization attained in the conventional ethics of duty [i.e., the Protestant Ethic]. Motives for action remain external to the morally responsible subject."[31] This is because utilitarianism only counsels that individuals pursue strategic actions for the satisfaction of pleasure. However, as pointed out by Alasdair MacIntyre among others, 'seek pleasure' is hardly a satisfactory guide for action.[32]

When motives are taken into consideration for ethical action in bourgeois moral philosophy (e.g., Kant), these motives are supposed to be scrubbed clean in that the only allowable motive is performance of duty. Other motives must be suppressed, therefore ethics is cut off from the interpretation of needs which would create motives for performance. "The limits of formalistic ethics can be seen in the fact that inclinations incompatible with duties must be excluded from the domain of the morally relevant, and they must be suppressed."[33]

Thirdly, Habermas further contends that those elements of bourgeois culture that remain—"denuded normative structures"—are not only "unsuited" to fill the gap left by the dissolution of pre-bourgeois traditions and of key components of bourgeois ideology, but even intensify the legitimation/motivation pressures. Habermas states that the most important residue of bourgeois tradition is "universalistic morality." Like Marx, Habermas contends that capitalism first created the conditions of universalistic morality through the ideology of exchange of equivalents. Although organized capitalism loses this ideological justification with the declining significance of the market, Habermas insists that a "collectively attained state of moral consciousness" can no more be simply disregarded, once practical discourse is unleashed, than scientific progress could be halted once theoretical discourse is unleashed. This is an aspect of a broader argument by Habermas that the development of science, post-auratic art, and universalistic morality are "irreversible developments" because each has an "internal logic." They each therefore present "cultural barriers" that can be broken only at the cost of "regressions . . . with extraordinary motivational burdens." In this regard, Habermas specifically mentions the irrationalism of fascism.[34]

In sum, the motivation-forming, meaning-giving pre-bourgeois traditions have been unable to withstand the impact of various kinds of rationalization. In addition, the "core components" of bourgeois belief that motivate action have lost their persuasiveness due to the development of the interventionist welfare state. What remains of bourgeois tradition is the universalistic framework for justifying moral belief. Universality is the legacy of bourgeois culture that cannot be erased. However, a review of the dominant ethical theories of bourgeois society indicates that they cannot produce a new interpretive framework in which universality can be connected with motive-formation. Instead, they stay at the level of a formalistic ethics that offers no clear guide to action because there is no theoretical space for the interpretation of needs which forge motivation. All of the above threaten the orienting interpretations that secure civil and familial-vocational privatism.

Habermas's theory is intriguing because he looks at the issue of legitimacy not only from the perspective of why people should obey but why they would obey. This sociological approach focuses our attention on the relationship between legitimacy and motivation, the conditions under which principles of legitimacy engage individuals and orient their actions. The inquiry into how motivations are elicited is also important because it leads into Habermas's most provocative hypothesis, that "values and norms in accordance with which motives are formed have an immanent relation to truth." By truth Habermas apparently means that reasons must be given for norms—or at least there is an implicit promise that reasons could be given—in order for norms to be effective, i.e., to call forth motivations by persons. This is particularly pressing in class societies. "Because the reproduction of class societies is based on the privileged appropriation of socially produced wealth, all such societies must resolve the problem of distributing the surplus social product inequitably and yet legitimately."[35] Habermas recognizes that at no time does the factual following of such norms rely solely on the idea that they are legitimate. But there must be some acceptance of their legitimacy—and therefore the promise that reasons could be given—or "the latent force embedded in the system of institutions is released."

Many of course reject out of hand this demanding conception of legitimacy. For example, some argue from a "functionalist point of view" that legitimacy exists if actions are in accord with legal procedures in an established order. The social grounding of this conception—known as decisionism—is simply that cohesion of an order requires that authority be placed somewhere. Decisionism is defended on the grounds that the function of the law is to "absorb uncertainty."[36] Habermas disputes the decisionist perspective, arguing that reference to procedures is not sufficient to produce legitimacy because the procedures themselves need moral grounding.

An alternative theory of legal legitimacy is the doctrine in modern natural right that motivation can be elicited by agreement based on interests, that is, the contractarian argument. This is an attempt to "empirically" ground norms. However, Habermas contends that this argument is also unconvincing. "A norm has a binding character—therein consists its validity claim. But if only empirical motives (such as inclinations, interests, and fear of sanctions) sustain the agreement, it is impossible to see why a party to the contract should continue to feel bound to the norms when his original motives change."[37] This was also the position of Emile Durkheim. Agreement based solely on interests is inherently unstable because interest positions frequently change. On the above perspective, when they do, the binding character of norms evaporates.

Therefore, according to Habermas, norms must be intersubjectively recognized if they are to be able to secure continuing motivations which are the basis of legitimacy. The "validity claim" of such norms is based on the implicit promise that a consensus could be brought about through argument and reasons "which may be questioned at any time."[38] Habermas acknowledges that practical discourse of this sort has been frequently declared impossible. "Anyone who still discusses the admissability of truth in practical questions is, at best, old-fashioned."[39] However, he insists that this opinion is a consequence of a narrow notion of rationality as only deductive argument, rather than discourse. In fact it is precisely this assumption that is the philosophical basis of Weber's decisionism.[40]

"Giving reasons" for the existing distribution of resources and for the goals of public policy is an increasing problem in advanced capitalism.

The less the cultural system is capable of producing adequate motivations for politics, the educational system, and the occupational system, the more must scarce meaning be replaced by consumable values. To the same extent, the patterns of distribution that arise from socialized production for non-generalizable interests are endangered. The definitive limits to procuring legitimation are inflexible normative structures that no longer provide the economic-political system with ideological resources, but instead confront it with exorbitant demands.[41]

Socialized production for "non-generalizable interests" cannot withstand the judgement of universalistic morality in the absence of traditional buffers.

One might immediately object that generalizable interests are not present in certain circumstances and areas. In this case, however, the universalization principle must still be employed to determine that fact. "[D]emarcating particular from generalizable interests in a manner that admits of consensus is possible only by means of discursive will-formation."[42] Where generalization is impossible, compromise is the result, or the establishment of a separate social area where strategically acting subjects can pursue their designs. However, the terms under which such a compromise is negotiated must themselves be determined in a universalizable manner in order to be legitimate. Universalism is a bone stuck in the throat of those who would defend the increasingly visible class-bias of the policies of the interventionist welfare state.

In this way it is the class structure of capitalism that provokes continuing normative crisis tendencies. "If this rough diagnosis is correct, a legitimation crisis can be avoided in the long run only if the latent class structures of advanced-capitalist societies are transformed or if the pressure for legitimation to which the administrative system is subject can be removed."[43] The latter option depends on nothing less than the emergence of a new mode of socialization of individuals, i.e., on the possibility of "uncoupling" the "integration of inner nature" from "norms that need justification." Habermas next considers whether such an uncoupling of socialization from normative discourse is possible.

Habermas begins his response by stating that classical social theorists such as Durkheim insisted that society is a "moral reality," that subjects "develop the unity of their person only in connection with identity-securing world-views and moral systems." Habermas argues that the primary goal of norms is to avoid the meaninglessness that comes from the separation of the person from society. "The fundamental function of world-maintaining interpretive systems is the avoidance of chaos, that is, the overcoming of contingency. The legitimation of orders of authority and basic norms can be understood as a specialization of this 'meaning-giving' function."[44] Religion originally allowed a meaning (explanation) for contingencies, thereby providing not only truth but consolation. Religion as the explainer of contingencies has now been displaced by scientific understanding and by a degree of technical control of nature which makes contingencies bearable.

However, Habermas argues, the growing complexity of society results in new contingencies and "suffering from uncontrolled societal processes." Social science cannot take on the role of worldviews because it has not produced technical control nor has it been able to "make the objective context of social evolution accessible." At the same time morality has become formalistic. If one accepts the idea that society coheres through moral integration, then the force of all these changes is the weakening of the bases of identity formation itself. "If world-views have foundered on the separation of cognitive from socially integrative components, if world-maintaining interpretative systems today belong irretrievably to the past, then what fulfills the moral-practical task of constituting ego- and group-identity?"[45]

Habermas raises the possibility that these multiple problems of social integration may be blunted by developments which separate identity-formation from normative integration altogether.[46] Habermas points to several examples in the history of ideas which suggests this tendency, for example, the "cynicism of a, as it were, self-denying bourgeois consciousness" of Nietzsche (and in a milder form, existentialism and positivism). Another example is elite theory and the elitist theory of democracy which denies that democracy has anything to do with formulating generalizable interests. "Political equality now means only the formal right to equal opportunity of *access* to power, that is, 'equal eligibility for election to positions of power.' Democracy no longer has the goal of rationalizing authority through the participation of citizens in discursive processes of will-formation. It is intended, instead, to make possible *compromises* between ruling elites."[47] Habermas says that in these phenomena we are either seeing the retreat of a class from universal demands that have become intolerable, or a general movement away from the historical mode of socialization of the species through norms that require justification. Habermas calls the latter the thesis of the "end of the individual."

Habermas argues that classic bourgeois society rested on individuation through socialization into a rational, independent practice. "If this form of reproduction were to be surrendered, together with the imperatives logically embedded in it, the social system could no longer establish its unity through formation of the identities of socially related individuals.

The constellations of general and particular would no longer be relevant for the aggregate state of the society."[48] This is the view of Niklas Luhmann, who argues that systems can stabilize themselves without recourse to individuals. Contemporary science reinforces the plausibility of this development by fostering an "objectivistic" self-interpretation of persons. Regarding the latter, Habermas quotes Albrecht Wellmer's remark that "even man has become an anthropomorphism in the eyes of man."[49]

At this point Habermas simply states that one must not allow one's methodological position to pre-decide the key issue of "whether the reproduction of social life is still bound to reason and, especially, whether generation of motives is still bound to internalization of norms that have need of justification."[50] Habermas argues that if the answer is negative, then "crisis theorems can no longer be constructed." He acknowledges that his own methodological choice is not guaranteed theoretical success. However, unlike Luhmann's systems theory, it does not prejudge the issue of whether a new mode of socialization has already emerged, that is, it allows us to investigate the grounds on which this may or may not have happened.

THE THEORY OF COMMUNICATIVE ACTION

Habermas's primary contribution in *Legitimation Crisis* is his focus on the motivational side of normative problems of advanced capitalism. Habermas argues that the legitimation problems of advanced capitalist societies depend upon the complex relationship between legitimation, motivation, and socialization (the formation of identity). A legitimation crisis of advanced capitalism actually depends on a motivation crisis insofar as the willingness to provide the economic-political system with supporting actions is "behaviorally" the ability of the system to motivate its population. Therefore an analysis of legitimation problems immediately turns to the question of whether the cultural system of society is able to elicit such supporting motivations. This gives greater theoretical depth to the recurring discussion of preference formation and the necessity of developing a sociology of justice.

Nevertheless, the argument in *Legitimation Crisis* is wanting in certain respects. The probability of a legitimation and motivation crisis is largely sketched-in rather than convincingly argued. For example, the idea that society is a moral reality—constructed on the notion of motive-formation as the internalization of norms—is more a gesture than an argument. Furthermore, the recalcitrance of culture to provide resources to the other subsystems is underspecified in *Legitimation Crisis*. In particular, there are

serious weaknesses in the argument that the motivation crisis is a consequence of the erosion of the bases of civil and familial-vocational privatism, which thereby deprives the political and economic subsystems of
necessary motivational inputs. That the "privatistic syndrome" partly
rests on pre-bourgeois traditions never rises much above the level of assertion. In fact, it is equally plausible that this loss of meaning leads to the
seeking of a meaningful life in private, particularistic groups, that is, it
leads to privatistic reactive identity formations. Habermas himself admits
this possibility, noting that it may be that certain groups "have already
begun the retreat to particular identities, settling down in the unplanned,
nature-like system of world society like the Indians on the reservations of
contemporary America."[51] Considering the phenomenon of young urban
professionals, on the one hand, and the proliferation of various personal-
ized mysticisms especially in the United States, on the other, privatism
would appear to have more motivational resources than those suggested by
Habermas in *Legitimation Crisis*. Many seem quite resigned to simply render unto Caesar that which is Caesar's.

The focus on normative issues itself obscures the broader difficulties
of culture, including science and art. Habermas later admitted that in *Legitimation Crisis* he did not clearly distinguish between the "legitimation/
motivation crisis," a consequence of cultural resistance to providing appropriate inputs for subsystems, and the "loss of meaning" that occurs
through the disintegration of the lifeworld by its "colonization" by subsystems.[52] The legitimation/motivation crisis is important but the greater
danger is colonization and loss of meaning that he discusses in his later
work. Although he says that "communicative action" and "normativistic
action" must not be conflated, he comes very close to doing so in *Legitimation Crisis*. The argument of *The Theory of Communicative Action* is clearer
to the extent that it focuses on loss of meaning.

The specific genesis and dynamic of subsystems also needs further explication. More to our present topic, class structure seems to be reduced to
the question of the generalizability or non-generalizability of interests.
The systems perspective leaves obscure other ways in which class structure
could be important for the dynamic of advanced capitalism. The increasing focus on systems theory in *The Theory of Communicative Action* actually further attenuates the notion of class structure. This is a topic to which
we will return.

To remedy these and other defects in his theory, Habermas started
anew with the two volumes of *The Theory of Communicative Action*.[53]
Therein his argument regarding the possibility of a legitimation/motivation

crisis is placed in the context of the broader cultural developments of modernization analyzed by Weber. Through this framework Habermas shows how the systems theory of society itself gains an empirical referent and analyzes the effects on the lifeworld of the expansion of media-driven subsystems. The distinction between system and lifeworld also allows Habermas to further specify the reasons for the emergence of opposition movements. Finally, the arguments of *The Theory of Communicative Action* provide the basis for Habermas's political proposals.

Habermas calls his new approach a "second attempt to appropriate Weber in the spirit of Western Marxism."[54] The first attempt is exemplified in the work of Georg Lukacs and the work of Max Horkheimer and Theodor Adorno. According to Habermas, Lukacs's theory of the reification was constrained by trying to connect reification to class consciousness. On the other hand, Horkheimer and Adorno's analysis of the "dialectic of enlightenment" was limited by their acceptance of Weber's perspective that instrumental reason is the only type of rationality.[55] In contrast, Habermas critically appropriates Weber's theory of societal rationalization in order to renew the theory of reification. To do this he attempts to demonstrate (1) that instrumental reason is not the only type of rationality and (2) that reification occurs because of the "selective rationalization" engendered by capitalism.

CULTURAL RATIONALIZATION AND SOCIETAL RATIONALIZATION

Following Weber, Habermas argues that the societal rationalization processes embodied in the capitalist economy and the modern state are only made possible by a prior cultural rationalization.[56] The systematization of religious worldviews leads to the differentiation of three "cultural value spheres," each exhibiting and developing its own "autonomous logic."[57] The three spheres that emerge from the fragmentation of religious worldviews are science, morality, and art. Cultural differentiation creates a "decentered understanding of the world" which makes possible an objectivistic view of facts, impersonal moral and legal relations, and frees subjectivity. Each of these spheres follows a distinctive type of rationality, which Habermas calls cognitive-instrumental rationality, moral-practical rationality, and aesthetic-expressive rationality, respectively.

From the beginning, this cultural rationalization is unsettling in two ways. First, although the inner logic of each sphere is set free, "the meaning-giving unity of metaphysical-religious worldviews thereby falls apart." Secondly, the elaboration of cultural contents within each sphere becomes the province of experts. Contrary to the hopes of the philosophes, the potential of the transformed cultural tradition to rationalize the various arenas of social activity is not automatically realized.[58] "As a result, the distance grows between the culture of the experts and that of the larger public. What accrues to culture through specialized treatment and reflection does not immediately and necessarily become the property of everyday praxis."[59] As Weber argued, this potential only becomes "empirically effective" when institutionalized in some fashion, including a combination of "external factors."[60] More specifically, Habermas states that the propagation of these new "structures of consciousness" occurs through three paths: social movements, cultural enterprises such as scientific communities and artistic markets, and—Weber's primary focus—the "institutionalization of purposive-rational action with structural effects on society as a whole," the capitalist economy and the modern state.[61]

Weber argued that purposive rationality (Habermas's cognitive-instrumental rationality) was motivationally based in the religious congregations and family socialization of the carrier strata of Calvinism. The religious and vocational orientation of the "calling" served their ideal and material interests, anchoring purposive-rational action in an "order of life" and thereby creating the cultural preconditions for the development of capitalism. These cultural conditions only became fully effective when societally institutionalized through law. Weber of course further argued that as capitalism developed, the Protestant ethic is eroded by a utilitarian attitude toward work and by hedonism, the famous "specialists without spirit, sensualists without heart."[62]

Weber believed that, once established, the capitalist enterprise and bureaucratically organized public administration grow because of their superior efficiency in the instrumental sense. According to Habermas, Weber could not see any way of institutionalizing moral-practical rationality because he could only imagine morality embodied in the salvation religions.[63] The institutionalization of cognitive-instrumental rationality and the fragmentation of culture therefore form the bases of Weber's loss of freedom (the "iron cage") and loss of meaning ("struggle among the gods") theses.

Unlike Weber, Habermas sees this development instead as selective rationalization; the rationalization potentials of modern differentiated culture have been insufficiently institutionalized. According to Habermas, why this imbalance has occurred cannot be explained by Weber because Weber's analysis is limited in two ways. First, Weber privileged one notion of rationality, the cognitive-instrumental, believing this to be the only form available given the fragmentation of substantive reason as a result of the differentiation of cultural value spheres and the "disenchanted" world of modern scientific understanding.[64] Secondly, according to Habermas, Weber (and many after him) understood conflicts in modern society as engendered by conflicting action orientations resulting from the fragmentation of culture. This refers to the apparent incompatibility of practice oriented by a scientific understanding of the world, versus action based on a normative understanding of the world, and each counterposed to the ineffability of aesthetic practice. Habermas argues that this focus on action orientations of individuals is simply too narrow for comprehending the dynamic of societal rationalization.

Habermas responds to the first limitation of Weber's theory by introducing the notion of "communicative action" to elaborate his conception of different types of rationality, an analysis we cannot fully pursue here. Briefly, Habermas contrasts communicative action to purposive-rational action in order to reveal additional dimensions of what should be considered societal rationalization. "I shall speak of communicative action whenever the actions of the agents involved are coordinated not through egocentric calculations of success but through acts of reaching understanding. In communicative action participants are not primarily oriented to their own individual successes; they pursue their individual goals under the condition that they can harmonize their plans of action on the basis of common situation definitions."[65] Habermas utilizes this distinction to argue that (1) in social life acting in the world first presupposes that a common definition of "the world" is agreed on, and (2) that there are crucial areas of social life that can only retain their coherence and be reproduced through communicative action. We will return to the latter argument in a moment.

Habermas argues that the second weakness of Weber's theory, his focus on action orientations, can only be remedied by resort to the systems theory of society developed by Talcott Parsons and by Niklas Luhmann. Weber's action theory did not allow him to properly understand the experiences of, and reactions to, the loss of freedom and loss of meaning characteristic of modern capitalist societies. The institutionalization of purposive-rational action actually led to the emergence of a new type of societal integration that bypasses action orientations of individuals altogether, through the development of "media-steered subsystems." To reveal this we must reconceptualize society in a dualistic fashion, as in certain respects a "system" and in other respects a "lifeworld." It is the dynamic of these two aspects of modern society that leads to an understanding of how capitalist society is only "selectively rationalized," of how selective rationalization engenders a perceived deterioration of social life and subsequent social conflicts, and to a consideration of a political project that can respond to these problems without sacrificing the gains of the cultural and societal rationalization that have already been achieved.

SOCIAL INTEGRATION AND SYSTEM INTEGRATION: LIFEWORLD AND SYSTEM

The overriding goal of Habermas's theoretical work is to find a way of combining the two leading approaches of social theory: the perspective that analyzes society as a meaningful whole for its participants (*Verstehen* theory) and the perspective that analyzes society as a system that is stabilized behind the backs of the participants (system theory). Habermas contrasts these two perspectives in a variety of places but *The Theory of Communicative Action* is Habermas's most complete attempt to combine them.[66] The two approaches to the study of society resolve into, respectively, a focus on the action orientations of society's members and a focus on how action consequences are coordinated without necessitating the will or consciousness of the participants. This is the distinction between the lifeworld, based on social integration, and system, based on system integration, that Habermas employs.

Contrary to some of his critics,[67] Habermas argues that this distinction is not simply methodological. All societies, not just capitalist societies, have systemic and lifeworld elements. For this reason Habermas proposes the general definition of society as "*systemically stabilized* complexes of action of *socially integrated* groups." However in pre-capitalist societies the two modes of societal integration—system integration and social integration—are closely tied together. It is only under capitalism that the system elements and lifeworld elements of society become "uncoupled" from each other through the generation of autonomous media-steered subsystems that have "structure-forming effect for the social system as a whole."[68] In this way, "the very object of the theory of society changes" with historical development.[69] The distinction between system and lifeworld is simultaneously a methodological and empirical distinction. It is an attempt to understand society as both a self-maintaining system and as a meaningful whole from the standpoint of participants.

A useful analogy may be the well known optical illusion of the picture that from one perspective appears as two heads in profile but from another perspective, by making a visual effort such that the foreground becomes background, the profiles disappear and we see a goblet. From one perspective society is a meaningful whole; the functional processes which maintain society "behind the backs" of the participants falls out of view. From the other perspective, the functional interconnections come into view but the meaning-giving aspects of social life are obscured. Habermas believes that this dualistic view of society will reveal the conflicts in capitalism which Weber described as loss of freedom and loss of meaning.

To follow Habermas's exploration along these lines it is necessary to first understand what he means by lifeworld. The lifeworld is broadly the background information presumed by the participants in any social action. The lifeworld cannot really be 'known' because it serves as the vehicle for all knowing. Individuals can never step outside their own lifeworld, no more than they can step outside of their language. It is "a reality that is at once unquestionable and shadowy." The lifeworld therefore forms "a context that, itself boundless, draws boundaries."[70] Although the lifeworld as a whole can never be placed in question, elements of the lifeworld can be and are placed in doubt. In these cases, the element is "thematized," made subject to argument as the participants attempt to re-establish their mutual definition of the situation, a prerequisite for successful cooperation. The lifeworld can therefore only be reproduced through communicative action, not purposive-rational action.

Drawing on the arguments of Mead, Habermas states that there are three "functional aspects" in which communicative action is necessary to reproduce the lifeworld: as "mutual understanding," communicative action maintains cultural knowledge over time; in "coordinating action," communicative action maintains social integration and "solidarity"; and in "socialization," communicative action is necessary for the formation of personal identity.

> The symbolic structures of the lifeworld are reproduced by way of the continuation of valid knowledge, stabilization of group solidarity, and socialization of responsible actors. . . . Corresponding to these processes of *cultural reproduction, social integration,* and *socialization* are the structural components of the lifeworld: culture, society, and person.[71]

It is important to note that by the term society here Habermas means "the legitimate orders through which participants regulate their memberships in social groups and thereby secure solidarity." Therefore normative coherence is only one aspect of the lifeworld that is reproduced through communicative action. Furthermore, the above account only concerns the reproduction of the symbolic structures of the lifeworld. Habermas insists that the "maintenance of the material substratum of the lifeworld" depends

on something else, "the medium of the purposive activity with which associated individuals intervene in the world to realize their aims."[72] This will
be the province of system processes.

Habermas argues that there is a tendency in modern societies for the
lifeworld to become increasingly "rationalized." This is a result of the
aforementioned increasing distance from substantive religious interpretations of the world. The institutionalized elaboration of the inner logic of
each cultural sphere displaces traditional understandings and consensus.
This opens the possibility of rationally motivated consensus over issues.[73]
Moreover, this rationalization leads to the "structural differentiation" of
the lifeworld itself. Increasingly the three structures of lifeworlds—culture, society, and person—become detached from each other.[74] Culture is
structurally differentiated from society in that institutions and worldviews
become uncoupled. Personality is structurally differentiated from society
by increased "contingency" in forming interpersonal relationships. Culture is structurally differentiated from personality in that the "renewal of
traditions depends more and more on individuals's readiness to criticize
and their ability to innovate." In addition, the rationalization of the lifeworld means that in each of these spheres we see a separation of form and
content and the development of the specialized tasks of "cultural transmission, social integration, and child rearing."[75] For example, there is a separation of form and content in society in that "principles of legal order and
of morality are established which are less and less tailored to concrete
forms of life." Furthermore, the task of social integration becomes specialized in jurisprudence.

The need for a systems-theoretical perspective emerges here. As the
lifeworld is rationalized in these multiple ways, agreement is less and less
ascribed by traditional interpretations. The need for consensus must be
achieved "through the interpretive accomplishments of participants, or
through a professionalized expert knowledge that has become customary
in a secondary sense."[76] This threatens to "overload" the capacity of coordination of action through agreement. Organizational forms are then developed that coordinate action through "media" that substitute for
language. This is the birth of subsystems of society steered through the
media of money and power.[77]

These "delinguistified" media make possible the full development of
societal spheres of purposive rationality.

> Media such as money and power attach to empirical ties; they en-
> code a purposive-rational attitude toward calculable amounts of
> value and make it possible to exert generalized, strategic influ-
> ence on the decisions of other participants while *bypassing*

processes of consensus-oriented communication. Inasmuch as they do not merely simplify linguistic communication, but *replace* it with a symbolic generalization of rewards and punishments, the lifeworld contexts in which processes of reaching understanding are always embedded are devalued in favor of media-steered interactions; the lifeworld is no longer needed for the coordination of action.[78]

Contrary to Weber it is not purposive-rational action orientations that need to be "institutionally and motivationally anchored in the lifeworld," rather these media need to be so anchored.[79] This is accomplished through formal law.

The development of media-driven subsystems allows the increasing complexity of society because media bypass the need for coordination through understanding. This establishes a new type of societal integration not based on shared understanding, unlike the lifeworld. Differentiated modern society therefore has two distinct principles of coherence or societal integration: "social integration" achieved through the coordination of action orientations via consensus, and "system integration" achieved through the "nonnormative steering of individual decisions," i.e., through media that coordinate social action through the interlinking of action consequences behind the backs of the participants.[80] The primary example is of course the market, but Habermas also includes public administration, steered by the medium of "power."

Through the development of media-steered subsystems, these two types of societal integration become "uncoupled" from each other. The conflicts that Weber envisioned are not between purposive rationality and other "action orientations" because the media coordinate action consequences, not action orientations.[81] Rather, Habermas argues that the "contradictions" of societal rationalization noted by Weber stem from the "competition" between the two types of societal integration, social integration through communicatively achieved understanding and system integration through media.[82]

THE COLONIZATION THESIS:
REIFICATION WITHOUT THE PROLETARIAT

The experience of the development of autonomous subsystems, the uncoupling of system and lifeworld, has been frequently described. From the perspective of the lifeworld, there is a peculiar "objectification" of social relations as the "social system definitively bursts out of the horizon of the lifeworld, escapes from the intuitive knowledge of everyday communicative practice." Social relations appear to "congeal into the 'second nature' of a norm-free sociality that can appear as something in the objective world."[83] As social domains are carved out by the media of money and power there is a "technicizing of the lifeworld," a development of "more and more complex networks that no one has to comprehend or be responsible for."[84]

Habermas believes that the lifeworld can only be reproduced through communicative action. Therefore the specific reproduction processes on which the lifeworld depends sets limits to the growth of subsystems. Social crises, conflicts, and resistance occur when subsystems grow such that they disrupt these communicative reproduction processes on which the coherence of the lifeworld depends. "Only an independent, *internal* resistance to functionally required revisions of one-sided views of the world and of society could explain crises, that is, disturbances that have a systematic character and represent something more than temporary disequilibria."[85] Disruption of the communicative reproduction of the lifeworld leads to "pathologies."

Habermas argues that advanced capitalist societies become increasingly dependent for their material reproduction on media subsystems, both money in the economic subsystem and power in the administrative subsystem of the interventionist welfare state. This mediatization of social life becomes a "colonization" of the lifeworld when "critical disequilibria" in the realm of material production flow over into the lifeworld, disrupting the communicative processes necessary for lifeworld reproduction and thereby disrupting social identity.[86]

In advanced capitalist societies disequilibria in the market are handled through the intervention of the state administration. The development of the welfare state takes the form of the creation of a new subsystem driven by the medium of power. Although the lifeworld "anchoring" of this medium differs from the anchoring of money, administration is also formally organized and therefore not dependent on achieved mutual understanding for its functioning. (By "formally organized" Habermas means these social relations are first institutionalized by positive law.) Bureaucracy in itself is not enough to generate the colonization of the lifeworld as long as the three key structural areas of the lifeworld—cultural reproduction, social integration, and socialization—are intact. It is the irresistable growth of the bureaucracy that creates problems: "Identity problems are unavoidable only if there is an *irresistable* tendency to an *ever-expanding* bureaucratization."[87]

We have still not explained why colonization has to happen, i.e., why economic and administrative subsystems push beyond what is necessary for the "institutionalization of money and power." As seen, Habermas agrees with Offe that the welfare state emerges to successfully fill in the "functional gaps" of the capitalist economy caused by economic disequilibria of "crisis-ridden growth," such as business cycles and insufficient infrastructure investment. The state does this through the manipulation of the boundary conditions within which the monetary subsystem operates, therefore without disturbing either the steering by the money medium or private control of investment.[88]

The welfare state and growth of public administration also occur because of the potential for class struggle over distribution. This potential is blocked by the development of various corporatist arrangements in which wage scales are set through bargaining mediated by the state and through the direct bureaucratic provision of use-values such as health care. In this way, "the social antagonism bred by private disposition over the means of producing social wealth increasingly loses its structure-forming power for the lifeworlds of social groups, although it does remain constitutive for the structure of the economic system."[89] With the "continuous rise in the standard of living" and other protections of private life from system imperatives, "conflicts over distribution also lose their explosive power."[90]

The welfare state is an accommodation with an autonomous subsystem steered by money. From the standpoint of the subsystems steered by money and power, the lifeworld is just another subsystem, an environment from which subsystems require inputs. These resources can only be extracted in the form of the medium of the subsystem in question.[91] The economy needs labor inputs which it obtains as wage labor, exchanging money which can be used for consumer goods. Workers are thereby transfigured into labor via money, a process Marx called "real abstraction." The rising standard of living and redistributive policies of the welfare state deemphasize the role of employee and enhance the role of consumer. In this way, class structuration in the lifeworld is obliterated. Thomas McCarthy refers to this process as "the disappearance of the proletariat into the pores of consumer society."[92]

The welfare state (administrative subsystem) has similar effects on the role of citizen, transforming citizens into "clients." The administrative subsystem needs legitimation which it obtains as "mass loyalty" through the provision of use-values and other social services that cannot be directly produced by the economic subsystem due to its operation through exchange-values. Public administration thereby transforms citizens into clients responding to legally anchored power. Habermas even refers to this clientelization of citizens as the "model case" of "colonization."[93] This is Habermas's version of the "welfare state compromise" that has been maintained since the end of World War II in advanced capitalist countries.

The question that Habermas asks is, if the activities of the interventionist state have pacified the role of employee by shifting the emphasis to the role of consumer, and if the administration of the welfare state has successfully transformed citizens into clients ("customers who enjoy the rewards of the welfare state"), why are there any conflicts at all? Habermas answers that even if there are no disequilibria in the subsystems, the continued existence of the welfare state compromise depends on growth of both the market and the welfare state. This growth leads to ever-increasing system complexity "which means not only an *extension* of formally organized domains of action, but an increase in their internal *density* as well." Even if we assume that there are no disequilibria in these systems, "capitalist growth triggers conflicts within the lifeworld chiefly as a consequence of the expansion and the increasing density of the monetary-bureaucratic complex; this happens, first of all, where socially integrated contexts of life are redefined around the roles of consumer and client and assimilated to systemically integrated domains of action."[94] Habermas says that historically this redefinition of roles has been successful where the material reproduction of the lifeworld is involved. In this case, welfare state "compensations" can be channeled ("canalized") through the roles of client and consumer where "privatized hopes for self-actualization and self-determination are primarily located."[95]

However, even if the important tasks of material production are manageable through the welfare state, conflicts persist because the very mode of further growth requires instrumentalities (further mediatization of the lifeworld) that threaten the specific mode of reproduction of the lifeworld, through communicative action. The ever-increasing density of the monetary-bureaucratic complex eventually affects the structural components of the lifeworld necessary for cultural reproduction, social integration, and socialization. These areas can only be reproduced through communicative action. Therefore conflict breaks out "along the seams between system and lifeworld."[96]

A sign of the encroachment of formally organized domains of action, media subsystems, is "juridification" of areas of social life that are communicatively structured.[97] For the welfare state to provide its services to clients they must first be redefined in the form of legal specifications in order to be "dealt with administratively." "Furthermore, indemnification of the life-risks in question usually takes the *form of monetary compensation.*" Juridification is the sign of encroachment because of the organization of subsystems through formal law.   Examples of increasing juridification of social domains that depend on communicative action are schools and families. This is the reason that educational and family policies have been prominent areas of political conflict.

In this way welfare policy mediatizes the contexts in which life is lived and makes sense; it undermines social integration by simultaneously individualizing, formalizing, and monetarizing aspects of life that depend on processes of understanding through communicative action. "The formalization of relationships in family and school means, for those concerned, an objectivization and *removal from the lifeworld* of (now) formally regulated social interaction in family and school. As legal subjects they encounter one another in an objectivizing, success-oriented attitude."[98] The consequence is the rise of "functional disturbances." These can be avoided only if certain areas of social life are protected from mediatization of action.

Habermas argues that the lifeworld of advanced capitalist societies is therefore endangered in two ways. First, it is endangered through "systemically induced reification" caused by media overflowing their bounds in material production. Secondly, it is endangered because of "cultural impoverishment" which results from the locking up of cultural rationalization in "expert cultures."   Everyday life has to try to get by with "traditionalist leftovers," with the "second nature" of traditions that have lost their force due to cultural rationalization.[99]

> Everyday consciousness sees itself thrown back on traditions whose claims to validity have already been suspended; where it does escape the spell of traditionalism, it is hopelessly splintered. In place of "false consciousness" we today have a "fragmented consciousness" that blocks enlightenment by the mechanism of reification. It is only with this that the conditions for a *colonization of the lifeworld* are met. . . . [L]ike colonial masters coming into a tribal society—[media] force a process of assimilation upon it. The diffused perspectives of the local culture cannot be sufficiently coordinated to permit the play of the metropolis and the world market to be grasped from the periphery.[100]

The dynamic of advanced capitalism results in widespread attempts to restore identity and meaning. These resources are not forthcoming because of the only partial rationalization of the lifeworld, therefore subsystems are able to colonize the lifeworld. This threatens the integrity of the life-world itself by assimilating to media the communicative structures that alone can reproduce the lifeworld. "[P]henomena of alienation and the unsettling of collective identity emerge."[101]

Habermas's analysis provides a basis for comprehending the many social struggles resisting these developments. "The issue is not primarily one of compensations that the welfare state can provide, but of defending and restoring endangered ways of life."[102] He refers to a "silent revolution" in values and attitudes, a "new politics" raising issues of "quality of life, equal rights, individual self-realization, participation, and human rights," even "cultural revolution."[103] Unlike the politics of production and distribution, this new movement is based on the participation of the new middle classes, youth, and the educated. "These phenomena tally with my thesis regarding internal colonization."

With this, a new line of conflict has emerged between the core strata directly involved in production and the welfare-state compromise, on the one hand, and the "variegated array of groups" on the "periphery," on the other. He mentions the antinuclear, peace, environmental, single-issue, local, squatter, commune, minority, fundamentalist, tax protest, "psychoscene," school protest, religious/linguistic/cultural, "and finally, women's" movements. Basically, he includes all movements not associated with the welfare state compromise and productivism. These groups proliferate in advanced capitalist societies because of "the painful manifestations of deprivation in a culturally impoverished and one-sidedly rationalized practice of everyday life. For this reason, ascriptive characteristics such as gender, age, skin color, neighborhood or locality, and religious affiliation serve to build up and separate off communities, to establish subculturally protected communities supportive of the search for personal and collective identity."[104] Habermas calls this "the revaluation of the particular, the natural, the provincial." The thrust of these movements is to clear the ground for "counterinstitutions" that will set limits on systemic penetration. This includes a "politics of the first person" and attempts to create "liberated areas" where identities are formed outside the domains of employee and client.[105]

Critical social theory today must concentrate on comprehending the various dislocations of welfare state capitalism that engender these movements. The "modern project" that Habermas is trying to rescue from "a capering deconstructivism" is to preserve the differentiations of rationality but also link them to everyday practice. In order to discover ways of resisting colonization, we must develop a new kind of analysis. "Rather than hunting after the scattered traces of revolutionary consciousness, it would have to examine the conditions for recoupling a rationalized culture with an everyday communication dependent on vital traditions."[106] This is the guiding intention behind Habermas's political proposals.

POLITICAL PROJECTIONS

The traditional socialist response to these problems is to argue for the reabsorption of the subsystems into the lifeworld by abolishing media, i.e., by eliminating the market economy and by democratizing public administration. Habermas opposes this response, calling it the "de-differentiation" of modern society. Abolition of subsystems would sacrifice the advances in societal complexity that have increased the capacity of society to satisfy the demands of material production. Habermas continually reminds us that the real material successes of the welfare state have been accomplished through societal differentiation into subsystems.[107] Furthermore, these subsystems arose partly as an answer to the potential overburdening of the increased communicative necessities of the partially rationalized lifeworld. Attempts at de-differentiation would therefore not only sacrifice efficiency but also endanger the further rationalization of the lifeworld. Finally, Habermas rejects the alienation problematic that underlies the project of de-differentiation, the notion of reabsorbing estranged powers. Habermas argues that this theoretical approach does not have the conceptual tools to distinguish between the necessary societal differentiation that complements the rationalization of the lifeworld, on the one hand, and the decay of traditional forms of life, on the other. The unity of a modern differentiated society must therefore be established through other means.

The socialist project is further weakened by the effacement of classes in lifeworld experience. Class conflict has been tamed through the standard of living ensured by the welfare state. New social divisions are indeed engendered by welfare state policies but they are not directly determined by class structure in the realm of production. Reification therefore has "class-unspecific effects." These new divisions do not result in class-based actors, nor can they be ameliorated by class-based policies. For this reason Habermas argues, citing Offe, that abstract labor no longer structures society in that the welfare state provision of use-values provokes conflicts that cannot be traced back to class positions.[108] The traditional socialist response of workers's self-management is unpersuasive for related reasons. Advanced capitalism simply does not allow a place for workers's self-management, a proposal which Habermas calls "nostalgia."[109]   Arguments for self-management depend on the notion of a societal "macrosubject," a conception which has no reality in a complex, differentiated society.[110]

Habermas's analysis of advanced capitalism was inspired by the apparent "crumbling of the welfare-state compromise" in the 1970s, signaled by the rise of both neoconservativism and the new social movements.[111] His political project is an attempt to come to grips with both the strengths and weaknesses of the welfare state, strengths often denied in traditional socialist theory. Habermas states that the development of the welfare state was guided by "a *specific* utopian idea" which became practically effective through the labor movement. The welfare state transformed the usual socialist vision in that emancipated, humane living conditions were no longer seen as requiring the replacement of 'heteronomous' labor by self-directed activity. Rather, the touchstone of this utopian vision was full employment and the other policies which created clients of the welfare state. However, since the 1970s the limitations of the welfare state have become obvious, yielding the present uncertainty of direction, which Habermas dubs "the new obscurity."[112]

Habermas argues that there are two problems with the further use of the welfare state "to foster and to tame the quasi-natural process of capitalistic growth": first, it does not have the power; secondly, it does not have the appropriate means. The power of the welfare state is diminished (a) by the globalization of capital versus the national state, (b) by the resistance of investors, (c) because the welfare state *does* increase the costs of the "valorization of capital," and (d) in that it must operate within the constraints of the private property system. Its political base is now dissolving as some do well and ally themselves against the poor, i.e., as the productivist bloc becomes defensive against the excluded and as the weakened market position of labor unions encourages them to become narrowly defensive of the interests of the still-employed.[113]

The interventionist welfare state does not have the means because of its bureaucratic mode of operation. As argued above, this disrupts the life-world of the citizenry, even though, Habermas states, it has created a more just distribution than before. Power is simply not an "innocent medium," a fact which is unappreciated by many social reformers. "In short, inherent in the project of the social state is a contradiction between goal and method. . . . Producing new forms of life is beyond the capacities of political power."[114]

Habermas does not, for all this, consider the welfare state to have been an historical mistake. "On the contrary, its institutions constitute, in no less a measure than the organizations of the democratic constitutional state, an achievement of the political system, for which in societies of our type there is no recognizable alternative—either in regard to the functions fulfilled by the social welfare state, nor in regard to the normatively justified demands it satisfies." However, given the effects of colonization, he reaches essentially the same conclusion as Offe.

> It is specifically this lack of alternatives, perhaps even the irreversibility of the still-debated structures of the compromise, that today pose for us the following dilemma: developed forms of capitalism can just as little afford to live without the welfare state as to live with its further expansion. The more or less befuddled reactions to this dilemma show that the political potential of the utopian laboring society to stimulate new suggestions is exhausted.[115]

Social Democrats typically react to this dilemma by defending the legitimacy of the welfare state, attempting to fine-tune the balance and restore equilibrium. They do not recognize the depth of the resistance to bureaucratization nor fully comprehend the waning of their political base.

Neoconservatives, on the other hand, have developed a different project comprised of supply-side economics to restore investment, neo-corporatism to reduce demands on government and eliminate ungovernability, and a cultural struggle against intellectuals purveying values perceived as obstructive of this project as a whole. This cultural strategy is reinforced by the promotion of patriotism, traditional values, etc., to "compensate for personal burdens on one's private life."[116] Habermas contends that the neoconservatives could actually succeed if "social darwinism" is persuasive and the excluded consequently ignored or repressed. This is a real possibility because, as in the periphery, the poor are no longer necessary for capitalist reproduction. However, the project would still leave important problems, because: "Such a decisive renunciation of the welfare state (class) compromise would have to leave gaps in the state's ability to function that could be closed only through repression or neglect."[117]

A third response to the dilemmas of the welfare state is the critique of growth by the new social movements. Habermas argues that the social democrats and neoconservatives are united in their acceptance of the idea that a balance can be restored between state and economy. The first group believes the problem is the unbridled economy; the latter thinks the problem is the unbridled state. Both assume that the lifeworld will be undamaged by these subsystems if this balance is found. In this way, social democrats and neoconservatives simply shuffle problems back and forth between the market and administration. On the other hand, new social movements recognize that social problems arise as a consequence of both "commodification and bureaucratization."[118] It is from reflection on these movements that Habermas derives an alternative political project.

The primary issue must be to correct the selective rationalization embodied in capitalist modernization which leads to colonization. Habermas therefore proposes the establishment of a new "balance of powers" (or "separation of powers") of the three types of social cohesion in advanced capitalism: money, power, and "solidarity" that comes from the securing of identity.[119] Habermas describes this new balance of subsystems and lifeworld in various ways: "democratic blocking," "restraining barriers," "indirect regulation" of the market, "curbing" both the market and administration, "socially contained" administration, struggle over "borders," control from "the outside" or "above," fight against the "demoralization of public conflicts," bring subsystems "into dependence on lifeworld imperatives," assert the "practically oriented demands of the lifeworld," and "modify the imperatives" coming from the subsystems.[120] Habermas argues that this project is a continuation of the Marxian tradition. In his interpretation, Marxism does not take the "dependence of the superstructure on the base" to be an "ontological constant" but "simultaneously explains and denounces this dependence."[121] He further argues that this project has the same intention that Marx expressed in *Capital* and elsewhere as the separation of the realm of freedom from the realm of necessity. "System and lifeworld appear in Marx under the metaphors of the 'realm of necessity' and the 'realm of freedom.' The socialist revolution is to free the latter from the dictates of the former."[122]

Crucial to this new balance is the further rationalization of the lifeworld. As stated above, this requires overcoming the dessication of everyday cultural life by freeing the cognitive potentials for cultural rationalization that have been locked up in expert cultures. Gaining access to these resources must be accomplished without destroying the differentiation of the three cultural value spheres or dispersing their contents. In Habermas's specifically political proposals, this is narrowed down to the institutionalization of moral-practical rationality.

The proposed institutionalization of moral-practical rationality is the fruit of Habermas's vigorous efforts to establish through the theory of communicative action that moral questions allow of rational argument. If moral positions do not allow of rational argument, then Weber's "polytheism" or "struggles" of "gods and demons" is inescapable. Habermas develops a self-described "cognitivist ethicist" position that tries to not prejudge the "good life" but nevertheless insists that certain principles—

specifically universalistic principles that are expressed in a theory of justice—must be included in all defensible forms of the good life.

The goal of institutionalizing moral-practical rationality resolves itself into the institutionalization of a kind of radical democracy. This radical democracy must limit itself in two ways. First, it must not be embodied in formal organizations because it would then fall prey to the medium of power. Its organizational forms must increase the capacity for collective action yet remain "below the threshold at which organizational goals become detached from the orientations and attitudes of organization members and become dependent on the self-maintenance imperatives of autonomous organizations."[123] Informal organizations pioneered by the new social movements have indicated the way. Secondly, it must be self-limiting in that it cannot seek the de-differentiation or absorption of subsystems. Habermas describes it as an attempt to continue the welfare state "at a higher level of reflection."[124] "The same combination of power and intelligent self-restraint that marks the political strategies of careful limitation and indirect regulation of capitalist growth needs to be taken back behind the lines of administrative planning."[125]

This new balance of power can be achieved by building up the resource of solidarity. Solidarity is the "measure" of social integration.

> The social integration of the lifeworld . . . takes care of coordinating actions by way of legitimately regulated interpersonal relations and stabilizes the identity of groups to an extent sufficient for everyday practice. The coordination of actions and the *stabilization of group identities* are measured by the *solidarity* among members.[126]

To the extent that the lifeworld is rationalized, there is a structural differentiation of processes of normative cohesion (social integration) from culture and personality, and a distancing of the form of legal and moral principles from the content of "concrete forms of life." Habermas argues that solidarity has been undermined by the collapse of traditional normative cohesion and also by the disappearance of class identities in the lifeworld.[127] The partial rationalization of the lifeworld is therefore itself one of the causes of the weakening of solidarity. Under these conditions—and in order to retain the gains of the structural differentiation of the lifeworld—solidarity must be reestablished through the institutionalization of rational discourses that can develop "the communicative force of production."[128] In a rationalized lifeworld, this can only be achieved by securing identities that are partly but crucially developed through a discourse on justice.

Habermas clarifies his previous argument regarding "generalizable interests" in a way that is quite similar to Offe's recent reflections on democratic preference formation. What is required is a public space for the "shared, reciprocal taking over of perspectives." "Justice and solidarity are two sides of the same coin" in that each one's voice is heard, thereby satisying "an individualistic understanding of equal rights" while also maintaining a sense of "belonging to an unlimited community of communication." "Only with the securing of the existence of the communication community, which demands of everyone, in the ideal assumption of roles, an unselfish, empathetic activity, can those relations of reciprocal recognition be reproduced, without which even the identity of each individual would disintegrate."[129] Importantly, Habermas insists that such argumentation is not a "decision procedure" leading to "resolutions"; it is a "procedure for resolving problems that leads to *convictions*."[130]

Habermas acknowledges that universalistic principles cannot create identities, which must always be situated and concrete. He therefore recognizes Hegel's criticism of Kant's universalism, that ethical identities must be grounded in on-going communities, as *Sittlichkeit*.[131] However, he states that there must be a "universalist core" to these concrete identities for this political project to succeed. Otherwise, radical democracy will result in a "generalized particularism."[132] He reinforces the discussion in *Legitimation Crisis* by insisting that universalistic principles are unavoidable in modern societies. These societies "can no longer be immunized against rational demands for legitimation. . . . If there is one thing that makes our neo-conservatives wild, it is this."[133] He nonetheless recognizes that legitimacy requires more than a naked universalism and that these discourses will at least require further "discourses of application" or "appropriateness."[134] This universalist core could be developed in the various social and political movements.

On the model of welfare state indirect intervention into the market, we must now curb, without destroying, media-steered administration. The resuscitated public sphere must focus on "influencing" the administration, which is also the key to sensitizing the economy to the needs of the lifeworld.[135] This goal requires counterposing "communicatively generated power" to administrative power that rests on extracting consent in the form of "mass loyalty."[136]

> The power produced through communicative action can exert an influence on the foundations of the evaluative and decision-making processes of public administration, without wanting to take them over altogether, so as to bring its normative demands to

bear in the only language that the besieged stronghold under-
stands: it cultivates the range of arguments that, though treated
instrumentally by administrative power, cannot be ignored by it,
in as much as administrative power is conceived along constitutional lines.[137]

We can influence administration through threats of "delegitimation."[138]
Habermas argues that subsystems cannot be completely uncoupled from
the lifeworld. Subsystems are anchored in the lifeworld by the fact that
they are formally organized through law. This is true of the monetary subsystem but is even more important for the medium of power. Unlike market
exchanges regulated by money, where actors are putatively equal, power in
administration disadvantages the subordinates and is therefore in need of
more immediate legitimation. Even if particular laws are conceived in a
decisionistic manner (as neutrally absorbing uncertainty), the legal system
from which they proceed must still be legitimated. In the normal course of
legal regulation the question of the legitimacy of the legal system as a
whole is "suspended," resulting in obedience on the basis of an implicit
promise that the legal system could be legitimated if called into question.
Habermas calls this suspension of the question of legitimation "second-
order traditionalism." However suspension is not abolition of the promise,
which may need to be redeemed under certain circumstances. The administrative subsystem will accept this legitimation as the limiting presuppositions of its activity. In this way, communicatively generated legitimacy,
rationally grounded in the general interest—or, failing that, in compromises grounded in universalistic procedures—combats administrative power
based on extracted mass loyalty.

Administration influences the results of a media-steered economy by
infrastructural investment, subsidies to specific industries it wants to encourage, tax penalties for practices it wishes to discourage, and broader
fiscal means. It thereby adjusts the "boundaries" within which the subsystem functions without disrupting the internal operation of the subsystem.
Habermas is now suggesting a similar approach to the colonizing administrative subsystem. We can alter the premises of its action without disrupting steering via the medium of power by reinvigorating and reformulating
the normative legal basis on which it operates. The analogy ends here,
however, because the mode of blocking the colonizing effects of administration, unlike the mode of administrative intervention in the economy,
cannot be accomplished by introducing yet another steering medium. "If
this 'regulation,' applied so very indirectly, is now supposed to extend to
the organizational performances of the state, the mode of influence may

not be specified again as indirect steering, for a new *steering* potential could only be furnished by *another* subsystem." An additional steering medium would simply intensify the colonization effects on the lifeworld. As Habermas expresses it, *"perceptions of crises in the lifeworld* cannot be translated without remainder into *systems-related problems of steering*."[139] Since we cannot solve the problem through additional steering, we must try to influence the dynamic of administration by transforming the type of legitimacy on which it now depends. Rather than mass loyalty procured by the administration through consumer goods, the clientelization of the citizen, and the dessication of politics through formal democracy, the institutionalization of a public sphere based on "free-floating communication" develops legitimacy based on generalizable interests and, where such an interest is lacking, on just compromises. In this way we again place in the forefront the issue of legitimacy—communicatively generated power— that is usually suspended by the administration but can never be eliminated insofar as the administration rests on constitutional, normative grounds, i.e., is anchored in the lifeworld. Habermas argues that this alters the context within which administrative decisionmaking operates, constraining it without disrupting its internal workings through the power medium. Subsystems only react to changes in their environments and therefore we influence them by altering their environments through the invigoration of normative, universalist discourse through the public sphere. We thereby "sensitize the self-steering mechanisms of the state and the economy to the goal-oriented outcomes of radical democratic will formation."

Habermas insists that this articulation of legitimacy through discourse in the public sphere be distinguished from legal "political *will-formation*."[140] Discourse can only unfold if it is not conflated with decision-making: it must be "unsubverted by power." Habermas is quite aware, however, that, "Discourses do not govern." Therefore, these discourses must somehow be connected with will-formation without being conflated with the latter.[141]

First of all, this requires an open break with the traditional imagery of revolutionary theory. The fact that complex modern societies lack "both summit and center" poses a problem for any conception of social consciousness as the "self-reflection of a societal macrosubject."[142] "Under these changed premises, there is no equivalent for the philosophy of the subject's model of self-influence in general and for the Hegelian-Marxist understanding of revolutionary action in particular."[143] Therefore, the radical democracy proposed by Habermas will actually be a kind of subjectless communication originating in various informal organizations diversely organized. In this way the pluralism of modernized lifeworlds—encouraged by the increasing structural differentiation of the lifeworld (the attenuation of the connections between culture, social identity, and personality), the abstract character of norms with the displacement of traditional understandings, cultural differentiation, and reactive identity formations—can be bridged.

> Even in modern societies, a diffuse common consciousness takes shape from the polyphonous and obscure projections of the totality. This common consciousness can be concentrated and more clearly articulated around specific themes and ordered contributions; it achieves greater clarity in the higher-level, concentrated communicative processes of a public sphere.[144]

Again, this public sphere will not attempt to steer society. As stated, power itself cannot bring forth "new forms of life" because it is a medium.[145] Public spheres will only bring rational normative considerations to bear on existing media-steered systems through indirect means. Presumably they will also try to free learning potentials through institutionalizing an arena in which expert cultures can be brought into everyday practice, although this part of Habermas's argument is submerged in the more directly political parts of his work. This renewed public sphere will seek to achieve "rational will-formation" through moral-practical discourse, with only a "virtual subject" that will influence administration and, through it, the economy. Solidarity will affect subsystem direction the way state administration affects the working of the market: through boundary manipulation to alter the shape of the field within which decisions are made without disrupting the media steering in each subsystem. Only this strategy will strengthen the communicative resources of the lifeworld without endangering the gains from social complexity, without destroying the structural differentiations of the rationalized lifeworld, and without adding to the burdens of colonization.

Although the long-term changes he envisions would be revolutionary, Habermas is firmly opposed to any idle talk about revolution. The complexity of modern societies requires caution. "One who uses the word 'revolutionary' in more than a metaphorical sense has to acknowledge that with the incalculability of interventions into deep-seated structures of highly complex societies, the risk of catastrophic alternatives ensuing also grows. To be sure, defeatism would be the wrong consequence to draw from this."[146] In one place Habermas even says that: "For academics, revolution is a notion of the nineteenth century."[147] He wants to rescue the intentions behind the socialist project but also make them compatible with the continued existence of complex society, of societies differentiated into media-steered subsystems. Habermas is particularly concerned that the socialist project not become idle moralism, a purely normative "ideal opposing an opaque reality." To avoid this, socialist arguments need to be reformulated as the "radically reformist self-criticism" of advanced capitalism.[148]

The prospects for success are uncertain. Social darwinism is a very powerful interpretation of society propagated by the right, and the isolation of the marginal, the impoverished, and the unemployed appears to be a successful strategy. The fundamentalism of the new social movements (the "Great Refusal") obstructs their alliance with social-democratic forces, without which, as Habermas says, "if we are realistic about it, nothing can be moved."[149]   However, Habermas says that one must not be concerned with conveying optimism or pessimism. The most that can be developed from a theoretical point of view is delineating the necessary conditions for communicative practice and discursive will-formation, to "put participants *themselves* in a position to actualize concrete possibilities for a better and less endangered life, in accord with their *own* needs and insights, and on their *own* initiative." The danger does not lie in utopia but only in too concrete a specification; at most we should show the conditions of a "highly developed communicative infrastructure of *possible* forms of life."[150] Anything else would contradict the radical democratic project itself.

REASON WITHOUT REVOLUTION?

In regard to our central topic, Habermas rejects the formation of class actors on grounds that are quite familiar. Like others, Habermas argues that individuals do not significantly forge their identities on the basis of their place in production. Various public policies create other bases for identity in advanced capitalism and efface the importance of place in production. Habermas frequently suggests, as do Jean Cohen and Andre Gorz, that production and identity should never have been theoretically linked in the analysis of capitalism in the first place. Consequently, Habermas rejects any notion of the working class as an inherently revolutionary subject. He says that he does not "dream of a revolutionary subject" of any sort and even argues that the rejection of the working class as the privileged subject of enlightenment has freed social theory for a more nuanced and rigorous analysis of contemporary capitalism and its sites of contestation.[151]

Building on his agreement with aspects of systems theory, Habermas rejects "macro-subjects" altogether. Instead, Habermas argues that we must pursue "the fundamental materialist question of how a differentiated social system that lacks both summit and center might still organize itself, once one can no longer imagine the 'self' of self-organization embodied in the form of macro-subjects such as the social classes of theories of class, or the people of popular sovereignty."[152] Suffice it to say, this is a complete rejection of any lingering romantic notions of world-historical subjects, the proletariat or the people. In a way Anthony Giddens's complaint that Habermas's theory lacks a "core" is affirmed here.[153]

The rejection of the proletarian macro-subject is of course the dominant theme of recent socialist theory. The crucial issue is whether Habermas rejects not only class formation but also any conceptionalization of capitalism itself as a class structured society. Habermas persistently empties the concept class of its contents. Besides the panoply of welfare state policies affecting life chances, many of the pressing concerns of citizens of advanced capitalist societies are the urban environment, nuclear energy, the possibility of war, and ecological issues, that is, they are issues that cut across class in affecting the conditions of life. Of course it is also an arguable position that these issues are primarily determined by the economic dynamic of advanced capitalism but these issues are not connected to differing life chances depending on production. Habermas further distances capitalism from class concepts by his view that economic growth is a consequence of the growth and application of politically supported scientific knowledge. Growth of science and technology are not only not fettered by capitalist relations of production but in fact are the privileged form of rationalization selected by capitalism.

Although Habermas bases his normative critique of capitalism on the suppression of generalizable interests, because of the considerations above he pointedly refuses the working class the role of bearer of these interests. "What today separates us from Marx are evident historical truths, for example that in the developed capitalist societies there is no identifiable class, no clearly circumscribed social group which could be singled out as the representative of a general interest that has been violated."[154] This is a part of his open and repeated rejections of the "productivist paradigm" and the utopia of a laboring society.[155]

Nevertheless, Habermas's alternative of "radical reformist" criticism leaves many crucial questions unanswered. There is a nagging ambiguity regarding the goals of radical will-formation and how discourse is to be connected with decisionmaking without conflating discourse and decision. Habermas's project can be clarified somewhat if we keep in mind its negative direction: we must limit, defend borders, check, etc. This is the implication of the proposal for a separation and balance of powers and is also in accord with the largely negatively expressed demands of social movements, as noted by Offe. However, Habermas is clearly uncomfortable with a merely defensive project and speaks of bringing system mechanisms back into "the horizon of the lifeworld."[156] He also acknowledges that the public spaces must still ultimately be connected to traditional democratic institutions, a position that brings him closer to traditional socialism.[157]

This could be understood in the following way. Habermas's point is that it is not another instrumental action that we want to further. Instead, we need to restore the lifeworld by protecting its reproductive processes from further erosion by media. To do this we must strengthen solidarity through communication in the public sphere. This will avoid social crisis, properly so-called, which only takes place in the lifeworld. When he writes of "strengthen[ing] the collective capacity for action" this only refers to the lifeworld's capacity for action. It is not intended to contradict the position that there is no capacity to control a differentiated society in its entirety. There is no macro-subject that could be the agency of such action.

However on this interpretation, the defensive nature of the project, its eschewing of instrumental goals in favor of communicative action, makes it appear empty in crucial respects. It opens Habermas's theory to the charge of *politique pour la politique* that is often leveled against Hannah Arendt's political vision.[158] The typical response to this charge is that this criticism relies on an instrumentalist conceptualization of politics, politics as making something. That is, there is a debilitating confusion here between *praxis* and *techne*. Therefore, Habermas is at least pointing out, yet again, that politics cannot be reduced to instrumental activity because social life cannot be reproduced solely through instrumentalism.

However, and this is the complaint variously articulated by sympathetic and less sympathetic critics alike, neither can politics exclude an instrumental dimension.[159]   Although we may not be able to influence administration and the economy directly, we do want to influence them. The recurring question is, in which direction and to what extent must we influence administration and the economy to achieve our goals of restoring the integrity of the lifeworld? The underlying ambivalence of specific formulations by Habermas stems from the recognition that a purely defensive project cannot be sustained without neglecting his own insights into the origins of the dilemmas of the welfare state.

This ambiguity has been extended, not reduced, by the large critical commentary on Habermas's theory. The chief problem with this program is stated bluntly by Giddens. "Aspects of the lifeworld have to be defended against the encroachments of political and economic steering-mechanisms. But how can such a defense be achieved without transforming those mechanisms themselves?"[160] In contrast, Albrecht Wellmer dismisses any strategy that would propose the triumph of the lifeworld over the system because in complex advanced societies system integration is necessary to help carry the load of "action coordination." In attempting to reiterate Habermas's position, Wellmer notes that the systemic mechanisms need to be anchored in the lifeworld. "Systemic integration, on the other hand, needs to be institutionalized and thereby anchored in the life-world: it *presupposes* forms of social integration and a legitimation of basic laws and institutions."[161] However, unsurprisingly Wellmer finds it difficult to stay with a project of mere anchoring, and seems to move in the same sentence from lifeworld autonomy to lifeworld triumph over the system. "Habermas reinterprets Marx's idea of an emancipated society: in an emancipated society the life-world would no longer be subjected to the imperatives of system maintenance; a rationalized life-world would rather subject the systemic mechanisms to the needs of the associated individuals."[162] Wellmer concludes by speaking of ending the dependence of the superstructure on the base and suggests that this project could perhaps still be called socialism.[163] The uncertainties of the project are simply restated.

It may help clarify the proposed relation between lifeworld and system if we briefly indicate the differences between Habermas and Arendt. Both attempt to resuscitate the noninstrumental aspects of public life for the same broad reason: they both believe that instrumentalist politics weakens the meaningfulness of life. However Arendt's theory focuses on human action, which does not allow her to entirely eliminate instrumental action without persisting ambiguities in her theory as a whole. On the other hand, Habermas's employment of systems theory, especially the concept of media, provides him with the conceptual means to relegate the instrumental dimension of social life to autonomous subsystems. The persuasiveness of his theory, then, depends on whether this specific compartmentalization of instrumental action and the communicative action which produces solidarity and meaning can be sustained.

The chief instrumental action of politics is material production and it this that Habermas relegates to autonomous subsystems. He has several reasons for doing so. First, Habermas repeatedly states the superior efficiency of media-steered subsystems—both the market and administration—for coordinating social activity in this domain. Secondly, he argues that rationalization of the lifeworld more and more requires achieved consensus through interpretive accomplishments by the participants, necessitating an unburdening of social communication. This is accomplished by turning over the coordination of certain areas of social activity to coordination by media. Thirdly, Habermas is convinced that class identifications have largely been eliminated from lifeworld experience by the activities of the welfare state, such that reification now manifests itself in class unspecific ways. In one place he even extends this anonymity of advanced capitalism to global capitalist processes. "Today, the agent of the expansion that Marx put so squarely on the map, is of course no longer the bourgeoisie of 1848; no longer a class that rules within national limits but rather an anonymous, internationally operating economic system that has ostensibly severed any ties it might once have had with an identifiable class structure."[164] It appears that, nationally and internationally, capitalism has become an anonymous, media-steered juggernaut.

This relegation of instrumental action to subsystems also informs Habermas's view of the type of normative grounding now needed by critical theory itself. Classical "ideology critique" was based on tracing social disruptions and disparities to the gap between ideals and action, a gap necessitated by social power based on nongeneralizable interests. Without an identifiable bourgeois class interest institutionalized in the social system and available to the lifeworld, this normative approach is displaced for three reasons. First, ideology critique has no place in a pluralistic situation tending toward relativism—where "consciousness turns cynical"[165]—and where a "philosophy of history" has collapsed. Secondly, ideology critique could only be socially effective where an audience of "political groups within the European working class movement" could orient their practice by it.[166] Thirdly, Marxists have been unable to "cash out" the expression 'socialism,' paradoxically because of an overly concrete guiding notion.[167] Given the pluralism of modern societies, moral theory must not attempt to project concrete notions of the good life but must confine itself to infusing existing social identities with universalistic principles. In this situation, the normative basis of critical theory must shift to an uncovering and analysis of those processes that obstruct the actualization of the universalistic presuppositions of rational consensus through discourse.

The key to Habermas's criticism of traditional socialist theory is the relegation of material production to subsystems. Unfortunately, the phrase material production is rarely given any specificity. In the places where he does mention specific administrative actions regarding the economy, the topics are infrastructural development, influencing business cycles, and protecting the legal requirements of market exchanges, none of which is contestable.[168] However, neither is this very illuminating. We need to further explore, e.g., the specific procedures of policy selection and implementation, as does Offe. These considerations complicate the explanation of administrative intervention and cannot be formulated solely through systems categories, especially that of a "media-steered" administration.[169]

To obscure matters even more, Habermas often refers to the crisis-ridden growth of the economy which must be moderated through administrative action. However he never adequately explains what causes these crises. In fact, this is a rather loose use of the term crisis itself, given his own theoretical strictures that crises can only properly be experienced in the lifeworld. For consistency he should only use the word "disequilibria."

The abstractness of Habermas's characterization of material production is directly a consequence of his adoption of systems theory. Thomas McCarthy has questioned this theoretical move, pointing out among other things that Habermas seems to have forgotten his own previous criticisms of the aridity of systems theory. For example, Habermas earlier criticized Parsons's theory of a "ridiculous imbalance between the towering mass of empty categorial boxes and the slim empirical content they accommodate."[170] McCarthy argues that it is not obvious why we need systems theory to get at the functional imperatives within society. He further argues that Habermas's adoption of systems theory makes it difficult for Habermas to specify his political proposals.[171] This leaves the puzzle of why Habermas has so thoroughly utilized systems-theoretic concepts in his mature social theory.

McCarthy believes that Habermas is attracted to systems theory because of its "theoretical virtuosity," however unfruitful it has proven to be in application.[172] However, it is clear that Habermas is also attracted to systems theory (1) because conceptualizing media as "delinguistified" action coordination provides an immediate contrast to linguistic (communicative) coordination, (2) in order to demonstrate the differentiation of societal processes of reproduction and thereby disabuse us of the notion of a societal (or social class) macrosubject, and (3) because he believes that a persuasive social theory must show its penetration by connecting its perspective and themes with the themes of other social theories, a goal he expresses as "a history of theory with a systemic intent."[173] Habermas specifically states that the latter was Parsons's own conception of social theory, with which Habermas clearly at least partly agrees.[174] Nevertheless, the abstractness of Habermas's account of material production creates doubts as to whether he has actually accomplished a critique of functionalist reason, in the specific sense of the word critique. He has indeed theorized the conditions of emergence of this kind of reason but he has only revealed some of its limitations.

The problem is that one cannot specify material production without including in one's theory the specific structures of private appropriation of socialized production (e.g., corporations), the structures and conscious strategies of transnational corporations, the structure of bureaucratic regulatory agencies, the structures and strategies of international development agencies, and the planned interventions of nation-states reacting to world market pressures. At the very least these are the pulleys and wheels over which the media of money and power move. In addition, such a theory would have to confront tendencies toward concentration of ownership and other topics long central, for good reason, to Marxian analysis. This would substantially corrupt Habermas's portrayal of the economy as an autonomous subsystem steered by media that only interacts with other areas of society as objectified 'environments.' McCarthy points out that Marx actually theorized the "internal workings and endogenously generated problems" of capitalism whereas systems theory only comprehends problems under the rubric of environmental "frictions" (Habermas's word).[175] We can also add that Habermas's own discussion of these problems in The *Theory of Communicative Action* falls below the specificity attained in *Legitimation Crisis*.

A related problem with the systems approach and a source of ambiguity is Habermas's uncertainty on whether systems processes can actually be understood from within the lifeworld. Various passages quoted above suggest that they cannot be, which is why systems theory had to be developed. On the other hand, Habermas sometimes suggests that subsystem activities and functions can indeed be brought into the lifeworld and that this is necessary if we are to exert any influence at all. McCarthy has again indicated the crucial ambiguity of Habermas on this point but Dieter Misgeld has more forcefully argued that there is a major epistemological problem of the systems approach as utilized by Habermas: how can we know about the workings of material production unless these can be brought into the lifeworld in some manner?[176] The alternative is to regard systems functions in the quasi-religious fashion of Friedrich Hayek: "It was men's submission to the impersonal forces of the market that in the past has made possible the growth of a civilization which without this could not have developed; it is by thus submitting that we are every day helping to build something that is greater than any one of us can fully comprehend."[177] Habermas could not agree with this position, partly because collective knowledge can arise on an intersubjective basis which, although not completely transparent to individuals nor completely clear, can serve for a generalized societal capacity for reflection. However, Habermas's systems-theoretic conception of autonomous media-steered subsystems sometimes comes too close to the hopelessly abstract vision of classical liberalism.

The abstractions of systems theory exclude one key relation in material production from view: social classes. If we at least grant that the structures of the economic and administrative subsystems themselves affect the coursing of media and therefore must be further specified to fully explain media dynamics, we can also grant that the elimination of class from social consciousness does not entail that class structures are irrelevant for analyzing the disequilibria of subsystems. A distinction between class relations (in subsystems) and class formation (in the lifeworld) can be renewed once again from this perspective. Habermas himself specifically criticizes both Parsons and Luhmann for neglecting class structure. For example, Habermas argues that Parsons's focus on the "integrative subsystem" privileges moral and legal development, "whereas the dynamics of the material reproduction of the lifeworld recede into the background, and with them the conflicts that arise from class structures and the political order."[178] He is even less equivocal regarding Luhmann's theory. After criticizing Marx for the alienation problematic that conflates societal differentiation with class division, he turns to Luhmann.

> Luhmann commits a complementary error. Faced with the new level of the differentiation of systems, he overlooks the fact that media such as money and power, via which functional systems set themselves off from the lifeworld, have in turn to be institutionalized in the lifeworld. This is why the class-specific distributive effects of the media's being anchored in property laws and constitutional norms do not come into view at all.[179]

Unfortunately, most of the time the same criticism could be leveled against his own theory. McCarthy is correct in stating that Habermas cannot convincingly explain why the colonization built on the ever-increasing density of bureaucratic activity need occur unless he were to discuss endogenous problems and structures more fully.[180]

This criticism must be qualified with the phrase "most of the time" because Habermas does frequently mention the continuing relevance of class structuration of material production even if these structures do not find expression in lifeworld experience, i.e., class formation in the usual sense of the phrase. For example, besides the many references in *Legitimation Crisis* to "latent classes," "latently continuing class struggle," or "class contradictions yielding class un-specific effects," we find similar statements in the later work *The Theory of Communicative Action*. In attempting to explain what sets in motion the monetary-bureaucratic complex, he mentions such causes as "containment of class conflict," "pathological side effects of a class structure," "dynamics of class opposition" that call forth bureaucratic measures with class un-specific effects, "pacifying the class conflict," and "social burdens resulting from class conflict."[181]

This does not present an immediate inconsistency in Habermas's theory because the "social antagonism bred by private disposition over the means of producing social wealth" has been pacified by the actions of the welfare state. Class structures exist but their force is blunted by the successful interception of the disequilibria they cause. It is for this reason that Habermas can argue that struggles over distribution and the "doctrinal significance" of "forms of ownership" have lost their currency.[182] We can nonetheless maintain, as in our discussion of Offe, that the way in which class relations set in train the interventionist and compensatory policies of the welfare state needs further explanation.

This is a rather pressing omission in Habermas's theory for the simple reason that his analysis of social conflict is predicated on the idea that the welfare state will survive. As he states, the crucial requirement is "that the social security system continues to hold good."[183] However, we have already seen that Habermas provides much evidence that the welfare state compromise is "crumbling." Habermas argues that the welfare state is in trouble partly because of the resistance of the bourgeoisie, groups whose identities and activities are at least partly rooted in the class structure, even if he describes these groups more anonymously. He frequently traces difficulties, quite correctly, to "the opposition of private investors," or "subjective perception of business interests."[184] He argues that the welfare state is hampered by the need to redistribute funds in a way that "barely touches the class-specific structure of property, particularly the distribution of the private ownership of the means of production." Habermas returns to these arguments again and again to show the limits of the "neo-Keynesian" strategies on which the welfare state compromise is constructed.

The major domestic problem of the welfare state is that it simply cannot produce enough jobs. More precisely, the labor market can no longer distribute labor appropriately to perform needed societal tasks.[185] As argued above, the strategy of neo-conservatives is to withdraw the state from this role and reduce legitimacy problems through social Darwinism, thereby marginalizing the unemployed.[186] We will ignore the fact that the rise of social Darwinism indicates the continuing relevance of *ideology critique.* The important point here is that Habermas himself argues that if this strategy is successful, struggles over distribution, theoretically laid to rest in *The Theory of Communicative Action,* will resurface. "It is obvious that neo-Keynesian economic policies are no longer sufficient to ensure the growth which is necessary to secure full employment, and to inhibit conflicts over distribution."[187] If the welfare state crumbles, these endogenous problems of capitalism, revolving around class structure, will lead to "some variant of traditional conflicts."[188]

With this topic, additional considerations emerge. Most importantly, it is fairly clear that the central factor for analyzing the prospects of the welfare state will be how global capitalism develops. There is no question that neo-conservatives utilize the pressures of globalism to reinforce their domestic agenda but the pressures are nonetheless real. In fact it is arguable that many of the defensive identity movements we are presently witnessing partly result from different countries attempting to manage the impact of transnational capitalism. Nevertheless, regardless of a few ambiguous comments suggesting the contrary, Habermas believes that the pressures of globalism are overstated. "The idea that the capacity to compete on an international scale—whether in markets or in outer space—is indispensable for our very survival is one of those everyday certitudes in which systemic constraints are condensed."[189] He does not, however, argue the point. Habermas's theory largely disregards economic global considerations because his social theory is based on the domestic compromises that produced the welfare state. The idea, for example, that the welfare state was only possible because these countries stand at the pinnacle of an international division of labor 'does not come into view at all.' This leaves the puzzle of why only a few nations in the world have been able to construct such successful (for the moment) welfare states. It is unlikely that more time will change this situation for other countries. Although world-systems theorists have not yet convincingly demonstrated the relation between a few successful welfare states and the international division of labor, it is a more persuasive approach than that of categorizing global capitalist pressures as somehow avoidable.

Both Habermas and Offe make a major mistake in this regard. Both suggest that if class or labor is less important to lifeworld experience then the dynamic of social structuration and social movements must be located in other dimensions. However, even if classes are no longer a part of the lifeworld this does not mean that production is also displaced from explanation. Habermas forgets his own arguments that media have structure-forming significance. He is driven to this inconsistency because (like Arendt) he believes that problems of production can be bracketed due to the successes of capitalism. In this he is mistaken, as his own analysis of the crumbling of the welfare state compromise reveals.

The lack of integration of Habermas's analysis of the welfare state compromise with his portrayals of a welfare state compromise under attack by class-based neo-conservatives may partly be a consequence of historical dating. In the late 1970s it was quite unforeseen how intense, widespread, and enduring would be the attack. It may be that the inconsistencies in Habermas's work result from a kind of historical layering of different arguments that have not been fully articulated with each other. Whether they can be integrated is an open question, but it would definitely entail going beyond the systems theoretical treatment of material production.

The under-specification of material production in Habermas's theory also stems partly from the fact that he focuses on, to use his own distinction, the "logic of development" rather than the "dynamics of development."[190] He is perfectly aware of this limitation.

> Theories, especially those of Marxist inspiration, ultimately only prove their worth by making a contribution to the explanation of concrete historical processes. I myself find it unfortunate that for the last two decades (if one disregards some shorter political writings) my interest has been taken up exclusively with problems which can be characterized in a broad sense as problems of theory construction.[191]

Habermas insists on the distinction between logic and dynamics to avoid teleological conceptions of history. The distinction also allows him to avoid the problems of circularity that are endemic to loose functionalist explanations.[192] Finally, Habermas insists on the distinction in order to avoid, as he put it in another context, "swimming in a sea of historical contingencies."[193]

It would be misleading, however, to suggest that analyzing the logic of development does not help explain the dynamic of development. For Habermas, the logic of cultural development through communicative action creates structural resistances to mediatization, constraining further development the same way that the physical structure of a species limits its possible evolutionary direction. In *Legitimation Crisis* Habermas theorized that this limit comes from the need for rational justification of action which increases with the displacement of traditional understandings and consensus. In *The Theory of Communicative Action* he argues that the constraint is more broadly the general reproduction requirement of the lifeworld through communicative action. When societal processes try to overcome these constraints, pathologies occur. This is expressed in *Legitimation Crisis* as "systematically distorted communication"; in *The Theory of Communicative Action* as cultural dessication, fragmentation of consciousness, reactive identities, etc. Habermas argues that this sort of "structuralism" is necessary for comprehending the welfare state.[194]

Nevertheless, even though it contributes to explanation, Habermas's concentration on the logic of development also opens him up to a charge he made against Mead.

> The material reproduction of society—securing its physical maintenance both externally and internally—is blended out of the picture of society understood as a communicatively structured lifeworld. The neglect of economics, warfare, and the struggle for political power, the disregard for dynamics in favor of the logic of societal development are detrimental, above all, to Mead's reflections on social evolution.[195]

Habermas himself complains in places that "we lack convincing analyses" and there is a general absence of "economic analysis with a lasting political impact."[196] We can simply state here that it is unlikely that systems theory will be helpful in this regard due to its focus on environments rather than the internal structural problems of capitalism, national and international.

The dynamic of development must also be exposed if we are to give adequate content to Habermas's conception of radical democracy. The pluralistic institutionalization of "free-floating, public communication" as a check on a decentered social system is simply unpersuasive unless the instrumental dimension is restored to this project, wrested back from complete absorption in subsystems. Habermas argues quite rightly that decisions must be left to the participants themselves. However, we can give more content to this political project if we acknowledge the persistence of class structures and their importance for the specific dynamics of material production, public administration, and colonization. Placing the questions as clearly as possible is a necessary part of the enlightenment of the participants that Habermas has always argued is the responsibility of a critical social theory.[197] The separation of discourse and decision presents puzzles that can only be solved if we acknowledge that some instrumental decisions must take place. A focus on the endogenous problems of capitalism, not just systems environments, would undoubtedly reveal the necessity of removing class structures if there is to be any possibility of continuing "the welfare state, grown reflexive."

Habermas's reflections are of the utmost importance for rethinking the direction of socialist theory. He recently referred to himself as "the last Marxist" and in the same place spoke of the "Marxian tradition, which I've quite fiercely decided to defend as a still-meaningful enterprise."[198] However, Habermas also argues that a "research tradition only remains alive when it can prove the validity of its old intention in the light of new experiences; and this cannot be done without abandoning outdated theoretical contents."[199] It is a chastened Marxism that he is defending, grounded in the firm belief that a social theory oversteps its bounds if it attempts "to project desirable forms of life into the future, instead of criticizing existing forms of life."

As intriguing as his analysis of the welfare state is, three general weaknesses persist in the proposed political project as developed thus far. Systems theory cannot sufficiently specify the dynamic and endogenous problems of either a capitalist economy or the interventionist welfare state. If systems imperatives are to be blocked, the ways in which class structures affect media-steering in both the market and administration must be analyzed. Furthermore, law does not merely mark off domains of "norm-free sociality." Law alters the flow of media, argued by Paul Hirst in regard to laws that define what can properly be considered property and laws that create the fictitious individual, i.e., corporations.[200] This raises a different dimension of juridification that cannot be captured by systems theory.

A renewed public sphere is undoubtedly necessary to overcome the fragmentation of consciousness that obstructs a vigorous response to systems imperatives. However, secondly, if we are to do away with the "fetishism of the labor market," the instrumental dimension of connecting discourse with binding decisions must be broached. Otherwise these public spaces will simply be overrun or impotent, as Nancy Fraser suggests.[201] "Cultural revolution" has never been enough. It must also be recognized that the Polish Solidarity movement's strategy of "intelligent self-restraint" could not be sustained in the long run.[202] Both this and the preceding weakness can only be remedied by unpacking the meaning of the metaphor "anchoring."

Finally, the welfare state's displacement of economic problems into the political and normative spheres must be reconsidered in the context of the globalization of capitalism. If capitalism has systemic imperatives, they now play themselves out on a global stage. World-system theory is the best-known attempt to analyze capitalism as such a transnational system. It is here that the system escapes the lifeworld if anywhere. We need to supplement Habermas's analyses of systemic colonization of the lifeworld with the historical effects of real colonization of nations and the continuing national lifeworld reactions against such colonization. We also need to observe the dynamic of contemporary capitalism from the perspective of those parts of the system where material progress has never been assured, to say the least.

Seven

World-System Theory and the Direct Producers: The Perspective of Immanuel Wallerstein

And mobilising ..

Class is a concept for analyzing social structure and the likely sites and issues of social conflict. In the preceding discussion the society to which
this concept is applied is the individual nation-state. The focus on nation-
states presumes that the primary unit of analysis of class structure and social conflict is the individual society, more or less coterminous with the
boundaries of the nation-state. World-system theory, especially the work
of its exemplar Immanuel Wallerstein, challenges this assumption by ques-
tioning our typical notion of society. In this way it provokes a fresh look at
the configuration of class relations, the multiple fracture lines of advanced
capitalism, and the classical Marxian theses regarding the future of capitalism. World-system theory forces us to consider the degree to which the
alleged eclipse of the importance of class structure and class identity in advanced capitalism may be merely a provincial, Eurocentric viewpoint. In
brief, this theory contends that the displacements of the welfare state do
not shape the experience of the vast majority of the direct producers of the
world nor can these differing experiences be analyzed exclusively of each
other. The dynamic of capitalism is global, not determined by processes of
individual societies bounded by nation-states. From this vantage point, the
historical trajectory of capitalism and the issues and agents of struggle
must be re-examined.[1]

To this end we will first explore Wallerstein's definition of a "world-
economy," as distinguished from other kinds of social systems, and the
rhythms and "secular trends" of this economy. We can then follow his
analysis of the contradictions of the capitalist world-economy, the diverse
"antisystemic movements" that emerge, and the relationship of class concepts to both. Finally, we will briefly examine the critical reception of
world-system theory and evaluate the strengths and weaknesses of this theory in helping us understand the sources of anticapitalist social conflict.

CAPITALISM AS A 'WORLD-ECONOMY'

Wallerstein argues that in order to reveal social dynamics, social theory must analyze "totalities."[2] The appropriate unit of social analysis is a social system, characterized by an "effective social division of labor" within which various areas "are dependent upon economic exchange with others for the smooth and continuous provisioning of the needs of the area."[3] Historically there have been three types of social systems: minisystems, world-empires, and world-economies. Minisystems are based on a coherent division of labor within a single cultural framework, for the most part simple agricultural societies. This type of social system no longer exists in that minisystems historically came under the 'protection' of neighboring empires and thereby lost their self-sufficiency.

The other types of social system are properly called world-systems, defined as a social system with a single division of labor but containing several cultural groups. There are only two kinds of world-system: those with a "common political system" and those without. Wallerstein calls the former a world-empire and the latter a world-economy. These are not "worlds" because their operations are global; rather, the phrase indicates the existence of a coherent and self-sufficient division of labor embracing several "cultural systems." It is only in the nineteenth century that the existing 'world-system' encompassed the entire globe.[4]

The present world-system is a world-economy that was established in the 16th century. It is not the first world-economy in history but it is the first to be stabilized. Earlier world-economies were transformed into world-empires by the development of a single polity embracing the whole division of labor. It is important to keep in mind this specific definition of a world-economy as a single division of labor operating through multiple cultures and multiple polities. Wallerstein argues that it is these characteristics that explain the particular dynamic of historical capitalism. As we shall see, this definition is very difficult to sustain and is actually called into question by other aspects of Wallerstein's theory as a whole. However the important point here is that Wallerstein contends that our typical notion of a more or less autonomous society, bounded by a nation-state and with a largely internally generated dynamic, is false. "Political structures do not contain 'economies'; quite the contrary: the 'world-economy' contains political structures, or states."[5]

In Wallerstein's account, the capitalist world-economy emerged as a response to certain problems of feudal production. Difficulties engendered by climatological events, technological limitations, and the exhaustion of the land for agricultural output were intensified by rising demands of the "ruling classes." This led to increased conflict between peasants and lords and conflict within the ruling classes themselves.[6] Wallerstein argues that if there had been a powerful empire on Europe's frontier, or if Europe had been politically more centralized, an empire might have developed instead of a world-economy.

Wallerstein develops a highly contentious thesis regarding the transition from feudalism to capitalism, a thesis that has important implications for the prospects of a progressive outcome in transcending capitalism. Contrary to the usual story or "myth," the transition to capitalism was not "the triumph of a new group" (capitalists) over the feudal nobility. Rather, market relations were actually developed by existing ruling groups attempting to reestablish declining revenues. "[T]here was a sort of creative leap of imagination on the part of the ruling strata. It involved trying an alternative mode of surplus appropriation, that of the market, to see whether it might serve to restore the declining real income of the ruling groups. This involved geographical expansion, spatial economic specialization, the rise of the 'absolutist' state—in short, the creation of a capitalist world-economy."[7] The transition is therefore characterized by "an essential *continuity* of the ruling families." This proved to be a good strategy in that the capitalist world-economy that emerged was superior to world-empires in producing a large surplus and therefore in restoring the revenues of the ruling strata.

By avoiding the establishment of a world-empire, the "singular feature" of the capitalist world-economy emerged: the "discontinuity between economic and political institutions."[8] It is this feature above all that produces the dynamism of capitalism. "It is only within the framework of such a historical system that persons or groups who give priority to the ceaseless accumulation of capital have been able to flourish."[9] This is so because in a system of multiple states the power of any particular state to interfere with production is limited. By definition no state can control the entire economy. Furthermore, any attempts by a state to hamper the activities of its domestic bourgeoisie can be resisted by transferring production to more congenial locations. Under these circumstances the distribution of the surplus generated by the social division of labor can only take place through the market, rather than through political authority.[10] "Once such a system was in place, capitalism could 'take off,' which is exactly what happened."

Wallerstein argues that in this way the capitalist world-economy emerged with the development of nation-states. Contrary to common conceptions, these states are not completely autonomous. Wallerstein contends that within the framework of a multiple state system "sovereignty" does not exist in the strong sense. "The states developed and were shaped as integral parts of an interstate system, which was a set of rules within which the states had to operate and a set of legitimations without which states could not survive."[11] The modern state is actually "defined by" its integration into the interstate system, which Wallerstein sometimes calls the "political superstructure of the capitalist world-economy."[12]

States do have real powers within the interstate system, even in the context of "a social division of labor whose boundaries are greater than those of any political entity." Territorial jurisdiction gives an individual state power to affect the movement of goods, money, and labor, and therefore some influence over the dynamic of the global social division of labor itself. These real, albeit limited, powers of individual states means that the market is not autonomous either. "No free market ever has existed, or could have existed, within a capitalist world-economy."

> The hypothetical free market is an intellectual construct which serves the same intellectual function as frictionless movement, as a standard from which to measure the degree of deviation. Rather, capitalists seek to maximize profit on the world market, utilizing whenever it is profitable, and whenever they are able to create them, legal monopolies and/or other forms of constraint of trade.[13]

There is no free market nor is any state permanently in favor of free trade. The position a state takes on the issue depends on its calculation of what will allow it to capture and retain the largest share of the surplus generated in the world-economy.[14]

In place of sovereign states and free markets, Wallerstein characterizes the capitalist world-economy as a "network of interlinked productive processes" called "commodity chains."[15] They are commodity chains because ultimately the final product is sold in the market to consumers. The phrase however does not imply that all the links in the chain of production of any particular commodity are forged by a market. On the contrary, Wallerstein argues that many of the links are actually nonmarket relations connecting phases of production, giving examples such as historical trading companies and today's "multinational" corporations.[16] Wallerstein even argues that profit in commodity production can be larger when all aspects are not commodified.[17] This is important for Wallerstein's conceptualization of the many kinds of exploited direct producers in the world, a discussion we will engage shortly.

To account for these nonmarket linkages, Wallerstein defines capitalism much more broadly than is customary in the Marxian tradition. In particular, capitalism does not require for its existence the full commodification of money, land, and labor. Wallerstein insists that we have ignored "the most obvious of all historical facts . . . that capitalist entrepreneurs have always operated *and flourished* in an arena in which some factors were 'free' but others were not (or were less so), in which the law of value was dominant in some but not in all sectors of the 'economy.'"[18] Further commodification of the factors of production is indeed a longterm "secular trend" of historical capitalism but Wallerstein argues, for reasons that we will clarify, that capitalism functions best with the partial freedom of these factors. In fact, further commodification of aspects of production signals the exhaustion of historical capitalism as a world-system.[19]

To clarify this, the market should not actually be thought of as an "institution" at all; it is a "structure molded by *many* institutions."[20] Wallerstein explicitly mentions four sets of institutions (properly so-called) which seek to shape the market: the multiple states; nations whether identified as independent states or not (including ethnic groups); classes in "evolving occupational contour and in oscillating degrees of consciousness"; and income-pooling households deriving their sustenance from several sources.[21] The market does not simply exist; it *emerges* as the mode of distribution in a social division of labor without a political center. It is manifested in the competition of various agents to control linkages in the social division of labor. It is for these reasons that historical capitalism is properly characterized by "the *partially* free flow of the factors of production and by the *selective* interference of the political machinery in the 'market.'"[22]

It follows that the separation of politics and economics into distinct analytical spheres is simply "liberal ideology."[23] The theoretical separation of state and economy implies that autonomous markets are the normal or paradigmatic functioning of capitalism. Wallerstein argues that both Adam Smith and Marx mistakenly believed that competitive markets are the typical mode of operation of capitalism and that monopolies therefore need additional explanation.[24] Following Fernand Braudel, Wallerstein argues instead that monopolies, and attempts to monopolize, are inherent to capitalism as an historical system. "The basic logic is that the accumulated surplus is distributed unequally in favor of those able to achieve various kinds of temporary monopolies in the market networks. This is a 'capitalist' logic."[25] In a truly competitive market, the rate of profit "by definition" is low. "Hence all participants in all markets are always seeking to promote monopolies for themselves and to break the monopolies of others."[26] However due to the irrepressibility of this kind of competition, monopolies are always eroded, a fact that Wallerstein refers to as "the normal entropy of monopolistic advantage within capitalism."[27] We should add that it is only for this reason that the law of value can have any theoretical purchase at all.

The global division of labor has multiple points of entry for attempts to steer portions of the surplus toward one's group. In the capitalist world-economy the absence of a central political authority means that distribution of the surplus results from competition over the various nodal points in the production of commodities. Some of his phrases to the contrary, for Wallerstein competition is still the key aspect of the capitalist world-economy. Although it is not completely clear in his theory, the competition is not primarily one of lowering costs by raising productivity but competition over positions in the world-economy that produce monopolistic and "quasi-monopolistic" advantage. Since this is the goal, Wallerstein has an atypically broader view of the arena, agencies, and institutions involved in this competition.

Competitive strategies especially focus on the individual state as one of the most organized and potentially powerful of agencies. Since the global division of labor runs through state boundaries, individual states have the capacity to try to capture an ever-larger portion of the surplus. States attempt to do this in various ways: through import/export controls, stimulation of technology (specifically rewarded in capitalism),[28] development of skilled labor, even direct intervention into other countries's affairs and military action. The successful employment of such tactics results in the accumulation of capital, which in turn has a cumulative effect on the political ability to employ these tactics. However, as long as the world-system does not become an empire, i.e., as long as there are multiple states, the competition continues. Therefore any special position in the economy that would result in the attainment of "quasi-monopolistic rents" is under incessant attack.

A state does not necessarily interfere with (or adjust) the market only in favor of "accumulators." Other groups can gain influence as well, which is Wallerstein's explanation of the rise of the welfare state in core countries. Furthermore, Wallerstein hastens to add that state machineries are not "manipulable puppets" of domestic forces.[29] States are constrained by the interests of the state apparatus itself and by the institutional compromises which made possible the construction of the particular state.

Nevertheless, since the tax revenues and popular support for regimes rest on successful accumulation, it is reasonable for the state to be responsive. Although Wallerstein includes this qualification, the general instrumentalist cast of his theory is a frequent object of criticism.

From Wallerstein's perspective, however, the charge of instrumentalism is fundamentally based on a false distinction. The specific contribution of the world-system approach is its insistence on the total intertwining of spheres that are usually analytically (and as disciplines) kept separate. The economic, the political, and the sociocultural aspects of social life "do not have separate 'logics.'" "[T]he intermeshing of constraints, options, decisions, norms, and 'rationalities' is such that no useful research model can isolate 'factors' according to the categories of economic, political, and social, and treat only one kind of variable, implicitly holding the others constant."[30] Wallerstein's frequent collaborator, Giovanni Arrighi, even accuses Marx of "following nineteenth-century liberal ideology" by portraying the world market as "operating over the heads rather than through the hands of state actors."[31] Therefore, contrary to those, like Juergen Habermas, who argue that contemporary capitalism is constituted by subsystems with autonomous logics, Wallerstein insists that "the whole is a seamless skein."

This does not mean that the capitalist world-system is an undifferentiated, competitive free-for-all. Capitalism must be conceived as a world-system with a specific history. This history had real effects that have crucially determined capitalism's global structure and delimit the options of states within it. A major characteristic of *historical* capitalism is the development of areas of the world-economy into "core," "periphery," and "semiperiphery," i.e., a hierarchy of production and exchange. At first the differences in political-economic capacities among regions were small, but geographical or historical advantages were slowly magnified to the point of the possibility of the "intrusion of force into the determination of price." Borrowing from Arghiri Emmanuel and Samir Amin, Wallerstein argues that these historically generated differentials created the basis for the operation of "unequal exchange."

> Starting with any real differential in the market, occurring because of either the (temporary) scarcity of a complex production process, or artificial scarcities created *manu militari*, commodities moved between zones in such a way that the area with the less 'scarce' item 'sold' its items to the other area at a price that incarnated more real input (cost) than an equally-priced item moving in the opposite direction. What really happened is that there was a

transfer of part of the total profit (or surplus) being produced from one zone to another. Such a relationship is that of coreness-peripherality. By extension, we can call the losing zone a 'periphery' and the gaining zone a 'core.'[32]

Wallerstein states that unequal exchange rests on the differing wage levels in the distinct parts of the world-economy, "in which a peripheral worker needs to work many hours, at a given level of productivity, to obtain a product produced by a worker in a core country in one hour."[33]

At first glance, there appears to be an affinity of the concept of unequal exchange with some of John Roemer's early models of the exchange of commodities containing unequal amounts of labor, an affinity noted in several places by Roemer himself.[34] However, at least in regard to Wallerstein's use of the concept, this is a mistaken impression. In Roemer's models, the transfer of surplus labor occurs because of the differing productivity of the initial capital endowments of the individuals involved in the exchange. In contrast, Wallerstein (and Samir Amin, whom he quotes) assumes equal productivity of those exchanging commodities. Unequal exchange is therefore a consequence of the sheer difference in wage levels—of the reward for this factor of production—and associated standards of living in non-core countries.

It is true that above Wallerstein confusingly speaks of a commodity as containing "more real input (cost)" than the other. In other places he also states that the origin of these differences lies in the "unequal amounts of social labor" contained in commodities from different areas and that unequal exchange allows "producers in core zones to gain additional competitive advantages in existing products" through "mechanization."[35] These remarks suggest that unequal exchange is not based solely on wage levels but on the differential productivity of the capital available in different locations of the world-economy. However, by "unequal amounts of social labor" Wallerstein apparently means that the structure of the household in peripheral areas allows the labor input into the commodity to be more than that of simply the specifically wage labor that is directly applied. This argument requires Wallerstein's thesis concerning the "semiproletarian household" and the central role it plays in historical capitalism.

Wallerstein argues that if the term proletarian is applied to households, not individuals, there are not many classical proletarian households in the world, that is, households that are reproduced solely through wage labor. Most of the world's population live in semiproletarian households, for Wallerstein the key category of direct producers. In these households wage work is combined with other sources of income and means of reproduction, such as "petty commodity production, rents, gifts and transfer payments, and (not least) subsistence production."[36]

Semiproletarian households are disproportionately found in the periphery and semiperiphery. The structure of the semiproletarian household allows people to offer their labor for less wages than are actually necessary to reproduce the household. These workers survive "*by virtue of* being embedded in these 'semiproletarian' extended households, benefitting from the income earned or goods produced (subsistence production, petty commodity production, rent) by other members of the household or by the wageworker at other times."[37] This is "super-exploitation" in that the wages "are insufficient for the reproduction of the labor force." Wallerstein argues that the explanation of low wages in the periphery is precisely the disproportionate existence of this type of household in which wages do not have to cover the total cost of reproducing the household.[38] This is therefore the origin of the differential in wages that makes unequal exchange possible.

Given the possibility of "superprofits," semiproletarianized households are the most functional for capitalism. According to Wallerstein, wage-labor is "a relatively *costly* mode of labor." The full-time wage laborer over a lifetime receives a larger share of the available surplus-value. It is also more costly in that proletarians are better able to organize to pursue their class interests and have higher "class consciousness." Wallerstein contends, therefore, that capitalism actually works best when the factor of production labor is embedded in only semiproletarianized households.[39]

As we will see, there are implications of this description of the semiproletarian household that are crucial for Wallerstein's argument regarding the trajectory of capitalism and also for how we conceive the direct producers in the world-economy. We will therefore fill out this analysis shortly. The important point here is that Wallerstein's conception of the semiproletarian household enables him to analyze unequal exchange as being based solely on differences in wage levels, not different levels of productivity. However, he does frequently mention as well the development of productive technology as part of the competitive advantages of the core.[40] Given these varying comments, it is unclear exactly what role unequal exchange on the basis of wage differentials plays in the contemporary reproduction of core and periphery. Unequal exchange on the basis of wage levels could be 'merely' a part of the historical development of capitalism, historically creating the differing capital endowments of core and periphery but having no real impact on the kind of unequal exchange—based on differing levels of productivity—that exists today. This would not deny

Wallerstein's argument that the global structural hierarchy of production in contemporary capitalism can only be understood on the basis of its historical development, but it would reduce the importance of wage differentials, contrary to Wallerstein's emphasis in so many places.

The most plausible interpretation of his argument is that unequal exchange on the basis of wage differences does indeed further develop the capacities of the core by creating more funds for technology, increasing the productive edge of core areas and thereby increasing the scope for unequal exchange on the basis of productivity. The increased surplus also creates the capacity and incentive to establish strong state machineries that can be utilized to reinforce the existing relationships, especially the "customary" differentials in the wages and standards of living in core and periphery.[41] Finally, the surplus obtained through unequal exchange under either definition allows core areas to create new products which yield a temporary monopoly or "quasi-monopoly" at one of the interstices of a commodity chain, providing even more opportunities to appropriate the surplus of the global division of labor as a whole.[42] Under this interpretation, unequal exchange is a concept comprising three avenues for appropriating the surplus of the periphery and semiperiphery: exploiting the difference in wage levels and standard of living, absorbing the surplus labor contained in commodities produced at differing levels of productivity, and deriving quasi-monopolistic "rents" from domination of links in a commodity chain, either through control of scarce technology and skills or through sheer political and commercial muscle. The combined result of these forces is the deepening polarization "not only in terms of distributive criteria (real income levels, quality of life) but even more importantly in the loci of the accumulation of capital."[43] It is not clear if this is what Wallerstein has in mind nor does this interpretation eliminate the problems of Wallerstein's theory, but it does make them manageable while we bring out the additional aspects of the theory.

There is an important corollary to Wallerstein's portrayal of the hierarchy of the capitalist world-economy that exemplifies his typical—but, contrary to some critics, not exclusive—emphasis on the importance of wage differentials and also accommodates the apparent recent success of some nations to escape peripheral status. Wallerstein argues that any industry becomes more competitive over time. As its quasi-monopolistic position is eroded, profits become smaller. These industries are then transferred to lower wage areas so that profits can be maintained. The semiperiphery is the area to which these formerly core processes are "demoted." Wallerstein gives contemporary examples of the automobile, steel, and electronics industries.[44] This allows some semiperipheral countries to give the appearance of development by taking advantage of the differential in wage costs.[45]

The location of production of a specific commodity is therefore not inherent in the commodity itself (e.g., raw materials, agricultural produce, consumer electronics). Instead, typically there are "product cycles" in which a product starts out as a core activity and tends to the periphery as the capacities to create it—technology and skills—are diffused.[46] Without the differential wage costs it would not be profitable to expand the division of labor in this way.[47] Since overall wage levels and relative accumulation between core areas and other parts of the world are not altered by these shifts of production and are in fact increasingly polarized, Wallerstein refers to these processes not as development but as "reshuffles" within the global division of labor.

PROBLEMS OF THE CAPITALIST WORLD-SYSTEM

Wallerstein argues that it is the ineluctable drive to accumulation that distinguishes capitalism from other modes of production. There had earlier been capitalists but they were in a situation such that their efforts were circumscribed and crushed. Only in the 16th century did the appropriate combination of structures develop that allowed capitalism to be stabilized as a system. Once established, "the search for maximum profit" forced the global expansion of the world-system, the continuing mechanization of work, and—very importantly—"the tendency to facilitate and optimize rapid response to the permutations of the world market by the proletarianization of labor and the commercialization of land."[48]

Competition in the market is the key to accumulation. There is no escape from this reality, no permanent monopolies of products, skills, or technology, no commanding political or military position safe from challenge. "Acute competition" is the "differentia specifica" of historical capitalism.[49] Those who would attempt to operate according to any principle other than accumulation through competition will be driven from the field. Wallerstein argues that this reveals the ultimate irrationality of capitalism, the "peculiar illogic" of a system "which makes accumulation an end in itself."[50]

The inescapability of competition is what causes the expansion of the system as a whole, the increased development of technology, and also leads to the contradictions of the system. According to Wallerstein, the "basic contradiction" of historical capitalism is that supply and demand are disjoined from each other, the "so-called anarchy of production." In a situation of one economy/multiple polities there is no central authority to guide investments. Investment decisions—supply—are made by individual producers. According to Wallerstein, this leads to a powerful tendency in capitalism for supply to expand without regard to demand. "The sum of the activities of the individual producers/entrepreneurs constantly increases world production, which means that continued profitability for all is necessarily a function of an *expanding* world demand."[51]

Demand is necessary for the realization of capital, the completion of the process of accumulation. The key issue for Wallerstein is, then, how a specific level and configuration of demand is established. Wallerstein says that formerly some believed that production itself creates demand, "but bitter experience has demonstrated that this is not true: demand is a function not of production but of how the revenues of enterprises are distributed, which is the intervening factor that determines demand." The level of wages is a consequence of political struggles in individual states, the outcomes of which are then politically solidified and not easy to change in the short run. These political struggles and consequent "political compromises" are conditioned by the strength of the contenders but are also constrained by the position of the individual nation in the capitalist world-economy. "The states 'lock in' demand by stabilizing (within a certain range) historic expectations of allocation of income."[52] These political compromises "last at least decades, if not more." In this way, the overall demand in the capitalist world-economy is a consequence of the outcomes of domestic struggles within individual states. "At any given time, therefore, world-wide demand is 'fixed'—the vector of the multiple state-side outcomes of their internal class struggles."

At regularly recurring intervals in historical capitalism, continually expanding production surpasses the relatively fixed demand agreements. "And therein lies the contradiction: world demand, the sum of the consequences of political decisions taken in each state, tends to remain stable over the middle run while world supply is hurtling toward ever greater production."[53] What follows is a realization crisis of capital accumulation based on insufficient demand. Wallerstein thus gives an 'underconsumptionist' interpretation of the problems of capitalism.

This disjuncture between supply and demand is the origin of "Kondratieff" cycles or waves, the "breathing mechanism" of the capitalist world-system.[54] Kondratieff cycles are longterm economic cycles composed of two phases, the expansionary phase (A-phase) and the contracting phase (B-phase), each full cycle lasting about 50–60 years. According to

Wallerstein's interpretation, the B-phase of the current Kondratieff began around 1967 so we can expect a new expansionary phase to begin sometime in the 1990s.[55]

Wallerstein argues that there are several typical responses to the consequent stagnation, i.e., to the latter end of the B-phase of a Kondratieff.[56] First, individual producers try to restore profitability by lowering costs of production, either through mechanization or through relocation to lower wage areas. Those who fail are bankrupted; this reduces supply but also reduces demand.[57] Secondly, in the core there are attempts to develop new products requiring scarce skills and technology. This is the origin of entirely new high profit core industries. Thirdly, global demand is increased through a reopening of the existing distribution arrangements. According to Wallerstein, in periods of stagnation it is common for struggles to emerge which result in the distribution of additional surplus to core workers and to the bourgeoisie of the semiperiphery and periphery. This raises immediate global demand but, since at any particular time the distribution of the surplus is a "zero-sum game," it is a loss in profits for the bourgeoisie in the core.[58] Finally, supply is cheapened by the expansion of the world economy into new areas, i.e., the incorporation of new zones into the social division of labor and the "proletarianization" of new groups of workers. These responses initiate a new Kondratieff cycle, although, as the word cycle suggests, they also set the stage for new problems in the future.

World-system theory states that "incorporation" of new geographical areas is the key to the "laws of motion" of historical capitalism. Contrary to those who argue that imperialism seeks cheap inputs and new markets, however, Wallerstein argues that the primary reason for incorporation is not to seek markets at all but to find "low-cost labor forces" for producing for existing markets. The low wages of the periphery do not really add much to global demand.[59]

Because of incorporation and other reasons, proletarianization is increasing. Capitalists seeking low-cost labor expand waged production into areas where the structure of the household permits wages below the costs of reproducing the household. Proletarianization is also increasing as the prospects for those living in rural areas declines due to demographic and ecological problems and the commercialization of land. This is progressively eliminating the basis for subsistence income and, among other things, increasing the number of agricultural proletarians.[60] Finally, Wallerstein strikingly insists that workers themselves demand that more of their reproduction costs be covered through wages.

One of the most effective and immediate ways for work-forces to increase real income has been the further commodification of their own labor. They have often sought to substitute wage-labour for those parts of the household production processes which have brought in low amounts of real income, in particular for various kinds of petty commodity production. One of the major forces behind proletarianization has been the world's work-forces themselves.[61]

For these reasons proletarianization increases even though "proletarianization has in the long term led to reduced profit levels in the capitalist world-economy." We will raise some difficulties and inconsistencies regarding the thesis of proletarianization shortly.

Wallerstein's crucial argument regarding the trajectory of historical capitalism is that there are limits to the repeated employment of these "recuperative mechanisms" of capitalism. "By the late nineteenth century, the capitalist world-economy had expanded its outer boundaries to cover the whole of the earth; by the late twentieth century, it had reached most of its inner geographical frontiers as well. There are now virtually no populations left to incorporate, and the structure must begin to collapse."[62] Wallerstein calls these eventually self-defeating tendencies of capitalism "secular trends."[63] The two key trends are "the commodification of everything" ("proletarianization") and the incorporation of all parts of the world into the world-economy ("geographical expansion"). Wallerstein argues that there are logical limits to the intensive (commodification) and extensive (incorporation) expansion of capitalism. As he puts it, "their curves tend toward asymptotes." "[T]here is an in-built limit to commodification—100 percent—and while we are still far from that, we have reached the point where that limit is visible, if remote."[64] Each new K-cycle moves us closer because in order to overcome economic contraction demand must be stimulated by redistributing the surplus to core workers and the bourgeoisie in the semiperiphery and periphery. This in turn requires geographical expansion to tap new sources of super-profits by incorporating labor whose full reproduction costs are not covered through wages. Therefore the limits of commodification result from the limits on the proletarianization of labor and the declining number of semi-proletarian households. For this reason Wallerstein says that, "a transition, a demise of an historical system, is less its breakdown than its fulfillment."[65]

For Wallerstein, as for Habermas in *Legitimation Crisis,* capitalism is a system that cannot reproduce itself from its own resources. It must continually incorporate noncapitalist or not fully capitalist sources to maintain itself. When these sources dry up, capitalism will collapse. It is in this way that capitalism is an historical system. It is not an unstructured set of eternal social laws, a film that can be run forwards or backwards without distinction. This world-system had a specific historical origin and developed a specific global structure that constrains its future trajectory.

Although, contrary to the Marxian tradition, historical capitalism cannot be characterized as a mode of production in which the factors of production are "free," the further freeing of the factors is indeed the overall secular trend of capitalism. As the capitalist world-system resists stagnation through further commodification, it more and more resembles Marx's vision of capitalism as an unstoppable system propelled forward by the "law of value." "The real crunch will come in the process of proletarianization, or, more generally, in the process of commodification—the quintessential way in which the success of the system is in fact its main destabilizing factor."[66] As these secular trends develop, all nations, even state socialist countries, are forced into increased "regard for the law of value." Capitalism may soon live up to its "ideal type": "In perhaps fifty years, and *for the first time,* the world-economy may *fully* operate according to the laws of value as outlined in Volume I of *Capital.*"[67] It is in this way that capitalism will die of its 'successes,' "its ability and its unquenchable thirst to commodify everything."[68]

According to Wallerstein, capitalism is only about halfway to the freeing of the factors of production. There will be one more Kondratieff cycle, after which proletarianization and commodification will have proceeded to their furthest possible extent. A transition to a new system will emerge by the end of the 21st or the beginning of the 22nd century. As in Marx's *Manifesto,* in places Wallerstein even adds a clarification thesis of his own: "the cash nexus, having become universal, will also become extremely visible. The system will not be able to survive the light of day."[69] Marx's vision of capitalism was not so much wrong as premature.

THE 'CLASSES' OF HISTORICAL CAPITALISM

Given his view that historical capitalism does not require the complete freedom of the factors of production, Wallerstein paints a varied picture of the world's "direct producers" or "working classes," insisting first of all on the plural. This has of course been presumed by our explication of his argument that a secular trend of capitalism is the increasing proletarianization of the world's direct producers. However, the direct producers share the important characteristic that, whether fully proletarian or not, they are all "exploited."

Wallerstein argues that capitalism is an exploitative system in the specific Marxian sense of appropriation of surplus value from the producers. In capitalism investment decisions are made on the basis of profitability. Profits emerge from absorbing the surplus of direct producers and also through unequal exchange in global markets. The "genius" of capitalism is precisely the "interweaving of these two channels of exploitation," of direct and mediated appropriation of surplus value.[70]

Wallerstein rejects the traditional conception of the proletarian as much too restrictive to capture the variety of direct producers in the world. The classical Marxian definition of proletarian cannot account for the persistence of the varied forms of production. "Nine-tenths of the world became 'questions,' 'anomalies,' 'survivals'—objectively progressive for a while perhaps, but destined to disappear, sociologically, analytically, politically."[71] In contrast, Wallerstein proposes that capitalism as an historical system—not as an abstract theory—has always functioned by exploiting wage labor ('free labor'), coerced labor, indebted peasant landowners, and even slaves. Furthermore, household labor, petty market production, subsistence gardens, etc., all contribute to the reproduction of the household in most households of direct producers in the world. Rather than defining away these households and varied forms of exploited labor, we should broaden our notion of the working classes.[72]

These truths have been especially obscured by the distinction between productive and nonproductive labor, the former associated with wage labor and the latter with labor in the household. The key to understanding the varied producing classes is to recognize that "surplus value" is not produced only in the wage relation. "I contend that when a product is produced for exchange, and value is created greater than the socially necessary amount needed to reproduce the labor that created the product, there is surplus value, whatever the nature of the social relation at the work place."[73] As mentioned earlier, Wallerstein argues that surplus value can be created without commodification of the intermediate steps in commodity production and is even maximized when these steps are not commodified. He supports this thesis by stating that even so-called "nonproductive" labor contributes to the production of value by a household. In fact, the work of the "housewife," young, and aged all produce "surplus-value."[74]

For Wallerstein, a surplus can be created and appropriated through various relations, not necessarily formal relations of ownership or nonownership of the means of production. This perspective allows him to include state socialist countries, coerced labor, and slave labor as part of the essential dynamic of historical capitalism.[75] For example, Wallerstein argues quite persuasively that the slave economy of the southern United States was an integral part of the capitalist world-economy at the time, producing a "surplus." (Revealingly, Wallerstein often uses the terms surplus and surplus-value interchangeably.) He adds that the difference between precapitalist and capitalist systems in this regard is that under the latter there is structural pressure for the maximization of exploitation over time.

In order to accumulate in a competitive situation it is necessary to reduce the costs of production. Consistent with his frequently narrow view of technology, Wallerstein argues that "[l]abour-power has always been a central and quantitatively significant element in the production-process."[76] Therefore the most important way of reducing costs is through pressure on the direct producer, "reducing his income to a minimum and allowing someone else to appropriate the remaining 'value' he has produced."[77] Resurrecting the much-maligned thesis of *The Manifesto,* Wallerstein even states that the capitalist world-system promotes not only increasing material polarization but also the "absolute immiseration" of the masses in the world.[78]

The thesis of absolute immiseration is one that, as Wallerstein says, "even orthodox Marxists tend to bury in shame." This is largely due to the fact of the development of the welfare state in core countries and the belief that the proper unit for analysis—and evaluation—of capitalism is the individual nation-state. However from the global perspective of world-system theory, this thesis must be reappraised. At least, given the desperate situation of the direct producers in most parts of the world and the increasing unemployment and declining real wages in some of the core countries, the possibility of a tendency to absolute material decline should not be rejected out of hand.

Although there may be other grounds for reconsidering this idea, Wallerstein's own attempt to reinstall the thesis of absolute immiseration involves him in a contradiction. As noted above, Wallerstein asserts that workers themselves seek commodification of labor-power in order to increase their "real income." Wage labor allows them to recover more of their costs of reproduction, i.e., without the subsidies of other family members and activities in the semiproletarian household. "They have understood, often better than their self-proclaimed intellectual spokesmen, how much greater the exploitation is in semi-proletarian than in more fully-proletarianized households."[79] However, this is a contradiction. If proletarianization is an increase in real income, and if increasing proletarianization is a secular trend, then the immiseration thesis must be false.[80]

If proletarianization is actually a material improvement for the direct producers, one can only rescue the thesis of material decline by rejecting the thesis of increasing proletarianization. It is not surprising therefore that Wallerstein appears to have modified his position on the key argument of increasing proletarianization. Specifically, Wallerstein suggests that the tendency to proletarianization might halt or at least slow down before reaching the "asymptote" of complete proletarianization of the world's labor-force. For example, Wallerstein and Joan Smith have recently argued that in New York City "non-wage remuneration" not only exists now but that such reproduction strategies will likely increase in core households and elsewhere with global restructuring.

> Thus, the core household type that is emerging does not take the form of the classical image of the "proletarian" household, one that draws all its income from wages and does not own the "means of production." Quite the contrary. The core household type of the majority who are above the poverty level but beneath the level of high wealth is a household that combines wage income, property that takes the form of means of production (not for the market but for the household) [i.e., tools, a car, lawnmower, washer and dryer, etc.], plus self-provisioning labor.[81]

For the poor in core countries, wage labor is to some degree replaced by welfare "transfers." With the trend toward increasing unemployment in the core, we might well expect that alternative survival strategies to wage labor will increase in frequency. "The peripheral household pattern seems to be in the process of becoming ever more encrusted for the large majority of world labor."[82] In the core and in the periphery, "the proletarian is condemned to remain a partial wage worker." These comments suggest that proletarianization is not growing at a rapid pace in the periphery either.

Wallerstein now emphasizes commodification rather than proletarianization. "Capitalism does indeed involve the 'commodification of everything,' and the cash nexus is its defining ideal. But it is not at all true that cash can only be obtained through wages." The thesis of 'commodification of everything' is much broader than proletarianization. In a recent statement he mentions as evidence "the extent of the mechanization of production; the elimination of spatial constraints in the exchange of commodities and information; the deruralization of the world; the near-exhaustion of the ecosystem; the high degree of monetarization of the work-process;

and consumerism (that is, the enormously expanded commodification of consumption)."[83]

Wallerstein can shift his focus from increasing proletarianization to increasing commodification because ultimately the important point for him is not the specific forms of labor but the increase in the stream of surplus value through the commodification of activities that were not previously commodified. The shift from proletarianization to commodification allows Wallerstein to accommodate the increase in petty market operations in the periphery and similar developments in the core. Along these lines in one place he proposes a broadened concept of proletarian as simply a producer who creates value, part of which must be surrendered to someone else.[84] However this only raises new difficulties for his theory. Such a reconceptualization deprives the semiproletarian household of its distinctiveness as a source of wage labor that is subsidized by other means of reproducing the household. If households in the core must also increasingly rely on activities to supplement wages, then the ground for unequal exchange based on wage differentials is undermined. We will return to these topics in our evaluation of Wallerstein's theory as a whole. Suffice it to say here that the elements of Wallerstein's analysis of the direct producers never quite congeal into a coherent argument.

In the above discussion, Wallerstein's explicit purpose is to show that surplus-value can be created in many ways and thereby account for the majority in the capitalist world-economy who do not fit the ideal-type of proletarian. From the other side, in analyzing the multiple strategies to appropriate part of this surplus-value, Wallerstein develops an equally expansive conception of the bourgeoisie. Members of the bourgeoisie are those who, because of their structural positions in the capitalist world-economy, tap the stream of surplus or surplus-value and use part of this surplus to invest for further accumulation. Wallerstein says this can occur "either as an individual or a member of some collectivity" but it is especially useful to think of the relation between bourgeois and proletarian as a collective rather than an individual relation.[85]

The existence of commodity *chains* allows many points of entry for appropriating the surplus of the direct producers. Those who appropriate surplus-value they did not create are bourgeois, regardless of their formal relation of ownership or nonownership. This is the obverse of the argument that those are proletarians who "yield part of the value they have created to others," regardless of actual formal ownership of means of production or petty market operations. Wallerstein argues that, like proletarians, the bourgeois combines several sources of income: from rent, trade, profits on production, "financial manipulation," etc. "Once these revenues are in money form, they're all the same for the capitalists, a means of pursuing that incessant and infernal accumulation to which they are condemned."[86]

The bourgeois is "condemned" to accumulate by the pressures of competition. Competition implies the fundamental fragmentation of the bourgeoisie that creates the principal contradiction of capitalism: the individual bourgeois interest leads to increasing supply and lowering costs which undercuts the interest of the class as a whole in maintaining adequate demand.[87] However, in addition to this essential fragmentation there are other important divisions within the bourgeoisie over appropriation of the surplus. Wallerstein argues that continuing struggles emerge from the fact that the classic owner/entrepreneur wishes most of all not to appropriate through competition in production at all but simply on the basis of structural position. That is, all bourgeois strive to become "rentiers," receiving income not from work but from ownership of some key aspect of a commodity chain. "Every capitalist seeks to transform profit into rent. This translates into the following statement: the primary objective of every 'bourgeois' is to become an 'aristocrat.'"[88] Rent increases the rate of profit compared to what capitalists would receive in a "truly competitive market." It is therefore similar to monopoly profits. Like monopoly profits, the structural positions on which rents are based must be politically protected in some fashion, a fact which Wallerstein refers to as the attempt "to transform achievement into status."

Wallerstein notes that the persisting attempts to turn profits into structural positions from which one can simply derive income without participating in competitive production is contrary to the usual historical account of the dissolution of rent with the rise of capitalism. The latter is part of the common understanding of the transition from feudalism to capitalism in which the productive bourgeoisie overthrew the rentier aristocrats.[89] To the contrary, Wallerstein insists that seeking to become a rentier is an ineradicable part of historical capitalism that creates very significant conflicts within the bourgeoisie. Not only does this reflect his view of the transition to capitalism, it also brings out once again Wallerstein's emphasis on battles over circulation.

The struggle over the division of the surplus that pits owner/rentiers against the members of the bourgeoisie engaged in production has been exacerbated by modern corporate forms. Wallerstein argues that the global percentage of the population who are bourgeois ("in one definition or another") is increasing, largely because of the importance of transnational corporations.[90] The corporate form of ownership emerged as a strategy of monopolistic control, a slow process because of the tendency for monopolistic positions to be eroded due to competition. With this form of enterprise came the well-known separation of ownership and control. This meant an increase in the "salaried bourgeoisie." In countries where state ownership is important there is a similar separation of ownership (by the people) and control, resulting in an "administrative bourgeoisie." Wallerstein argues that as these developments continue, "the role of the legal owner becomes less and less central, eventually vestigial."[91]

Although he calls them bourgeois, Wallerstein argues that this "new social stratum" cannot be adequately characterized by using "nineteenth-century categories of analysis." The salaried bourgeoisie is not bourgeois as a result of ownership but because these individuals share in the surplus generated by the direct producers and, to a degree, enjoy the standard of living of the bourgeoisie. The salaried bourgeois's claim to part of the surplus is based on the rather dubious concept (in Wallerstein's opinion) of "human capital," i.e., specialized training and skills. The new middle classes have education and professional credentials that allow them to appropriate part of the surplus value. As non-owners they cannot pass structural rent positions from property on to their children, however they do try to ensure "privileged access to the 'better' educational institutions."[92]

Like Offe, Wallerstein doubts that scarce professional skills are really being developed in these better educational institutions. The facts are that there are simply too few positions to go around for the professionally credentialled. Therefore, contrary to assertions of "meritocracy" and "careers open to talent," these amount simply to closure strategies regarding structural positions from which one can claim some of the surplus. Wallerstein argues that the reality of the situation explains the social struggles over education and believes that these struggles will continue and intensify. The entire argument is quite similar to some of Erik Olin Wright's analyses.

Due to the increasing importance of institutions that maintain capitalism (corporations, the state) and to the increasing resistance of the working classes, various groupings in the salaried bourgeoisie are becoming structurally more important and successfully demand a redistribution of the surplus in their direction. Wallerstein describes this as the "janissarization of the ruling classes." He considers this to be politically destabilizing for several reasons: as the rewards of the top are reduced, so are the corresponding motivations; the bourgeoisie is less cohesive and cannot act as purposefully as it once could; and the resources for further "cooptation" are progressively reduced.[93] This tendency is particularly acute in the United States where the professional middle classes are a higher percentage of the population.[94] Wallerstein even states that due to the rise of the salaried bourgeoisie, the state cannot ensure property rights as well as it used to: "the state is increasingly barred from awarding past-ness, encrusting privilege and legitimating rent." It is for this reason that he declares that "property is becoming ever less important as capitalism procedes on its historical trajectory."[95]

Wallerstein's analysis of the contemporary bourgeoisie is essentially the mirror-image of his conception of the direct producers or proletariat in the expanded definition. Although there are specific distinctions regarding the bases of their claims to a portion of the surplus—ownership, corporate management, professional credentials from the right schools, management of a state enterprise—the bourgeoisie is the class that appropriates the surplus. As he often argues that proletarianization is increasing, Wallerstein also insists that bourgeoisification is increasing in the sense that "[t]he percentage of upper strata involved in market surplus-extraction operations has been growing, and an ever greater percentage of their income has in fact been coming from current market operations."[96] The mirror-image is important for Wallerstein's argument that, in spite of the varied forms of creation of the surplus by the direct producers and the varied bases for appropriation of the surplus by fractions of the bourgeoisie, the structural polarity of capitalism exists and is increasing. "Indeed, Marx's original insight that the operation of the capitalist system created two clear and polarized classes is in fact affirmed and not disconfirmed by the evidence. . . . [T]he slow but steady commodification of the workforce as well as of the managerial sectors has in fact diminished the 'social veil' that blurred class structure."[97]

However, the attempt at symmetry creates ambiguities and inconsistencies in Wallerstein's account of the bourgeoisie. First of all, Wallerstein defines the bourgeois not only as one who appropriates a portion of the surplus but one who also "is in the position to invest . . . some of this surplus in capital goods."[98] Although this would apply to the owning/rentier bourgeois, it is difficult to see how this necessarily applies to the salaried bourgeois or the administrative bourgeois. One may be able to argue a functionally equivalent activity of these other two fractions but one would also have to demonstrate that their investing activities are driven by a need to compete. Such a thesis is possible but it would require much more argument than Wallerstein presents.

Secondly, Wallerstein contrasts the rentier bourgeois to the salaried bourgeois on the criterion of present performance in competitive production: the rentier appropriates on the basis of ownership of some factor nec-

essary for completion of a commodity chain, whereas the salaried bourgeois in some way contributes to production. However Wallerstein also argues that the salaried bourgeois gains a position from which she or he can
claim part of the surplus not because of "merit," but because he or she has
attended the right schools or has professional credentials.

This is not necessarily a contradiction. Even if positions are limited
and one uses indefensible means to obtain such a position, this does not entail that one does not work once one gains the position. But it does seem to
be an admission that the salaried bourgeois, like the owner/rentier, is in
some ways appropriating on the basis of structural position, not merit nor
simply for contribution to production. It would be clearer to say that all
fractions of the extended bourgeoisie—and here we could also include the
administrative bourgeois in state enterprises—appropriate partly because
of their position in the social division of labor, not solely on the grounds of
contribution. This would not only clarify Wallerstein's portrayal, it could
be deepened by the arguments of Offe and some of Wright's critics on the
difficulty of measuring contribution to production.[99] It would probably
also be closer to the truth of the matter.

CLASS ANALYSIS AND ANTISYSTEMIC MOVEMENTS

Wallerstein's discussion of classes is somewhat loose partly because he is
suspicious of formal models of class structure. "Class analysis loses its
power of explanation whenever it moves towards formal models and away
from dialectical dynamics."[100] Instead of formal models Wallerstein focuses on the imperative of accumulation and consequent group formations
and strategies, stressing the mutability of classes. "[C]lasses do not have
some permanent reality. Rather they are formed, they consolidate themselves, they disintegrate or disaggregate, and they are re-formed."[101] He
argues that we can theoretically and practically bring out the antisystemic
aspects of, for example, racial conflict without resorting simply to "some
stupid insistence on the priority of class analysis." He emphasizes that
"class consciousness," although important when it occurs, is situational,
depending on revolutionary situations or in developing challenges to specific groups.

Wallerstein argues that although capitalism is certainly properly described in terms of social class, class consciousness is "latent most of the
time." The struggle over the disposition of the stream of surplus value is
refracted through ethnic identification, race, subnational identities and
parties, and, above all, the nation-state. The fundamental structure of the

capitalist world-system is a world-economy which operates through a multiplicity of nation-states. The consequence is that for both the proletariat and the bourgeoisie, class interests stemming from position in the world-economy must largely be pursued through the individual nation-state, with a corresponding effect on consciousness. "[T]he antinomy of class—*an sich* in a world-economy, but *fuer sich* in the states—forces *most* expressions of consciousness to take a national/ethnic/race form."[102] Class demands can therefore emerge as claims of peoples or nations, depending on the situation or tactics. Capturing this mutability, Wallerstein refers to status groups and political parties as the "blurred collective representation of classes."[103] Nevertheless, Wallerstein says that if we focus on the struggle to accumulate and the resistance to the burdens entailed by accumulation, "one is able to make a great deal of sense out of the political history of the modern world" and the "hydra-headed monster" of historical capitalism.[104]

Given these specific relations of historical capitalism, a panoply of "antisystemic movements" has developed which Wallerstein orders through an explication of the two "world revolutions" of 1848 and 1968. Although there have been many rebellions in the history of the capitalist world-system, Wallerstein argues that only these two revolutionary upsurges challenged the fundamental structures of the capitalist world-system.[105] These world revolutions were successful in that they gave birth to enduring antisystemic movements and also transformed the terrain and organizational forms for future struggles.

The revolution of 1848, the "springtime of nations," encouraged the idea of the self-determination of nations and widespread struggles for popular sovereignty within nation-states.[106] The failure of spontaneous uprisings for these principles in 1848 taught the lesson that "social transformation" required political and cultural organization, leading to the "institutionalization" of the first types of antisystemic movements. It also created a broad consensus that the proper middle run objective of these movements should be political organization for the seizure of state power.[107]

The revolution of 1848 produced two major antisystemic movements, the social movement (labor and/or socialist) and nationalist movements. "Both kinds of movements sought to achieve, in some broad sense, 'equality.' In fact, both kinds of movements used the three terms of the French revolutionary slogan of 'liberty, equality, and fraternity' virtually interchangeably."[108] The emergence of dual movements was a consequence of the two avenues of exploitation and conflict within the capitalist world-system: conflict within the nation-state, and conflict among the core, periphery, and semiperiphery. The social movement focused on "the oppression of the proletariat by the bourgeoisie" and struggled for improvement in the lives of laborers. Nationalist movements, on the other hand, were struggles for "oppressed peoples" or "minorities," defined by linguistic, ethnic, or colonial status. Both of these movements sought state power to achieve their goals because of the promise of immediate benefits and also because of the absence of an alternative entry point for challenging the capitalist world-system.[109]

Over the next century the movements of 1848 were remarkably successful at achieving their goals of state power, establishing themselves as the social democrats in Western Europe, the socialist countries, and post-liberation nationalist governments in various former colonies. Wallerstein insists that each type of movement in power could claim at least one significant "reform": the social democrats firmly established the welfare state; the communists nationalized the means of production, providing a real increase in social security, and laid the basis for very rapid industrialization; and national liberation movements completed the "indigenization of personnel," especially in government but also to a degree in economic and cultural positions.[110]

Overall, however, the strategy of seizing state power has proven to have several limitations. First, the struggle for political power typically requires a coalition including those who are not antisystemic. Secondly, as suggested above, there are real limits on the power of states in the world-economy and the interstate system. Therefore hopes were necessarily disappointed. Thirdly, Wallerstein frequently argues that the successful seizure of state power in the name of oppressed peoples can be relatively easily accommodated by the interstate system. In this way it turns into a reform of the world-system, not its alteration. For all these reasons, the strategy of seizure of state power has been at best a "cul-de-sac" for antisystemic movements.[111]

In response to these limitations of the classical antisystemic movements in contesting the dynamic of the capitalist world-system, a variety of new antisystemic movements developed, institutionalized, according to Wallerstein, in 1968.[112] There are three basic forms of these new movements, corresponding to the three older and immediately successful antisystemic movements. In the social-democratic West various movements of women, students, ethnic and racial minorities, and environmentalist groups have risen to challenge the project of social democracy. In the socialist countries Wallerstein mentions the radical dissidents who partly laid the groundwork for the reforms of Gorbachev, "extra-party, human rights" organizations, and the supporters of the Cultural Revolution in China in the 1960s. In fact, he calls the revolutions of 1989 the "continuation of 1968."[113] In the Third World the dilemmas of successful national liberation movements—the "unfulfilled revolution"—stimulated a variety of anti-Western and anti-universalist movements, including religious fundamentalism.[114]

For much of their history these new social movements have been sharply critical of the older antisystemic movements. Wallerstein argues that the Vietnam War pointedly revealed that the older movements had not only *not* altered the system but that some elements of the old left benefitted from and participated in the exploitation of other groups in the capitalist world-system. Furthermore, the older movements now in power did not know how to respond to the newer concerns of gender, ethnicity, and social issues brought to the forefront by changes in capitalist production, especially in the core countries. "[T]hey found themselves to a significant degree locked into reflecting this traditional central core of the working class whose numbers were no longer growing. They found it far more difficult to appeal politically to the three growing segments of the wage-labor force: the salaried professionals, the 'feminized' service-sector employees, and the 'ethnicized' unskilled or semi-skilled labor force."[115] Overall the new movements argued that the older movements, once in power, had simply lost their oppositional character. For their part, the classical movements charged that the new movements were divisive, middle class, and "anti-worker."

Historically, the concerns represented by the new movements had been regarded as secondary by the old left. The latter argued for concentrating on the "primary oppressed," either the working class in core movements or the nation in national liberation movements in the periphery and semiperiphery. This sortition of multiple oppressions into primary and secondary is precisely the central challenge of the new social movements, on the grounds that a majority group struggling against oppression does not really exist in either the core or the periphery. It was increasingly acknowledged that the "world's laboring strata" were not tending toward the "ideal-type of the 'proletarian' as traditionally conceived. The reality of capitalism was far more occupationally complex than that."[116] Similarly, all nationalist movements were immediately faced with the claims of domestic minorities for national expression. It is very easy to see that the logic of demands for national expression leads to an "unending cascade" of minorities, for which the strategy of seizure of state power by a specific group can offer no relief.

The denial of majority status for the groups at the center of classical social movements signaled the end of the notion of a primary struggle. For this reason, Wallerstein refers to 1968 as the "ideological tomb of the concept of the 'leading role' of the industrial proletariat."[117] After 1968, no oppressed group would "ever again accept the legitimacy of 'waiting' upon some other revolution."[118] This opened up the possibility of new perspectives and new strategies.

Like Offe and Habermas, Wallerstein includes a wide number of groups and issues among the new social movements, including gender, age, ethnicity, race, ecology, religions, human rights, and various dissident groups.[119] Regardless of the extreme diversity of these groups, Wallerstein argues that there are a few common themes. First, the three main new antisystemic movements—the twins of the three older antisystemic movements now in power—are decidedly anti-bureaucratic. According to Wallerstein, this is a response to the bureaucratization of social democratic parties, post-liberation governments, and state socialist countries and a response to the inefficacy of bureaucratic organs for furthering antisystemic struggle, as compared to the alternative demonstrated effectiveness of direct action.[120]

A second common theme, related to the first, is the rejection of state power as an immediate goal. It is not that the seizure of state power by older movements was a mistake; they really had no other option with any promise of success. However, although Wallerstein recognizes that state power is indeed one of the few levers of power in the world-economy, he doubts that the world-economy will be transformed through individual state action. He argues that the global character of capitalism has even made state ownership of production not as important nor as revolutionary as expected by older movements. Antisystemic movements must ultimately recognize the fact that "the seizure of state power by these movements is simply not a sufficient condition to permit the passage from a capitalist world-economy to a socialist world order."[121]

The challenge to the utility of state power is part of a broader "skepticism" regarding the "liberal consensus." "The Revolution of 1968 challenged . . . above all the belief that the state was a rational arbiter of conscious collective will."[122] Consequently, a third and most distinctive theme of the newer social movements is the importance of cultural struggle, broadly conceived. Wallerstein argues that this new focus on culture is partly inspired by "disillusionment with the efficacy of transforming the world by altering its economic or political forms." The object of the attack is "Enlightenment universalism," which Wallerstein frequently refers to as "the geoculture of the capitalist world-economy" and sometimes even by the classical term "ruling ideas."[123]

Wallerstein calls universalism "the keystone of the ideological arch of historical capitalism." Universalism facilitates the smooth functioning of global capitalism through "the creation of a world bourgeois cultural framework that could be grafted onto 'national' variations."[124] It became the mark of forward-looking persons in various parts of the world, associated with modernization, science, technology, and rationality itself. In this way universalism as Western science creates cadres who are separated from the unenlightened masses, participating in the fruits of exploitation and thus increasing security from revolts. As Wallerstein puts it, "scientific culture" became the "fraternal code" of those participating in the accumulation of capital, a source of "class cohesion for the upper stratum."[125]

Wallerstein contends that universalism can serve as the "veil" of exploitation in more ways than this. For example, it establishes the illusion of meritocracy. Universalism offers a ready explanation if a country does not progress. "[T]he universal work ethic justifies all existing inequalities, since the explanation of their origin is in the historically unequal adoption by different groups of this motivation."[126] In this way a culture of poverty argument is used to justify the impoverishment of countries, as well as of individuals of all countries. Meritocracy is not only compatible with the continued existence of hierarchy but reinforces it by providing a justification. Furthermore, universalism and scientific culture have facilitated and disguised the fundamental irrationality of capitalism: "The great emphasis on the rationality of scientific activity was the mask of the irrationality of endless accumulation."[127]

Wallerstein extends this argument concerning the ideological function of universalism to the concept of truth itself. He asserts that the search for truth, as a support for universalism, is a "self-interested rationalization." "Truth as a cultural ideal has functioned as an opiate, perhaps the only serious opiate of the modern world." However, ultimately Wallerstein's animus toward universalism and the search for truth is not epistemological but political: "The search for truth, proclaimed as the cornerstone of progress, and therefore of well-being, has been at the very least consonant with the maintenance of a hierarchical, unequal social structure in a number of specific respects."[128]

To some extent Wallerstein recognizes that any critique of universalism is problematic, demonstrated by the fact that the critique formulated by new social movements actually flows in two opposite directions. In the first instance, one can criticize capitalist universalism on the grounds that it overlooks the fact that the subordination of women and minorities is essential to the operation of capitalism as an historical system. Wallerstein seems to employ this sort of critique in his discussion of sexism and racism. For example, Wallerstein argues that racism has been a "cultural pillar of historical capitalism" in that it has been utilized as an ordering device for the re-creation of and justification of income differentials in occupational categories and in different regions of the world. However, the force of this criticism itself rests on the principle of universality, i.e., its moral force comes from criticizing the system for not living up to its universalistic pretensions (e.g., equality).

This is not the kind of critique in which Wallerstein is interested. In fact he repeatedly attacks Marx for employing this sort of critique. Wallerstein derides Marx's alleged allegience to Enlightenment universalism, especially to the universalist demands for liberty, equality, fraternity. According to Wallerstein, Marx typically relied on an immanent critique that merely sought to demonstrate the failure of universalist liberalism to live up to its own principles.[129] He thereby remained in the ideological ambit of universalism.

In contrast, the newer antisystemic movements promote a more provocative critique of universalism that can be broadly characterized as identity politics. Although he recognizes its manifestation in debates over gender and ethnicity, Wallerstein's major focus in this regard is on what he calls the "civilizational project" of various cultures in the world. The increasing emphasis on this form of cultural struggle has a clear material base among "elements economically and politically more marginal to the functioning of the system and less likely to profit, even eventually, from the accumulated surplus."[130] These movements reassert the value of non-European civilizations, again with special stress on the plural. In differing circumstances this cultural resistance has a "conservative" or a "radical tone." Either way, it is "a rejection of the hypothesis that capitalism in its only concrete existing form, a world-economy in fact dominated by the 'West,' [is] morally or politically 'better' than alternative historical systems."

A final aspect of the critique of universalism is "the 'new science,'" "a direct attack on the oldest intellectual pillar of the modern world-system, Baconian-Newtonian science."[131] The new science challenges traditional science on a number of grounds: its presumptions of equilibrium (rather than disequilibrium); its projection of isolated units (rather than seeing interaction as basic to analysis); its atemporal approach (rather than a universe crucially determined by time and recognition of a kind of "time internal to structures"); the separation of science and society (i.e., the "two cultures" argument); and its quest for universal laws (rather than the recognition that comprehending reality means appreciating diversity).[132] To the degree that Marxist social theory itself has pursued "eternal laws, symmetry, reversibility, and, therefore, the certainty of the future" it must be "cast out."

Wallerstein directly connects the emergence of a new science with the crisis of capitalism and the emergence of new antisystemic movements. He argues that it is only because historical capitalism is reaching a crisis that "the most basic consensuses are open for discussion for the first time since they were established." The new science is connected with the "civilizational project" in an obvious way: "Insofar as the crisis of the world-system is reflected in the 'civilizational project,' the world is rediscovering its wealth of alternative formulations of knowledge."[133] However, the "paradigms" of previous movements were ideologically intertwined with the Baconian worldview. Therefore Wallerstein argues that the crisis of the sciences is above all a crisis of the antisystemic movements themselves as they seek a new path beyond historical capitalism.[134]

ANTISYSTEMIC MOVEMENTS, CONTEMPORARY CAPITALISM, AND REVOLUTION

According to Wallerstein, recent directional tendencies of the capitalist world-economy have created new possibilities for antisystemic movements. Partly as a consequence of the successful seizure of the state by the classical social movements, there have been a number of changes in the world-system, amounting to a "structural transformation of the capitalist world-economy." First, there has been a "widening" and "deepening" of "stateness." By this Wallerstein means that an increased number of 'peoples' since World War II have achieved a nation-state expression. He is also referring to the increased internal strength of states relative to local organizations. However, Wallerstein also acknowledges the increasing density of the interstate system itself. The multitude of interstate organizations, the United Nations and regional agencies, international meetings, and other interstate relations entail a further decline in the sovereignty of nation-states. The effect of these simultaneous trends is the representation of more peoples in a denser interstate network.[135]

A second change in the world-economy, again in partial response to the successes of social movements, is intensification of the transnationalization of production. Of course the global coordination of production by large firms is not new. However, Wallerstein argues that the global social division of labor has been rapidly increasing in scale. "The transnational corporations' reconstruction of the world-scale division and integration of labor processes fundamentally alters the historical possibilities of what are still referred to, and not yet even nostalgically, as 'national economies.'"[136] Although the transnational character of capitalism is the key assumption of world-system theory, this aspect of capitalism has also clearly deepened and widened in recent years.

Thirdly, accompanying the extension of the division of labor, capital has become much more centralized through transnational financial agencies. The transnationalization of production creates an obvious problem for states in that production is coordinated by transnational corporations whereas states are still responsible for the labor forces that are employed in these activities. The resulting "massive contradictions" have encouraged the development of agencies for global financing. The intensified transnationalization of production has created a situation in which states must appeal to international lending agencies, which in turn are a kind of a "world ruling class in formation." The general response of these agencies is of course to require a lowering of the overall costs of production in the borrowing states, i.e., austerity. Wallerstein argues therefore that we are witnessing "the simultaneous growth in massive centralizations of capital and a sort of deconcentration of capital (called deindustrialization in present core areas of the axial division of labor)."[137] All of the above changes together create a fundamental "reconstitution of terrain" on which struggles over the system now proceed.

For example, the increasing density of state regulation has intensified the enduring issue of the relation of states to individual liberties. This is the impetus behind the increased demands for the defense of human rights against the predations (or perceived predations) of states, including demands for workers' rights and those of various other "status-groups."[138] This is part of a general restlessness of "civil society" and "increasingly 'anti-state' consciousness of the mass of the population." The deconcentration of production and resulting austerity regimes have increased the numbers of "official paupers" in the core itself, especially women, the young, and the elderly. This leads to legitimacy problems of states caused by the "structured incapacity of states to take care of their own" and widespread discontent by the clients of various state bureaucracies.[139] Overall

Wallerstein argues that these phenomena expose world-wide "contradictions between relations of rule and relations of production."

Wallerstein states that there is even some evidence that these changes may resurrect overt class struggle. One consequence of the social democratic welfare state in the West was increased inequality within the global proletariat, extending the possibility of unequal exchange. Capital responded by attempting to reduce labor inputs in the core and by relocating industry to more congenial climes. Wallerstein suggests that a possible consequence of this continuing relocation is that nationalist movements in peripheral countries may increasingly emphasize a class-conscious dimension.[140] In fact, he contends that since 1968 there has overall been a marked increase in the "unruliness of labor" and consequently a "growing frustration experienced by the functionaries of capital in their global search for safe havens of labor discipline." This unruliness of labor, seemingly contradicted by the experiences in the core, must be seen in a global perspective. Although the relocation of capital subdues labor militancy in the places it abandons, it increases it in its new locations. From this world-system standpoint, "We may well say that since 1968 the functionaries of capital have been 'on the run.'"[141]

The deconcentration of production seems to have especially shifted the "epicenter of 'classically' framed and conducted class conflict—direct, organized, large-scale capital-labor struggles" to the semiperiphery.[142] However, growing unemployment has also led to a reopening of fundamental questions in the core itself. Although the movements of 1968 were successful in the longterm in shifting the focus of the Left toward previously subordinate groups and issues, they have demonstrably failed in regard to the material improvement of any but a minority in the newer social movements. This failure of new left tactics has occasioned something of a rapproachment with the old left. This development contributes to Wallerstein's belief that, although conflicting tendencies exist, 1968 was a "rehearsal . . . of things to come."[143]

According to Wallerstein, there is no doubt that the historical system of capitalism will be replaced. It will perish of the intensive and extensive development of capitalism itself, i.e., of the secular trends of the "commodification of everything" and of the incorporation of new zones into the world-economy. It will also be pushed in this direction by the "social power" of labor in a globally differentiated but interdependent production process. The trends of commodification, incorporation, and the simultaneous centralization of capital and deconcentration of production are inalterable.[144]

What will replace capitalism is, however, a completely open question. Along with his other criticisms, Wallerstein attacks Marx for accepting the Enlightenment faith in progress, a faith that led Marx to conclude that capitalism was historically progressive. Wallerstein insists that, on this, "Marx was unequivocally wrong"; capitalism in many ways and for the vast majority transformed the world for the worse.[145] If we reject this inheritance of the Enlightenment, a progressive outcome to the impending transition is not preordained.

This denial of historical progress does not imply a denial of historical determinism. Wallerstein believes that determinism is inscribed in the systematicity of the world-system itself. "When a historical system is functioning normally—whatever the system, and thus including the capitalist world-economy—it seems to me that, almost by definition, it operates overwhelmingly as something that is determined. What does the word system mean if not that there are constraints on action? If these constraints didn't work, it would not be a system and it would rapidly disintegrate."[146] While functioning the system is also shored up by the "dominant ideology," which means that an historical system is in considerable measure "held together by the willing adherence of its members and not merely by overt force."

However, Wallerstein's view of the manner in which history is determined is almost the opposite of G. A. Cohen. Cohen believes that history is noncontingent in regard to epochal changes, although he is unsure of the ways in which the theses of historical materialism apply to nonepochal change. Influenced by the work of Braudel, Wallerstein argues that human activity is indeed governed by longterm cycles about which one can do very little.[147] But Wallerstein further contends that when the contradictions of the system intensify, this creates "a situation in which free will prevails." Determinism and cycles are internal to systems; there is no deterministic relation between systems.

Adapting bifurcation theory from the new science, Wallerstein argues that when a social system exhausts its capacity for renewal, necessity gives way to freedom. Bifurcation theory proposes that "systems move away from equilibrium states" and, as they do, small fluctuations lead to ever greater variations. Wallerstein extends this to historical systems: as capitalism reaches the limits of its recuperative mechanisms, small inputs can have greater and greater influence over possible trajectories. "It is on these occasions that it can be truly said that 'man makes his own history.'"[148] Wallerstein's historical vision is, then, one of long periods of determinism (cycles, ideology) followed by short periods of transition to the new, about which we can exercise choice. In brief, he suggests a resolution of the hoary issue of determinism versus freedom by assigning them different temporal periods.

Given this view, the direction of the future depends crucially on the outcomes of several basic debates within the antisystemic movements, including their very form of association itself. The above discussion has shown the extreme diversity of the "world family of antisystemic movements." Wallerstein argues that in contrast to earlier strategies of unification, today it is widely believed that the multiplicity of movements in the world must simply be accepted.[149] Even if it were possible, for several reasons it would be undesirable to reduce this multiplicity through a unified organization. First, as stated, a well-defined majority that could be accorded priority simply does not exist. "[I]t is important to remember that it is not the case that *some* movements are 'universalistic' and *others* 'particularistic.' *All* existing movements are in some ghetto."[150] Secondly, the distrust of organization is in general salutary, as shown by the limitations of the seizure of state power and by the bureaucratization of earlier movements. Thirdly, particularism is itself part of the goal of a robust civil society that will be able to check state power and ensure liberty of a variety of sorts.

This dilemma of appropriate organization is further intensified by a nagging ambivalence concerning universalism. In a discussion reminiscent of Habermas, Wallerstein argues that the abstract and irresistable forces of global capitalism continually engender particularistic defensive responses. Utilizing the classical sociological categories, Wallerstein describes the capitalist world-system as a society (*Gesellschaft*) that has destroyed traditional communities (*Gemeinschaften*). However, contrary to the classical view of modernization, new communitarian projects proliferate in an attempt to restore meaning in the midst of this maelstrom.

> [T]hey are the common consequence of the relentless spread of the ever more formally rational and ever more substantively irrational historical social system in which we all find ourselves collectively trapped. They represent screams of pain against the irrationality that oppresses in the name of a universal, rationalizing logic. Had we really been moving from *Gemeinschaft* to *Gesellschaft,* all this would not be occurring. We should instead be bathing in the rational waters of an Enlightenment world.[151]

Instead, the abstract universalizing of global capitalism has provoked what appears to be a "worldwide cultural rebellion."

In this way the capitalist world-economy generates a dichotomy between universality and particularity which creates additional uncertainties for antisystemic movements. On the one hand, universalism has been exposed as compatible with oppression. On the other, to simply accept multiple civilizations is to "risk immolation in archaisms" that could be "crippling because non-growing." Wallerstein raises the possibility of "a long period of confusion and the erratic emergence of new mysticisms" and even "mindless cultural pluralism."[152] To this point, the antisystemic movements are "unsure how to respond to the liberal dream of more science and more assimilation."

These considerations have led to doubts among antisystemic movements even regarding appropriate middle run objectives. Wallerstein insists that some kind of joint activity is necessary for a progressive outcome and therefore the various movements must strive for transnational, especially "trans-zonal," links in order to form an "alliance of the multiple groups of the oppressed." Although this is exceedingly difficult, given the differences among the everyday concerns of the oppositional movements in the different zones of the world-economy, Wallerstein is optimistic.[153]

The major problem is formulating an alternative to the strategy of seeking state power. Wallerstein says that it is clear that there are other sources of power than state power, such as "control of economic institutions," "control of cultural institutions," the threat of disruption, etc. The earlier generation of antisystemic movements usually regarded "power other than in state-machineries [as] a lesser form required *in order that* one be in a position to control the state." Wallerstein rather vaguely recommends that control of state power today be relegated to at most a tactic of social movements, not their primary objective.[154] Like many others who have raised the issue, he points to the respect for limits expressed by the Solidarity movement in its first phase. However, he also realistically notes that it is difficult to see how this revaluation of multiple sites of struggle for power can be articulated with an effective political project.

The question of antisystemic strategy is further complicated by Wallerstein's view of the transition from capitalism itself. According to Wallerstein, the real goal should not actually be "controlled transformation" of the system at all but rather "acceleration" of its "decadence." "One of the strongest and perhaps least useful heritages of the Enlightenment is the feeling that since change is possible, it is only possible or optimally possible through rational social planning."[155] Wallerstein argues that decadent transitions are preferable first of all because of the inherent threats to freedom contained in controlled anything, endemic to organization of any kind, including antisystemic movements. A second reason is that antisystemic movements themselves contain elements that are seeking advantage, and in transitional periods (Russia and eastern and central Europe could be recent examples) these elements seek controlled transformation precisely in order to maintain hierarchy and privilege for themselves. Wallerstein argues that the most dangerous moment comes when change is inevitable and therefore everyone starts to support it. "[T]he most obvious technique for the holders of current power to construct new veils would be to take the lead themselves in destroying the old system in the name of constructing the new. I believe this is what happened in the so-called transition from feudalism to capitalism, although I know this is a controversial position."[156] Some of these elements in the present are likely to be from the administrative and salaried bourgeoisie. They will insist, for example, on the unavoidability of hierarchy in order to preserve a role for their privileged position. To forestall this possibility, the internal struggles of the antisystemic movements are of the utmost importance.

Therefore, for all its dangers, Wallerstein prefers the disintegration of the present system to its controlled transformation.

> We must lose our fear of a transition that takes the form of crumbling, of disintegration. Disintegration is messy, it may be somewhat anarchic, but it is not necessarily disastrous. "Revolutions" may in fact be "revolutionary" only to the degree they promote such crumbling. Organizations may be essential to break the crust initially. It is doubtful they can actually build the new society.[157]

It is this path of disintegration that is most likely to lead to a "relatively egalitarian, relatively democratic world order."

Wallerstein usually describes this world order as socialism, sometimes defined as "production for use" but more specifically as a kind of market socialism. Again following Braudel, Wallerstein argues that competitive markets are clear, predictable, nonexploitative (low-profit), open modes of social interchange.[158] Bringing our discussion around full circle, he suggests that the problem of capitalism is not markets but the continual striving for monopolistic advantage. "It will in fact only be with a socialist world-system that we will realize true freedom (including the free flow of the factors of production)."[159]

In several places Wallerstein states that his theorizing is an attempt to present an "alternative organizing myth" to the prevailing one regarding the development and progressive nature of historical capitalism. More recently he rejects the word myth in favor of "metahistory" or "heuristic theory." By this Wallerstein means that the role of social theory is political, to develop perspectives that demonstrate the absence of "substantive rationality" in historical capitalism and to help "illuminate the historical choices" that he believes are on the horizon "rather than presume to make them."[160]

Perhaps by its very nature this approach to social theory is not very satisfying and Christopher Chase-Dunn, another world-system theorist, insists that it is time for world-system theory to go beyond merely heuristic theory.[161] Wallerstein himself admits the ambiguities of his analyses and proposals. However, he asserts that, given the circumstances, "it is as concrete as one can be in the midst of a whirlpool."[162] Regardless of the general obscurity of our situation, "we are condemned to act."

CRITICISMS OF WALLERSTEIN'S THEORY

It is not surprising that there are numerous criticisms of a theory as bold, frequently obscure, and inconsistent as Wallerstein's world-system theory. The most immediate problem is the assertion that there are cyclical movements in historical capitalism. Aristide Zolberg rejects the assertion outright. He objects to the general reliance of world-system theory on "extremely abstract properties such as 'rhythms' and 'cycles,'" arguing rather persuasively that: "Cycles of *something* are always to be found."[163] Even some world-system theorists, such as Chase-Dunn, admit the hypothetical character of the various cycles argued by world-system theory. Similarly Thomas Shannon, a sympathetic critic, points to the difficulty of operationalizing the concept of cycles and indicates disagreements over their duration.

In response to these doubts, Wallerstein suggests that the problem lies in the collection of appropriate data. However, the cycles integral to world-system theory actually present a logical problem. A primary objective of any cyclical theory must be not only to reveal regularity but also explain why the periodicity itself is constant. In the case of world-system theory, the Kondratieff waves allegedly occur every 50 or 60 years. The contraction phase is ended both by the development of new technologically sophisticated production processes employed by the core and also by political struggles to redistribute the appropriated surplus in order to stimulate demand, that is, political intervention contributes to the beginning of a new Kondratieff expansion. However on this explanation, if Kondratieff waves are to be convincing one would have to show why appropriate political intervention constantly occurs at 50–60 year intervals. Not only economic (price movements, investment) cycles must be proven; political interventions must also evince a remarkable regularity since these are a crucial determinant of the Kondratieff dynamic.

The only attempt at hypothesizing political regularity of this type is the proposed hegemonic cycles of the interstate system. However, hegemonic cycles are unusable for this purpose in that they have a much longer periodicity than Kondratieffs and are even more speculative. "In only a very rough sense is this [hegemony] a cycle because its periodicity is very uneven."[164] In fact, there have only been three hegemons since the sixteenth century: the Netherlands, Great Britain, and the United States. Wallerstein himself argues that the concept of hegemonic cycles should not be stressed overly much.[165] Therefore this is not promising for helping explain the more immediate periodicity of K-waves.

This is a very serious weakness in Wallerstein's theory because the existence of K-waves is crucial for Wallerstein's diagnosis of and prognosis for capitalism. Wallerstein argues that in the immediate future there will be an economic upturn, based on the beginning of a new Kondratieff expansion. He is somewhat inconsistent as to whether this will be "more spectacular" or "more 'glorious'" than the post-war expansion or "not quite as spectacular."[166] Regardless, Wallerstein states that this will be the final K-wave because the secular trends engendered by the repeated expansions will have reached their asymptotes. This cannot be persuasive unless the existence and periodicity of K-waves are better formulated.

A related problem is Wallerstein's insistence on secular trends. If cycles are not clearly established, neither are secular trends. If anything, having abolished the teleology of progress Wallerstein tries to bring teleology back in as secular trends. We have already noted that Wallerstein has recently shifted his argument from proletarianization to simply commodification. However, although Wallerstein indicates several developments typically mentioned in regard to the transnationalization of production and fluidity of global finance, it is difficult to give content to the phrase "the commodification of everything." It is tolerably clear to say that geographical incorporation of new areas has limits. But Wallerstein's frequent statements that we are approaching asymptotes in regard to commodification, or that the limit on proletarianization is "100%," are completely uninstructive mathematical analogies.

Wallerstein is pushed to such analogies in his attempt to delineate necessity in history. The concept system does indeed imply some kind of necessity. However, one can rebut the systematicity of the world-system itself. Theda Skocpol, for example, criticizes Wallerstein's reliance on "system-maintenance arguments" because of their functionalist or teleological basis.[167] Zolberg, on the other hand, does not reject the use of systems concepts in general but argues that the world system is much too broad a formulation, resulting in an unhelpful abstraction or universal. Zolberg says that "petty materialism" and "systems analysis" simply result in an "impossible hybrid paradigm" and praises Braudel's history in contrast for its relative lack of systematicity.[168]

Closer to Wallerstein's own perspective, Etienne Balibar rejects similar aspects of Wallerstein's theory on the grounds that the global economy is not in itself a social unit. Social units should be distinguished from the economic unity of the world today. He proposes that the "overall movement of the world-economy is the random *result* of the movement of its social units rather than its cause."[169] Contrary to Wallerstein, Balibar argues that transnational economic forces, on the one hand, and domestic social relations, on the other, create a conflict-ridden situation that is "not immediately totalizable."

In related attacks on the systematicity of the world-system, many critics insist that Wallerstein's system-theory leads him into class reductionism, a "systematic neglect of political structures and processes."[170] The recommended alternative to Wallerstein's view is always a variant of the autonomy of the political: "intersecting structures" with "autonomous logics"; "relative independence of political and economic development"; "political structure as an irreducible and relatively autonomous systemic element"; "two separate but interactive explanatory logics, i.e., sets of premises and conceptual apparatus."[171] The political is asserted to have its own logic because of the solidity of the governmental apparatus, historically circumscribed, or because of its specific concerns, such as national security.[172] One can easily anticipate that Wallerstein's rejoinder to this criticism would be that the separation of polity and economy is liberal ideology. We need not rehearse that debate here.

However, it is important to point out that Wallerstein's attempt to describe historical capitalism in a holistic fashion does lead him into a central inconsistency that bears on this discussion. Wallerstein insists on the economic, political, and cultural unity of the system. "I assume that a historical system must represent an integrated network of economic, political, and cultural processes the sum of which hold the system together."[173] As noted, Wallerstein sometimes emphasizes the unity of the interstate system to the point of calling it a "political superstructure." Similarly he also asserts the existence of a "geoculture" that furthers Western liberal universalism.[174] To reinforce these points he occasionally even uses the traditional Marxian phraseology of ruling class and ruling ideas.

The problem with this emphasis on unity is that it contradicts Wallerstein's own concept of a world-system. Wallerstein distinguishes world-systems from minisystems by the criterion that the former operate through many cultures. Furthermore, Wallerstein's fundamental notion of a world-economy distinct from a world-empire requires the separation of politics and economy.[175] In short, Wallerstein undermines his own specific notion of world-economy by insisting too much on the integration of economics, politics, and culture.

Wallerstein's original definition of a world-economy as a single social division of labor operating through multiple cultures and multiple polities is much more intriguing than a system that is substantially economically, politically, and culturally unified. The functional unity of all major dimensions of society is a part of the Marxian heritage that has obstructed analysis of how the disjunctions between these social dimensions can unleash murderous impulses in the world. Wallerstein is correct to challenge the idea of independent logics of spheres that are then only contingently related to each other. However, we must not overstate the case for unity. His theory is most powerful when we recognize several dimensions of human life, each requiring resources from the others. To be sure, these aspects of society should be conceived as operating through, not above or behind each other. Nevertheless, an over-emphasis on unity compromises this perspective.

Wallerstein honestly admits that overcoming the distinctions between polity, economy, and culture is the "hardest nut to crack."[176] The basic problem with Wallerstein's approach is that a critique not only criticizes theoretical categories but is also intended to lay bare the conditions for the existence and general plausibility of these categories. It is in this way that one shows the limits of theoretical categories, not by mere exhortation or by theoretical (and verbal) fiat. One must show the reasons a certain theoretical categorization has been so ubiquitous and why it is so difficult to escape. Wallerstein cannot carry through this critique because he has not well articulated his conception of the differentiated unity of historical capitalism.

Another area of dispute—and perhaps most damaging to world-system theory—is the origin of the surplus or surplus value. The fact that Wallerstein uses the two terms interchangeably without explanation already indicates a problem. Leaving aside the previously discussed deficiencies of the labor theory of value, the primary issue is the role of technology in producing a surplus. As noted earlier, Wallerstein usually speaks of technology not in regard to increased efficiencies but as creating temporary monopolistic positions through dominance of a portion of a commodity chain or through the establishment of a new commodity chain. Furthermore, Wallerstein's conception of unequal exchange does not rest on the idea of different levels of productivity, but largely on different general wage levels. Robert Brenner argues that from this perspective capitalism "appears to be essentially one more system based primarily on the extraction of what we have called absolute surplus labor."[177]

Brenner argues that capitalism is distinguished from precapitalist forms by its "*systematic* tendency" for economic development, especially through "what might be called (after Marx's terminology) relative as opposed to absolute surplus labor." For Wallerstein, on the other hand, "the growth of the world division of labor *is* the development of capitalism."

> In essence, his view of economic development is *quantitative* . . . Wallerstein does not, in the last analysis, take into account the development of the forces of production through a process of accumulation by means of innovation ('accumulation of capital on an extended scale'), in part because to do so would undermine his notion of the essential role of the underdevelopment of the periphery in contributing to the development of the core, through surplus transfer to underwrite accumulation there.[178]

To the contrary, Brenner insists that the source of accumulation under capitalism is the development of relative surplus labor caused by competitive pressures to raise the productivity of labor through technological innovation.[179] Competitive pressure is only channelled in this direction if the factors of production are free. In conditions of coerced labor there is actually an opposite tendency to utilize the extant surplus to strengthen the ability to coerce labor, i.e., to strengthen the means for exploitation through extraction of absolute surplus labor. Therefore, in the situation of coerced labor, the surplus is not ploughed back into improvement of the productive forces.[180]

Brenner contends that underdevelopment is largely a consequence of the history of class relations in underdeveloped countries and the logic of modes of surplus extraction that flows from these relations. He does not "deny that there was a long-term transfer of surplus away from the periphery" but argues that this transfer stems from a "different dynamic" than the one argued in world-system theory.[181] The relative stagnation of productivity under conditions of coerced labor is counterbalanced by the capacity of the dominant class to lower labor costs by reducing the subsistence of laborers. Consequently, the overall market for both capital and consumer goods has been quite small. This "class-structured character of the profit opportunities" in coerced labor situations has meant little capital investment and a reliance on the core for efficient production of goods for the relatively small domestic market. "In other words, the development of underdevelopment was rooted in the class structure of production based on the extension of absolute surplus labour, which determined a sharp *disjuncture* between the requirements for the development of the productive forces (productivity of labour) and the structure of profitability of the economy as a whole."[182] Contrary to Wallerstein's view of core accumulation as "a 'primitive accumulation of capital' extracted from the periphery," analyses of development and underdevelopment must "specify the particular, historically developed class structures" through which the processes of accumulation must proceed.[183]

According to Brenner, if one argues that participation in the world market underdevelops a country, a number of unhelpful political conclusions follow: strategies for "autarchic" development; assertions that the primary fault line is between core and periphery, which results in recommendations of a coalition with national bourgeoisies; "Third-worldist ideology"; arguments for "socialism in one country"; and the argument that the core proletariat has been "bought off" by the surplus.[184] Wallerstein's occasional collaborator, Samir Amin, draws precisely these conclusions in making his argument for "delinking," relating it to China's historic path of "self-reliance."[185]

In another place Brenner also rejects the underconsumptionist explanation of capitalism's difficulties that underlies the theory of Wallerstein and others. Brenner agrees that there is presently a capitalist crisis caused by the decline of profitability. However, he criticizes theories of Fordism and post-Fordism which emphasize demand problems allegedly resulting from the erosion of an institutional framework that maintained high wage levels and consumption. Brenner argues that demand does not simply rest on institutional forms distributing the surplus through wages, i.e., demand should not be conflated with wage levels. Demand is also generated by investment which stimulates demand for capital goods, not immediately consumer goods. Although it is unclear, Brenner's analysis suggests instead that the origin of the decline of profitability must be sought in the dynamic of investment necessitated by the specific social relations of competitive capitalism.[186]

There is support for Brenner's general critique of world-system theory in that the statistics do not appear to bear out the thesis that development of the core rests on the underdevelopment of the periphery. In response,

Chase-Dunn acknowledges that the percentage of surplus from the periphery is smaller than that produced in the core itself but asserts that it is still qualitatively important for maintaining labor peace in the core, helping during economic slumps, and reducing conflict among core states. Wallerstein himself states that the question is still open.[187] On the other hand, this concession has been explicitly rejected by Samir Amin. He insists that "the view that value belongs only to the process of production is an 'alibi' of Western-centered Marxism, which makes it possible to eliminate the problem of imperialism."[188] It is for good reason that Charles Tilly refers to theoretical struggles over the relative importance of production versus circulation as "that bloody field."[189]

Wallerstein acknowledges the difficulties of the issues involved. He says that the "complex lines delimiting the spheres of necessary labor, relative surplus value, and levels of livelihood" are "poorly understood theoretically."[190] However, once one admits the possibilities of technology for creating a surplus, the concept of unequal exchange is devalued. We must then re-examine the importance of the institutional frameworks of individual states and also focus attention on exactly how labor is oppressed in these countries, revealing the avenues labor has for resistance, challenge, and change. The deconcentration of production in the world does indeed appear to establish a global division of labor. In whatever way conceived, this means that the options for individual states are increasingly constrained by transnational economic forces. However, these forces will always be refracted through the specific class relations in individual nations.

Finally, it needs to be noted that, regardless of his occasional strong statements to the contrary, Wallerstein is himself quite ambivalent about Enlightenment universalism, resulting in frequent inconsistencies in his arguments. As noted, he often refers to the slogan of "liberty, equality, fraternity" as liberal ideology and condemns Marx for accepting it. On the other hand, Wallerstein is as likely as not to invoke the slogan and these values himself. In one place Wallerstein even argues that "liberty, equality, fraternity" was not actually a slogan of triumphant capitalism but a slogan of the first antisystemic movement against capitalism. In another place he rightly states that there will always be a continuing tension between the universal and the particular, and then speaks of "particularisms whose object (avowed or not) would be the restoration of the universal reality of liberty and equality." In fact, Wallerstein suggests that a promising strategy for social movements would be an insistence on equality on the local level, in the sense of attempting to retain more of the surplus generat-

ed at each link in a commodity chain. Finally, and most recently, Wallerstein vigorously argues for democracy and human rights.[191]

These rampant inconsistencies result from the fact that—as Wallerstein notes in regard to the national expression of peoples—even claims
for the protection of diversity unavoidably appeal to universalistic principles.[192] As Habermas contends, this appears to be a logical necessity of
'making a claim' at all. Universalism is simply not that easy to escape.
For related reasons Wallerstein insists that the new science is a scientific
critique of science, backing away somewhat from the relativism entailed by
his criticism of truth as an opiate.[193] It is simply difficult to argue that
truth is an opiate and then expect anyone to accept this statement as true.

If universalism is not pure bourgeois ideology, if the new science is
still science, if the institutions of individual states continue to have an important role to play, and if the world-system is not a political, economic,
and cultural unity, it is unclear in what ways the new antisystemic movements should be regarded as antisystemic. Even if one attempts to evade
this question by arguing that there will be an economically legislated last
crisis of some sort—as Wallerstein comes close to doing—or simply
hopes that the various extant movements will rattle the system apart, disintegration is not likely to turn out well. If there are dangers in the revolutionary model of the transition from feudalism to capitalism, the transition
from slave society to feudalism was equally unattractive. The decay of
Rome led to the Dark Ages.

Perhaps the greatest strength of Wallerstein's theory is that it contributes to an expanded notion of the direct producers that forces us to
grapple with many phenomena of the world today as something other than
survivals. Under certain reasonable definitions, exploitation can take
place outside of the wage labor relationship. Although Wallerstein's apparent retraction of the thesis of increasing proletarianization weakens
other aspects of his theory, it does appear to be true that in the core more
and more individuals need to supplement wage labor with other activities
and income to reproduce their households. Besides self-provisioning labor
and nonmarket labor exchanges, there seems to be increased reliance on
transfer payments, income pooling in extended households, and petty market operations. It is at least an arguable and interesting hypothesis that
these reproduction strategies will increase with permanent unemployment
in the core as well as the periphery. In this regard, Wallerstein's arguments
can be added to those previously discussed which suggest a decline in the
formative effects of wage labor.

Some may object that Wallerstein's portrayal of the direct producers is much too broad to be useful. A concept that contains too much is empty. Furthermore, the rejection of the importance of specifically wage labor in defining capitalism would have many powerful reverberations that must be confronted at the outset. The priority of the wage relation is the basis for many theses in Marxian historiography and social analysis. It governs the portrayal of the transition from feudalism to capitalism (the freeing of labor to work for wages), the argument for the progressive character of capitalism (a type of freedom), the explanation for the emergence of popular forms of government (abstract freedom of individuals), and the analysis of the specific dynamic of the capitalist process of production (exploitation is hidden by the free labor contract). If anything, the classical definition of capitalism underpins the separation of polity and economy, in that, as Marx put it, "other than economic pressure" is no longer necessary for exploitation.

However, some of these arguments are only important for establishing the history of capitalism, not its future. Secondly, it is actually rather strained to analyze, for example, Southern slavery as separate from the capitalist mode of production. If one defines capitalism according to the wage relation, one must resort to theoretical constructions of 'dominant' forms within a 'social formation' which always seem rather cobbled together. In this respect Wallerstein's argument is simpler and more persuasive. Thirdly, as discussed in several places in previous chapters, the decline of the formative effects of wage labor does not entail that the fundamental class relation of capitalism—the private appropriation of the fruits of social labor—has lost any of its currency for determining the multiple problems and trajectory of contemporary capitalism.

Another strength of Wallerstein's analysis is his insistence on the role of the state in the multidimensional competition that constitutes the global market. However, it is precisely because of this role that the apocalyptic extension of the cash nexus—the commodification of everything—is in doubt. For one thing, as argued by Offe and Habermas, the activities of the state are decommodified. One could respond that states are increasingly bypassed by global economic forces. This is an arguable position. But if we accept that the forces operate through, not above nor behind, existing institutional frameworks, it is equally plausible to predict serious and continuing battles to restrain these forces. Struggles against commodification will keep pace with forces for commodification for the simple reason that a society based solely on the cash nexus could not endure a single day. A society of strategically acting individuals is inconceivable. To use Habermas's term, the pathologies would be overwhelming long before that.

In one place Wallerstein states that world-systems analysis is not a theory, but a protest.[194] It works as a protest. Wallerstein's refusal to regard coerced labor, religious fundamentalisms in all parts of the world, and ethnic strife to the point of genocide as simply anomalies destined to disappear is important and realistic. We are, as he says, in the midst of a worldwide cultural rebellion and it no doubt draws much of its sustenance from an expanding global division of labor, an economic order that operates through multiple cultures and multiple polities. The dynamic of the historical period in which we live comes from the tensions of this fractured global society. However, this cultural rebellion is not simply aimed at the West; it is being fought out today domestically in almost every country in the world in the form of proliferating bigotries. Wallerstein's work provokes discussion that may help us to eventually uncover the causes of the death of progress. But for this, we will need theories.

Eight

Contemporary Capitalism and Its Discontents

Socialism aims at the abolition of class relations, the form of inequality in our historical epoch that more than any other determines our collective possibilities. Traditionally this project has been understood as 'universalization,' the furthering and deepening of the bourgeois revolution by extending it to all social spheres. Capitalism itself has promoted universalization by generalizing the commodity form, creating a global economy, breaking down cultural isolation, and establishing a common discourse on a kind of political freedom and equality. Socialism has generally been conceived as the completion of this revolution, building on the groundwork of capitalism. Since the proletariat has also been regarded as the vehicle of socialism, the universalizing impulse has manifested itself in strategies of purifying this agent, showing possible ways of ameliorating alternative, obstructive identities. Class formation has meant identifying and furthering the processes through which the proletariat can actualize its concept.

This strategy has been driven by two important beliefs. The first is that, although the proletariat is an abstraction, it is a 'real abstraction.' The labor theory of value proposes that commodities are only comparable in that they contain labor. Commodification transforms concrete labor into abstract labor, thereby establishing the respective values of the things exchanged. This process allows capitalist commodity markets to form an autonomous realm of social relations, i.e., an economy. Only in this way could the law of value emerge as the independent regulator of social life.

Besides the technical and logical problems of the labor theory of value, and the difficulties of relative surplus value, this theory is unpersuasive to the extent that the value of a commodity is determined by noneconomic factors. It is now abundantly clear that noneconomic factors are ineliminable in capitalist society. Individual states in domestic and foreign policy, transnational institutions such as the International Monetary Fund, national and global corporations, trade unions, the National Zapatista Liberation Army, currency speculators, and innumerable other agencies all seek more or less successfully to alter the value of commodities. To the degree that this is true, the dynamic of capitalism does not rest on the real abstraction of the transformation of concrete labor into abstract labor. Indeed, the distinction between labor and labor-power itself depends on the fact that the application of labor, and therefore the labor content of any particular commodity, is not simply given. For all of these reasons, we must conclude that labor is irreducibly concrete and therefore the proletariat is in this respect only an ordinary abstraction.

In addition to Marx's theoretical understanding of the processes of abstract labor, there is a second basis for his belief that the concept of the proletariat would be increasingly realized. The ineluctable proletarianization of the producers of the world would simplify and clarify class relations. Against some of his own earlier theses, Wallerstein provides persuasive evidence that this is not the case. If we look at the United States alone we see that the survival strategies of producers under pressure are becoming increasingly multiform, including transfer payments and public services such as Medicaid, insurance claims, petty commodity trading such as garage sales and flea markets, small time speculation (baseball cards, collectables), direct labor for oneself and direct exchange of labor with family and friends, begging, criminal activities, and various other extensions of the informal economy. Increasing proletarianization is no longer a tenable thesis even in the metropoles.

Abstractions must be evaluated by their usefulness; the proletariat is no longer a useful abstraction. This is an enormous blow to the Marxian theory of history. Marxian theory requires that the proletariat overthrow capitalism. Marx expected that, under appropriate historical conditions, the proletariat would develop the class capacities to do so. However, abstractions do not act. Unless one believes in a breakdown theory, without the proletariat the fettering of the forces of production becomes equally abstract. Deprivations, antagonisms, and struggles exist, but not contradictions. Without an agent, the case for socialism more and more appears to rely on moral exhortation.

Given this confusing theoretical situation, it is important to note certain recurring themes in recent Marxian discussion. First, the expansiveness and multiple displacements of the capitalist welfare state make the topic of sheer ownership or nonownership of property less fruitful for orienting socialist strategy. The forms of ownership are so diverse and the rights of property so complex and subject to legal interpretation that the bourgeoisie also increasingly seems to be a relatively unhelpful abstraction. Furthermore, state intervention has altered the grounds for existence of both classes through public provision of services, tax policy and fiscal manipulation, and the horizontal cleavages stimulated by public policy in general. The commodification activities of states are such that political power is immediately involved in reproducing the relations between capital and labor and the conditions under which investment and appropriation take place. As neoconservatives know, the market is not natural. Today domestically, and even to a considerable degree transnationally, it is more than ever a political design for the social relations among individuals. It is precisely for the reason that the market is not natural that neoconservatives must maintain the incessant drumbeat that it is.

A second theme is, somewhat paradoxically, that the socialist strategy of seizing state power is exhausted. The paradox is alleviated if we recognize that the extension of state activities entails increased pressure for the cooperation or at least the acquiescence of various social sectors. The vision of the state as a self-contained entity that simply orders things done, backed up by the threat of force, is misleading. Offe persuasively argues that the interventionist state cannot perform its tasks without the cooperation of many of the affected. More generally, Habermas insists on the importance of eliciting motivations for society to function. We cannot assume that such motivations will be forthcoming. Although we must be careful not to overstate the need for cooperation, in a complex and interdependent society there are limits to the strategy of divide and rule.

If this is true, then there is promise in the nonstate socialist strategy of influencing policy through the mobilization of civil society. However, the feasibility of this approach depends on clarifying the conditions of emergence of alternative kinds of power and of noncapitalist veto groups. Furthermore, the dependence of state on society and the variety of forces included under the rubric of civil society create the real possibility of stalemate, collapse, and political reaction. Disintegration could lead to something worse than capitalism. It would likely reinforce the fascist forces in the world, in either their velvet or genocidal variants.

A third recurring theme is the increased emphasis of Marxian theorists on normative questions. In Marxian theory the revolutionary agent is usually conceived in a more or less utilitarian fashion, as shown in G. A. Cohen's rational adaptive practices interpretation of history, in Wright's attempts to reveal the interest structure of contemporary capitalism, and in the ubiquity of the word 'interest' in Marxian discussion. Even many of those who reject the proposition that class position automatically results in political interests base their emendation of Marxian theory on the category interest, merely insisting that interest is formed on other grounds. In fact most Marxian analyses of revolutionary agency are essentially guided by the prospects of the emergence of a kind of collective utilitarianism, that people will revolt because it is in their interest to do so. Many have demonstrated that such a class interest can only exist in the abstract and as such cannot motivate individual action. Rational choice theorists have further shown that fragmentation and paralysis are the lot of a collection of self-interested individuals.

However, since people do act collectively, it is quite reasonable to investigate normative motivations for participation. It is true that moral exhortation alone will not challenge capitalism but this is too simplistic a way of putting the issue. Normative commitments partially form one's very identity and thereby help an individual make sense of her or his life. Norms help create meaning, an apparently universal desire that must not be underestimated. The concept of self-interest immediately begs the question of the self one is attempting to advance. "What shall I do" is inseparable from the question "who am I?" Morals, meaning, and identity are inextricably bound together and form powerful, in fact inescapable, motivations. Therefore an analysis of the generation and flux of moral commitment—a sociology of injustice—is a necessity if we are to comprehend the possibilities of challenging capitalism.

This brings us to the extremely important theme of identity and the politics that flows from this inexhaustible source. We can be agnostic on the degree to which capitalism is a self-regulating system and still recognize that there are many forces in the world that evade traditional strategies of control. These anonymous forces in turn intensify the desire for comprehending one's place in the world. Although the transnationalization of production does not mean that various groups will simply stop trying to influence the dynamic of capitalism, it does mean at the least that the consequences of this struggle will be increasingly difficult to anticipate and largely unintended. As capitalism becomes more universal it becomes more mysterious. Habermas argues that myth-making in archaic societies is a response to "the experience of being delivered up unprotected to the contingencies of an unmastered environment."[1] This would help explain the explosion of mythical—and even magical—thinking in the world today.

The overarching conclusion that can be derived from the theories we have discussed is that class formation has been exhausted as a topic and point of departure for socialist theory. The universalization expressed in the political strategy of class formation is fatally flawed. As Marx frequently indicated—in the critique of representation in his work on Hegel, in his analysis of labor in *Capital,* in his critique of equality in the *Gotha Programme*—naked universalization is abstract, empty, and alienating. Since the social and political relations of capitalism are not exclusive enough to produce stable class identities, it is not surprising that identities are formed through other more immediate ascriptive and quasi-ascriptive relations such as family, gender, geographical location, nation, religion, age, and language. Contrary to what used to be sociological dogma, ascriptive identities persist and appear to even be strengthened in capitalism because of its general displacements and deprivations: the universalism of capitalism produces an ascriptive reaction.

Given the immense strength of ascriptively defined groups as a consequence of the dislocations of capitalism, the tenuous and ephemeral character of class subjectivity when achieved, and the electoral dynamic of capitalist democracies which continually disorganizes identities, socialist political practice may be better directed toward attempts to further direct democracy and functional representation of groups in the institutions of government. Direct democracy has been often argued but functional representation requires a few remarks here. Functional representation of a variety of existing groups directly in national political institutions will alter the political terrain on which the struggle over class relations takes place. It cannot but have the effect of increasing the voices and considerations that shape public policy. It is much more direct than electoral struggle, less alienating than the abstract inclusion in a polity under the rubric of citizenship, and, a fundamental point according to Schumpeter and Przeworski, it holds out the prospect of immediate benefits for the represented groups. It is no secret that functional representation of certain groups, representatives of various bourgeois fractions, already exists through interest group activity in legislatures and especially in executive agencies. Rather than decrying this in the name of universality, we should extend it by insisting on the institutional representation of more groups.

It goes without saying that these groups are not class groups. However, although a class subject does not exist this does not mean that the construction of identities is completely open. Class subjects may not exist but class relations do. A socialist movement will only be established by continually demonstrating that, although the elimination of capitalist relations is not a sufficient condition to satisfy their demands, it is still a necessary condition. Class struggle has to be refocused as a struggle against class relations, without the comfort of a possible universal class emerging.

In his analyses of contemporary political struggles Marx did not suggest that socialists wait for a pure revolutionary agent to emerge. We must create political institutional arenas—direct democracy and functional representation—in which the socialist case can be more directly discussed and in which the groups participating in the discussion have immediate institutional power.

The institutionalization of functional representation of groups is not unproblematic. All proposals for functional representation from feudalism through John C. Calhoun to neo-corporatism immediately raise the question of which groups shall be included in the counsels of government and which ones not.[2] However, socialists have no reason to fear this question. Who is to be included in decisionmaking is simply the question of democracy itself. Given the dilemmas of the electoral road to socialism, we might well reconsider the various historical forms (and imagined forms) of direct representation of communities and social groups, such as feudal political structure, modern corporatism and neocorporatism, direct democracy, and the various schemes of workers's councils expressed in utopian socialist, guild socialist, and anarcho-syndicalist literature. There were good reasons why the question of whether or not to participate in electoral politics was so hotly debated by earlier generations of socialists. If electoral socialism is a deadend, we must recover that debate. Both Przeworski and Poulantzas argue that political forms structure the field of struggles only to the point where these struggles transform those forms. Functional representation draws on existing identities to directly challenge the prevailing political forms. These identities, although not class identities, are a direct consequence of the howling winds of capitalism.

Some will reject this proposal on the grounds that capitalism is mutable and will find a way around any political restrictions placed on it. Capitalism is indeed flexible; contrary to predictions, it accommodated universal suffrage and the development of trade unions. However capitalism is not a spirit that mysteriously affects institutions but stands apart from them. It is protean but it is not immaterial. Capitalism works through historically developed institutions. Capitalism has been flexible to the degree that it has been able, when necessary, to develop new institutional forms for its expansion and vigor, such as the corporate form itself. New historical forms entail real struggles, not shadow-plays. Determinism in history is in some important measure an artefact of hindsight. It is by recognizing this that we rescue previous struggles from, as E. P. Thompson famously put it, "the enormous condescension of posterity."[3] It is also by this that we overcome the illusion that capitalism is invincible. If capitalism requires institutional embodiment and needs the state, then struggles over state forms continue to be important.

A moment of universality must be retained insofar as socialism is the elimination of class inequality. Equality is an inescapable question in socialist theory and, as we have seen, has received increased attention. Even if one argues, as Marx did in *The Critique of the Gotha Programme,* that the ultimate goal is not equality but individuality, any argument for why we should respect individuality would seem to logically require a defense of equality, of recognition of the equal dignity and worth of all individuals.

There is, nevertheless, a danger in focusing too much on the question of equality. Marx may have been reticent in discussing the injustice of capitalist exploitation not simply for the philosophical reasons often given. He may have rejected this approach on the grounds that communism is not an attempt to arrive at a more just distribution of the products of labor but an attempt to direct the productive resources of society such that needs can be satisfied. That is, communism is especially concerned with the development and deployment of the productive forces in a substantively rational way.

Therefore, socialism is also about, to use Przeworski's phrase, feeding everyone. Any attractive version of socialism requires that we neither completely separate nor conflate bread and morals. The lack of necessities deprives people of the most immediate forms of freedom, security, and dignity, i.e., freedom from want. However, it is not preordained that this kind of freedom is necessarily compatible with other kinds of freedom. There is no guarantee that all values will fit together in a seamless whole. It is this that gives the human condition its tragic nature. The inevitable conflicts between various values can only be negotiated in an open and democratic practice.

Finally, although the proletariat is not the protagonist of history, Marx understood that insofar as the discussion of socialism is severed from the question of agency it becomes merely moral exhortation. The content of socialism itself partly emerges with the forces that struggle for it. It is only for this reason that socialism has even the possibility of being democratic and authentic. In the struggle for a democratic socialism, ends and means cannot be separated. Therefore the question of the addressee of critical theory is unavoidable.

Unfortunately, the proletariat can no longer serve as that addressee. The proletariat is a kind of Sorelian myth, "that is to say, an arrangement of images capable of evoking instinctively all of the sentiments which correspond to the various manifestations of the war waged by socialism against modern society."[4] All those who have been inspired by Marxian theory have felt the power of this myth. However, it has lost the combat with other myths in the world today, myths evocative of nation and blood and other determinants of the community of the morally worthy. We do not create the circumstances within which we struggle. The grounds of these other, destructive and dehumanizing, myths must be engaged rather than merely railed against or theoretically ignored. The grounds of engagement are, as Habermas and other Marxian theorists state, principles of universality. These principles are neither intended to nor capable of eliminating other bases of concrete identities. But they are still the irreplaceable source of illumination of the meaning of an emancipated—unfettered—society.

Many today argue that the Marxian socialist project is fundamentally mistaken because material production does not give history any coherence. The dissipation of the illusion of the inevitability of progress is interpreted to mean that history is meaningless. History is considered, as Macbeth said of life, "a tale told by an idiot, full of sound and fury signifying nothing." However, this position conflates history and progress. The animating thesis of the present work has been that the displacements of conflict in contemporary capitalism to the state, to the lifeworld, and to identity politics are *displacements,* and therefore these phenomena are grounded in the material conditions of production. It is only by comprehending these developments as displacements that we can gain some insight into the dynamic of contemporary capitalism and evaluate the possibilities of its transformation.

It is indeed true that Marx had two theories of history—conditions and agency—weakly sutured together by the role of the proletariat. It is also true that the meaning of history can never be given from the outside, that meaning emerges as human beings live their lives and is always open to reconstruction. It is difficult to provide a unified field theory which would clearly and logically bind together the elemental forces of "men make their own history" and "the circumstances directly encountered, given, and transmitted from the past." Perhaps it is only in their simultaneous mutual repulsion and inseparability that the truth lies. However, the Marxian thesis that it is in this conjunction that history makes sense is still as productive a hypothesis as the postmodern alternatives. The latter only lead into a 'wilderness of mirrors' from which there is no escape.

Notes

CHAPTER ONE

1. "Critique of Hegel's Doctrine of the State," in *Karl Marx: Early Writings* (New York: Vintage Books, 1975), pp. 146–147. Cf. *The Politics of Aristotle*, edited by Ernest Barker (London: Oxford University Press, 1958), p. 298: "In the state, as in other natural compounds, [there is a distinction to be drawn between 'conditions' and 'parts':] the conditions which are necessary for the existence of the whole are not organic parts of the whole system which they serve. The conclusion which clearly follows is that we cannot regard the elements which are necessary for the existence of the state, or of any other association forming a single whole, as being 'parts' of the state or of any such association." (The addition belongs to Barker.) Aristotle subsequently excludes "the class of mechanics" from the state with an ideal constitution: p. 302.

2. In op. cit., p. 256.

3. Anthony Giddens, *The Class Structure of the Advanced Societies* (New York: Harper Torchbooks, 1975), p. 10; Barry Hindess, *Politics and Class Analysis* (New York: Basil Blackwell, Inc., 1987), pp. 1–2; Erik Olin Wright, Andrew Levine, and Elliott Sober, *Reconstructing Marxism* (London: Verso, 1992), pp. 174–175.

4. *The Eighteenth Brumaire of Louis Bonaparte* (New York: International Publishers Co., Inc., 1963), p. 15.

5. Princeton: Princeton University Press, 1978.

6. Ibid., pp. 34–35, p. 32. Also, G. A. Cohen, *History, Labour, and Freedom: Themes From Marx* (Oxford: Oxford University Press, 1988), p. 4.

7. *Karl Marx's Theory of History*, p. 134: "[T]he nature of a set of productive relations is explained by the level of development of the productive forces embraced by it (to a far greater extent than vice versa)." In a footnote to this statement, Cohen adds: "Some such qualifying phrase is always to be understood whenever the primacy thesis is asserted." The "1859 Preface" is in Marx, *A Contribution to the Critique of Political Economy* (New York: International Publishers, Inc., 1970); originally published in 1859.

8. *Karl Marx's Theory of History*, pp. 161–162. Alan Carling summarizes

255

Joshua Cohen's objection that this is circular, in Carling, "Analytical Marxism and Historical Materialism: The Debate on Social Evolution," *Science and Society* Volume 57, Number 1 (Spring 1993), pp. 34–37. G. A. Cohen's response to Joshua Cohen and others is in *History, Labour, and Freedom*, Chapter 5, written with Will Kymlicka.

9. *Karl Marx's Theory of History*, p. 150. He holds out the possibility that Marx was mistaken about history being a coherent story.

10. Ibid., pp. 152–153, p. 155.

11. Ibid., p. 153. And it is sometimes technically unfeasible to do so: p. 155. He does acknowledge Rome as a counter-example.

12. *History, Labour, and Freedom*, p. 8; *Karl Marx's Theory of History*, p. 266, pp. 271–272, and Chapter X; "Reply to Elster on 'Marxism, Functionalism, and Game Theory,'" in *Marxist Theory*, edited by Alex Callinicos (New York: Oxford University Press, 1989), p. 100.

13. *Karl Marx's Theory of History*, p. 149, p. 153, pp. 292–293.

14. Ibid., pp. 203–204. Cf. pp. 148–149.

15. "Reply to Elster on 'Marxism, Functionalism, and Game Theory,'" p. 97 footnote 13. Cf. *Karl Marx's Theory of History*, p. 148.

16. *History, Labour, and Freedom*, p. 15. The charge "utopian" is from p. 19.

17. "Rationality and Class Struggle," in *Marxist Theory*, p. 27. The phrase is adopted by Cohen in response to their critique.

18. Ibid., pp. 38–40.

19. "The Social Basis of Economic Development," in *Analytical Marxism*, edited by John Roemer (New York: Cambridge University Press, 1986), p. 35.

20. Ibid., p. 26.

21. Ibid., p. 29.

22. Ibid., p. 31; pp. 27–28.

23. Ibid., p. 26. For this reason Brenner argues that "property relations" should be called "relations of reproduction": p. 46.

24. Ibid., p. 51, p. 53. In footnote 13 on pages 46–48 Brenner directly engages Cohen's argument.

25. Levine and Wright, op. cit., pp. 40–41, p. 33.

26. Ibid., p. 32. All of the participants in this discussion are well aware of the

'free rider' problem raised by attempts at collective action, which indicates that individuals will not necessarily revolt even if it is in their self-interest to do so: Cohen, *History, Labour, and Freedom*, pp. 55–56, p. 56 footnote 6, pp. 111–112; Wright, Levine, and Sober, op. cit., pp. 44–45. We will discuss the issue in a later chapter.

27. Levine and Wright, op. cit., p. 42; pp. 32–33. The quote is Cohen, *Karl Marx's Theory of History*, p. 204 footnote 2.

28. Op. cit., p. 43. Wright, Levine, and Sober agree with this rejection, a rejection virtually universal among Marxian theorists today. They call it "empirically unfounded and theoretically defective": op. cit., p. 34.

29. Levine and Wright, p. 46.

30. "Agrarian Class Structure and Economic Development in Pre-Industrial Europe," in *The Brenner Debate*, edited by T. H. Aston and C. H. E. Philpin (New York: Cambridge University Press, 1985), p. 14. The essay was originally published in 1976 in *Past and Present*.

31. Ibid., p. 12. On empirical grounds Brenner also rejects the common argument that the existence of towns explains the differential impact: pp. 38–40.

32. Ibid., p. 18.

33. Ibid., pp. 41–42. The particular structure of the village in turn partly depended on the conditions of its foundation, whether independent or colonial. Brenner notes that the success of the French peasantry in protecting their independent property led to the backward character of French agriculture: p. 62.

34. *Free to Lose: An Introduction to Marxist Economic Philosophy* (Cambridge, MA: Harvard University Press, 1988), p. 122.

35. Op. cit., pp. 44–45.

36. *History, Labour, and Freedom*, p. 24. See also Carling's comments, op. cit., pp. 37–40.

37. *History, Labour, and Freedom*, pp. 25–27.

38. Ibid., p. 133 footnote 2.

39. Ibid., p. 102, p. 92, and passim.

40. "Reply to Elster," p. 98. Cf. *Karl Marx's Theory of History*, pp. 148–150.

41. "Reply to Elster," p. 97. Elster's statement occurs in "Marxism, Functionalism, and Game Theory: The Case for Methodological Individualism," in *Marxist Theory*, p. 48. The case for the application of rational choice theory and methodological individualism to Marxian theses, promoted by Elster and others, will be discussed in Chapter Four.

42. *History, Labour, and Freedom*, p. 16.

43. Ibid., p. 19.

44. *Karl Marx's Theory of History*, pp. 148–149; "Reply to Elster," pp. 96–97; *History, Labour, and Freedom*, pp. 14–15. Carling raises the same issue: op. cit., pp. 49–50.

45. "Reply to Elster," p. 98. For further discussion of this issue Wright, Levine, and Sober's analysis of "precipitating events" and "fundamental causes" is relevant: op. cit., pp. 151–155.

46. Op. cit., pp. 80–83.

47. Ibid., p. 90–91. As they say in another place, "Incompatibility is always a matter of *degree*." p. 20 footnote 13. They also note, like many others including Cohen (*History, Labour, and Freedom*, p. 112), that even if class capacities were developed a revolution may not take place due to the "transition costs" to socialism: pp. 43–44. We will explore this argument as developed by Adam Przeworski later.

48. Ibid., p. 96. Their later comments on causality in regard to "limits" and "selection" are relevant here. They argue that it is unwise to argue that "causes" that *limit* possible selections are "more fundamental" or "more important" than choices within the imposed limits. This suggests that neither the level of the forces of production (which sets the limits) *nor* class capacities (which determines the choice within the limits) should be considered more fundamental or important than the other. See pp. 147–151.

49. Cohen, *History, Labour, and Freedom*, p. 132; Wright, Levine, and Sober, op. cit., p. 96 and p. 97.

50. Carling, op. cit., pp. 44–46.

51. Ibid., p. 51.

52. *Reconstructing Marxism*, pp. 25–29, p. 21. Carling also notes the ambiguity in Cohen's account: op. cit., pp. 48–49. Like Wright, Levine, and Sober, Carling argues that 'use-fettering' is theoretically more fruitful.

53. *History, Labour, and Freedom*, pp. 111–112, p. 114. Wright, Levine, and Sober agree: p. 26. On the word 'develop,' *History, Labour, and Freedom*, p. 115.

54. He explicitly borrows this argument from Joseph Schumpeter: *History, Labour, and Freedom*, p. 117.

55. Ibid., p. 113.

56. Ibid., pp. 120–121. An example of a present restriction on utilization that may lead to long-term development is patents. See Jon Elster and Karl Ove

Moene, editors, *Alternatives to Capitalism* (Cambridge: Cambridge University Press, 1989), p. 5.

57. Op. cit., pp. 28–29.

58. *Karl Marx's Theory of History*, p. 297.

59. Ibid., pp. 304–306.

60. Ibid., p. 306–307. This argument is quite reminiscent of the work of Herbert Marcuse.

61. *History, Labour, and Freedom*, pp. 120–121. Also ibid., p. 113: "[U]nder different arrangements the same forces of production could be used to bring about a benign realignment of labour, leisure, and education." 'Better way of life' partially means "increased leisure," "freedom from unwanted activity": *Karl Marx's Theory of History*, p. 323, p. 320, p. 304.

62. *History, Labour, and Freedom*, p. 156 footnote 3.

63. Op. cit., p. 35. After all of this discussion it appears that Cohen's answer as to how capitalism fetters the forces of production is "fettering of some or other kind." *History, Labour, and Freedom*, p. 121.

64. *Karl Marx's Theory of History*, p. 320. This may be an example of "scarcity" being "imposed" by the ruling class, as argued by Levine and Wright: op. cit., pp. 39–40.

65. Besides where this is mentioned in passing in some of the passages quoted above, see *History, Labour, and Freedom*, p. 109: "different feasible relations."

66. Op. cit., p. 100.

67. Erik Olin Wright, "Class Analysis, History and Emancipation," *New Left Review* Number 202 (November/December 1993), p. 20. This is also the thrust of Ellen Meiksins Wood's critique of the "new 'true socialism'": *The Retreat From Class: A New 'True' Socialism* (London: Verso, 1986).

CHAPTER TWO

1. *Classes* (London: Verso, 1985), p. 13. For example, it is disconcerting for academic Marxists to not be able to say with any conviction to which class they themselves belong.

2. Ibid., p. 7.

3. "Rethinking, Once Again, the Concept of Class Structure," in Wright et al., *The Debate on Classes* (London: Verso, 1989), pp. 271–272, p. 272 footnote 2.

4. *Classes*, pp. 32–33.

5. Ibid., p. 33.

6. "Rethinking, Once Again, the Concept of Class Structure," pp. 269–270.

7. Ibid., p. 301.

8. Poulantzas, *Classes in Contemporary Capitalism* (London: New Left Books, 1975); Barbara and John Ehrenreich, "The Professional-Managerial Class," in *Between Labor and Capital*, edited by Pat Walker (Boston: South End Press, 1979): pp. 5–45. Poulantzas argues that the "new petty bourgeoisie" forms a unified class with the traditional petty bourgeoisie because of the "affinity" of the "ideological effects" caused by their respective social structural determinations: op. cit., p. 287. See Wright's discussion and criticisms of this argument in *Class, Crisis, and the State* (London: Verso, 1979), pp. 39–41 and pp. 58–59.

9. *Class, Crisis, and the State*, p. 73. In a footnote on this page he argues that these criteria are "non-arbitrary" in that they can be related to the "C + V + S = total value" formula from Marxian political economy: control over constant capital (physical means of production), control over variable capital ("labor"), and control over surplus value (investment). We can ignore Wright's conflation here of labor and labor-power.

10. Ibid., pp. 64–71.

11. He borrows this idea from Poulantzas as well: ibid., pp. 39–40 and pp. 79–80. The argument that a mode of production can in some way "contain" other subordinate modes of production is rather contentious because it always appears ad hoc. We will return to the issue in the later chapter on "world-system" theory as formulated by Immanuel Wallerstein.

12. Ibid., p. 63, pp. 74–82.

13. Ibid., p. 81, p. 82.

14. Ibid., p. 82 footnote 70. Wright acknowledges that the definition of autonomy for semi-autonomous workers is particularly troublesome.

15. Ibid., p. 98.

16. In one place Wright explains the various terms used in class analysis. He argues that there is a complex "dialectical" relationship between "class structure," "class formation," and "class struggles": ibid., p. 102. Wright distinguishes these three concepts in the following way: class structure refers to the relations *between* classes in a society; class formation refers to the social relations *within* a class which have consequences on the capacity of a class to engage in class struggles for class interests, i.e., consequences for class capacities (ibid., pp. 98–99 footnote

84); and class struggles dialectically link class interests to class capacities. (Ibid., p. 102.) Nevertheless, although he wants to maintain some kind of distinction between class capacities and class formation, Wright often confusingly uses the two terms interchangeably. Most of the time he defines class formation as the "formation of collective actors organized around class interests within a class structure." ("Rethinking, Once Again, the Concept of Class Structure," p. 272 footnote 2; *Classes*, p. 10.) It will not hamper the present discussion if we use the terms class formation and class capacities interchangeably.

17. *Class, Crisis, and the State*, pp. 98–102.

18. Ibid., p. 106, p. 105.

19. *Classes*, p. 14.

20. Ibid., p. 286. Peter Meiksins points out that Wright finds it difficult in practice to stick with this position. In his empirical investigations of class consciousness, Wright *expects* to find a close relation between class location and class consciousness. When he does not, he refers to the vicissitudes of class formation. However, if there is always a gap between class structure and class formation then *any close* relationship between location and consciousness should *also* have to be explained by political and ideological processes of class formation. If we truly believe, as Wright states, that the relation between structure and formation is "contingent," then we should not expect anything at all. See Meiksins's comments: "A Critique of Wright's Theory of Contradictory Class Locations," in *The Debate on Classes*, pp. 181–183, and p. 175. Also see Meiksins's elaboration of his own position in "Beyond the Boundary Question," *New Left Review* Number 157 (May/June 1986), pp. 101–120.

21. *Class, Crisis, and the State*, pp. 100–101. Although Wright is not so careful here (see ibid., p. 102 footnote 91), I am purposely leaving out legal divisions in classifying workers—argued by Meiksins in "'Beyond the Boundary Question," p. 115—or other political mediations in order to conform to Wright's intention to explain as much as possible before introducing politics or ideology. The various mediations between class structure and class formation are at the heart of many alternative perspectives on class formation that will be discussed in later chapters. Here we will focus on Wright's argument.

22. *Class, Crisis, and the State*, pp. 108–110. Wright discusses the difference between immediate and fundamental interests in ibid., pp. 88–91.

23. "Reconsidering, Once Again, the Concept of Class Structure," p. 304.

24. *Classes*, p. 51.

25. Ibid., p. 46, pp. 52–57; "Rethinking, Once Again, the Concept of Class Structure," pp. 304–305.

26. "Rethinking," p. 304.

27. "A General Framework for the Analysis of Class Structure," in *The Debate on Classes*, pp. 5–6; *Classes*, pp. 56–57.

28. *Classes*, p. 56.

29. *History, Labour, and Freedom: Themes From Marx* (Oxford: Clarendon Press, 1988), p. 231.

30. John E. Roemer, *Free To Lose: An Introduction to Marxist Economic Philosophy* (Cambridge, MA: Harvard University Press, 1988), p. 49.

31. *The Politics of Aristotle*, edited by Ernest Barker (London: Oxford University Press, 1958), p. 23. Marx quotes Aristotle on the matter in *Capital* Volume 1 (New York: International Publishers, 1967), p. 85 footnote 1. In *Capital* Marx frequently quotes Aristotle's economic insights.

32. Wright discusses this argument in "The Value Controversy and Social Research," in *The Value Controversy*, Ian Steedman et al. (London: Verso, 1981), pp. 41–43.

33. Ian Steedman, "Ricardo, Marx, Sraffa," in ibid., p. 13, p. 17.

34. Cohen, *History, Labour, and Freedom*, p. 226.

35. Ibid., pp. 226–227. Capitalists qua "owners" do not produce anything.

36. Ibid., p. 209. Guglielmo Carchedi argues, to the contrary, that the labor theory of value is perfectly consistent: "Classes and Class Analysis," in *The Debate on Classes*, p. 113.

37. See the discussions of Morishima by Wright, "The Value Controversy and Social Research," p. 42 footnote 9; Pradeep Bandyopadhyay, "Critique of Wright 2: In Defense of a Post-Sraffian Approach," in *The Value Controversy*, pp. 104–108; and, Jon Elster, *Making Sense of Marx* (New York: Cambridge University Press, 1985), p. 141. Debates over the labor theory of value are extensive, continuing, and often hard-fought. The most one can do here is indicate a few recent articles that will give a sense of the present state of the discussion to a broader audience: David Laibman, "The Falling Rate of Profit: A New Empirical Study," *Science and Society* Volume 57, Number 2 (Summer 1993), pp. 223–233; Murray E. G. Smith, "Productivity, Valorization and Crisis: Socially Necessary Unproductive Labor in Contemporary Capitalism," *Science and Society* Volume 57, Number 3 (Fall 1993), pp. 262–293; and, Michael Perelman, "The Qualitative Side of Marx's Value Theory," *Rethinking Marxism* Volume 6, Number 1 (Spring 1993), pp. 82–95.

38. Roemer, op. cit., pp. 53–54.

39. Elster, op. cit., p. 141.

40. *Classes*, p. 75. Cf. Wright, "Exploitation, Identity, and Class Structure: A Reply to My Critics," in *The Debate on Classes*, p. 199 footnote 16. This argument is not entirely accurate regarding the unemployed—one of Wright's examples—however, because without a "reserve army of labor," the bargaining position of capitalists would be altered for the worse.

41. *Classes*, p. 77.

42. Ibid., pp. 74–75. As we will see, this is similar to Wallerstein's argument. Wright's actual definition is uncertain. On succeeding pages in *Classes*, Wright argues that the criterion is 'more than one produces' (p. 75) and then "price" which "exceed[s] its costs of production." This very important difference was quickly seized by Wright's critics, discussed shortly.

43. Ibid., p. 72.

44. Ibid., pp. 73–104; "Exploitation, Identity, and Class Structure," pp. 191–192; "Rethinking," 306–307. Actually Wright mentions a fourth "asset" that is irrelevant for exploitation under capitalism because in capitalism, unlike feudalism, everyone owns it: one's labor-power: ibid., pp. 77–78.

45. *Classes*, p. 79, pp. 78–82; "Exploitation, Identity, and Class Structure," pp. 199–201.

46. Ibid., p. 81.

47. *Classes*, p. 76; "Exploitation, Identity, and Class Structure," p. 192; "Rethinking," p. 307.

48. *Classes*, p. 106.

49. Ibid., p. 87, p. 91, p. 125.

50. Ibid., p. 145.

51. Ibid., pp. 278–280, p. 187 footnote 2.

52. Ibid., pp. 89–91.

53. Ibid., pp. 84–86. Wright's overall analysis is again based on the notion that multiple modes of production are contained in the typical contemporary capitalist social formation: statist production and democratic socialism are present in kernel, as capitalism was allegedly present within feudalism. As stated in a previous note, this formulation seems to stretch the concept "mode of production" to the point where it loses its shape.

54. Ibid., p. 125.

55. Ibid., p. 125, pp. 90–91. Again this argument is remarkably similar to that of Wallerstein.

56. Ibid., pp. 125–126.

57. Ibid., p. 288.

58. Ibid., p. 289. He more recently discusses class alliances in "Class Analysis, History and Emancipation," *New Left Review* Number 202 (November/December 1993), pp. 34–35.

59. *Classes*, p. 126.

60. Ibid., p. 289. Wright uses the terms "alliance" and "class formation" somewhat interchangeably here: pp. 125–126, pp. 288–289.

61. Ibid., p. 290. For other examples, see Meiksins, "Beyond the Boundary Question," p. 115.

62. Carchedi, op. cit., p. 111; Meiksins, "A Critique of Wright's Theory of Contradictory Class Locations," p. 176; Johanna Brenner, "Work Relations and the Formation of Class Consciousness," in *The Debate on Classes*, pp. 188–189.

63. "Exploitation, Identity, and Class Structure," p. 192 footnote 2; pp. 192–199. Also see note 42, supra.

64. "Rethinking," pp. 308–310. However, he still holds out the possibility that there are circumstances where monopolization could result in surplus appropriation: ibid., pp. 312–313. He also briefly discusses problems of calculating the surplus in "Class Analysis, History, and Emancipation," p. 30 footnote 15.

65. "Class Analysis, History and Emancipation," pp. 32–33; "Exploitation, Identity, and Class Structure," p. 192.

66. Meiksins, "A Critique," p. 177.

67. Ibid., pp. 179–180.

68. "Rethinking," p. 347.

69. Ibid., p. 306.

70. Ibid., pp. 312–313.

71. Meiksins, "A Critique," p. 177; Meiksins, "Beyond the Boundary Question," p. 111, p. 107; Martin Oppenheimer, *White Collar Politics* (New York: Monthly Review Books, 1985), pp. 15–17. Carchedi also criticizes Wright's individualistic premises in general: op. cit.

72. Wright, "Rethinking," p. 280.

73. Ibid., p. 278.

74. For a representative view, see Sandy Carter, "Class Conflict: The Human Dimension," in *Between Labor and Capital*, pp. 97–119.

75. Barbara and John Ehrenreich, op. cit., pp. 29–30.

76. *The Class Structure of the Advanced Societies* (New York: Harper Torchbooks, 1975), p. 187, p. 195.

77. "Rethinking," p. 289.

78. Ibid., pp. 298–299; "Exploitation," pp. 210–211.

79. Respectively, "Exploitation," p. 206, and "Rethinking," p. 280.

80. "Rethinking," p. 282.

81. Ibid., pp. 286–287.

82. Ibid., pp. 299–300.

83. "Exploitation," p. 210; "Rethinking," pp. 281–282; *Class, Crisis, and the State*, pp. 88–91.

84. "Rethinking," p. 285. In the most prominent place, Weber defines class according to common "life chances" for possession of goods and income "under the condition of the commodity or labor markets." "But always this is the generic connotation of the concept of class: that the kind of chance in the *market* is the decisive moment which presents a common condition for the individual's fate. 'Class situation' is, in this sense, ultimately 'market situation.'" [Emphasis in original.] In *From Max Weber: Essays in Sociology*, edited by H. H. Gerth and C. Wright Mills (New York: Oxford University Press, 1958), pp. 181–182. See all of "Class, Status, Party," in ibid., pp. 180–195.

However, Weber's usage is not very systematic. For example, he appears to alter his definition of class in an aside concerning another topic in ibid., p. 301: "The specific and typical cases of class situation today are ones determined by markets. But such is not necessarily the case: class situations of landlord and small peasant may depend upon market relations only in a negligible way." The prior definition is the one to which theorists typically appeal when they contrast Weber with Marx.

85. Op. cit., p. 78.

86. "Rethinking," p. 313.

87. *Classes*, p. 106; "Rethinking," pp. 318–319.

88. Op. cit., pp. 108–109. A similar example is used by Uwe Becker, "Class Theory: Still the Axis of Critical Social Scientific Analysis?" in *The Debate on Classes*, pp. 148–149.

89. "Rethinking," p. 284.

90. Ibid., p. 284. Wright also argues that there is a general interest in expanding one's capacity to act: *Classes*, p. 28.

91. For starters, see Allen Wood, "Marx and Equality," in *Analytical Marxism*, edited by John Roemer (New York: Cambridge University Press, 1986), pp. 283–303.

92. *Marxism and Class Theory: A Bourgeois Critique* (New York: Columbia University Press, 1979), p. 25.

93. "Constructing the (W)right Classes," in *The Debate on Classes*, p. 261.

94. Parkin, *Marxism and Class Theory*, pp. 70–71.

95. Becker, op. cit., p. 143; Johanna Brenner, op. cit., p. 185; Andre Gorz, *Farewell to the Working Class: An Essay on Post-Industrial Socialism* (Boston: South End Press, 1982), p. 7.

96. Van Parijs, "A Revolution in Class Theory," in *The Debate on Classes*, p. 230.

97. Ibid., p. 234.

98. Gorz, for one, argues that "full employment" is "absolutely impossible" today: op. cit., p. 3.

99. Stinchcombe, "Education, Exploitation, and Class Consciousness," in *The Debate on Classes*, p. 170.

100. Op. cit., pp. 150–152.

101. Paul Hirst, "Economic Classes and Politics," in *Class and Class Structure*, edited by Alan Hunt (London: Lawrence and Wishart, 1977), p. 131. Cf. Antony Cutler, Barry Hindess, Paul Hirst, and Athar Hussein, *Marx's 'Capital' and Capitalism Today* Volume One (London: Routledge and Kegan Paul, 1977), pp. 188–189, and pp. 232–238.

102. Laclau and Mouffe, *Hegemony and Socialist Strategy: Towards a Radical Democratic Politics* (London: Verso, 1985), p. 83.

103. Agnes Heller, *The Theory of Need in Marx* (London: Allison and Busby, 1976), pp. 57–60. "One may search in vain for the concept of 'class interest' in works such as the *Grundrisse, Capital, Wages, Prices, and Profit*, or *Theories of Surplus Value*: it does not appear once, not even with reference to class struggle." (p. 60.) On social need: "This is in no way, however, an autonomous structure, 'suspended above' the members of a class or of a society. The need of the individual is what he knows and feels to be his need—he has no other needs." (p. 71.)

104. Cohen and Howard, "Why Class?," in *Between Labor and Capital*, p. 81. As stated in the article, this part was written by Cohen. The idea that capitalism itself creates the logic of calculation of interests is a lively topic, discussed in Martin Carnoy, *The State and Political Theory* (Princeton: Princeton University Press, 1984, Chapter One. Cf. Jane J. Mansbridge, ed., *Beyond Self-Interest* (Chicago: The University of Chicago Press, 1990).

105. Ibid., p. 86.

106. Op. cit., p. 151.

107. "Rethinking," p. 323. Earlier in the same place he says that he intended to map interests in order to better analyze the possibilities of class formation, and concludes that "That aspiration has yet to be fulfilled." Ibid., p. 270.

108. Ibid., pp. 324–336. Meiksins argues also that some of these are "ambiguous class positions": "Beyond the Boundary Question," p. 113.

109. "Rethinking," p. 273 footnote 3.

110. Op. cit., p. 144.

111. "Class Analysis, History and Emancipation," p. 21. See also his acknowledgement of the power of Becker's argument: "Rethinking," p. 313 footnote 58.

112. Op. cit., pp. 28–29.

113. Gorz does accept the thesis of deskilling: ibid., p. 28 footnote 4. He admits that this is partially a self-criticism.

114. Ibid., p. 41 and p. 48.

115. Ibid., p. 29.

116. Ibid., pp. 48–50.

117. Ibid., p. 65, p. 52.

118. Ibid., p. 67.

119. Ibid., p. 70, pp. 68–69, p. 72.

120. Ibid., p. 70.

121. Ibid., p. 67.

122. Ibid., p. 73.

123. Ibid., p. 74, p. 73.

124. Ibid., p. 75.

125. Ibid., p. 70.

126. Ibid., p. 81.

127. Cohen and Howard, op. cit., p. 79.

128. Cohen and Howard, op. cit., p. 81. Cf. Jean Cohen, *Class and Civil Society: The Limits of Marxian Critical Theory* (Amherst, MA: The University of Massachusetts Press, 1982), p. 24.

129. Cohen, op. cit., p. 192.

130. Ibid., p. 150.

131. Ibid., p. 61.

132. Cohen and Howard, op. cit., p. 80.

133. Cohen, op. cit., p. 192.

134. Ibid., p. 194; Cohen and Howard, op. cit., pp. 80–81.

135. Ibid., p. xiii.

136. Ibid., p. 177; Cohen and Howard, op. cit., pp. 82–83 footnote 14.

136. Cohen, op. cit., p. 190.

138. Ibid., p. 35. As we will see in a later chapter, this is also a concern of Claus Offe and Juergen Habermas, who use the same phrase "de-differentiation."

139. For extended arguments on this theme see Jean Cohen, "Why More Political Theory?" *Telos* Number 40 (Summer 1979): pp. 70–94; and Jean Cohen, "Rethinking Social Movements," *Berkeley Journal of Sociology* Volume 28 (Fall 1983): pp. 97–113. The most complete statement is Jean L. Cohen and Andrew Arato, *Civil Society and Political Theory* (Cambridge, MA: The MIT Press, 1992).

140. Cohen, *Class and Civil Society*, p. 188.

141. Ibid., p. 74.

142. Cohen and Howard, pp. 82–83.

143. Cohen, *Class and Civil Society*, pp. xii-xiii, p. 183, and passim.

144. Giddens, op. cit., p. 192 and p. 132, respectively.

CHAPTER THREE

1. For an extensive discussion of the question of political representation of the proletariat, with all the appropriate exegeses of Marx's work, see John F. Sitton, *Marx's Theory of the Transcendence of the State* (New York: Peter Lang Publishers, 1989), especially Chapter 9: "The Political 'Secret' of the Proletariat."

2. Gramsci, *Selections from the Prison Notebooks*, edited by Quintin Hoare and Geoffrey Nowell Smith (New York: International Publishers, 1971): p. 243.

3. Anderson, "The Antinomies of Antonio Gramsci," *New Left Review* Number 100 (November 1976/January 1977): p. 28.

4. In this chapter we are concerned with Marxian arguments concerning citizenship and its affect on working class experience and practice. However, it is worth noting that two prominent non-Marxian sociologists who have explicated the concept of citizenship agree that the institutionalization of citizenship affects the existence of classes. T. H. Marshall argues that although the extension of the meaning and practices of citizenship has not eliminated inequality, the remaining inequality probably does not constitute "class distinctions" in any strong sense. Those class distinctions that remain are relatively unimportant. See "Citizenship and Social Class," *Class, Citizenship, and Social Development: Essays by T. H. Marshall* (Garden City, NY: Doubleday and Company, Inc., 1964), p. 115.

Building on the work of Marshall, Reinhard Bendix even argues that the working class movement itself was originally a response to political exclusion, i.e., "political alienation": "Rather than engage in a millenarian quest for a new social order, the recently politicized masses protest against their second-class citizenship, demanding the right of participation on terms of equality in the political community of the nation state. If this is a correct assessment of the impulses and half-articulated longings characteristic of much popular agitation among lower classes in Western Europe, then we have a clue to the decline of socialism. For the civic position of these classes is no longer a pre-eminent issue in societies in which the equality of citizenship has been institutionalized successfully." In Bendix's analysis, the working class project of socialism was actually a disguised plea for civic equality. The "civic incorporation of the lower classes" allows them to pursue their interests through political associations and the franchise. See *Nation-Building and Citizenship* (New York: John Wiley and Sons, Inc., 1964), pp. 73–74 and pp. 79–80.

5. Lukacs, *Lenin: A Study on the Unity of His Thought* (Cambridge, MA: The MIT Press, 1971), p. 65–66.

6. "Ideology and Ideological State Apparatuses (Notes towards an Investigation)," in *Lenin and Philosophy and Other Essays* (New York: Monthly Review Press, 1971), pp. 127–186. Althusser states that Gramsci had a similar perspective: ibid., p. 142 footnote 7.

7. Lukacs, *Lenin*, p. 66. In all quotes, emphases are in the original.

8. Lukacs, "Towards a Methodology of the Problem of Organization," In *History and Class Consciousness* (Cambridge, MA: The MIT Press, 1971), p. 319.

9. Sartre, *The Communists and Peace* (New York: George Braziller, Inc., 1968), pp. 125–126.

10. Ibid., p. 130. Again on p. 88: "If the working class wants to detach itself from the Party, it has only one means at its disposal: to crumble into dust."

11. Luxemberg, "The Russian Revolution," in *The Russian Revolution and Leninism or Marxism?* (Ann Arbor, MI: University of Michigan Press/Ann Arbor Paperbacks, 1961), p. 65.

12. See Luxemburg's comment: "the political struggle is conducted not by the masses through direct action, but in conformity with the structure of the bourgeois state, in the representative fashion, by the pressure exercised upon the legislative body." Quoted by Adam Przeworski, *Capitalism and Social Democracy* (Cambridge: Cambridge University Press, 1985), p. 13.

13. Pashukanis, *Law and Marxism: A General Theory* (London: Ink Links, 1978), p. 123.

14. Ibid., p. 112, p. 121.

15. Ibid., p. 115.

16. Marx, *Capital* Volume 1 (New York: International Publishers, 1967), p. 176.

17. Op. cit., pp. 40–41.

18. This leads to the famous statement of Marx regarding the relation between the specific mode of extraction of surplus labor and the political form of the society; *Capital* Volume III (New York: International Publishers Co., Inc, 1967), pp. 791–792: "The specific economic form, in which unpaid surplus-labour is pumped out of direct producers, determines the relationship of rulers and ruled, as it grows directly out of production itself and, in turn, reacts upon it as a determining element. Upon this, however, is founded the entire formation of the economic community which grows up out of the production relations themselves, thereby simultaneously its specific political form. It is always the direct relationship of the owners of the conditions of production to the direct producers—a relation always naturally corresponding to a definite stage in the development of the methods of labour and thereby its social productivity—which reveals the innermost secret, the hidden basis of the entire social structure, and with it the political form of the relation of sovereignty and dependence, in short, the corresponding specific form of the state. This does not prevent the same economic basis—the same from the standpoint of its main conditions—due to innumerable different empirical circumstances, natural environment, racial relations, external historical influences, etc., from showing infinite variations and gradations in appearance, which can be ascertained only by analysis of the empirically given circumstances."

19. Pashukanis, op. cit., pp. 141–143. The functionalism of this argument is unhelpful.

20. Hirst, *On Law and Ideology* (Atlantic Highlands, NJ: Humanities Press, 1979), p. 52.

21. As Hirst puts it, "Seeking to assign law an essence-in-origin necessarily gives it a single content." Op. cit., p. 111. See also Hugh Collins, *Marxism and Law* (New York: Oxford University Press, 1982), pp. 108–111.

22. Hirst, op. cit., p. 114, pp. 136–137.

23. Ibid., p. 113.

24. *Capital* III, p. 791. For full quote, see footnote 18 above.

25. Samuel Bowles and Herbert Gintis, *Democracy and Capitalism* (New York: Basic Books, 1987).

26. William H. Sewell, Jr., "Artisans, Factory Workers, and the Formation of the French Working Class, 1789–1848" in *Working-Class Formation*, edited by Ira Katznelson and Aristide Zolberg (Princeton, NJ: Princeton University Press, 1986), p. 59; Michelle Perrot, "On the Formation of the French Working Class," in ibid., p. 95; Amy Bridges, "Becoming American: The Working Classes in the United States before the Civil War," in ibid., p. 165.

27. Op. cit., p. 60.

28. Hobsbawm, "Labor and Human Rights," in *Workers: Worlds of Labor* (New York: Pantheon Books, p. 309; Marshall, op. cit., p. 104. An interesting recent exploration of the relation between rights and the sphere of the political and whether "human rights is a form of politics" is Claude Lefort, "Politics and Human Rights," in *The Political Forms of Modern Society* (Cambridge, MA: The MIT Press, 1986), pp. 239–272.

29. Steven Lukes, *Marxism and Morality* (Oxford: Oxford University Press, 1985); Norman Geras, "The Controversy About Marx and Justice," *New Left Review* Number 150 (March/April 1985), pp. 47–85; G. A. Cohen, *History, Labour, and Freedom: Themes from Marx* (Oxford: The Clarendon Press, 1988).

30. Marx, *The German Ideology*, in *Collected Works* Volume 5 (New York: International Publishers, 1976), p. 323.

31. Collins, op. cit., pp. 124–128.

32. This is not to deny the innumerable ways in which ruling groups try to exclude others in practice. The important question is why these attempts are successful, 'why the weaker class is weak.'

33. Poulantzas, *State, Power, Socialism* (London: New Left Books/Verso, 1980), pp. 50–51.

34. Ibid., pp. 16–17.

35. Ibid., p. 64.

36. Poulantzas, *Political Power and Social Classes* (London: New Left Books, 1973), p. 126, pp. 126–129; *State, Power, Socialism*, p. 64.

37. *Political Power and Social Classes*, p. 63.

38. *Classes in Contemporary Capitalism* (London: New Left Books, 1975), p. 21.

39. *State, Power, Socialism*, pp. 65–66.

40. *Political Power and Social Classes*, p. 130; *State, Power, Socialism*, pp. 69–70, p. 66.

41. *Political Power and Social Classes*, pp. 130–131.

42. *State, Power, Socialism*, p. 66.

43. *Political Power and Social Classes*, p. 133.

44. *State, Power, Socialism*, p. 70, p. 72.

45. Ibid., p. 75.

46. *Political Power and Social Classes*, p. 86.

47. Ibid., p. 86.

48. Ibid., p. 90 footnote 40.

49. *Classes in Contemporary Capitalism*, p. 210.

50. Ibid., p. 14.

51. Ibid., p. 20.

52. Ibid., pp. 210–216.

53. Ibid., p. 228.

54. Ibid., p. 224, pp. 236–237.

55. Ibid., pp. 30–31.

56. Ibid., p. 30.

57. Ibid., pp. 16–17.

58. Adam Przeworski, "Proletariat into a Class: The Process of Class Formation from Karl Kautsky's *The Class Struggle* to Recent Controversies," *Politics and Society* Volume 7, Number 4 (1977), p. 369.

59. *State, Power, Socialism*, pp. 54–62. The state's apparatuses "are molded in such a way that they exercise power over the ensemble so constituted: they realize the very material frame of reference or space-time matrix that is implied by the relations of production." Ibid, p. 65.

60. Ibid., pp. 251–265, p. 257.

61. Ibid., p. 30.

62. *Political Power and Social Classes*, p. 115 footnote 24.

63. Op. cit., p. 75.

64. Przeworski, "Proletariat into a Class: The Process of Class Formation from Karl Kautsky's *The Class Struggle* to Recent Controversies," *Politics and Society* Volume 7, Number 4 (1977), p. 368.

65. Ibid., p. 343.

66. Ibid., p. 358, p. 361.

67. Ibid., p. 365.

68. Ibid., p. 385.

69. Ibid., p. 367.

70. Ibid., p. 371, pp. 370–372.

71. Ibid., p. 367.

72. Ibid., p. 386.

73. Ibid., pp. 388–389; pp. 386–390.

74. *Capitalism and Social Democracy*, pp. 7–10.

75. Ibid., p. 10. Adam Przeworski, "Material Bases of Consent: Economics and Politics in a Hegemonic System," *Political Power and Social Theory* Volume 1, edited by Maurice Zeitlin (Greenwich, CN: JAI Press, Inc., 1980), p. 30.

76. *Capitalism and Social Democracy*, pp. 12–13. Joseph Schumpeter, *Capitalism, Socialism, and Democracy* (New York: Harper Colophon Books, 1975), p. 317.

77. Przeworski, *Capitalism and Social Democracy*, pp. 14–15.

78. Ibid., p. 30, pp. 241–242.

79. Ibid., p. 28, pp. 24–28.

80. Adam Przeworski and John Sprague, *Paper Stones: A History of Electoral Socialism* (Chicago: University of Chicago Press, 1986).

81. Ibid., pp. 99–132.

82. *Capitalism and Social Democracy*, p. 43.

83. Ibid., p. 129.

84. Przeworski, "Proletariat into a Class," pp. 399–400.

85. Ibid., p. 388.

86. Katznelson, *City Trenches: Politics and the Patterning of Class in the United States* (New York: Pantheon Books, 1981), p. 55.

87. Katznelson, "Working-Class Formation: Constructing Cases and Comparisons," in *Working-Class Formation*, p. 26.

88. Martin Shefter, "Trade Unions and Political Machines: The Organization and Disorganization of the American Working Class in the Late Nineteenth Century," in ibid., p. 273.

89. Amy Bridges, op. cit., pp. 160–161; Katznelson, *City Trenches*, p. 71.

90. Shefter, op. cit., pp. 209–213, p. 247; Alan Dawley and Paul Faler, "Working Class Culture and Politics in the Industrial Revolution: Sources of Loyalism and Rebellion," *Journal of Social History* Volume 9, Number 4 (June 1976), pp. 474–475, p. 477.

91. Zolberg, "How Many Exceptionalisms?" in *Working-Class Formation*, p. 450.

92. Shefter, op. cit., p. 242, p. 263.

93. Nolan, "Economic Crisis, State Policy, and Working-Class Formation in Germany, 1870–1900," in *Working-Class Formation*, p. 361.

94. *Capitalism and Social Democracy*, pp. 99–100.

95. Katznelson, "Working-Class Formation," p. 14; *City Trenches*, p. 201.

96. "Working-Class Formation," p. 18, p. 22.

97. Katznelson, *City Trenches*, p. 207.

CHAPTER FOUR

1. Jon Elster, "Marxism, Functionalism, and Game Theory: The Case for Methodological Individualism," in *Marxist Theory*, edited by Alex Callinicos (New York: Oxford University Press, 1989), p. 49. The same is asserted in John Roemer, " 'Rational Choice' Marxism: Some Issues of Method and Substance," in *Analytical Marxism*, edited by John Roemer (New York: Cambridge University Press, 1986): p. 192. See also Roemer's introduction to the latter work, p. 1. Jon Elster and John Roemer are the two uncontestable figures of this approach. It is clear from Roemer's titles that 'analytical Marxism' and 'rational choice Marxism' are equally acceptable, although the former lays a somewhat broader net. Erik Olin Wright prefers analytical Marxism for this reason: Wright et al., *The Debate on Classes* (London: Verso, 1989), p. 54 footnote 4.

A comment by Vicky Prehoditch, from a different context, is the source of the title of this chapter.

2. *Reconstructing Marxism* (London: Verso, 1991), pp. 5–6, p. 108. For the specific criticism of Lukacs, see ibid, pp. 103–105; and Alex Callinicos, "Introduction: Analytical Marxism," in *Marxist Theory*, pp. 14–15.

3. Roemer, *Free to Lose* (Cambridge, MA: Harvard University Press, 1988), p. 176. As quoted in Chapter Two, Guglielmo Carchedi criticizes this perspective: "Classes and Class Analysis," in *The Debate on Classes*, pp. 105–125. See also Michael Buroway's criticism of Wright's theoretical approach in ibid., "The Limits of Wright's Analytical Marxism and An Alternative," pp. 78–99. Finally, see W. Suchting's broad criticism of the book *Reconstructing Marxism*: "Reconstructing Marxism," *Science and Society* Volume 57, Number 2 (Summer 1993): pp. 133–159; and the response: Wright, Levine, and Sober, "Reconstructing Marxism: A Reply," *Science and Society* Volume 58, Number 1 (Spring 1994): pp. 53–60.

The following statements from prominent practitioners of analytical Marxism are typical of the perceived relation to Marxism. First, Adam Przeworski: "[I]f one accepts the methodological validity of individualistic postulates, most if not all traditional concerns of Marxist theory must be radically reformulated. Whether the eventual results will confirm any of the substantive propositions of Marxist theory of history and whether the ensuing theory will be in any distinct sense 'Marxist,' I do not know." "Marxism and Rational Choice," *Politics and Society* Volume 14, Number 4 (1985), p. 400, and p. 390. Jon Elster is more forthright: "It is not possible today, morally or intellectually, to be a Marxist in the traditional sense. . . . But, speaking now for myself only, I believe it is still possible to be a Marxist in a rather different sense of the term. I find that most of the views that *I* hold to be true and important, I can trace back to Marx." *Making Sense of Marx* (Cambridge: Cambridge University Press, 1985), p. 531; and p. xiv. Also, see Roemer, "Introduction," in *Analytical Marxism*, pp. 1–2; and Wright, Levine, and Sober, *Reconstructing Marxism*, pp. 179–191.

4. Elster, "Marxism, Functionalism, and Game Theory," p. 48. The preceding quote is from the same page.

5. Jon Elster, *Making Sense of Marx*, p. 5.

6. Ibid., p. 359.

7. Adam Przeworski, "Marxism and Rational Choice," pp. 386–387. Also, see his statement: "Let me join in the pleas for a methodological individualism." In "The Ethical Materialism of John Roemer," *Politics and Society* Volume 11, Number 3 (1982), p. 313. On the other hand, see Przeworski's criticism of the conception of the individual employed by game theory, *Democracy and the Market* (Cambridge: Cambridge University Press, 1991), p. 38 footnote 48; and his argument that methodological individualism is not necessarily required for game theory: "Marxism and Rational Choice," p. 401 footnote 1.

The limits of methodological individualism are also explored by Wright, Levine, and Sober, *Reconstructing Marxism*, pp. 107–127.

8. Przeworski, "Marxism and Rational Choice," p. 386. See also John Roemer, " 'Rational Choice' Marxism," p. 193.

9. *Democracy and the Market*, p. 30.

10. Roemer, "New Directions in the Marxian Theory of Exploitation and Class," *Politics and Society* Volume 11, Number 3 (1982), p. 257. This essay is reprinted in *Analytical Marxism*, pp. 81–113. My references will be to the original in *Politics and Society*. The article is a truncated version of the argument developed in Roemer, *A General Theory of Exploitation and Class* (Cambridge, MA: Harvard University Press, 1982).

11. "New Directions in the Marxian Theory of Exploitation and Class," p. 259.

12. *Free to Lose*, pp. 20–25.

13. "New Directions," pp. 261–263.

14. Ibid., p. 265.

15. Elster, *Making Sense of Marx*, pp. 181–182 (he quotes Marx here); Immanuel Wallerstein, "Dependence in an Interdependent World: The Limited Possibilities of Transformation Within the Capitalist World Economy," in *The Capitalist World Economy: Essays by Immanuel Wallerstein* (New York: Cambridge University Press, 1979), p. 71.

16. Elster, *Making Sense of Marx*, p. 183.

17. "New Directions," p. 266.

18. Ibid., p. 275.

19. Ibid., p. 276.

20. Ibid., p. 279. On socialist exploitation, ibid., pp. 283–284.

21. Roemer, "Reply," *Politics and Society* Volume 11, Number 3 (1982), pp. 376–377.

22. "Should Marxists Be Interested in Exploitation?," in *Analytical Marxism*, p. 280. Here he also speaks of a "fetishism of labor" and the confusion between socialism and "industrial democracy." There are additional comments in *Free to Lose*, p. 107.

23. Roemer, "New Directions," pp. 266–268.

24. Przeworski, "The Ethical Materialism of John Roemer," p. 295.

25. Roemer, "Reply," p. 376.

26. Roemer, "Should Marxists Be Interested in Exploitation?," p. 269. Elster makes a similar argument: *Making Sense of Marx*, p. 199.

27. *Free to Lose*, p. 51, p. 57, p. 89, and passim; and Roemer, "Should Marxists Be Interested in Exploitation?" It should also be noted that Roemer's conception of what makes inequality of property unjust is the differential in welfare it entails. In his more recent discussions of socialism and public ownership he focuses especially on distribution of property in that it affects distribution of welfare. See *Free to Lose*, pp. 148–171 and pp. 175–176.

28. Ibid., pp. 127–131; "Should Marxists Be Interested in Exploitation?"

29. Elster argues that the procedure is generally ill-defined: *Making Sense of Marx*, p. 203.

30. *Free to Lose*, pp. 134–135.

31. Ibid., p. 90.

32. Roemer, "Should Marxists Be Interested in Exploitation?," p. 262.

33. G. A. Cohen, "The Labour Theory of Value and the Concept of Exploitation," in *History, Labour, and Freedom: Themes from Marx* (Oxford: Clarendon Press, 1988), pp. 234–235. Cf. p. 298 for his strongest statement on the matter.

34. Elster, "Marxism, Functionalism, and Game Theory," pp. 84–85. See footnote for the reference to Kolakowski; and *Making Sense of Marx*, p. 177 footnote 1. Also see an earlier argument of Elster, quoted by Cohen in "Reply to Elster on 'Marxism, Functionalism, and Game Theory,'" in *Marxist Theory*, p. 104 footnote 20.

35. Cohen, "Reply to Elster," p. 103.

36. *Making Sense of Marx*, pp. 228–229, pp. 174–175. In the latter place Elster objects that Roemer's conception transforms exploitation into a property (B is exploited) rather than a relation (A exploits B). Elsewhere Elster proposes a further way of looking at exploitation as "taking unfair advantage" of someone. This is distinguished from mere coercion in that one willingly enters the situation but the distributional consequences of the arrangement are morally suspect. Whether exploitation is occurring, however, seems to depend upon specifying an additional distributional criterion that is being violated. See "Roemer versus Roemer: A Comment on 'New Directions in the Marxian Theory of Exploitation and Class,'" *Politics and Society* Volume 11, Number 3 (1982), pp. 364–365.

37. *Free to Lose*, p. 85. Elster agrees with this assessment: *Making Sense of Marx*, p. 323.

38. Roemer, *Free to Lose*, p. 3; Elster, *Making Sense of Marx*, pp. 529–530. See also Cohen, "Freedom, Justice, and Capitalism," in *History, Labour, and Freedom*, p. 297 but also the entire chapter pp. 286–304.

39. Roemer, "Reply," p. 394, p. 385; *Free to Lose*, p. 144.

40. Roemer, "Should Marxists Be Interested in Exploitation?," footnote 34 pp. 279–280; *Free to Lose*, pp. 85–89.

41. "The Ethical Materialism," p. 307.

42. Przeworski, "Marxism and Rational Choice," p. 382; Elster, "Marxism, Functionalism, and Game Theory," p. 66.

43. Elster, *Making Sense of Marx*, p. 344, p. 347. He argues that, among other things, the concept class interest must be defined in terms of specific time preferences. Elster's discussion is hampered by his apparent intent to find a transhistorical definition of class, quite contrary to the usual position of Marx. See ibid., p. 322, pp. 318–344. It is true that Marx sometimes used the concept class in transhistorical fashion, for example in *The Manifesto*. However he also often spoke of class (as opposed to Estate) as specific to capitalism and one can easily argue that this is his most defensible and useful meaning.

44. Ibid., p. 350.

45. Ibid., p. 361.

46. Ibid., pp. 362–366.

47. Ibid., pp. 391–394.

48. Allen Buchanan, "Revolutionary Motivation and Rationality," *Philosophy and Public Affairs* Volume 9, Number 1 (1979), p. 67.

49. Ibid., p. 72.

50. Ibid., p. 74 and p. 81.

51. Ibid., pp. 78–80.

52. Ibid., p. 65 footnote 11; pp. 63–65. On p. 65 Buchanan insists that it is not only rational for individual utility-maximizers to abstain from collective action but abstention is also rational even for those motivated by a desire to maximize group-utility. "Each maximizer of group utility would reason as follows. Regardless of whether I contribute or not, either enough others will contribute or they won't. If the former, then my costs of contribution would do no good, while constituting a subtraction from the utility the group gains from G. If the latter, then my costs of contribution are again a subtraction from the group's utility. So maximizing group utility requires that I be a free rider. And again, since every other maximizer of

group utility reasons in the same way, the good *G* will not be secured." This argument is weak in that it is entirely unclear under what definition of group utility an individual's contribution would be a subtraction from group utility.

53. Elster, *Making Sense of Marx*, pp. 367–368.

54. Elster's work is filled with numerous gratuitous insults in which many of Marx's views are called "absurd," "silly," and "pointless." Elster even says that: "In one sense, therefore—the sense that to him was the most important—Marx's life and work were in vain." *Making Sense of Marx*, p. 531. This puzzling "rhetorical strategy" is explored in David Schweikert, "Reflections on Anti-Marxism: Elster on Marx's Functionalism and Labor Theory of Value," *Praxis International* Volume 8, Number 1 (April 1988): pp. 109–122.

55. "Marxism and Rational Choice," p. 401 footnote 1.

56. Ibid., p. 380, p. 381.

57. Ibid., p. 382.

58. Ibid., p. 382.

59. "The Ethical Materialism," p. 311.

60. Ibid., p. 307 footnote 26. To clarify, this does not mean that social structure is intentional; Przeworski allows for the importance of "unanticipated" consequences of action: "Marxism and Rational Choice," p. 400.

61. "Marxism and Rational Choice," p. 381.

62. Ibid., p. 381, p. 393. See Ellen Meiksins Wood, "Rational Choice Marxism: Is the Game Worth the Candle?," *New Left Review* Number 177 (September/October 1989): pp. 41–88.

63. *Democracy and the Market*, p. 38 footnote 48. One can acknowledge this and still appreciate, as Przeworski clearly does, the methodological usefulness of rational choice theory. This does not therefore contradict his previously quoted objection to the insistence on immediate descriptive realism.

64. "The Ethical Materialism," p. 310 footnote 30.

65. "Marxism and Rational Choice," p. 397, pp. 399–400, pp. 384–385; *Democracy and the Market*, p. 38.

66. "Marxism and Rational Choice," p. 401, p. 397.

67. Ibid., p. 399.

68. Ibid., p. 399.

69. *Democracy and the Market*, pp. 11–12.

70. "Marxism and Rational Choice," p. 390.

71. *Democracy and the Market*, p. 64 footnote 20; cf. "Marxism and Rational Choice," p. 391. In the former place he says that workers are not properly in a prisoners dilemma; in the latter he does describe it as a prisoners dilemma.

72. Elster, *Making Sense of Marx*, pp. 358–365, especially p. 364.

73. Przeworski, "The Ethical Materialism," pp. 293–294. See also Przeworski, *Capitalism and Social Democracy* (New York: Cambridge University Press, 1985), pp. 99–100. For a fuller treatment see Przeworski, "Proletariat into a Class: The Process of Class Formation from Karl Kautsky's *The Class Struggle* to Recent Controversies," *Politics and Society* Volume 7, Number 4, pp. 343–401.

74. Przeworski, "Marxism and Rational Choice," p. 394.

75. "Marxism and Rational Choice," pp. 393–394; "The Material Bases of Consent: Economics and Politics in a Hegemonic System," *Political Power and Social Theory* Volume 1 (1980), edited by Maurice Zeitlin (Greenwich, CN: JAI Press, Inc.), pp. 26–27.

76. "The Material Bases," p. 27.

77. Roemer, *Free to Lose*, pp. 70–71. We will discuss Offe's argument in the next chapter.

78. In "The Material Bases" he mentions "multiple constraints" on capitalist decisionmaking, including competition: p. 26. Also, "Marxism and Rational Choice," pp. 393–394. On p. 391 ibid., in parentheses he suggests that capitalists are at least sometimes not in a comfortable pre-strategic situation and the illustration he uses in making a point about *worker* collective action is about the strategic problems of a price war among gasoline station owners.

79. Przeworski, "The Ethical Materialism," p. 298. Cohen cites Elster as having a similar position and agrees, with qualifications, with this assessment: "Reply to Elster," p. 98.

80. "The Ethical Materialism," pp. 298–299.

81. Przeworski, ibid., p. 297. Roemer responds that he also considers this "social democratic game" in his book: "Reply," pp. 384–385.

82. The three key articles containing these arguments are: Przeworski, "Material Bases of Consent," pp. 21–66; Przeworski (with Michael Wallerstein), "Material Interests, Class Compromise, and the State," in *Capitalism and Social Democracy*, pp. 171–203; and Przeworski and Wallerstein, "Democratic Capitalism at the Crossroads," *democracy* Volume 2, Number 3 (July 1982): pp. 52–68.

83. *Democracy and the Market*, p. 130.

84. Ibid., p. 133.

85. Ibid., p. 129.

86. "The Ethical Materialism," p. 305.

87. Cohen, "Freedom, Justice, and Capitalism," in *History, Labour, and Freedom*, p. 298; cf. *History, Labour, and Freedom*, p. 226.

88. On socialism as industrial democracy, see Roemer, *Free to Lose*, p. 107. For Roemer directly challenging the ethical arguments of defenders of capitalism, see ibid., Chapter 10, pp. 148–171.

89. G. A. Cohen, *History, Labour, and Freedom*, p. 291.

90. For various commentaries on the importance of this distinction: Geoff Hodgson, "Critique of Wright 1. Labour and Profits," in Ian Steedman et al. *The Value Controversy* (London: Verso Books, 1981), p. 94; Harry Braverman, *Labor and Monopoly Capital* (New York: Monthly Review Press, 1974), p. 54 and passim; Samuel Bowles and Herbert Gintis, *Democracy and Capitalism* (New York: Basic Books, 1987), p. 69.

91. Claus Offe, " 'Ungovernability': The Renaissance of Conservative Theories of Crisis," in *Contradictions of the Welfare State*, edited by John Keane (Cambridge, MA: The MIT Press, 1984), p. 83.

92. Roemer, *Free to Lose*, p. 86; "Should Marxists Be Interested in Exploitation?," pp. 278–280.

93. *Free to Lose*, p. 171.

94. Karl Polanyi, *The Great Transformation* (Boston: Beacon Press, 1944), pp. 68–76.

95. An important additional question is noted by Roemer himself: if a labor market is unnecessary for exploitation, then why has capitalism used this mechanism? *Free to Lose*, pp. 97–99.

96. Ellen Meiksins Wood, "Rational Choice Marxism," p. 79.

97. Roemer, "Reply," p. 379, including a footnote criticizing Wright's misinterpretation.

98. Daniel R. Sabia, Jr., "Rationality, Collective Action, and Karl Marx," *American Journal of Political Science* Volume 32, Number 1 (February 1988), p. 51.

99. For criticisms of game theory as applied to historical materialism and Cohen's defense of—anathema to rational choice theory—"functional explana-

tion," see Cohen, "Reply to Elster." For appeal to rationality of human beings in support of the development of the productive forces see Cohen, "Human Nature and Social Change in the Marxist Conception of History," in *History, Labour, and Freedom*, pp. 83–106. Generally, see Chapter One above.

100. Cohen, *History, Labour, and Freedom*, p. 140.

101. Elster, ed., "Introduction," in *Rational Choice* (New York: New York University Press, 1986), p. 18. Buchanan poses the following challenge to Marxian theorists: "A Marxian . . . who wishes to argue that the public goods problem is avoided because each proletarian maximizes group utility would have to provide an account of how the proletarian comes to desire to maximize his class's interest rather than his own." Buchanan, op. cit. p. 65 footnote 11. Exploration of the conditions under which specific identities are formed would begin to meet this challenge.

102. "Introduction," p. 24. As noted, Przeworski explicitly rejects the conception of social relations to which Elster resorts in the next sentence.

103. E.g. Elster, *Making Sense*, pp. 363–364.

104. See ibid., where Elster does consider justice to be part of revolutionary motivation: pp. 529–530.

105. Alasdair MacIntyre, *After Virtue* Second Edition (Notre Dame, IN: University of Notre Dame Press, 1984), p. 224. For Elster on rational desire and the principle of "ought implies can," see "Introduction," in *Rational Choice* p. 22. For what seems to be a criticism of the principle "ought implies can," see Elster, *Making Sense of Marx*, p. 201. It is possible that there is a "Damned If You Do, Damned If You Don't Game" of which I am unaware.

106. Elster, "Introduction," p. 24.

107. Ibid., pp. 22–24.

108. Claus Offe and Helmut Wiesenthal, "Two Logics of Collective Action," in *Disorganized Capitalism* [essays by Claus Offe], edited by John Keane (Cambridge, MA: The MIT Press, 1985), p. 183.

109. Sabia, op. cit., pp. 50–71.

110. Elster, "Marxism, Functionalism, and Game Theory," p. 72. For a discussion of the conditions under which cooperation might emerge, see Elster, *Making Sense of Marx*, pp. 360–366.

111. Elster, *Making Sense of Marx*, p. 378.

112. "Marxism, Functionalism, and Game Theory," p. 67 footnote 46.

113. Elster, *Making Sense of Marx*, p. 366.

114. Ibid., p. 359.

115. Quoted by Przeworski in *Democracy and the Market*, p. 188. See William Hinton's similar observation in "Impressions of Manila," *Monthly Review* Volume 45, Number 1 (May 1993), p. 15: "Some recent visitors from East Germany said they thought socialism was bad, a dead-end, until they saw the end result of capitalism in Manila. Manila was a real eye-opener. Every one who came to the conference from China thought China's young generation should come en-masse and have a look."

116. Przeworski and Wallerstein, "Democratic Capitalism at the Crossroads," pp. 52–68.

117. *Democracy and the Market*, p. 33, p. 34.

118. Respectively: Margaret Levi, Review of Roemer, *American Political Science Review* Volume 78, Number 1 (March 1984), p. 293; Ellen Meiksins Wood, "Rational Choice Marxism," p. 83.

119. See the overview in Richard J. Bernstein, *Beyond Objectivism and Relativism: Science, Hermeneutics, and Praxis* (Philadelphia: University of Pennsylvania Press, 1983).

120. *Free to Lose*, p. 177.

121. E.g. ibid., p. 144.

122. Polanyi, *The Great Transformation*, p. 129. In this place Polanyi is actually reporting the utopian socialist Robert Owen's conception of the situation, with which Polanyi clearly agrees.

123. *Making Sense*, pp. 530–531. For an overview of Marxian economic crisis theory, see ibid., pp. 154–165. Ellen Meiksins Wood has criticized, however, the movement toward making socialism merely a normative ideal: *The Retreat from Class: A New 'True' Socialism* (London: Verso, 1986). I take the phrase 'right' and 'interest' from the first page of Rousseau's *Social Contract*.

124. *Capitalism and Social Democracy*, pp. 243–245. See also Allan Wood's rebuttal of the idea that Marx was concerned with eliminating inequality: "Marx and Equality," in *Analytical Marxism*, pp. 283–303. However, see also Przeworski's more recent discussion of socialism and its prospects in *Democracy and the Market*, pp. 100–135.

125. *Capitalism and Social Democracy*, p. 246; pp. 239–248; "The Ethical Materialism," pp. 305–306. This is similar to G. A. Cohen's conception of the way in which capitalism could be said to be fettering the forces of production, discussed in Chapter One above.

126. *Capitalism and Social Democracy*, p. 244.

127. Cohen, "The Future of a Disillusion," *New Left Review* Number 190 (November/December 1991), pp. 12–15.

CHAPTER FIVE

1. Frances Fox Piven and Richard Cloward, *The New Class War* (New York: Pantheon Books, 1982).

2. Offe, *Contradictions of the Welfare State* [edited and introduced by John Keane](Cambridge, MA: The MIT Press, 1984), p. 38. In this and all quotes all emphases are Offe's.

3. Offe, *Disorganized Capitalism* (Cambridge, MA: The MIT Press, 1985), p. 2.

4. Offe, "Political Authority and Class Structures—An Analysis of Late Capitalist Societies," *International Journal of Sociology* Spring 1972, p. 97.

5. Offe (essay co-authored with Gero Lenhardt), *Contradictions of the Welfare State*, p. 115 footnote 7.

6. Offe, *Contradictions*, pp. 38–39.

7. Ibid., p. 54 and passim.

8. Offe, "Structural Problems of the Capitalist State. Class Rule and the Political System. On the Selectiveness of Political Institutions," *German Political Studies* Volume I (Beverly Hills, CA: Sage Publications, 1974), p. 33. See also John Keane's "Introduction" to Offe, *Contradictions*, p. 15.

9. Offe, *Contradictions*, p. 48; *Disorganized Capitalism*, p. 335 footnote 4.

10. *Contradictions*, p. 49. See also, "Political Authority and Class Structures," p. 100; and "Structural Problems of the Capitalist State," p. 37 and p. 53.

11. *Contradictions*, p. 122.

12. Ibid., pp. 239–240, p. 255, pp. 266–267. Keane, "Introduction," to *Contradictions of the Welfare State*, p. 15. See also Keane, "The Legacy of Political Economy: Thinking With and Against Claus Offe," *Canadian Journal of Political and Social Theory* Volume 2, Number 3 (Fall 1978), pp. 49–92.

13. Offe, *Contradictions*, p. 149, p. 266, and pp. 179–206. Piven and Cloward make a similar argument in op. cit.

14. *Disorganized Capitalism*, p. 71. See also ibid., p. 11.

15. *Contradictions*, p. 200–201. For a similar argument see Friedrich Hayek, *The Road to Serfdom* (Chicago: The University of Chicago Press, 1944), p. 76.

16. *Contradictions*, p. 149 and p. 197.

17. Ibid., p. 197. For related comments see ibid., p. 266, where Offe mentions the "purgative effects generated by the old business cycles of the capitalist econo-

my"; ibid., p. 122 where he speaks of the "periodic destruction of large parts of value through unfettered economic crises"; and ibid., p. 149.

18. Ibid., p. 266.

19. Ibid., p. 123, p. 240.

20. Ibid., p. 244. This is a central argument of Offe, raised in several places. See also: ibid., p. 50, p. 285, p. 77, and p. 166; Offe, *Disorganized Capitalism*, pp. 191–192; and Offe, "The Theory of the Capitalist State and the Problem of Policy Formation," in *Stress and Contradiction in Modern Capitalism: Public Policy and the Theory of the State*, edited by Leon Lindberg et al. (Lexington, MA: Lexington Books/D.C. Heath, 1975), p. 143.

21. Offe, *Contradictions*, p. 151 and p. 200.

22. For example: Samuel Bowles and Herbert Gintis, *Democracy and Capitalism* (New York: Basic Books, 1987), pp. 88–90; Charles Lindblom, *Politics and Markets* (New York: Basic Books, 1977), especially Chapter 13 "The Privileged Position of Business," pp. 170–188; and, of course, the various works by Adam Przeworski discussed in Chapter Four above.

23. *Contradictions*, p. 120. See also *Disorganized Capitalism*, p. 87.

24. *Contradictions*, p. 124 and p. 57.

25. Ibid., p. 194.

26. "The Theory of the Capitalist State and the Problem of Policy Formation," pp. 127–134.

27. Ibid., p. 130.

28. Ibid., p. 132.

29. Ibid., p. 134. See also, *Contradictions*, pp. 124–125 and p. 266; and *Disorganized Capitalism*, p. 86 and p. 271.

30. *Contradictions*, p. 175.

31. "The Theory of the Capitalist State," p. 134.

32. *Contradictions*, pp. 123–125.

33. Ibid., p. 123.

34. "The Theory of the Capitalist State," pp. 132–133.

35. Ibid., p. 134.

36. *Contradictions*, pp. 93–96.

37. Ibid., p. 94 and p. 263.

38. *Contradictions*, p. 99; Karl Polanyi, *The Great Transformation* (Boston: Beacon Press, 1944), p. 72 and passim.

39. Polanyi, op. cit., p. 72.

40. *Contradictions*, p. 51.

41. Offe, "Political Authority and Class Structures," p. 79.

42. Offe, *Contradictions*, pp. 65–87.

43. Ibid., p. 198.

44. Ibid., p. 112; Offe, "Introduction to Part III," in *Stress and Contradiction in Modern Capitalism*, p. 255.

45. Offe, *Contradictions*, p. 168 and pp. 112–113.

46. Offe, *Disorganized Capitalism*, pp. 308–309 and p. 311. In direct relation to corporatism, see Offe, *Contradictions*, p. 72: " 'consensus' becomes the decisive bottleneck."

47. Respectively: Offe, *Contradictions*, p. 73; ibid., p. 125; Offe, *Disorganized Capitalism*, p. 243. Also, *Contradictions*, p. 167: "neocorporatist methods of interest intermediation."

48. Offe, *Contradictions*, p. 125; ibid., p. 167; "Political Authority and Class Structures," p. 101.

49. A particularly acute critic of the exaggeration of the importance of corporatism is Leo Panitch, "Recent Theorizations of Corporatism: Reflections on a Growth Industry," *British Journal of Sociology* Volume 31, Number 2 (June 1980), pp. 159–187. However, Offe insists on its expansive character: *Disorganized Capitalism*, pp. 240–241 and pp. 300–316.

50. *Disorganized Capitalism*, p. 244; *Contradictions*, pp. 188–189.

51. Offe, *Disorganized Capitalism*, p. 242.

52. See Panitch, op. cit.

53. Respectively, Offe, *Contradictions*, p. 73 and pp. 291–292.

54. Offe, *Disorganized Capitalism*, pp. 248–253; also, *Contradictions*, pp. 291–292.

55. Offe, *Disorganized Capitalism*, pp. 253–254; also, ibid., p. 236 and p. 247.

56. Ibid., p. 231.

57. Ibid., p. 230.

58. Ibid., p. 304.

59. Ibid., pp. 305–306. For a related argument, Offe, "The Theory of the Capitalist State," pp. 136–141.

60. Offe, *Disorganized Capitalism*, pp. 307–308.

61. Ibid., p. 302.

62. Offe, *Contradictions*, p. 264; ibid., p. 165. For the absence of "decision rules," see Offe, "The Theory of the Capitalist State," pp. 135–136.

63. Ibid., p. 128.

64. Offe, "Introduction to Part III," p. 256.

65. Offe, *Contradictions*, pp. 264–265.

66. Offe, "New Social Movements: Challenging the Boundaries of Institutional Politics," *Social Research* Volume 52, Number 4 (Winter 1985), p. 818.

67. Ibid., p. 819.

68. Offe, *Contradictions*, pp. 128–129.

69. Ibid., p. 44.

70. Offe, *Disorganized Capitalism*, p. 168.

71. Offe, "New Social Movements," p. 845.

72. *Contradictions*, p. 42 and pp. 285–286; *Disorganized Capitalism*, pp. 142–143. See also Claus Offe and Rolf G. Heinze, *Beyond Employment: Time, Work, and the Informal Economy* (Philadelphia: Temple University Press, 1992).

73. *Disorganized Capitalism*, p. 166, pp. 81–85, and p. 61; *Contradictions*, p. 285. This is recently stated a little more cautiously: Offe and Heinze, *Beyond Employment*, pp. 31–32.

74. *Disorganized Capitalism*, p. 38.

75. *Contradictions*, p. 197, p. 48, and pp. 282–285; *Disorganized Capitalism*, p. 132. See also "Political Authority and Class Structures," p. 95: "The relationship between income and life chances has thus become more tenuous."

76. *Disorganized Capitalism*, pp. 52–53. Again, see *Beyond Employment* for varieties of supplementation.

77. Ibid., p. 282; also, ibid., p. 240.

78. "Political Authority and Class Structures," p. 95 and p. 102; *Disorganized Capitalism*, p. 3; Offe, *Industry and Inequality: The Achievement Principle in Work and Social Status* (New York: St. Martin's Press, 1977), p. 100 and p. 102.

79. "Political Authority and Class Structures," p. 84; *Contradictions*, p. 187.

80. *Disorganized Capitalism*, pp. 218–219.

81. Ibid., pp. 183–184.

82. Ibid., p. 137.

83. Ibid., p. 126, p. 138, and pp. 106–107.

84. Ibid., p. 138.

85. Ibid., p. 139; see also ibid., p. 134.

86. Ibid., pp. 138–139.

87. *Industry and Inequality*, p. 56.

88. *Disorganized Capitalism*, p. 63.

89. Ibid., p. 156.

90. "Political Authority and Class Structures," p. 102.

91. *Contradictions*, p. 203.

92. "New Social Movements," p. 856.

93. Ibid., p. 846.

94. These comments are from a revised version of the above essay "New Social Movements," published in *Changing Boundaries of the Political*, Charles S. Maier, ed. (Cambridge: Cambridge University Press, 1987), p. 73–74. All other citations from this article are from the original.

95. *Contradictions*, p. 176. See also: ibid., p. 189; *Disorganized Capitalism*, p. 36; and, *Industry and Inequality*, passim.

96. *Contradictions*, pp. 266–267; *Disorganized Capitalism*, pp. 86–87 and pp. 271–272.

97. "Introduction to Part III," p. 255.

98. "New Social Movements," p. 834 footnote 19; *Contradictions*, p. 128 and pp. 264–265.

99. "New Social Movements," p. 834.

100. *Contradictions*, pp. 111–112 and pp. 264–265.

101. "New Social Movements," p. 836; *Contradictions*, pp. 168–169.

102. *Disorganized Capitalism*, p. 279.

103. *Contradictions*, p. 292 and p. 250; *Disorganized Capitalism*, p. 257 and p. 342 (note 11). For Panitch's critical view, see op. cit.

104. *Contradictions*, p. 250.

105. *Disorganized Capitalism*, p. 99. See also, ibid, p. 65, p. 72, p. 75, p. 77, pp. 97–100, p. 153, and p. 167; and, *Contradictions*, p. 237 and pp. 296–297. *Beyond Employment* is his fullest treatment of this question.

106. *Disorganized Capitalism*, p. 94. The discussion of "cooperation circles" in *Beyond Employment* is still quite tentative. However, Offe and Heinze state, as others have before them, that: "What is realistic cannot be known until what is actually unrealistic has been discovered in practice." P. 216.

107. See Juergen Habermas, "New Social Movements," *Telos* Number 49 (Fall 1981), pp. 33–38. An issue of *Social Research* Volume 52, Number 4 (Winter 1985) is devoted to the analysis of new social movements, with articles by leading theorists such as Jean Cohen, Charles Tilly, Klaus Eder, Alain Touraine, and Offe.

108. *Disorganized Capitalism*, p. 149.

109. Offe, "New Social Movements," p. 850.

110. Ibid., p. 853.

111. Offe, ibid., p. 847.

112. *Contradictions*, pp. 266–267.

113. Ibid., p. 190; "New Social Movements," p. 830.

114. Offe, "New Social Movements," p. 853.

115. *Disorganized Capitalism*, pp. 277–278.

116. Offe, "New Social Movements," p. 826.

117. *Contradictions*, p. 250. This also seems to be the thrust of Sheldon Wolin's essay, "Democracy and the Welfare State: The Political and Theoretical Connections Between Staatsraeson and Wohlfahrtsstaatsraeson," *Political Theory* Volume 15, Number 4 (November 1987), pp. 467–500.

118. *Contradictions*, p. 173.

119. Offe, "New Social Movements," p. 837.

120. Ibid., pp. 831–832 and pp. 836–837.

121. Ibid., p. 836.

122. Ibid., p. 838.

123. Ibid., p. 851.

124. Ibid., pp. 832–833.

125. Ibid., pp. 830–831.

126. Jean Cohen, "Strategy or Identity: New Theoretical Paradigms and Contemporary Social Movements," *Social Research* Volume 52, Number 4 (Winter 1985), pp. 669–670.

127. *Contradictions*, p. 294.

128. Ibid., pp. 294–297.

129. Offe, "New Social Movements," p. 857 and p. 866.

130. Ibid., pp. 864–868, p. 853; *Contradictions of the Welfare State*, pp. 294–295. See two contemporaneous articles on German politics relevant to the topic: Frieder Otto Wolf, "Eco-Socialist Transition on the Threshold of the 21st Century," *New Left Review* Number 158 (July/August 1986), pp. 32–42; Werner Huelsberg, "After the West German Elections," *New Left Review* Number 162 (March/April 1987), pp. 85–99.

131. *Contradictions*, p. 286. In *Beyond Employment* Offe and Heinze argue that links between organized labor, the Greens, and others in the new social movements might be forged through the project of developing non-market cooperation circles: p. 216.

132. *Contradictions*, pp. 152–154, p. 157, pp. 287–288.

133. Offe, "Democracy Against the Welfare State?" *Political Theory* Volume 15, Number 4 (November 1987), p. 519. For other reflections on the welfare state, see the article in the same issue, Sheldon Wolin, "Democracy and the Welfare State: The Political and Theoretical Connections Between Staatsraeson and Wohlfahrtsstaatsraeson," pp. 467–500.

134. Offe, "Democracy Against the Welfare State?," p. 521 and p. 523.

135. Ibid., pp. 524–525 and p. 527.

136. Ibid., p. 528 and p. 527.

137. Ibid., p. 526.

138. Ibid., p. 533, pp. 526–533.

139. Ibid., p. 513.

140. Ibid., pp. 529–535.

141. Ibid., p. 514.

142. Ibid., pp. 532–533.

143. Offe believes that the resurgence of methodological individualism is helpful for macrosociology. However, he also believes that this theoretical development is amenable to a "sociology of knowledge interpretation" in that (1) its resurgence is itself connected with some of the processes argued above; and (2) it is no accident that methodological individualism has renewed currency at the same time that postmodern criticisms of subjectivity are also prevalent. He calls these "twin phenomena": p. 514 and p. 537 footnote 40.

144. Ibid., p. 527.

145. Ibid., p. 528.

146. Ibid., p. 528. However, in the same article he also suggests that health care can be subject to the same deterioration as costs rise: p. 534.

147. Ibid., p. 530.

148. Ibid., p. 510.

149. Respectively: *Contradictions*, p. 94 and p. 77; "Structural Problems of the Capitalist State," pp. 46–47; *Contradictions*, p. 171; *Disorganized Capitalism*, pp. 201–202, p. 207, and passim.

150. *Disorganized Capitalism*, p. 30; also, ibid., p. 2. In another place (ibid., p. 173) in direct opposition to his argument that work is no longer a unified category because service work has a different rationality, Offe strongly suggests that a conceptual distinction between "blue-collar" and "white-collar" is a mistake because it does not acknowledge the common experiences of job insecurity and deskilling. This may not be a contradiction, depending on how white-collar is defined, but again it does reveal uncertainty on a central support of his position.

151. *Contradictions*, p. 83.

152. *Disorganized Capitalism*, pp. 56–57.

153. *Industry and Inequality*, pp. 28–29.

154. Ibid., pp. 36–37 and p. 54.

155. *Disorganized Capitalism* p. 179.

156. Jean Cohen, *Class and Civil Society: The Limits of Marxian Critical Theory* (Amherst, MA: University of Massachusetts Press, 1982), p. 227.

157. *Contradictions*, p. 153 and pp. 262–264.

158. Mike Davis, *Prisoners of the American Dream: Politics and Economy in the History of the US Working Class* (London: Verso, 1986), pp. 206–220.

159. Claus Offe and Ulrich K. Preuss, "Democratic Institutions and Moral Resources," in *Political Theory Today*, edited by David Held (Stanford: Stanford University Press, 1991), p. 165. See also the article by Bernard Manin on the relation between democracy, deliberation, and preference formation: "On Legitimacy and Political Deliberation," *Political Theory* Volume 15, Number 3 (August 1987): pp. 338–368.

160. Ibid., p. 170–171.

161. Ibid., p. 165.

162. For a discussion of Arendt's own argument of the interrelation between political institutions and judgement based on the experience of multiple perspectives, see Sitton, "Hannah Arendt's Argument for Council Democracy," in *Hannah Arendt: Critical Essays*, edited by Lewis P. Hinchman and Sandra K. Hinchman (Albany, NY: State University of New York Press, 1994), pp. 307–329.

CHAPTER SIX

1. "A Philosophico-Political Profile," *New Left Review* 151 (May/June 1985), p. 78.

2. Respectively, Boston: Beacon Press, 1984 and 1987.

3. On his explication of his intentions: interview, "The Dialectics of Rationalization [1981]," in *Autonomy and Solidarity*, edited by Peter Dews (London: Verso Books, 1992), pp. 104–105. One should add that Habermas is trying to rethink the normative grounds of critical social theory without recourse to a "philosophy of history": ibid. 108–109, 111–113. Habermas himself acknowledges the difficulty, complexity, and "rougher discourse" of *The Theory of Communicative Action*; he says the book is a "monster" and "hopelessly academic": ibid., pp. 129, 104, and 108, respectively.

4. Ibid., 108.

5. *Legitimation Crisis* (Boston: Beacon Press, 1975), p. 33.

6. Ibid., pp. 50–51.

7. Ibid., pp. 52–53.

8. Ibid., p. 55–56.

9. Ibid., p. 38.

10. Ibid., p. 39.

11. Ibid., p. 61.

12. Ibid., p. 62, p. 69.

13. Ibid., p. 69.

14. Ibid., p. 69.

15. Ibid., p. 36.

16. Ibid., pp. 71–72. The argument reminds one of Edmund Burke's characterization of nature and tradition as "wisdom without reflection": *Reflections on the Revolution in France* (Indianapolis: The Liberal Arts Press, Inc., 1955), p. 37.

17. *Legitimation Crisis*, p. 72.

18. Ibid., p. 73.

19. Ibid., p. 72. This contrasts with Przeworski's argument that there is some content to the bourgeois claim to be acting in the general interest, based on its structural control over investment.

20. Ibid., p. 70.

21. Ibid., p. 74.

22. Ibid., p. 73. Also, p. 93: "The substitutive relation between the scarce resources, value and meaning, is therefore decisive for the prediction of crisis."

23. Ibid., p. 73.

24. Ibid., pp. 74–75.

25. Ibid., p. 75.

26. Ibid., p. 76.

27. Ibid., pp. 79–80.

28. Ibid., pp. 77–80.

29. Ibid., p. 83. Habermas speaks of various developments "weakening the socialization effects of the market."

30. Ibid., p. 88.

31. Ibid., p. 89.

32. MacIntyre, *A Short History of Ethics* (New York: The Macmillan Company, 1966), pp. 80–82.

33. *Legitimation Crisis*, p. 89.

34. Ibid., p. 84.

35. Ibid., pp. 95–96.

36. Ibid., p. 99.

37. Ibid., p. 104.

38. Ibid., p. 105.

39. Ibid., p. 123.

40. Ibid., pp. 105–107.

41. Ibid., p. 93.

42. Ibid., p. 112.

43. Ibid., p. 93.

44. Ibid., p. 118. He quotes Peter Berger on this issue. "The ultimate danger of such separation, however, is the danger of meaninglessness. This danger is the nightmare par excellence, in which the individual is submerged in a world of disorder, senselessness, and madness."

45. Ibid., p. 120.

46. Ibid., p. 122.

47. Ibid., pp. 123–124.

48. Ibid., p. 125.

49. Ibid., p. 125. Wellmer is quoting Horkheimer and Adorno.

50. Ibid., p. 141.

51. Ibid., p. 121.

52. "A Reply to My Critics," in *Habermas: Critical Debates*, edited by John B. Thompson and David Held (Cambridge, MA: The MIT Press, 1982), pp. 280–281.

53. *Reason and the Rationalization of Society*, p. xxxix.

54. *Lifeworld and System: A Critique of Functionalist Reason,* p. 302.

55. On both: *Reason and the Rationalization of Society*, pp. 366–386.

56. What follows is Habermas's own reading of Weber. Other interpretations are not of immediate relevance.

57. *Reason and the Rationalization of Society*, 176.

58. Ibid., p. 244; on Condorcet, *Reason and the Rationalization of Society*, 150–151. Also, "Modernity—An Incomplete Project," in *Interpretive Social Science: A Second Look*, edited by Paul Rabinow and William M. Sullivan (Berkeley: University of California Press, 1987), p. 149; and *Lifeworld and System*, 326–327.

59. "Modernity—An Incomplete Project," p. 149.

60. *Reason and the Rationalization of Society*, p. 187 and p. 216.

61. Ibid., p. 217.

62. On the importance of "carrier strata": ibid., pp. 199, p. 203, pp. 216–230. For Weber's original argument, see *The Protestant Ethic and the Spirit of Capitalism* (New York: Charles Scribner's Sons, 1958), especially pp. 180–183.

63. *Reason and the Rationalization of Society*, pp. 239–241.

64. Ibid., pp. 221–222. However, Habermas notes that Weber could not avoid implicitly appealing to a broader conception of reason because of Weber's criticism of the "iron cage": p. 222. One of the best brief expressions of the former metaphysical unity of science, morals, and art is in Keats's "Ode on a Grecian Urn": " 'Beauty is truth, truth beauty,' that is all ye know on earth, and all ye need to know."

65. *Reason and the Rationalization of Society*, pp. 285–286.

66. *Legitimation Crisis*, pp. 1–8; *Reason and the Rationalization of Society*, pp. 107–111; *Lifeworld and System*, pp. 113–118 and p. 200; and in many interviews, e.g., "The Dialectics of Rationalization," p. 105. These contrasting perspectives are succinctly expressed by Thomas McCarthy in the "Introduction" to *Reason and the Rationalization of Society*, xxvi–xxvii: "From one point of view, society is conceptualized as the lifeworld of a social group in which actions are coordinated through harmonizing action orientations. From another point of view, society is conceptualized as a self-regulating system in which actions are coordinated through functional interconnections of action consequences. Habermas considers either of these conceptual strategies, taken by itself, to be one-sided. The theory of society requires a combination of the two—of the internalist perspective of the participant with the externalist perspective of the observer, of hermeneutic and structuralist analysis with systems-theoretic and functionalist analysis, of the study of social integration with the study of system integration. . . . Neither point of view is merely a point of view; each is a response to something in the social object, in the one case to the fundamentally symbolic nature of social action, in the other to the latent functions it fulfills."

67. For example, Anthony Giddens: "Reason Without Revolution? Habermas's *Theorie des kommunikativen Handelns*," in *Habermas and Modernity*, edited by Richard J. Bernstein (Cambridge: The MIT Press, 1985), p. 119.

68. *Lifeworld and System*, p. 165. For the broad definition of society, ibid., p. 152. For the discussion of precapitalist and capitalist societies as analyzed through these categories, ibid., pp. 153–172.

69. Ibid., p. 301.

70. Ibid., p. 132.

71. Ibid., pp. 137–138.

72. Ibid., p. 138.

73. *Reason and the Rationalization of Society*, p. 340.

74. *Lifeworld and System*, pp. 145–146.

75. Ibid., p. 146.

76. *Reason and the Rationalization of Society*, p. 340.

77. *Lifeworld and System*, pp. 183–184.

78. Ibid., p. 183.

79. *Reason and the Rationalization of Society*, pp. 341–342.

80. *Lifeworld and System*, p. 150.

81. Interview, "Discourse Ethics, Law, and *Sittlichkeit* [1990]," in *Autonomy and Solidarity*, pp. 262–263.

82. *Reason and the Rationalization of Society*, pp. 342–343.

83. *Lifeworld and System*, p. 173.

84. Ibid., pp. 183–184.

85. Ibid., p. 294. In *Legitimation Crisis* this was discussed as the resistance of the "socio-cultural system" to being "randomly functionalized."

86. *Lifeworld and System*, p. 305.

87. Ibid., p. 311.

88. Ibid., pp. 343–344.

89. Ibid., p. 348.

90. Ibid., pp. 349–350.

91. Ibid., p. 322.

92. "Introduction," in *Reason and the Rationalization of Society*, p. xix.

93. *Lifeworld and System*, p. 322.

94. Ibid., pp. 350–351.

95. Ibid., p. 356.

96. Ibid., p. 395.

97. Ibid., pp. 356–357, p. 363.

98. Ibid., p. 369.

99. Ibid., pp. 327–328.

100. Ibid., p. 355.

101. Ibid., p. 386.

102. Ibid., pp. 391–392.

103. For the last phrase, see Habermas, *The Philosophical Discourse of Modernity* (Cambridge: The MIT Press, 1990), p. 365.

104. *Lifeworld and System*, p. 395.

105. Ibid., p. 396. The work of Andre Gorz fits in well with this analysis. See especially, *Farewell to the Working Class: An Essay on Post-Industrial Socialism* (Boston: South End Press, 1982).

106. *Lifeworld and System*, pp. 355–356. For the phrase "a capering deconstructivism," "A Philosophico-Political Profile," p. 97.

107. Interview, "Political Experience and the Renewal of Marxist Theory [1979]," in *Autonomy and Solidarity*, p. 82; "Conservative Politics, Work, Socialism, and Utopia Today [1983]," in ibid., pp. 138–139; and "The Dialectics of Rationalization," pp. 107–108, also p. 116: "Let's give our Marxist hearts a shock: capitalism was quite a success, at least in the area of material reproduction, and it still is."

108. Habermas, "The New Obscurity: The Crisis of the Welfare State and the Exhaustion of Utopian Energies," in *Philosophy and Social Criticism* 11 (1986), pp. 3–4. The article by Claus Offe that he cites here is, "Work: The Key Sociological Category?" published in Offe, *Disorganized Capitalism* (Cambridge: The MIT Press, 1985): pp. 129–150.

109. "What Does Socialism Mean Today? The Rectifying Revolution and the Need for New Thinking on the Left," *New Left Review* 183 (September/October 1990), pp. 13–14, and p. 15. Also, "The New Obscurity," p. 13. This is Gorz's opinion as well: op. cit., pp. 48–50.

110. "What Does Socialism Mean Today?," p. 16. See also *The Philosophical Discourse of Modernity*, pp. 342–349.

111. "The Dialectics of Rationalization," p. 106, p. 108.

112. "The New Obscurity," p. 3, pp. 5–6.

113. Ibid., pp. 6–8.

114. Ibid., pp. 8–9.

115. Ibid., pp. 9–10.

116. Ibid., p. 11.

117. Ibid., p. 12.

118. Ibid., p. 13.

119. "What Does Socialism Mean Today?," p. 19; "A Philosophico-Political Profile," p. 103; *The Philosophical Discourse of Modernity*, p. 364.

120. Respectively: "Discourse Ethics, Law, and *Sittlichkeit*," pp. 265–266; *The Philosophical Discourse of Modernity*, p. 364, and "The Dialectics of Rationalization," p. 108; "What Does Socialism Mean Today?," p. 17; ibid., pp. 17–18; "The New Obscurity," p. 13; "What Does Socialism Mean Today?," p. 19; ibid., p. 17, interview, "Ideologies and Society in the Post-War World [1977]," in *Autonomy and Solidarity*, p. 53, and interview, "Conservatism and Capitalist Crisis [1978]," in ibid., p. 72; "What Does Socialism Mean Today?," p. 19; "A Philosophico-Political Profile," p. 103; "Further Reflections on the Public Sphere," in *Habermas and the Public Sphere*, edited by Craig Calhoun (Cambridge: The MIT Press, 1992), p. 444, and make them "prevail," ibid., p. 444 and p. 455; and, "Concluding Remarks," in *Habermas and the Public Sphere*, p. 469 (or "counter" or "redirect").

Some of Habermas's sympathetic critics have added, develop "[l]ifeworld contexts, freed from system imperatives": Andrew Arato and Jean Cohen, "Civil Society and Social Theory," in *Between Totalitarianism and Modernity*, edited by Peter Beilharz, Gillian Robinson, and John Rundell (Cambridge, MA: The MIT Press, 1992), p. 210; make the subsystems "sensitized to [lifeworld] goals": "Editor's Introduction," in *Autonomy and Solidarity*, p. 15; and, "subject the systemic mechanisms to the needs of the associated individuals": Albrecht Wellmer, "Reason, Utopia, and the *Dialectic of Enlightenment*," in *Habermas and Modernity*, p. 57.

121. "A Philosophico-Political Profile," p. 96. Alternatively: "not an ontological statement about social being" but a "seal that must be broken," "What Does Socialism Mean Today?," p. 16. The lifting of this "spell" will free use-values: "A Philosophico-Political Profile," p. 103.

122. *Lifeworld and System*, p. 340. Also, "Political Experience and the Renewal of Marxist Theory," p. 94.

123. "The New Obscurity," p. 15.

124. Ibid., p. 14.

125. "What Does Socialism Mean Today?," p. 18. also, "The New Obscurity," p. 13.

126. *Lifeworld and System*, p. 140.

127. "Further Reflections on the Public Sphere," pp. 444–445.

128. Ibid., p. 447.

129. "Discourse Ethics, Law, and *Sittlichkeit*," pp. 251–252. This is, of course, very Arendtian: see Hannah Arendt, "Truth and Politics," in *Between Past and Future: Eight Exercises in Political Thought* (New York: Penguin Books, 1977), p. 241.

130. "Discourse Ethics, Law, and *Sittlichkeit*," p. 255.

131. "Further Reflections on the Public Sphere," p. 444. See also, "Editor's Introduction" to *Autonomy and Solidarity*, pp. 38–41. Finally, see "Morality and Ethical Life: Does Hegel's Critique of Kant Apply to Discourse Ethics?," in Habermas, *Moral Consciousness and Communicative Action* (Cambridge, MA: The MIT Press, 1990), pp. 195–215.

132. "Further Reflections on the Public Sphere," p. 445 and p. 451; "Editor's Introduction," p. 39. See also *The Philosophical Discourse of Modernity*, p. 365, and interview, "On Morality, Law, Civil Disobedience, and Modernity," in *Autonomy and Solidarity*, p. 223.

133. Interview, "Life-Forms, Morality and the Task of the Philosopher," in *Autonomy and Solidarity*, pp. 201–202. This interview was conducted by Peter Dews and Perry Anderson.

134. "Discourse Ethics, Law, and *Sittlichkeit*," pp. 250, 251, 253, and 267.

135. "Concluding Remarks," p. 470.

136. "Discourse Ethics, Law, and *Sittlichkeit*," p. 263. Habermas credits the idea of communicatively generated power to Arendt.

137. "What Does Socialism Mean Today?," p. 18.

138. "Further Reflections on the Public Sphere," p. 452; "Concluding Remarks," p. 470. Communicative power affects administration not by directly intervening in it but by depriving it of normative grounds for action. "The normative grounds which are supposed to justify the posited norms in the language of politics are considered by the administration as restrictions and subsequent rationalizations of decisions which have been generated elsewhere. At the same time, normative grounds are the only currency in which communicative power can make itself

effective. It can operate on the administrative system in such a way that it rations the stock of grounds from which administrative decisions, which stand under constitutional restrictions, are obliged to nourish themselves. Not everything which the administrative system could do is permissible, if the prior political communication and will-formation has [sic] discursively devalued the requisite grounds." "Discourse Ethics, Law, and *Sittlichkeit*," p. 265.

139. *The Philosophical Discourse of Modernity*, p. 363, p. 365. See also, "Discourse Ethics, Law, and *Sittlichkeit*," p. 263.

140. "Discourse Ethics, Law, and *Sittlichkeit*," p. 256. This is an enduring theme in Habermas's work, shown, for example, in the author's introduction to *Theory and Practice* (Boston: Beacon Press, 1973).

141. "Further Reflections on the Public Sphere," pp. 451–452. This also keeps the door open for civil disobedience. "What Does Socialism Mean Today?," p. 18.

142. *The Philosophical Discourse of Modernity*, p. 345; "What Does Socialism Maen Today?," p. 16.

143. Ibid., p. 361.

144. Ibid., p. 359. Habermas uses the singular and the plural—"public sphere" or "public spheres"—interchangeably.

145. Ibid., p. 364. "The New Obscurity," p. 15.

146. "A Reply to My Critics," p. 223. For similar comments: "The New Obscurity," p. 14, "A Philosophico-Political Profile," p. 104, and "Conservatism and Capitalist Crisis," p. 73.

147. "Concluding Remarks," p. 469.

148. "What Does Socialism Mean Today?," pp. 10–11, 14–16, and 21.

149. "A Philosophico-Political Profile," p. 101. See also, "The New Obscurity," p. 13.

150. Both, "The New Obscurity," p. 17.

151. "A Philosophico-Political Profile," p. 104; "Reply," p. 222.

152. "What Does Socialism Mean Today?," p. 16.

153. Giddens, "Labour and Interaction," in *Habermas: Critical Debates*, p. 159.

154. "Reply," p. 221.

155. "A Philosophico-Political Profile," p. 78; "What Does Socialism Mean Today?," p.11.

156. "What Does Socialism Mean Today?," p. 16.

157. Ibid., p. 18.

158. Martin Jay, "Hannah Arendt: Opposing Views," *Partisan Review* XLV, Number 3 (1978), p. 353. See also, Benjamin I. Schwartz, "The Religion of Politics: Reflections on the Thought of Hannah Arendt," *Dissent* VII (March/April 1970).

159. Thomas McCarthy, "Complexity and Democracy, or the Seducements of Systems Theory," *New German Critique* Number 35 (Spring/Summer 1985), pp. 43–45; Arato and Cohen, op. cit., pp. 211–213; Giddens, "Reason Without Revolution?," p. 121.

160. "Reason Without Revolution?," p. 121.

161. Op. cit., pp. 54–55, p. 62.

162. Ibid., p. 57.

163. Ibid., p. 66.

164. "What Does Socialism Mean Today?," p. 9; also pp. 11–12.

165. "Further Reflections on the Public Sphere," p. 442.

166. "The Dialectics of Rationalization," p. 99.

167. "A Philosophico-Political Profile," p. 92.

168. *Lifeworld and System*, p. 344. This is not true of *Legitimation Crisis*.

169. See Offe's collections of essays, *Contradictions of the Welfare State* (Cambridge, MA: The MIT Press, 1984) and *Disorganized Capitalism* (Cambridge, MA: The MIT Press, 1985).

170. Cited by McCarthy, "Complexity and Democracy," p. 46. The original has been translated slightly differently but the meaning is the same: Habermas, *On the Logic of the Social Sciences* (Cambridge, MA: The MIT Press, 1988), p. 188. A similar criticism has been made by others against the theory of Nicos Poulantzas.

171. "Complexity and Democracy," pp. 42–43.

172. Ibid., p. 47. See Habermas's glowing comments on the conceptual skill of Talcott Parsons, *Lifeworld and System*, pp. 199–200, and the same on Luhmann, *The Philosophical Discourse of Modernity*, pp. 384–385.

173. *Reason and the Rationalization of Society*, p. 140.

174. *Lifeworld and System*, p. 200.

175. "Complexity and Democracy," p. 51.

176. Ibid., p. 43. Dieter Misgeld, "Critical Hermeneutics versus Neoparsonianism?," *New German Critique* Number 35 (Spring/Summer 1985): pp. 55–82.

177. *The Road to Serfdom* (Chicago: The University of Chicago Press, 1944), p. 204. It goes without saying that, besides its abstract formulation, this defense of the market is often simply a transparent attempt to justify the existing distribution of power.

178. *Lifeworld and System*, p. 285.

179. *The Philosophical Discourse of Modernity*, pp. 354–355.

180. "Complexity and Democracy," p. 51. David Held criticizes Habermas for utilizing "'unreconstructed' systems concepts and assumptions": "Crisis Tendencies, Legitimation and the State," in *Habermas: Critical Debates*, p. 189. Giddens specifically focuses on the overreliance on Parsons: "Labour and Interaction," pp. 159–160. Habermas's use of Weber has provoked a particularly strong reaction from Giddens, another theorist often 'accused' of being a Weberian: "Too much Weber! Too little Marx!": "Reason Without Revolution?," p. 120.

181. Respectively: *Lifeworld and System*, p. 302; ibid., p. 303; ibid., p. 332; ibid., pp. 364 and 391–392; ibid., p. 347. In an early interview he states: "I am using the word 'class' in its Marxist sense. Class structures persist as long as the means of production and socially useful labor-power are deployed according to preferences which reflect sectional interests in society." "Ideologies and Society in the Post-War World," p. 49. In "Life-Forms, Morality and the Task of the Philosopher" he was criticized by his interviewers Perry Anderson and Peter Dews for a lack of specificity in describing social structures in his mature social theory: p. 206. In the response to the criticisms of Giddens in *Habermas: Critical Debates*, Habermas says "I am attempting to arrive at a suitable approach to the critical analysis of class structures through integrating these three concepts [force, power, and legitimate domination]": "A Reply to My Critics," p. 269.

182. Respectively, *Lifeworld and System*, pp. 348–350, and "What Does Socialism Mean Today?," p. 17.

183. "Conservatism and Capitalist Crisis," p. 69.

184. "The New Obscurity," p. 7.

185. "A Philosophico-Political Profile," p. 102; "The Dialectics of Rationalization," pp. 140–141 and 142–143.

186. Habermas refers to "social Darwinism" frequently: "Conservative Politics, Work, Socialism and Utopia Today," pp. 136, 141, and 146; "The New Obscurity," pp. 11–12; *The Philosophical Discourse of Modernity*, p. 367; and, "What Does Socialism Mean Today?," p. 20.

187. "Conservative Politics, Work, Socialism and Utopia Today," p. 135.

188. "The Dialectics of Rationalization," 117–118.

189. *The Philosophical Discourse of Modernity*, pp. 366–367. See also his ambivalent comments in "What Does Socialism Mean Today?," p. 17, and "The New Obscurity," p.7.

190. *Reason and the Rationalization of Society*, pp. 194–195 and 197.

191. "A Philosophico-Political Profile," p. 89.

192. *Reason and the Rationalization of Society*, p. 219.

193. "The Dialectics of Rationalization," p. 114.

194. Ibid., p. 113.

195. *Lifeworld and System*, p. 110.

196. Respectively, "Political Experience and the Renewal of Marxist Theory," p. 83; and "Concluding Remarks," p. 470. Habermas is capable of outlining how dynamics can fill the explanatory gaps, as demonstrated by his brief sketch in *Lifeworld and System*, pp. 314–318.

197. "Ideologies and Society in the Post-War World," pp. 58 and 61; "Conservatism and Capitalist Crisis," p. 67; "Life-Forms, Morality and the Task of the Philosopher," p. 202. This is contrary to Misgeld's assertion that Habermas has abandoned this dimension of critical social theory.

198. "Concluding Remarks," pp. 469 and 464, respectively.

199. Interview, "Critical Theory and Frankfurt University," in *Autonomy and Solidarity*, p. 211; "A Philosophico-Political Profile," p. 92.

200. *On Law and Ideology* (Atlantic Highlands, NJ: Humanities Press, 1979).

201. Nancy Fraser, "Rethinking the Public Sphere: A Contribution to the Critique of Actually Existing Democracy," in *Habermas and the Public Sphere*, pp. 134–136. Andrew Arato and Jean Cohen argue that it may be possible to insert democratic spaces *inside* system domains. They claim that the present institutions are themselves 'colonized' and their present form could be altered without disrupting media-steering: op. cit., p. 214.

202. Specifically used as a model by Arato and Cohen in op. cit., p. 216. The article is from 1988. On the other hand, Oliver MacDonald predicted that this "restraint" by Solidarity could not be sustained: "The Polish Vortex: Solidarity and Socialism," *New Left Review* Number 139 (May/June 1983), pp. 5–48.

CHAPTER SEVEN

1. Although there are many people utilizing and elaborating the perspective of capitalism as an historical world-system, for purposes of economy this chapter focuses on the work of Immanuel Wallerstein. Unlike other accounts, we will center on works other than his multi-volume general history. Furthermore, the positions of others elaborating world-system theory will be discussed only where directly relevant.

Two general introductions should be mentioned for additional reading on world-system theorists as a whole: Thomas Richard Shannon, *An Introduction to the World-System Perspective* (Boulder, CO: Westview Press, 1989), and Christopher Chase-Dunn, *Global Formation: Structures of the World-Economy* (Cambridge, MA: Basil Blackwell, 1989). Also we must not overlook the contributions of one of the first to develop a world system perspective, Oliver C. Cox: Herbert M. Hunter and Sameer Y. Abraham, editors, *Race, Class, and the World System: The Sociology of Oliver C. Cox* (New York: Monthly Review Press, 1987).

2. *The Capitalist World-Economy: Essays by Immanuel Wallerstein* (Cambridge: Cambridge University Press, 1979), p. 4. Wallerstein approvingly quotes Georg Lukacs's argument that the superiority of Marxian theory lies in its focus on totality: ibid., p. 2.

3. Ibid., pp. 5–6. See also ibid., pp. 155–156. Wallerstein argues that the vague term 'society' begs the question of the proper unit of analysis and that social science would benefit by eliminating the term altogether: ibid., p. 153; *The Politics of the World-Economy: The States, the Movements, and the Civilizations* (Cambridge: Cambridge University Press, 1984), p. 2; and *Unthinking Social Science: The Limits of Nineteenth Century Paradigms* (Cambridge: Polity Press, 1991), pp. 244–248.

4. *The Politics of the World-Economy*, p. 13, p. 165.

5. "Crisis as Transition," in Samir Amin, Giovanni Arrighi, Andre Gunder Frank, and Immanuel Wallerstein, *Dynamics of Global Crisis* (New York: Monthly Review Press, 1982), pp. 13–14. [Although there is considerable overlap in perspective, different parts of this book were written by the individual co-authors. Their agreements and disagreements are stated in the introduction and conclusion of the work.] Cf. *The Politics of the World-Economy*, p. 14; *The Capitalist World-Economy*, p. 66.

6. *The Modern World-System: Capitalist Agriculture and the Origins of the European World-Economy in the Sixteenth Century* (New York: Academic Press, Inc., 1974), p. 37; *The Capitalist World-Economy*, p. 161.

7. *The Capitalist World-Economy*, p. 161. For further arguments along these lines, and for the use of the word "myth," see *Unthinking Social Science*, pp. 57–58. In this place Wallerstein raises the possibility that his account sounds too "volun-

taristic." He nonetheless reaffirms that this was a "strategy" to restore revenues, whether the strategy was "found" or "emerged." See also *Historical Capitalism* (London: Verso, 1983) where he says, "Without suggesting that anyone consciously verbalized any such attempt. . . ": p. 42; again on p. 43: "No one may have verbalized the intent . . ." On occasion he also straightforwardly defends teleological explanations: "What could be more plausible than a line of reasoning which argues that the explanation of the origin of a system was to achieve an end that has in fact been achieved?": p. 41.

8. *The Capitalist World-Economy*, p. 37.

9. *Dynamics of Global Crisis*, 13–14.

10. *The Capitalist World-Economy*, p. 159; *Dynamics of Global Crisis*, p. 14.

11. *Historical Capitalism*, pp. 56–57. "All of these constraints ran counter to the official ideology of sovereignty. Sovereignty however was never really intended to mean total autonomy. The concept was rather meant to indicate that there existed limits on the legitimacy of interference by one state-machinery in the operations of another." Cf. Anthony Giddens, *The Nation State and Violence* (Berkeley: The University of California Press, 1987).

12. *The Politics of the World-Economy*, p. 50.

13. *The Capitalist World-Economy*, p. 149; *Dynamics of Global Crisis*, p. 13.

14. Especially if it has "hegemony" over the world-economy. For arguments, see: *Historical Capitalism*, pp. 58–60; and *The Politics of the World-Economy*, pp. 44–46.

15. *The Politics of the World-Economy*, pp. 2–3.

16. Ibid., p. 3. Wallerstein usually rejects the word "multinational" in favor of the adjective 'transnational,' which better supports his attempt to free theory from concentrating on individual nation-states.

17. *Historical Capitalism*, p. 16.

18. *Dynamics of Global Crisis*, pp. 23–24.

19. *The Capitalist World-Economy*, p. 149; *Historical Capitalism*, p. 16.

20. *The Capitalist World-Economy*, p. 285. Poulantzas's intriguing distinction between 'institutions' and 'structures' might be helpful here: *Political Power and Social Classes* (London: New Left Books, 1973), p. 115 footnote 24.

21. *Historical Capitalism*, p. 64.

22. *The Politics of the World-Economy*, p. 43.

23. Giovanni Arrighi, Terence K. Hopkins, and Immanuel Wallerstein, *Anti-*

systemic Movements (London: Verso, 1989), p. 46. [All parts of this work are under joint authorship therefore I regard the arguments as jointly held.]

24. *Unthinking Social Science*, p. 203.

25. Ibid., p. 247. Wallerstein mentions that Braudel would limit the word 'capitalist' to the highest, speculative, multidimensional, and monopolistic level of the world-system: ibid., pp. 210–211. For Braudel's intriguing argument see *The Wheels of Commerce* Volume 2 of *Civilization and Capitalism 15th–18th Century* (New York: Harper and Row, 1982), pp. 455–457 and pp. 374–457 passim; and *The Perspective of the World* Volume 3 of *Civilization and Capitalism 15th–18th Century* (New York: Harper and Row, 1984), pp. 622–623.

26. *Geopolitics and Geoculture: Essays on the Changing World-System* (Cambridge: Cambridge University Press, 1991), p. 39.

27. Ibid., p. 53.

28. *Unthinking Social Science*, p. 233.

29. *The Capitalist World-Economy*, p. 20, p. 70 (on welfare states), p. 121. His response to the charge of 'instrumentalism' is found also in *The Politics of the World-Economy*, p. 30.

30. *Unthinking Social Science*, p. 242, p. 264. Cf. *Geopolitics and Geoculture*, p. 38, where he uses the phrase "subsystems with autonomous logics." Also, *Unthinking Social Science*, p. 241: "We know where all these divisions of subject matter came from. They derive intellectually from the dominant liberal ideology of the nineteenth century which argued that state and market, politics and economics, were analytically separate (and largely self-contained) domains, each with their particular rules ('logics')." Wallerstein mentions the importance of the fact that Braudel established a separate academic home for his perspective: ibid., p. 189. Wallerstein is criticized by Aristide Zolberg for doing the same: "Origins of the Modern World System: A Missing Link," *World Politics* Volume 33 (1981), p. 256.

31. "Marxist Century—American Century: The Making and Remaking of the World Labor Movement," in Samir Amin, Giovanni Arrighi, Andre Gunder Frank, and Immanuel Wallerstein, *Transforming the Revolution: Social Movements and the World-System* (New York: Monthly Review Press, 1990), p. 64. [As in *Dynamics of Global Crisis*, although there is agreement on perspective, each section was written by one of the individual authors. Agreements and disagreements are outlined in the introduction and conclusion of the work.]

32. *Historical Capitalism*, pp. 31–32, p. 30.

33. *The Capitalist World-Economy*, p. 71, p. 18. In a footnote on page 71 Wallerstein quotes Samir Amin at length, in which Amin insists that unequal exchange

takes place on the basis of "equal productivity." See also ibid., p. 84, and *The Politics of the World-Economy*, p. 15.

34. John Roemer repeatedly mentions the possible application of his models for elucidating "unequal exchange": "New Directions in the Marxian Theory of Exploitation and Class," *Politics and Society* Volume 11, Number 3 (1982), p. 286; "Should Marxists Be Interested in Exploitation?," in *Analytical Marxism*, edited by John Roemer (Cambridge: Cambridge University Press, 1986), p. 269; and *Free to Lose: An Introduction to Marxist Economic Philosophy* (Cambridge: MA: Harvard University Press, 1988), p. 106. It is not actually clear that Roemer's equilibrium models of a subsistence economy are applicable to this situation.

35. Respectively, *The Politics of the World-Economy*, p. 15, and *Historical Capitalism*, p. 32.

36. Etienne Balibar and Immanuel Wallerstein, *Race, Nation, Class: Ambiguous Identities* (London: Verso, 1991), p. 130. [Half of these individual essays were written by Wallerstein and half by Balibar. They are not co-authored.] *Historical*, pp. 23–24: Wallerstein states that less than half of the households of the world are fully proletarianized. This seems to be the dimension he has in mind when he says that the factors of production are less than half 'freed.'

37. *Dynamics of Global Crisis*, p. 21. *Race, Nation, Class*, p. 34; *The Politics of the World-Economy*, p. 19.

38. *Race*, p. 130. Wallerstein specifically calls this "surplus value." Cf. *Historical*, p. 32; also ibid., pp. 21–28. Finally, *The Capitalist*, pp. 125–127 and pp. 264–265.

39. *The Capitalist*, p. 290; *Unthinking Social Science*, p. 164; *Historical Capitalism*, p. 27.

40. *Unthinking*, p. 233. Wallerstein often speaks of the increased efficiencies stemming from technology: *Unthinking*, p. 111; *Geopolitics*, p. 164. He also mentions it in regard to the stagnation of soviet-style economies: ibid., p. 94.

41. *Historical Capitalism*, p. 33. This position is similar to that in feminist politics known as "comparable worth." Some occupations have historically been paid lower simply because they are disproportionately filled with women.

42. *The Capitalist World-Economy*, p. 88; *The Politics of the World-Economy*, pp. 3–4; *Historical Capitalism*, pp. 32 and 37.

43. *Historical Capitalism*, p. 30. Shannon gives a brief overview of the ambiguities and discussion of the concept of unequal exchange in op. cit., pp. 30–31 and pp. 148–149. Recently, Wallerstein is more cautious on the issue, speaking of "some form of unequal exchange (not necessarily as defined originally by Arghiri Emmanuel)": *Unthinking Social Science*, p. 268.

44. *Historical Capitalism*, p. 35. Cf. *The Politics of the World-Economy*, p. 103 and *The Capitalist World-Economy*, p. 68.

45. *The Capitalist World-Economy*, pp. 85–86 and p. 61. See also his articles criticizing the concept of 'development' in *Unthinking Social Science*: pp. 41–124.

46. *Historical Capitalism*, p. 36; *The Capitalist World-Economy*, p. 71; *The Politics of the World-Economy*, p. 16. In *Global Formation*, Chase-Dunn refers to some recent discussion of 'product cycle' theory: p. 234 and p. 251.

47. *The Capitalist World-Economy*, pp. 70–71.

48. Ibid., p. 134, pp. 272–273.

49. *Historical Capitalism*, p. 33. Cf. *The Politics of the World-Economy*, p. 3.

50. *Dynamics of Global Crisis*, p. 12. He says that the cultural principle inculcated by this capitalist "civilization" is correspondingly the "cosmology of 'more'": *The Politics of the World-Economy*, p. 165, p. 98.

51. *The Politics of the World-Economy*, p. 98; ibid., p. 16; *Dynamics of Global Crisis*, pp. 15–16.

52. *The Capitalist World-Economy*, p. 275; see also *The Politics of the World-Economy*, pp. 98–100. Wallerstein cites Emmanuel on the "ethical" determination of wages, i.e., the "moral and historical" mediation of the level of wages in a particular state. However, this 'moral' mediation is also conditioned by the world economic position of the particular state: *The Capitalist World-Economy*, p. 70, p. 84. Arghiri Emmanuel's argument is made in *Unequal Exchange: A Study of the Imperialism of Trade* [with additional comments by Charles Bettleheim] (New York: Monthly Review Press, 1972).

53. *Dynamics*, p. 16; cf. *The Politics*, pp. 6, 16; *Historical*, pp. 17–18.

54. *Historical*, pp. 34–35.

55. *Dynamics*, pp. 38–40; *The Capitalist*, pp. 61–62, p. 97; *The Politics*, p. 16 and p. 59.

56. *The Politics*, pp. 16–17; cf. ibid., p. 53 and p. 100.

57. *Dynamics*, pp. 17–19; *Historical*, pp. 34–35.

58. *Historical*, p. 61; *The Politics*, p. 100.

59. Ibid., pp. 38–39; *The Capitalist*, p. 83.

60. *The Capitalist*, pp. 128–129. Cf. ibid., pp. 145–146.

61. *Historical*, pp. 36–37.

62. *Dynamics*, pp. 22–23. Cf. *The Politics*, p. 104.

63. There is some confusion in this concept. Sometimes Wallerstein refers to three secular trends, mechanization, proletarianization, and incorporation: *The Politics*, pp. 103–104. However, in other places he also mentions the secular trends of "contractualization," "politicization," and "janissarization of the ruling classes": *The Capitalist*, pp. 278–279.

64. *Dynamics*, p. 22, p. 25.

65. *Geopolitics and Geoculture*, p. 46.

66. *Dynamics*, p. 23.

67. *The Politics*, p. 55. See also ibid., p. 126 ("ideal type"), and *Dynamics*, p. 41 ("regard for the law of value"). Arrighi says something similar in "Marxist Century—American Century: The Making and Remaking of the World Labor Movement," in *Transforming the Revolution*, p. 73.

68. *The Politics*, p. 143, p. 133, and p. 24; *Dynamics*, p. 33.

69. *The Capitalist*, p. 129, p. 67.

70. *The Capitalist*, p. 162, pp. 106–107; *The Politics*, pp. 153–154.

71. *Unthinking*, pp. 160–161.

72. *Unthinking*, pp. 250–251. Cf. *The Capitalist*, pp. 9 and 17.

73. *The Capitalist*, p. 276. In *Unthinking Social Science*, pp. 154–155, Wallerstein presents this gloss on certain passages of Marx to bolster his position: "Note once again that all these forms of production are considered to have created 'surplus-value' once they enter the 'circuit' of capital. 'The character of the process of production from which they originate is immaterial.'"

74. *Race, Nation, and Class*, p. 35. Wallerstein argues that although the distinction between productive and unproductive labor is not the origin of "sexism," it did mark its "institutionalization": *Historical Capitalism*, pp. 22–26.

75. Often the labor is indeed coerced: *The Politics*, pp. 154–155; on slavery in the United States, *The Capitalist*, p. 220.

76. *Historical*, p. 21.

77. *The Politics*, p. 3.

78. On "absolute immiseration," *Historical*, pp. 100–101; *Race, Nation, Class*, pp. 127–129: *Dynamics*, pp. 25–26; and *Historical*, pp. 100–105. On polarization and suggested absolute immiseration, *Geopolitics and Geoculture*, pp. 176–177. Wallerstein admits that figures concerning polarization need to be improved: *Un-*

thinking Social Science, pp. 269–270. On the other hand, Christopher Chase-Dunn denies absolute immiseration but agrees that polarization has occurred: op. cit., p. 10.

79. *Historical*, pp. 36–37. Wallerstein is no more gentle with the workers themselves than with their 'spokesmen': "by their own efforts, workers become proletarianized, and then shout victory!" In *Race*, p. 131.

80. In one place he says that this "has meant an increase in money income (if not at all necessarily an increase in real income)": *The Politics*, p. 102. But see *Race, Nation, Class*, p. 131.

81. Immanuel Wallerstein and Joan Smith, "Conclusion: Core-Periphery and Household Structures," in *Creating and Transforming Households: The Constraints of the World-Economy*, "coordinated" by Wallerstein and Smith (Cambridge: Cambridge University Press, 1992), p. 260. "In a capitalist society, wages can never be the sole or even principal mode of payment of the vast majority of the world workforce. Wages must always be combined with other forms of income. These other forms of income are never negligible." Ibid., p. 254. Also, in the slightly earlier work: Smith, Wallerstein, and Hans-Dieter Evers, "Introduction," in *Households and the World-Economy*, edited by Smith, Wallerstein, and Evers (Beverly Hills: Sage Publications, 1984), p. 10: "As areas within the core itself become dominated by these 'marginalized' labor processes we can expect to see greater dependence on these apparently anomalous structures." On New York City, ibid., p. 9.

82. Wallerstein and Smith, "Conclusion," p. 261, pp. 256–262.

83. "The Agonies of Liberalism: What Hope Progress?," *New Left Review* Number 204 (March/April 1994), p. 14.

84. *The Capitalist*, pp. 288–289.

85. *The Capitalist*, p. 292 and pp. 285–286. In the latter place Wallerstein uses the phrases "surplus value" and "surplus" interchangeably.

86. *Race*, pp. 131–132. Cf. *The Politics*, p. 128.

87. *Historical*, p. 17.

88. *Race*, pp. 146–148, p. 133; *The Capitalist*, pp. 286–288. The attempt to turn 'achievement' into 'status' comes under particular pressure in economic downturns, not to mention revolutions like the English Civil War: ibid. In recent times, the political pressures of workers on 'rights to property' also encourage the increased "bourgeoisification of the capitalist class": "Feudal-aristocratic idleness becomes too obvious and too politically dangerous."

89. *Race*, p. 146.

90. Ibid., p. 143. Also, *The Politics*, p. 23.

91. *Race*, p. 149.

92. Ibid., pp. 140–141, pp. 149–150.

93. *The Capitalist*, pp. 163 and 279. *Dynamics*, p. 32. Also, in ibid., p. 24, Wallerstein suggests that education is a kind of claim on property.

The original 'janissaries' were a special corps of slaves extracted by the Ottoman Empire from its subject Christian territories or through war, beginning around the late 14th century. The slaves were raised as Moslems and served as the elite infantry and artillery forces for the Ottoman Empire. Their importance allowed them to increase their privileges and political power to the point of deposing a Sultan in 1622. See the account by Perry Anderson, *Lineages of the Absolutist State* (London: Verso, 1974), pp. 366–367 and pp. 381–382.

94. *The Politics*, p. 64. This "enormous economic drain" is aiding the loss of hegemony of the United States to Japan in particular: *Geopolitics and Geoculture*, p. 43; cf. *The Politics*, p. 45.

95. Both in *Race*, p. 150.

96. *Unthinking*, p. 165.

97. *The Politics*, p. 101.

98. *The Capitalist*, p. 286.

99. Offe, *Industry and Inequality: The Achievement Principle in Work and Social Status* (New York: St. Martin's Press, 1977). For Wright's critics, see Chapter Two above. This illustration may clarify the comment. The number of tenure-track college and university positions is less than the number of qualified people to fill them. Attending the 'right' schools and getting the 'right' degrees are closure strategies that aid in obtaining a position. This does not necessarily imply that those few who obtain these positions do no work when they get there.

100. *The Capitalist*, p. 222.

101. Ibid., p. 224, pp. 222–227, p. 230, p. 198; *The Politics*, p. 183, pp. 78–79, p. 8.

102. *The Politics*, p. 8, pp. 35–36; *Dynamics*, p. 26, p. 30; *The Capitalist*, p. 61, p. 196; *Antisystemic Movements*, p. 23, p. 26.

103. *The Capitalist*, p. 181.

104. *Historical*, pp. 64–65; *Unthinking*, p. 166.

105. *Antisystemic Movements*, p. 97.

106. For the phrase "springtime of nations": *Transforming*, p. 16; for the leading ideas, *Antisystemic*, p. 97.

107. *Antisystemic*, pp. 98–99.

108. *Geopolitics*, p. 68. Also, *Historical*, p. 67.

109. *The Politics*, p. 21, p. 35, and p. 140.

110. *Transforming*, pp. 29–34; *Geopolitics*, p. 75.

111. *Geopolitics*, p. 64. See also, *The Politics*, pp. 138–141, and *Historical*, pp. 69–70 and pp. 91–92. However, Wallerstein is by no means completely consistent on the issue. See *The Politics*, pp. 108–109: "The importance of antisystemic movements is not in the reforms they achieve or in the regimes they establish. Many of these regimes are in fact parodies of their stated objectives. The importance of these movements is in terms of the changes they bring about in the world-system as a whole. They transform not primarily the economics but rather the politics of the capitalist world-economy. Joined with the more narrowly socioeconomic trends previously described, this secular increase of the strength of antisystemic movements undermines the viability of the world-system." His more common position appears in the other citations.

112. *Antisystemic*, p. 98; *Geopolitics*, p. 65.

113. "The Agonies of Liberalism," p. 13.

114. *Geopolitics*, pp. 75–76; *Antisystemic*, p. 34–35.

115. *Antisystemic*, p. 88. Wallerstein also notes the division within the "tertiary sector" between highly paid professionals and lower paid clerks: ibid., pp. 83–88. Cf. ibid., p. 102. On Vietnam, ibid., pp. 35–36. See also *Transforming*, pp. 40–41.

116. *Geopolitics*, pp. 72–73.

117. Ibid., p. 72; *Antisystemic*, p. 104.

118. *Geopolitics*, p. 74.

119. *Antisystemic*, p. 114; *Geopolitics*, pp. 75–76.

120. *Anti-Systemic*, pp. 37–38.

121. *Geopolitics*, p. 64; *The Politics*, pp. 140–141; *The Capitalist*, pp. 68–69, p. 74, p. 91.

122. *Geopolitics*, p. 11. "What 1968 represented was the institutionalization of a deep skepticism about the liberal consensus that had previously dominated all the cultural, intellectual, and political institutions of the Western world and, indeed, of large parts of the periphery." Ibid., p. 54.

123. *Geopolitics*, pp. 11–12, p. 217, p. 193, and p. 173; *Historical*, p. 75.

124. *Historical*, p. 83, p. 81.

125. Ibid., p. 84, p. 82. In the process, the masses are deprived of potential leaders.

126. *Geopolitics*, pp. 174–175. Racism and sexism are not antithetical to universalism but rather these together form a "symbiotic pair": ibid., p. 167; *Historical*, p. 85. Also, *The Politics*, p. 56.

127. *Historical*, p. 85.

128. Ibid., pp. 78–82, p. 103. Although this claim may appear excessive, it should be recalled that Hannah Arendt also criticized "truth" as corrupting of authentic political experience. However, apparently unlike Wallerstein, she argued that 'truth' had its place outside of the political realm. See "Truth and Politics," in *Between Past and Future: Eight Exercises in Political Thought* (New York: Penguin Books, 1968), pp. 227–264.

129. *Race*, pp. 126–127; *Geopolitics*, p. 224; *Historical*, p. 86.

130. *Historical*, pp. 89–90; *Geopolitics*, p. 224.

131. *Geopolitics*, p. 13.

132. *Unthinking*, pp. 32–34; *Geopolitics*, p. 13, p. 119.

133. *Geopolitics*, p. 119, p. 221. "The concept of civilization (singular) is a Newtonian idea." Ibid., p. 234.

134. *Historical*, pp. 92–93; *Unthinking*, p. 34; *Geopolitics*, p.221.

135. *Antisystemic*, pp. 42–46, pp. 50–51. Wallerstein et al. mention that there are, nonetheless, countertendencies that cannot be ignored. The most important of these is the rise of various "pan-" movements—the women's movement, peace movements, pan-Islam, pan-Africanism—which relate "communities of believers/practitioners" without regard to state boundaries or interstate relations.

136. Ibid., p. 48.

137. Ibid., pp. 48–50, pp. 111–112.

138. Ibid., p. 93, pp. 113–114.

139. Ibid., p. 113, p. 95, pp. 91–93. This is related to the secular trend of "contractualization": *Geopolitics*, pp. 41–42. Rudolf Meidner discusses how even the 'Swedish model' has been undermined partly but importantly by the globalization of capital: "Why Did the Swedish Model Fail?," *Socialist Register 1993*, edited by Ralph Miliband and Leo Panitch (London: The Merlin Press, 1993), pp. 211–228.

140. *Antisystemic*, p. 112, p. 41. Arrighi argues that the capital/labor relation is becoming increasingly prominent as the locus of struggle: "In this sense they [the movements] will all be workers' movements." *Transforming*, p. 185. According to Arrighi, the resort to financial speculation reveals the growing "social power of labor": ibid., pp. 79–80.

141. *Antisystemic*, p. 105.

142. Ibid., p. 90.

143. *Antisystemic*, pp. 110–111, pp. 106–108, p. 89; *Geopolitics*, p. 76; *Transforming*, pp. 45–46.

144. *Antisystemic*, p. 94. On the generally increasing social power of labor, see Arrighi's essay in *Transforming*, pp. 54–95.

145. *Unthinking*, p. 167, p. 183, p. 205; *Geopolitics*, p. 121; *Historical*, pp. 97–110.

146. *Race*, p. 231, p. 229.

147. Wallerstein's insistence on the role of cycles and secular trends stems from the work of Fernand Braudel, although Braudel himself appears to use the term "secular trends" to refer to very longterm, gradual price changes. Braudel concludes that although present-day capitalism is facing a crisis more serious than 1929, he does not believe it is in danger of collapse. Braudel, *The Perspective of the World*, p. 626. Also, ibid., p. 80: "Is this a short-term conjunctural crisis, as most economists seem to think? Or have we had the rare and unenviable privilege of seeing with our own eyes the century begin its downward turn? If so, the short-term policies admirably directed toward immediate ends, advocated by our political leaders and economic experts, may turn out to be powerless to cure a sickness of which our children's children will be very lucky to see the end." Braudel believes Wallerstein's analysis to be "extremely stimulating" but "a little too systematic, perhaps": ibid., p. 70. On Braudel's use of the term "secular trend," see ibid., pp. 76–78.

148. *Geopolitics*, pp. 234–237, pp. 13–15, p. 106. But, unsurprisingly, mankind does not make history just as it pleases: "To say a transition is stochastic is not to say that anything and everything is possible. The possible vectors are not infinite but are located within a range created by the sum of existing realities. Ergo the choices we have today are quite different from those available in say AD 1450 or 500 BC. The arrow of time is irreversible and cumulative—but not inevitably progressive." In *Unthinking*, p. 263. Also ibid., p. 254.

149. *Geopolitics*, p. 74, p. 82, pp. 121–122. A very interesting article on this topic, discussing the groups around the "People's Plan for the Twenty-First Century (PP21)," is Martin Hart-Landsberg, "Post-NAFTA Politics: Learning from Asia," *Monthly Review* Volume 46, Number 2 (June 1994) pp. 12–21.

150. *Transforming the Revolution*, p. 53.

151. *Unthinking*, pp. 75–76.

152. *Geopolitics*, p. 56, p. 198, p. 224, p. 45, p. 182. "This is a sort of ultimate abandonment of rationality, a game I for one am not ready to play." Ibid., p. 235. See also, *Historical*, p. 86.

153. *Geopolitics*, p. 81, pp. 24–25, p. 128. Wallerstein suggests the necessity of "fusing currents" but this is not much more than a metaphor: ibid., p. 157. When Wallerstein uses the phrase "family of antisystemic movements" he is not referring to Ludwig Wittgenstein's famous conceptual argument of "family resemblances." Wallerstein explains that he is thinking of how families do not always agree but try to present a common front against enemies: *Transforming*, pp. 51–52.

Wittgenstein, on the other hand, argued that in attempting to understand the employment of words like "game" we should not seek a common element. The same word is used not because of some element common to all 'games' but rather because one game resembles another in a certain respect while another game might resemble the second in a different respect, like two members of a family might share the same nose but a third, with a distinctive nose, might share the color of eyes with one of the previous two. We recognize them as a family because of these overlapping characteristics, not because all share the same characteristic: *Philosophical Investigations* Third Edition (New York: Macmillan Publishing, 1968), pp. 31e–32e. Wittgenstein's analogy might actually serve Wallerstein's purposes better.

154. *Unthinking*, p. 36; *Geopolitics*, pp. 78–79; on Solidarity, ibid., pp. 22–23. Samir Amin, for one, argues against relying on "the autonomy of a shattered and fragmented civil society," saying that this strategy is "too heavily biased by antistatism to really be up to the real [sic] historical challenge." *Transforming*, p. 131. See also the intriguing but pessimistic discussion of social movements by Andre Gunder Frank and Marta Fuentes, "Civil Democracy: Social Movements in Recent World History," in ibid., pp. 139–180.

155. *Geopolitics*, p. 229, p. 80. *Unthinking*, p. 23; p. 36: "It is in the acceleration of the decadence of the present system and not in its controlled transformation, to use Amin's distinction, that the prospects of creating a truly socialist world-historical system lie." Samir Amin uses the distinction in relation to the project of "delinking" in his contribution to *Dynamics of Global Crisis*, pp. 218–225.

156. *Geopolitics*, p. 227–228, p. 46; *Unthinking*, pp. 28–30. Amin openly prefers the transitional 'model' of from antiquity to feudalism to the transition from feudalism to capitalism: *Dynamics of Global Crisis*, p. 225.

157. *Unthinking*, p. 169; *Geopolitics*, pp. 135–136.

158. *Unthinking*, p. 215, p. 167, p. 206. See the articles in ibid., "Capitalism: the

Enemy of the Market?," pp. 202–206; and "Braudel on Capitalism, or Everything Upside Down," pp. 207–217.

159. *The Capitalist*, p. 134.

160. *Unthinking*, p. 60, p. 184, p. 78. "An Agenda for World-Systems Analysis," in *Contending Approaches to World System Analysis*, edited by William R. Thompson (Beverly Hills: Sage Publications, 1983), p. 302. "Social scientific theorizing" is "nothing but the effort to systematize our mythology": in ibid., p. 304. He also states that historical myths are "fundamental means of organizing our knowledge of the world": in "The World-System: Myths and Historical Shifts," in *The Global Economy: Divergent Perspectives on Economic Change*, edited by Edward W. Gondolf, Irwin M. Marcus, and James P. Doughterty (Boulder, CO: Westview Press, 1986), pp. 15–16.

161. Op. cit., p. 1.

162. "The Agonies of Liberalism," pp. 16–17. The entire quote reads: "You may think that the programme I have outlined for judicious social and political action over the next twenty-five to fifty years is far too vague. But it is as concrete as one can be in the midst of a whirlpool. First, make sure to which shore you wish to swim. And second, make sure that your immediate efforts seem to be moving in that direction. If you want greater precision than that, you will not find it, and you will drown while you are looking for it."

163. Aristide Zolberg, " 'World' and 'System': A Misalliance," in *Contending Approaches to World System Analysis*, p. 275, p. 278; Chase-Dunn, op. cit., p. 49; Shannon, op. cit., pp. 160–163. See Braudel's discussion of Kondratieffs, secular trends, and other cycles in *The Perspective of the World*, pp. 71–88.

164. Chase-Dunn, op. cit., p. 50.

165. *The Politics*, p. 46. For discussion of hegemonic cycles, see Chase-Dunn, op. cit., pp. 166–198; George Modelski, "Of Politics, Portugal, and Kindred Issues: A Rejoinder," in *Contending Approaches to World System Analysis*, pp. 291–298.

166. *Geopolitics*, p. 43, p. 131, p. 55.

167. Theda Skocpol, "Wallerstein's World Capitalist System: A Theoretical and Historical Critique," *American Journal of Sociology* Volume 82, Number 5 (March 1977), p. 1078, pp. 1086–1089. Stanley Aronowitz criticizes Wallerstein on similar grounds: "A Metatheoretical Critique of Immanuel Wallerstein's *The Modern World-System*," *Theory and Society* Volume 10, (1981), pp. 508–509. Aronowitz's conclusion that Wallerstein's account of the transition from feudalism does not proceed from "internal contradictions of a system" but from "pure contingency" is accurate with this qualification: Wallerstein argues that a system's contradictions lead to its "exhaustion" of possibilities. At *this* point, contingency (or 'free will') reigns. The

major weakness of functional explanations is, as noted succinctly by Charles Tilly, that "Functional explanations . . . are notoriously difficult to verify or falsify and slip into tautology with great ease." Tilly, *Big Structures, Large Processes, Huge Comparisons* (New York: The Russell Sage Foundation, 1984), p. 126.

168. Zolberg, "Origins of the Modern World System," p. 257; and Zolberg, " 'World' and 'System': A Misalliance," p. 286. In the latter article Zolberg also criticizes Modelski's use of systems concepts. In turn, Modelski defends his "Parsonian" notion of world-system: op. cit., p. 291.

Zolberg argues that, "The search for a social system that is 'real' and 'self-contained' leads to infinite regress in space and time." In " 'World' and 'System': A Misalliance," p. 272. Considering Andre Gunder Frank's present position that the world-system stretches back 5000 years, this criticism seems sound: Frank and Barry K. Gills, "The Five Thousand Year Old World System: An Interdisciplinary Introduction," *Humboldt Journal of Social Relations* Volume 18, Number 2 (Spring 1992) [paper version while article forthcoming]. See also the comments on Frank's position, in "Conclusion: A Friendly Debate," *Transforming the Revolution*, p. 182.

169. *Race*, pp. 6–7. Balibar admits that identifying these 'units' is still a problem. R. W. Connell also criticizes Wallerstein's over-emphasis on the unity of the capitalism: "Class Formation on a World Scale," *Review* Volume VII, Number 3 (Winter 1984), pp. 436–437.

170. Zolberg, "Origins of the Modern World System," p. 255; also, "reductionist tendency" (p. 255). Skocpol criticizes Wallerstein's "reduction . . . of politics to world market-oriented class interest": op. cit, p. 1080 and p. 1086. David P. Rapkin also refers to Wallerstein's "economic reductionism": "The Inadequacy of a Single Logic: Integrating Political and Material Approaches to the World System," in *Contending Approaches to World System Analysis*, p. 246. Finally, Robert Brenner speaks of the "economic determinism that pervades all aspects of Wallerstein's theoretical framework": "The Origins of Capitalist Development: A Critique of Neo-Smithian Marxism," *New Left Review* Number 104 (July/August 1977), p. 61.

171. Respectively: Skocpol, op. cit., pp. 1087–1088; Zolberg, "Origins of the Modern World System," p. 263 and p. 275; Rapkin, op. cit., pp. 241–242, and p. 256 (in which he mentions "subsystems"). Zolberg does allow that certain arguments of Wallerstein are an "illustration of mutually reinforcing political and economic causation with which I have no quarrel": "Origins," p. 271. On the other hand, Chase-Dunn's attempt to rescue the "one logic" view through assertions of "interdependent determinants" is rightly rejected by Zolberg as too vague: Zolberg, " 'World' and 'System,'" p. 275. Rapkin says something similar about Chase-Dunn's analysis of hegemony: Rapkin, op. cit., p. 264.

172. Rapkin argues that neglect of the latter topic is Wallerstein's "chief failing": op. cit., pp. 259–260.

173. *Unthinking*, p. 230. He calls this thesis "banal."

174. *Geopolitics*, p. 11.

175. Indeed he argues on occasion that transnational financial agencies may serve as a "structural replacement of the colonial empires": *Antisystemic*, p. 49. Cf. ibid., p. 112. The weakness of his position is best shown by the fact that Wallerstein himself appeals to the existence of a distinct political "logic" on occasion. In discussing intra-elite struggles so as to distinguish them from class struggle, Wallerstein argues that the "logic" of seeking political "command" differs from the "logic" of seeking economic "command." The main reason is that economic power is cumulative in a way that political power is not. The distinction between the two types of 'command' leads to intra-elite conflict because of the "transterritoriality" of the former, whereas the latter is limited to a specific territory: *Antisystemic*, pp. 61–63. In another place Wallerstein et al. even call "non-market constraints" "artificial": ibid., pp. 38–39.

Zolberg states that Wallerstein faces the same difficulty when he indicates Christianity as the cultural unifier of Europe: "Origins of the Modern World System," p. 260.

176. *Unthinking*, pp. 270–271; ibid., p. 4.

177. Brenner, op. cit., pp. 60–61. Brenner also criticizes Wallerstein's use of the notion of "unequal exchange" to ground his position, although Brenner does not explicitly reject the concept itself: p. 63. Similarly, Balibar criticizes Wallerstein for concentrating on "extensive" exploitation and ignoring "what Marx calls . . . 'relative surplus value'" generated through technology: *Race*, p. 11.

178. Brenner, op. cit., pp. 30–31, p. 54. 'Neo-Smithian' in that expanding the division of labor is considered the primary source of surplus.

179. Ibid., p. 32.

180. Ibid., pp. 36–37. Brenner also argues that systematically increasing productivity only begins when individuals have been "freed" from owning means of production. As argued in Chapter One above, where peasants own their own plots it is rational to diversify production and they are not subject to competitive pressures. Although this is an aspect of the class relations that block development, we can neglect this part of Brenner's argument here.

181. Ibid., p. 84.

182. Ibid., p. 85.

183. Ibid., p. 91, p. 61.

184. Ibid., pp. 91–92.

185. "Crisis, Nationalism, and Socialism," in *Dynamics of Global Crisis*, pp. 192–193. Amin argues that the "main contradiction" is not capital/labor but that "between imperialism and the popular forces in the periphery" (p. 189). He even accepts the phrase and project of "socialism in one country": "If socialism in one (backward) country is impossible, socialism itself is impossible" (p. 223, pp. 218–219). This is connected with his above-mentioned idea of "decadence" as the best transition: ibid., p. 225. He modifies this in "The Social Movements in the Periphery: An End to National Liberation?," in *Transforming the Revolution*, p. 115: not socialism, but "anticapitalism" is possible through delinking, and "delinking" is "relative," not "autarchy" (p. 126). He may be thinking of China's present road, debated by others recently in *Monthly Review*: Zongli Tang, "Is China Returning to Semi-Colonial Status?," pp. 77–86, and William Hinton, "Can the Chinese Dragon Match Pearls with the Dragon God of the Sea? A Response to Zongli Tang," pp. 87–104: Volume 45, Number 3 (July/August 1993).

186. Brenner and Mark Glick, "The Regulation Approach: Theory and History," *New Left Review* Number 188 (July/August 1991), pp. 45–119, especially pp. 91–96. On pp. 62–63 they mention the possibility of what Wallerstein calls semiproletarian labor and argue that it would emphasize "extensive" (as opposed to capital-intensive) accumulation. In passing it should be noted that Samir Amin, Andre Gunder Frank, and Giovanni Arrighi believe that problems of capitalism are a crisis of profits, not demand. Wallerstein, on the other hand, says that there is no essential difference, they are two sides of the same coin, because it is a crisis of the realization of capital either way: "Conclusion: A Friendly Debate," in *Dynamics of Global Crisis*, p. 234.

187. Chase-Dunn, op. cit., p. 26 and p. 42. Shannon, op. cit., cites Wallerstein, pp. 151–152. Connell, op. cit., argues the same, p. 430.

188. *The Law of Value and Historical Materialism* (New York: Monthly Review Press, 1978), p. 11. Ibid., pp. 116–117: "It is interesting to observe that, whatever the school or the line of research, the arguments brought against analyses which are based squarely on class struggle on the world scale are always the same. They include dogmatic assertion of exclusive interest in production relations (reduced, in fact, to relations within the elementary unit of advanced capitalism), which makes it possible to evade, under the pretext of 'anti-circulationism,' analyses of the collective and worldwide genesis of surplus value. . . . Indeed, these critics forget the ABCs of Marxism: value is not a category of the process of production but of the whole process of production and circulation, since value does not exist without exchange. The dogmatism in question conceals a basic economism . . ."

189. Tilly, op. cit., p. 68.

190. *Antisystemic*, p. 73. On ibid., p. 76, he refers to the "abstruse matters of 'necessary labor' and 'relative surplus value.'"

320 RECENT MARXIAN THEORY

191. Respectively: *Unthinking*, p. 79; *Geopolitics*, p. 199; *Unthinking*, pp. 122–123; and "The Agonies of Liberalism," pp. 16–17. See also, *Race*, p. 127; *Transforming*, p. 10 and p. 45; and *Geopolitics*, pp. 81–82. Amin openly insists that a measure of universalism is necessary: "The unity of the world, despite the polarization between centers and peripheries on which it is built, requires that the core dimension of any culture that wishes to build a better future based on the solution of the real problems of today be universalist. Diversity must serve the universalism that is to be built, not be contrasted with it as its polar opposite." In *Transforming*, p. 134.

192. *Historical*, pp. 87–88, pp. 85–86.

193. *Geopolitics*, p. 233; *Unthinking*, p. 31.

194. *Unthinking*, p. 237.

CHAPTER EIGHT

1. *Reason and the Rationalization of Society* (Boston: Beacon Press, 1984), pp. 46–47.

2. Calhoun, *A Disquisition on Government and Selections from the Discourse* (Indianapolis: The Bobbs-Merrill Company, 1953).

3. E. P. Thompson, *The Making of the English Working Class* (New York: Vintage Books, 1963), p. 12. From a very different philosophical perspective, Ernesto Laclau has a similar purpose: *New Reflections on the Revolution in Our Time* (London: Verso, 1990), p. 216.

4. *From Georges Sorel: Essays in Socialism and Philosophy*, edited and introduced by John L. Stanley (New York: Oxford University Press, 1976), p. 211.

Works Cited

Althusser, Louis. *Lenin and Philosophy and Other Essays*. New York: Monthly Review Press, 1971.

Amin, Samir. *The Law of Value and Historical Materialism*. New York: Monthly Review Press, 1978.

Amin, Samir, Giovanni Arrighi, Andre Gunder Frank, and Immanuel Wallerstein. *Dynamics of Global Crisis*. New York: Monthly Review Press, 1982.

———. *Transforming the Revolution: Social Movements and the World-System*. New York: Monthly Review Press, 1990.

Anderson, Perry. *Lineages of the Absolutist State*. London: Verso, 1974.

———. "The Antinomies of Antonio Gramsci." *New Left Review* Number 100 (November 1976-January 1977): pp. 5–78.

Arato, Andrew, and Jean Cohen. *Civil Society and Political Theory*. Cambridge, MA: The MIT Press, 1992.

———. "Civil Society and Social Theory." In *Between Totalitarianism and Modernity*, edited by Peter Beilharz, Gillian Robinson, and John Rundell. Cambridge, MA: The MIT Press, 1992: pp. 199–219.

Arendt, Hannah. *Between Past and Future: Eight Exercises in Political Thought*. New York: Penguin Books, 1977.

Aristotle. *The Politics of Aristotle*, edited by Sir Ernest Barker. London: Oxford University Press, 1958.

Aronowitz, Stanley. "A Metatheoretical Critique of Immanuel Wallerstein's *The Modern World-System*." *Theory and Society* Volume 10 (1981): pp. 503–520.

Arrighi, Giovanni, Terence K. Hopkins, and Immanuel Wallerstein. *Antisystemic Movements*. London: Verso, 1989.

Balibar, Etienne, and Immanuel Wallerstein. *Race, Nation, and Class: Ambiguous Identities*. London: Verso, 1991.

Bandyopadhyay, Pradeep. "Critique of Wright 2: In Defense of a Post-Sraffian Approach." In *The Value Controversy*, Steedman et al.: pp. 100–129.

Becker, Uwe. "Class Theory: Still the Axis of Critical Social Scientific Analysis?" In *The Debate on Classes*, Wright et al.: pp. 127–153.

Bendix, Reinhard. *Nation-Building and Citizenship*. New York: John Wiley and Sons, Inc., 1964.

Bernstein, Richard J. *Beyond Objectivism and Relativism: Science, Hermeneutics, and Praxis*. Philadelphia: University of Pennsylvania Press, 1983.

———, ed. *Habermas and Modernity*. Cambridge: The MIT Press, 1985.

Bowles, Samuel, and Herbert Gintis. *Democracy and Capitalism*. New York: Basic Books, 1987.

Braudel, Fernand. *The Perspective of the World*, Volume III of *Civilization and Capitalism 15th–18th Century*. New York: Harper and Row, 1984.

———. *The Wheels of Commerce*, Volume II of *Civilization and Capitalism 15th–18th Century*. New York: Harper and Row, 1982.

Braverman, Harry. *Labor and Monopoly Capital*. New York: Monthly Review Press, 1974.

Brenner, Johanna. "Work Relations and the Formation of Class Consciousness." In *The Debate on Classes*, Wright et al.: pp. 184–190.

Brenner, Robert. "Agrarian Class Structure and Economic Development in Pre-Industrial Europe." In *The Brenner Debate*, edited by T. H. Ashton and C. H. E. Philpin. New York: Cambridge University Press, 1985: pp. 10–63.

———. "The Origins of Capitalist Development: A Critique of Neo-Smithian Marxism." *New Left Review* Number 104 (July/August 1977): pp. 25–92.

———. "The Social Basis of Economic Development." In *Analytical Marxism*, edited by Roemer: pp. 23–53.

———, and Mark Glick. "The Regulation Approach: Theory and History." *New Left Review* Number 188 (July/August 1991): pp. 45–119.

Bridges, Amy. "Becoming American: The Working Classes in the United States before the Civil War." In *Working-Class Formation*, edited by Katznelson and Zolberg: pp. 157–196.

Buchanan, Allen. "Revolutionary Motivation and Rationality." *Philosophy and Public Affairs* Volume 9, Number 1 (1979): pp. 59–82.

Burke, Edmund. *Reflections on the Revolution in France*. Indianapolis: The Liberal Arts Press, Inc., 1955.

Buroway, Michael. "The Limits of Wright's Analytical Marxism and an Alternative." In *Debate on Classes*, Wright et al.: pp. 78–99.

Calhoun, Craig, ed. *Habermas and the Public Sphere*. Cambridge: The MIT Press, 1992.

Calhoun, John C. *A Disquisition on Government and Selections from the Discourse*. Indianapolis: The Bobbs-Merrill Company, Inc., 1953.

Callinicos, Alex, ed.. *Marxist Theory*. New York: Oxford University Press, 1989.

———. "Introduction: Analytical Marxism." In *Marxist Theory*, edited by Callinicos: pp. 1–16.

Carchedi, Guglielmo. "Classes and Class Analysis." In *The Debate on Classes*, Wright et al.: pp. 105–125.

Carling, Alan. "Analytical Marxism and Historical Materialism: The Debate on Social Evolution." *Science and Society* Volume 57, Number 1 (Spring 1993): pp. 31–65.

Carnoy, Martin. *The State and Political Theory*. Princeton: Princeton University Press, 1984.

Carter, Sandy. "Class Conflict: The Human Dimension." In *Between Labor and Capital*, edited by Walker: pp. 97–119.

Chase-Dunn, Christopher. *Global Formation: Structures of the World-Economy*. Cambridge, MA: Basil Blackwell, 1989.

Cohen, G. A. *History, Labour, and Freedom: Themes From Marx*. Oxford: Clarendon Press, 1988.

———. *Karl Marx's Theory of History: A Defense*. Princeton: Princeton University Press, 1978.

———. "The Future of a Disillusion." *New Left Review* Number 190 (November/December 1991): pp. 5–20.

———. "Reply to Elster on 'Marxism, Functionalism, and Game Theory.'" In *Marxist Theory*, edited by Callinicos: pp. 88–104.

Cohen, Jean. *Class and Civil Society: The Limits of Marxian Critical Theory*. Amherst, MA: University of Massachusetts Press, 1982.

———. "Rethinking Social Movements." *Berkeley Journal of Sociology* Volume 28 (Fall 1983): pp. 97–113.

———. "Strategy or Identity: New Theoretical Paradigms and Contemporary Social Movements." *Social Research* Volume 52, Number 4 (Winter 1985): pp. 663–716.

———. "Why More Political Theory?" *Telos* Number 40 (Summer 1979): pp. 70–94.

———, and Dick Howard. "Why Class?" In *Between Labor and Capital*, edited by Walker: pp. 67–95.

Collins, Hugh. *Marxism and Law*. New York: Oxford University Press, 1982.

Connell, R. W. "Class Formation on a World Scale." *Review* Volume VII, Number 3 (Winter 1984): pp. 407–440.

Cutler, Antony, Barry Hindess, Paul Hirst, and Athar Hussein. *Marx's 'Capital' and Capitalism Today* Volume One. London: Routledge and Kegan Paul, 1977.

Davis, Mike. *Prisoners of the American Dream: Politics and Economy in the History of the US Working Class*. London: Verso, 1986.

Dawley, Alan, and Paul Faler. "Working Class Culture and Politics in the Industrial Revolution: Sources of Loyalism and Rebellion." *Journal of Social History* Volume 9, Number 4 (June 1976): pp. 466–480.

Dews, Peter, ed. *Autonomy and Solidarity*. London: Verso Books, 1992.

Ehrenreich, Barbara, and John Ehrenreich. "The Professional-Managerial Class." In *Between Capital and Labor*, edited by Walker: pp. 5–45.

Elster, Jon. *Making Sense of Marx*. London: Cambridge University Press, 1985.

———, ed. *Rational Choice*. New York: New York University Press, 1986.

———. "Introduction." In *Rational Choice*, edited by Elster: pp. 1–33.

———. "Marxism, Functionalism, and Game Theory: The Case for Methodological Individualism." In *Marxist Theory*, edited by Callinicos: pp. 48–87.

———. "Roemer versus Roemer: A Comment on 'New Directions in the Marxian Theory of Exploitation and Class.'" *Politics and Society* Volume 11, Number 3 (1982): pp. 363–373.

———, and Karl Ove Moene. *Alternatives to Capitalism*. Cambridge: Cambridge University Press, 1989.

Emmanuel, Arghiri. *Unequal Exchange: A Study of the Imperialism of Trade* [with additional comments by Charles Bettleheim]. New York: Monthly Review Press, 1972.

Frank, Andre Gunder, and Barry Gills. "The Five Thousand Year Old World System: An Interdisciplinary Introduction." *Humboldt Journal of Social Relations* Volume 18, Number 2 (Spring 1992) [paper version while article 'forthcoming'].

Fraser, Nancy. "Rethinking the Public Sphere: A Contribution to the Critique of Actually Existing Democracy." In *Habermas and the Public Sphere*, edited by Craig Calhoun: pp. 109–142.

Geras, Norman. "The Controversy about Marx and Justice." *New Left Review* Number 150 (March/April 1985): pp. 47–85.

Gerth, H. H., and C. Wright Mills, editors. *From Max Weber: Essays in Sociology*. New York: Oxford University Press, 1958.

Giddens, Anthony. *The Class Structure of the Advanced Societies*. New York: Harper Torchbooks, 1975.

———. *The Nation-State and Violence*, Volume Two of *A Contemporary Critique of Historical Materialism*. Berkeley: University of California Press, 1987.

———. "Labour and Interaction." In *Habermas: Critical Debates*, edited by Thompson and Held: pp. 149–161.

———. "Reason Without Revolution? Habermas's *Theorie des communikativen Handelns*." In *Habermas and Modernity*, edited by Bernstein: pp. 95–121.

Gorz, Andre. *Farewell to the Working Class: An Essay on Post-Industrial Socialism*. Boston: South End Press, 1982.

Gramsci, Antonio. *Selections from the Prison Notebooks*, edited by Quintin Hoare and Geoffrey Nowell Smith. New York: International Publishers, 1971.

Habermas, Juergen. *Communication and the Evolution of Society*. Boston: Beacon Press, 1979.

———. *Legitimation Crisis*. Boston: Beacon Press, 1975.

————. *Moral Consciousness and Communicative Action*. Cambridge: The MIT Press, 1990.

————. *On the Logic of the Social Sciences*. Cambridge, MA: The MIT Press, 1988.

————. *The Philosophical Discourse of Modernity*. Cambridge: The MIT Press, 1990.

————. *Theory and Practice*. Boston: Beacon Press, 1973.

————. *The Theory of Communicative Action* Volume One: *Reason and the Rationalization of Society*. Boston: Beacon Press, 1984.

————. *The Theory of Communicative Action* Volume Two: *Lifeworld and System: A Critique of Functionalist Reason*. Boston: Beacon Press, 1987.

————. *Toward a Rational Society*. Boston: Beacon Press, 1970.

————. "Concluding Remarks." In *Habermas and the Public Sphere*, edited by Calhoun: pp. 462–479.

————. "Further Reflections on the Public Sphere." In *Habermas and the Public Sphere*, edited by Calhoun: pp. 421–461.

————. "Modernity—An Incomplete Project." In *Interpretive Social Science: A Second Look*, edited by Paul Rabinow and William M. Sullivan. Berkeley: University of California Press, 1987: pp. 141–156.

————. "The New Obscurity: The Crisis of the Welfare State and the Exhaustion of Utopian Energies." *Philosophy and Social Criticism* 11 (1986): pp. 1–17.

————. "New Social Movements." *Telos* Number 49 (Fall 1981): pp. 33–38.

————. "A Philosophico-Political Profile." *New Left Review* Number 151 (May/June 1985): pp. 75–105.

————. "A Reply to My Critics." In *Habermas: Critical Debates*, edited by Thompson and Held: pp. 219–283.

————. "What Does Socialism Mean Today? The Rectifying Revolution and the Need for New Thinking on the Left." *New Left Review* Number 183 (September/October 1990): pp. 3–21.

Hart-Landsberg, Martin. "Post-NAFTA Politics: Learning from Asia." *Monthly Review* Volume 46, Number 2 (June 1994): pp. 12–21.

Hayek, Friedrich. *The Road to Serdom*. Chicago: The University of Chicago Press, 1944.

Held, David. "Crisis Tendencies, Legitimation and the State." In *Habermas: Critical Debates*, edited by Thompson and Held: pp. 181–195.

Heller, Agnes. *The Theory of Need in Marx*. London: Allison and Busby, 1976.

Hindess, Barry. *Politics and Class Analysis*. New York: Basil Blackwell, Inc., 1987.

Hinton, William. "Can the Chinese Dragon Match Pearls with the Dragon God of the Sea? A Repsonse to Zongli Tang." *Monthly Review* Volume 45, Number 3 (July/August 1993): pp. 87–104.

————. "Impressions of Manila." *Monthly Review* Volume 45, Number 1 (May 1993): pp. 9–20.

Hirst, Paul. *On Law and Ideology.* Atlantic Highlands, N.J.: Humanities Press, 1979.

————. "Economic Classes and Politics." In *Class and Class Structure,* edited by Alan Hunt. London: Lawrence and Wishart, 1977: pp. 125–154.

Hobsbawm, Eric. *Workers: Worlds of Labor.* New York: Pantheon Books, 1984.

Hodgson, Geoff. "Critique of Wright 1: Labour and Profits." In *The Value Controversy,* Steedman et al.: pp. 75–99.

Huelsberg, Werner. "After the West German Elections." *New Left Review* Number 162 (March/April 1987): pp. 85–99.

Hunter, Herbert M., and Sameer Y. Abraham, eds. *Race, Class, and the World System: The Sociology of Oliver C. Cox.* New York: Monthly Review Press, 1987.

Jay, Martin. "Hannah Arendt: Opposing Views." *Partisan Review* XLV, Number 3 (1978): pp. 348–368.

Katznelson, Ira. *City Trenches: Politics and the Patterning of Class in the United States.* New York: Pantheon Books, 1981.

————. "Working-Class Formation: Constructing Cases and Comparisons." In *Working-Class Formation,* edited by Katznelson and Zolberg: pp. 3–41.

————, and Aristide Zolberg, eds. *Working-Class Formation.* Princeton, N.J.: Princeton University Press, 1986.

Keane, John. "Introduction." In *Contradictions of the Welfare State,* by Offe: pp. 11–34.

————. "The Legacy of Political Economy: Thinking With and Against Claus Offe." *Canadian Journal of Political and Social Theory* Volume 2, Number 3 (Fall 1978): pp. 49–92.

Kitching, Gavin. *Karl Marx and the Philosophy of Praxis.* London: Routledge, Chapman, and Hall, 1988.

Laclau, Ernesto. *New Reflections on the Revolution of Our Time.* London: Verso, 1990.

————, and Chantal Mouffe. *Hegemony and Socialist Strategy: Towards a Radical Democratic Politics.* London: Verso, 1985.

Laibman, David. "The Falling Rate of Profit: A New Empirical Study." *Science and Society* Volume 57, Number 2 (Summer 1993): pp. 223–233.

Lefort, Claude. *The Political Forms of Modern Society.* Cambridge, MA: The MIT Press, 1986.

Levi, Margaret. "Review of Roemer." *American Political Science Review* Volume 78, Number 1 (March 1984): pp. 293–294.

Levine, Andrew, and Erik Olin Wright. "Rationality and Class Struggle." In *Marxist Theory,* edited by Callinicos: pp. 17–47.

Lindblom, Charles. *Politics and Markets*. New York: Basic Books, 1977.

Luhmann, Niklas. *Political Theory in the Welfare State*. New York: Walter de Gruyter, 1990.

Lukacs, Georg. *History and Class Consciousness*. Cambridge, MA: The MIT Press, 1971.

————. *Lenin: A Study on the Unity of His Thought*. Cambridge, MA: The MIT Press, 1971.

Lukes, Steven. *Marxism and Morality*. Oxford: Oxford University Press, 1985.

Luxemburg, Rosa. *The Russian Revolution and Leninism or Marxism?* Ann Arbor, MI: University of Michigan Press/Ann Arbor Paperbacks, 1961.

MacDonald, Oliver. "The Polish Vortex: Solidarity and Socialism." *New Left Review* Number 139 (May/June 1983): pp. 5–48.

MacIntyre, Alasdair. *After Virtue* Second Edition. Notre Dame, IN: University of Notre Dame Press, 1984.

————. *A Short History of Ethics*. New York: The Macmillan Company, 1966.

Maier, Charles S., ed. *Changing Boundaries of the Political*. Cambridge: Cambridge University Press, 1987.

Manin, Bernard. "On Legitimacy and Political Deliberation." *Political Theory* Volume 15, Number 3 (August 1987): pp. 338–368.

Mansbridge, Jane J., ed. *Beyond Self-Interest*. Chicago: University of Chicago Press, 1990.

Marshall, T. H. *Class, Citizenship, and Social Development: Essays by T. H. Marshall*. Garden City, N.Y.: Doubleday and Co., Inc., 1964.

Marx, Karl. *Capital* Volumes 1–3. New York: International Publishers, 1967.

————. *A Contribution to the Critique of Political Economy*. New York: International Publishers, Inc., 1970.

————. *The Eighteenth Brumaire of Louis Bonaparte*. New York: International Publishers Co., Inc., 1963.

————. *The German Ideology*. In *Collected Works* Volume 5. New York: International Publishers, 1976.

————. *Karl Marx: Early Writings*, introduced by Lucio Colletti. New York: Vintage Books, 1975.

McCarthy, Thomas. "Complexity and Democracy, or the Seducements of Systems Theory." *New German Critique* Number 35 (Spring/Summer 1985): pp. 27–53.

————. "Translator's Introduction." To *Reason and the Rationalization of Society*, by Habermas: pp. v-xxxvii.

Meidner, Rudolf. "Why Did the Swedish Model Fail?" In *Socialist Register 1993*, edited by Ralph Miliband and Leo Panitch. London: The Merlin Press, 1993: pp. 211–228.

Meiksins, Peter. "Beyond the Boundary Question." *New Left Review* Number 157 (May/June 1986): pp. 101–120.

———. "A Critique of Wright's Theory of Contradictory Class Locations." In *The Debate on Classes*, Wright et al.: pp. 173–183.

Misgeld, Dieter. "Critical Hermeneutics versus Neoparsonianism?" *New German Critique* Number 35 (Spring/Summer 1985): pp. 55–82.

Modelski, George. "Of Politics, Portugal, and Kindred Issues: A Rejoinder." In *Contending Approaches to World System Analysis*, edited by Thompson: pp. 291–298.

Nolan, Mary. "Economic Crisis, State Policy, and Working-Class Formation in Germany, 1870–1900." In *Working-Class Formation*, edited by Katznelson and Zolberg: pp. 352–393.

Offe, Claus. *Contradictions of the Welfare State*. Cambridge, MA: The MIT Press, 1984.

———. *Disorganized Capitalism*. Cambridge, MA: The MIT Press, 1985.

———. *Industry and Inequality: The Achievement Principle in Work and Social Status*. New York: St. Martin's Press, 1977.

———. "Democracy Against the Welfare State? Structural Foundations of Neo-conservative Political Opportunities." *Political Theory* Volume 15, Number 4 (November 1987): pp. 501–537.

———. "Introduction to Part III." In *Stress and Contradiction in Modern Capitalism: Public Policy and the Theory of the State*, edited by Leon Lindberg et al. Lexington, MA: Lexington Books/D.C. Heath, 1975: pp. 245–259.

———. "New Social Movements: Challenging the Boundaries of Institutional Politics." *Social Research* Volume 52, Number 4 (Winter 1985): pp. 817–868.

———. "Political Authority and Class Structures—An Analysis of Late Capitalist Societies." *International Journal of Sociology* Spring 1972: pp. 73–108.

———. "Structural Problems of the Capitalist State. Class Rule and the Political System. On the Selectiveness of Political Institutions." *German Political Studies* Volume I. Beverly Hills, CA: Sage Publications, 1974: pp. 31–57.

———. "The Theory of the Capitalist State and the Problem of Policy Formation." In *Stress and Contradiction in Modern Capitalism: Public Policy and the Theory of the State*, edited by Leon Lindberg et al. Lexington, MA: Lexington Books/D.C. Heath, 1975: pp. 125–144.

———, and Rolf G. Heinze. *Beyond Employment: Time, Work, and the Informal Economy*. Philadelphia: Temple University Press, 1992.

———, and Ulrich K. Preuss. "Democratic Institutions and Moral Resources." In *Political Theory Today*, edited by David Held. Stanford: Stanford University Press, 1991: pp. 143–171.

Oppenheimer, Martin. *White Collar Politics*. New York: Monthly Review Press, 1985.

Panitch, Leo. "Recent Theorizations of Corporatism: Reflections on a Growth Industry." *British Journal of Sociology* Volume 31, Number 2 (June 1980): pp. 159–187.

Parkin, Frank. *Marxism and Class Theory: A Bourgeois Critique.* New York: Columbia University Press, 1979.

Pashukanis, Evgeny B. *Law and Marxism: A General Theory.* London: Ink Links, 1978.

Perelman, Michael. "The Qualitative Side of Marx's Value Theory." *Rethinking Marxism* Volume 6, Number 1 (Spring 1993): pp. 82–95.

Perrot, Michelle. "On the Formation of the French Working Class." In *Working Class-Formation*, edited by Katznelson and Zolberg: pp. 71–110.

Piven, Frances Fox, and Richard Cloward. *The New Class War.* New York: Pantheon Books, 1982.

Polanyi, Karl. *The Great Transformation.* Boston: Beacon Press, 1944.

Poulantzas, Nicos. *Classes in Contemporary Capitalism.* London: New Left Books, 1975.

———. *Political Power and Social Classes.* London: New Left Books, 1973.

———. *State, Power, Socialism.* London: New Left Books/Verso, 1980.

Przeworski, Adam. *Capitalism and Social Democracy.* Cambridge: Cambridge University Press, 1985.

———. *Democracy and the Market.* Cambridge: Cambridge University Press, 1991.

———. "The Ethical Materialism of John Roemer." *Politics and Society* Volume 11, Number 3 (1982): pp. 289–313.

———. "Marxism and Rational Choice." *Politics and Society* Volume 14, Number 4 (1985): pp. 379–409.

———. "The Material Bases of Consent: Economics and Politics in a Hegemonic System." *Political Power and Social Theory* Volume 1, edited by Maurice Zeitlin. Greenwich, CN: JAI Press, Inc., 1980: pp. 21–66.

———. "Proletariat into a Class: The Process of Class Formation from Karl Kautsky's *The Class Struggle* to Recent Controversies." *Politics and Society* Volume 7, Number 4 (1977): pp. 343–401.

———, and John Sprague. *Paper Stones: A History of Electoral Socialism.* Chicago: University of Chicago Press, 1986.

———, and Michael Wallerstein. "Democratic Capitalism at the Crossroads." *democracy* Volume 2, Number 3 (July 1982): pp. 52–68.

Rapkin, David P. "The Inadequacy of a Single Logic: Integrating Political and Material Approaches to the World System." In *Contending Approaches to World System Analysis*, edited by Thompson: pp. 241–268.

Roemer, John, ed. *Analytical Marxism.* New York: Cambridge University Press, 1986.

———. *Free to Lose: An Introduction to Marxist Economic Philosophy*. Cambridge, MA: Harvard University Press, 1988.

———. *A General Theory of Exploitation and Class*. Cambridge, MA: Harvard University Press, 1982.

———. "New Directions in the Marxian Theory of Exploitation and Class," *Politics and Society* Volume 11, Number 3 (1982): pp. 253–287.

———. " 'Rational Choice' Marxism: Some Issues of Method and Substance." In *Analytical Marxism*, edited by Roemer: pp. 191–201.

———. "Reply." *Politics and Society* Volume 11, Number 3 (1982): pp. 375–394.

———. "Should Marxists Be Interested in Exploitation?" In *Analytical Marxism*, edited by Roemer: pp. 260–282.

———. "Introduction." In *Analytical Marxism*, edited by Roemer: pp. 1–7.

Rose, David, and Gordon Marshall. "Constructing the (W)right Classes." In *The Debate on Classes*, Wright et al.: pp. 243–265.

Sabia, Daniel R. Jr. "Rationality, Collective Action, and Karl Marx." *American Journal of Political Science* Volume 32, Number 1 (February 1988): pp. 50–71.

Sartre, Jean-Paul. *The Communists and Peace*. New York: George Braziller, Inc., 1968.

Schumpeter, Joseph. *Capitalism, Socialism, and Democracy*. New York: Harper Colophon Books, 1975.

Schwartz, Benjamin I. "The Religion of Politics: Reflections on the Thought of Hannah Arendt." *Dissent* VII (March/April 1970): pp. 144–161.

Schweikert, David. "Reflections on Anti-Marxism: Elster on Marx's Functionalism and Labor Theory of Value." *Praxis International* Volume 8, Number 1 (April 1988): pp. 109–122.

Sewell, William H. Jr. "Artisans, Factory Workers, and the Formation of the French Working Class, 1789–1848." In *Working-Class Formation*, edited by Katznelson and Zolberg: pp. 45–70.

Shannon, Thomas Richard. *An Introduction to the World-System Perspective*. Boulder, CO: Westview Press, 1989.

Shefter, Martin. "Trade Unions and Political Machines: The Organization and Disorganization of the American Working Class in the Late Nineteenth Century." In *Working-Class Formation*, edited by Katznelson and Zolberg: pp. 197–276.

Sitton, John F. *Marx's Theory of the Transcendence of the State*. Bern and New York: Peter Lang Publishers, 1989.

———. "Hannah Arendt's Argument for Council Democracy." In *Hannah Arendt: Critical Essays*, edited by Lewis P. Hinchman and Sandra K. Hinchman. Albany, NY: State University of New York Press, 1994: pp. 307–329.

Skocpol, Theda. "Wallerstein's World Capitalist System: A Theoretical and Historical Critique." *American Journal of Sociology* Volume 82, Number 5 (March 1977): pp. 1075–1090.

Smith, Joan, Immanuel Wallerstein, and Hans-Dieter Evers. "Introduction." In *Households and the World-Economy*, edited by Smith, Wallerstein, and Evers. Beverly Hills: Sage Publications, 1984: pp. 7–13.

Smith, Murray E. G. "Productivity, Valorization and Crisis: Socially Necessary Unproductive Labor in Contemporary Capitalism." *Science and Society* Volume 57, Number 3 (Fall 1993): pp. 262–293.

Social Research Volume 52, Number 4 (Winter 1985).

Sorel, Georges. *From Georges Sorel: Essays in Socialism and Philosophy*, edited and introduced by John L. Stanley. New York: Oxford University Press, 1976.

Steedman, Ian. "Ricardo, Marx, Sraffa." In *The Value Controversy*, Steedman et al.: pp. 11–19.

———, et al. *The Value Controversy*. London: Verso Books, 1981.

Stinchcombe, Arthur. "Education, Exploitation, and Class Consciousness." In *The Debate on Classes*, Wright et al.: pp. 168–172.

Suchting, W. "Reconstructing Marxism." *Science and Society* Volume 57, Number 2 (Summer 1993): pp. 133–159.

Tang, Zongli. "Is China Returning to Semi-Colonial Status?" *Monthly Review* Volume 45, Number 3 (July/August 1993): pp. 77–86.

Thompson, E. P. *The Making of the English Working Class*. New York: Vintage Books, 1963.

Thompson, John B., and David Held, eds. *Habermas: Critical Debates*. Cambridge, MA: The MIT Press, 1982.

Thompson, William R., ed. *Contending Approaches to World System Analysis*. Beverly Hills: Sage Publications, 1983.

Tilly, Charles. *Big Structures, Large Processes, Huge Comparisons*. New York: The Russell Sage Foundation, 1984.

Van Parijs, Philippe. "A Revolution in Class Theory." In *The Debate on Classes*, Wright et al.: pp. 213–241.

Walker, Pat, ed. *Between Labor and Capital*. Boston: South End Press, 1979.

Wallerstein, Immanuel. *The Capitalist World-Economy: Essays by Immanuel Wallerstein*. New York: Cambridge University Press, 1979.

———. *Geopolitics and Geoculture: Essays on the Changing World-System*. Cambridge: Cambridge University Press, 1991.

———. *Historical Capitalism*. London: Verso, 1983.

———. *The Modern World-System: Capitalist Agriculture and the Origins of the European World-Economy in the Sixteenth Century*. New York: Academic Press, Inc., 1974.

————. *The Politics of the World-Economy: The States, the Movements, and the Civilizations*. Cambridge: Cambridge University Press, 1984.

————. *Unthinking Social Science: The Limits of Nineteenth Century Paradigms*. Cambridge: Polity Press, 1991.

————. "An Agenda for World-Systems Analysis." In *Contending Approaches to World System Analysis*, edited by Thompson: pp. 299–308.

————. "The Agonies of Liberalism: What Hope Progress?" *New Left Review* Number 204 (March/April 1994): pp. 3–17.

————. "The World-System: Myths and Historical Shifts." In *The Global Economy: Divergent Perspectives on Economic Change*, edited by Edward W. Gondolf, Irwin M. Marcus, and James P. Dougherty. Boulder, CO: Westview Press, 1986: pp. 15–24.

————, and Joan Smith. "Conclusion: Core-Periphery and Household Structures." in *Creating and Transforming Households: The Constraints of the World-Economy*, coordinated by Smith and Wallerstein. Cambridge: Cambridge University Press, 1992: pp. 253–262.

Weber, Max. *The Protestant Ethic and the Spirit of Capitalism*. New York: Charles Scribner's Sons, 1958.

Wellmer, Albrecht. "Reason, Utopia, and the *Dialectic of Enlightenment*." In *Habermas and Modernity*, edited by Bernstein: pp. 35–66.

Wittgenstein, Ludwig. *Philosophical Investigations* Third Edition. New York: Macmillan Publishing, 1968.

Wolf, Frieder Otto. "Eco-socialist Transition on the Threshold of the 21st Century." *New Left Review* Number 158 (July/August 1986): pp. 32–42.

Wolin, Sheldon. "Democracy and the Welfare State: The Political and Theoretical Connections Between Staatsraeson and Wohlfarhtstaatsraeson." *Political Theory* Volume 15, Number 4 (November 1987): pp. 467–500.

Wood, Allen. "Marx and Equality." In *Analytical Marxism*, edited by Roemer: pp. 283–303.

Wood, Ellen Meiksins. *The Retreat From Class: A New 'True' Socialism*. London: Verso, 1986.

————. "Rational Choice Marxism: Is the Game Worth the Candle?" *New Left Review* Number 177 (September/October 1989): pp. 41–88.

Wright, Erik Olin. *Class, Crisis, and the State*. London: Verso Books, 1978.

————. *Classes*. London: Verso, 1985.

————, ed. *The Debate on Classes*. London: Verso Books, 1989.

————. "Class Analysis, History and Emancipation." *New Left Review* Number 202 (November/December 1993): pp. 15–35.

————. "Exploitation, Identity, and Class Structure: A Reply to My Critics." In *The Debate on Classes*, edited by Wright: pp. 191–211.

————. "Rethinking, Once Again, the Concept of Class Structure." In *The Debate on Classes*, edited by Wright: pp. 269–348.

————. "The Value Controversy and Social Research." In *The Value Controversy*, Steedman et al.: pp. 130–162.

Wright, Erik Olin, Andrew Levine, and Elliott Sober. *Reconstructing Marxism*. London: Verso, 1992.

————. "Reconstructing Marxism: A Reply." *Science and Society* Volume 58, Number 1 (Spring 1994): pp. 53–60.

Zolberg, Aristide. "How Many Exceptionalisms?" In *Working-Class Formation*, edited by Katznelson and Zolberg: pp. 397–455.

————. "Origins of the Modern World System: A Missing Link." *World Politics* Volume 33 (1981): pp. 253–281.

————. "'World' and 'System': A Misalliance." In *Contending Approaches to World System Analysis*, edited by Thompson: pp. 269–290.

Index

Absolute immiseration, 216, 309*n74*
Action
  administrative, 191
  anti-capitalist, 16
  avoidance, 116
  capacity for, 57
  chosen, 158
  class, 45, 86–95, 91, 98
  collective, 33, 35, 69, 73, 75, 86–95,
    96, 98, 101, 103, 106, 107, 145,
    163–165, 257*n26, 278n52*
  communicative, 152, 169, 172, 175,
    180, 189
  consequences of, 279*n60, 295n66*
  coordinated, 169, 170
  economic courses of, 6
  ethical, 158
  forbidden, 158
  guides for, 158
  human, 89
  individual, 89, 91
  instrumental, 190
  large scale, 102
  motivation for, 96, 99, 159
  normativistic, 164
  organized domains of, 174
  orientation, 167, 295*n66*
  political, 51
  purposive-rational, 166, 167, 169
  rational justification of, 196
  revolutionary, 12
  social, 89, 104, 132, 169
  theory, 152
Adorno, Theodor, 165
Alienation, 85, 86, 176, 177, 193

  of bourgeois society, 39
  and exploitation, 83
  of labor, 44, 45
  political, 269*n4*
  in work, 44
Althusser, Louis, 52
Altruism, 100
Amin, Samir, 206, 207, 241, 242,
  306*n33, 315n155, 315n156,*
  319*n186*
Anderson, Perry, 50–51
Arendt, Hannah, 188, 189, 313*n128*
Aristotle, 106, 255*n1, 262n31*
Arrighi, Giovanni, 206, 319*n186*
Authority
  and class position, 38
  neutrality of, 57
  political, 56, 59, 124, 202
  public, 57, 120
  rationalization of, 162
  relations, 23, 28, 38, 97
  sovereign, 114, 147
  state, 123
Autonomy, 23
  absolute, 116
  defining, 260*n14*
  economic, 51, 60
  individual, 44, 45, 59
  labor, 96
  of the personality, 55
  political, 51
  relative, 116, 118
  state, 110, 116
  values of, 135
  in work, 127